D0138260

A Guide to the Blues

A Guide to the BLUES

HISTORY, WHO'S WHO, RESEARCH SOURCES

AUSTIN SONNIER, JR.

Greenwood Press
Westport, Connecticut • London

Library of Congress Cataloging-in-Publication Data

Sonnier, Austin M.
A guide to the blues : history, who's who, research sources / Austin Sonnier, Jr.
p. cm.
Includes bibliographical references, discography, filmography, and index.
ISBN 0–313–28724–4 (alk. paper)
1. Blues (Music)—History and criticism. 2. Blues musicians—Biography. I. Title.
ML3521.S58 1994
781.643′09—dc20 93–30773

British Library Cataloguing in Publication Data is available.

Library of Congress Catalog Card Number: 93–30773
ISBN: 0–313–28724–4

First published in 1994

Greenwood Press, 88 Post Road West, Westport, CT 06881
An imprint of Greenwood Publishing Group, Inc.

Printed in the United States of America

The paper used in this book complies with the Permanent Paper Standard issued by the National Information Standards Organization (Z39.48–1984).

10 9 8 7 6 5 4 3 2 1

Every reasonable effort has been made to trace the owners of copyright materials in this book, but in some instances this has proven impossible. The author and publisher will be glad to receive information leading to more complete acknowledgments in subsequent printings of this book and in the meantime extend their apologies for any omissions.

To my mother and father,
Austin and Mayola Sonnier

CONTENTS

FIGURES

ACKNOWLEDGMENTS

During the many years I worked on this project, there were many people whose enthusiasm, kindness, support, cooperation, generosity, knowledge, and assistance in a variety of contexts were invaluable to me. I would like to extend my gratitude to those kind folks for their help and friendship. Special thanks are due to Bruce Iglaure, Shirley and Richard House, Robert Sacre, Fritz and Franziska Svacina, David and Susan Melman, Robert McGuire, Maat, Sandy Hebert LaBry, Jacques Depoorter, Gloria Adams, and the Cameron Organization. I would also like to thank my editors, Barbara A. Rader, Marilyn Brownstein, Richard Sillett, Maureen Melino, and all of the others at Greenwood for their support and cooperation. I am particularly indebted to my wife, Nellie, and sons Austin III and David for their kindness and understanding during the course of my researching and writing this book. Most of all I am indebted to all the men and women who have lived and are living the "blues life." Without them this work would not exist.

INTRODUCTION

The blues is a breath of fresh air
In a world that's filled with sorrow
It's a breath of clean air
In a world that's full of horror
Like a mojo in the pocket
It'll keep you sane till tomorrow.[1]

The blues is a noble spirit that is able to communicate more than one emotion at the same time. It is in one breath hot, cold, uplifting, and down. The blues is a way of life for some; for others it is an escape from life. But for all who are acquainted with the blues, it is, as the song goes, "a breath of fresh air." The blues is not merely a marriage of words and music. Its lyrics tell one story and its music tells another. It penetrates deeply into the soul and pulls out what does not belong there, replacing it with what does. It is a good-time music that sings of life and at the same time cries about and laughs at life's problems.

Exactly when the blues first surfaced is not known, but blues artists recall hearing it in several areas of the United States right after the turn of the century. Pioneer New Orleans jazz drummer Warren "Baby" Dodds remembered hearing the blues in that city in the 1890s. Composer/pianist Ferdinand "Jelly Roll" Morton commented on hearing pianists Game Kid and Mamie Desdoumes play the blues in New Orleans at the turn of the century. Gertrude "Ma" Rainey, the great blues singer from Columbus,

1. Lyrics by Austin Sonnier, Jr.

Georgia, said that she first heard the blues in 1902. Musician/composer/author William Christopher Handy, who was born in 1873, claimed to have heard the blues for the first time in 1903 while waiting for a train in Tutwiler, Mississippi. It was not until 1912, though, that the first published sheet music of a blues song appeared. The two songs, "Dallas Blues" and "Memphis Blues," were the first titles to use the term "blues" and to incorporate the form that identifies the music. The first blues recording, "Crazy Blues," sung by Mamie Smith, was made in 1916.

Nobody actually knows where the blues began, but its roots go back to August 1619, when a Dutch ship dropped off twenty Africans at Jamestown, Virginia, and started the black man's journey through America. Judging from most accounts, the blues seems to have surfaced in different areas of the South around 1900. The two most heavily saturated areas of blues involvement seem to have been the Mississippi Delta and New Orleans. Both claim to be the birthplace of the blues. The Mississippi Delta stands out as being the more probable birthplace simply because the blues moved ahead there, undiluted, and fed the talents of giants like Robert Johnson, Son House, and Charley Patton, while New Orleans abandoned the blues early in its development for the magic of another sound called jazz. Whatever the case may be, the blues thrived and was nurtured by the laughter and cries of a displaced people.

As the blues gradually moved to different parts of the United States, it began to take on different sophistications. Its coat of armor remained the same, but the type of polish for it changed with the area. As it became more urban, it moved from the vocal/guitar stylings of itinerant griots (oral historians) to the slick delivery of electronics, brass, and woodwinds.

This work is designed not only to offer the reader historical and musical insight but also to introduce some of the musicians who have made, or are currently making, blues music accessible to the world. I have attempted to trace the music from its African roots through its many stages of growth and influences up to its present state. Some of the major areas of blues activity are discussed, and analysis of music factors inherent in the blues form is touched upon.

The musicians that appear in the bibliography section were chosen because of their life-long devotion to playing the blues and the style in which they have chosen to champion the music. This collection of musicians represents the full range of the blues experience from is purest Mississippi Delta forms through its movement through rhythm-and-blues, soul, and rock. Additional work by and about these musicians is also listed in the selected filmography, bibliography, and discography, which can be found in Part II of this work.

The individual biographies offer a look at some of the artists' work that is, in most cases, currently available on the market. The selected discography, on the other hand, includes not only the artists' current material but also works that (1) are out of circulation, (2) contain the same material but have been released by different record labels and index numbers, (3) are by the artist as a sideman on other musicians' recordings, and (4) are part of anthologies and collections. Titles which appear in both the biography section and the discography are there solely for the convenience of the reader.

In addition to the many men who played the blues in the work camps, in honky-tonks, at house parties, and on city street corners, there was also a "sorority" of women blues singers who dominated the field in the 1930s. These women, dubbed "classic blues singers," were the first to record, develop shows, and perform on the road with bands. These female blues singers were responsible for introducing the blues to a much larger audience through their access to the recording studio, radio broadcasts, and theater appearances.

Survival of the blues, as well as of any other form of music, depends on the lives of those musicians who play the music and sing the songs. A large part of this work is dedicated to biographical sketches of these men and women. Because this music survived as an oral tradition up to the first quarter of this century, information on a large number of these musicians is sketchy. In those cases I have chosen to utilize whatever information is available and offer apologies for not being as complete on some entries as on others.

Somewhere along the way, years ago, I can remember hearing someone say: "Music is a message from the gods. When you hear music, you hear the gods speaking. It's the only way that they've chosen to talk to us." This book is about the blues message and about the men and women who have been chosen by the gods to deliver that message to the world.

Part I

HISTORY, DEVELOPMENT, AND INFLUENCE

1

AFRICAN INFLUENCES: A PRE-HISTORY

Not until recently were historians forced to embrace the reality that Africa has a rich history of its own, independent of European discovery and intervention. Africa was considered the "dark" continent by those Europeans who were restricted to coastal areas by powerful African nations and later by an ignorance that kept the continent and the realities of its ways of life, religion, economics, politics, and education at arm's length from the rest of the world. One can safely say that the history of Africa is among the most challenging of modern studies. Conventional documents are scarce and concern, in most instances, events of relatively small historical significance. Unfortunately, early written records are in Arabic or, as in the case of the inscriptions on the monuments at Meroe, are undeciphered. Historians and writers using African sources have to rely on the oral tradition, which requires an intimate knowledge of West African languages, anthropology, archaeology, and linguistics.

From the ninth to the sixteenth centuries three of the largest and most famous African kingdoms flourished in the western Sudan, an area known to the Muslims as the Land of the Black People. These kingdoms of Ghana, Mali, and Songhay played an extremely important part in the history of Africa. Having connections with North Africa and the Near East, these states served as a channel through which ideas and merchandise passed between the West Africans and the Arabs, as well as between the West Africans and the Europeans to the north. Pilgrims' travels to Mecca constantly brought the African rulers and their courts into contact with the latest developments in the Islamic world. The caravan routes that crossed the Sahara not only brought Arab and European culture to the black world, but also transported the treasures of black Africa all the way to the Mediterranean world.

Among the three states of the western Sudan, the earliest to rise to fame and fortune was Ghana. Because of its position between the gold deposits of the South and the salt deposits of the North, Ghana profited mightily from exchange between the two regions. All throughout the Middle Ages and up to the discovery of America, Ghana was one of the principal providers of gold to the Mediterranean world. Gold built the power possessed by Ghana and the power of the Mandingo empire.

In 1054 Ibn Yasin, the Almoravid ruler of North Africa, began his march south in an effort to chastise pagans and to make converts to Islam. This marked the beginning of Ghana's downfall, even though it was not until 1076 that another Almoravid ruler, Abu Bakr, could take the capital of Ghana itself. The Almoravids extended their supreme authority over the blacks of Ghana, devastated their land, plundered their property, and compelled a great number of them to become Muslims. The authority of the kings of Ghana having been destroyed, Ghana's neighbors, the Sosso, overran the country and reduced its inhabitants to slaves. By the thirteenth century the state and cities of Ghana were far gone in decay.

By 1213, according to respectable tradition, Allokoi Keita had founded the Mandingo state that would later be known as Mali. Twenty-five years later his successor, Sundiata, defeated the Sosso rulers who had earlier established themselves in Ghana. In 1240, after two years of fighting, Sundiata took the existing capital city of Ghana from the Sosso, destroyed it, and established the first of his capitals (Niani or Jeriba) in the south on the upper Niger. Sundiata and his successors continued to dominate most of the western Sudan for another hundred years.

Meanwhile, far to the east, another great savannah region was undergoing the same detribalization and centralizing process. The states and empires of the Hausa and the Fulani of Kanem, Darfur, and Bornu rose out of the turmoil. In this crystallizing process one strong force and ruling people rivaled, succeeded, or coexisted with another. Sometimes the governing powers overlapped in time and place; sometimes one continued in power under a different name or dynasty. In a limited sense the Mandingo empire of Mali can be said to have succeeded Ghana, Songhay, and Mali, and Bornu succeeded Kanem. In this restructuring of power there were definite parallels with contemporary Europe, as can be seen in the organization of a central power and the establishment of a background of class systems, trade, and agriculture.

Timbuktu and Djenne, both to become famous throughout the Islamic world for their commerce and learning, seem to have grown into cities by the twelfth century. In 1307 the most renowned of all the kings of the old Sudan, Mansa Kankan Musa, inherited power over Mali and began to extend its dominion. By 1324 Mali had enclosed within its governing system the approaches to the salt deposits of Taghaza on the northern edges of the Sahara, as well as the approaches to the gold country near the southern border of the savannah. To the east Mali encompassed the copper mines and the caravan center of Takedda, and to the west it reached as far as the Atlantic. When Mansa Musa died in 1332, he left behind him an empire that was as remarkable for its size as for its wealth, one that provided a striking example of the capacity of the black African for political organization.

The Songhay empire of middle Niger came to power after Mali had passed its highest point of development, and it carried the civilization of the western Sudan further toward maturity. Sonni Ali became king in 1464 and made Songhay the most powerful state in the Sudan during his time. He extended the boundaries of Songhay by seizing Djenne and Timbuktu from their Mandingo rulers and making these cities part of his dominion.

Mohammed Askia Ishak, Sonni Ali's successor, took the throne in 1493 and reigned for thirty-five momentous years. He pushed the frontiers of the Songhay empire as far as Segu to the west and the sub-Saharan region of Air to the northeast. Yet his greatest triumph was to provide Songhay with an administrative system that marked new advances toward a truly centralized state. But in 1591 the Moroccan armies of El Mansur emerged from the Sahara, captured Gao and Timbuktu, scattered the forces of Songhay, and plundered the state. Decline set in. Timbuktu and Djenne retained their tradition and practice of scholarship, but within narrower limits. By 1600 the great days of the western Sudan were over.

Within the framework of the newly defined political boundaries, four distinct cultural areas developed in the region south of the Sahara. Each cultural area still continues to have a good deal of homogeneity, and each bears contrasts in some rather specific ways when compared with its neighbors. The western part of the tip of southern Africa is called the Khoi-San area and is inhabited by Bushmen and Hottentots. The Bushmen are a somewhat different group, racially, being shorter than the average black African and of a lighter-colored skin. The Hottentots are evidently the result of a racial mixture between black Africans and Bushmen. This area has a culture dependent mainly on nomadic gathering of food.

The eastern part of Africa's southern tip, from Ethiopia southward, is called the Eastern Cattle Area. Its cultures are complex and revolve around cattle, the chief economic item and symbol of wealth. Some of the tribes are fond of war; some, like the Watusi and the Masai, are very tall and, by virtue of their size, rule over neighboring peoples of smaller stature.

The southern coast of the western extension of the continent, which includes Ghana, Nigeria, the Ivory Coast, and Liberia, is known as the Guinea Coast. This area lacks cattle and is characterized by an elaborate political organization that gave rise to powerful kingdoms before the imposition of European rule.

The Congo area, north of the Khoi-San and centered in the Congo Republic, has to some extent a combination of Eastern Cattle Area and Guinea

Coast traits. It included a number of Pygmy and Negrito people who lived in relative isolation in the jungle. The Congo area probably has the most highly developed visual art tradition in Africa. In fact, the Pygmies may have been the inventors of both counterpoint and polyrhythm in the dawn of African time. Even on this most musical of continents the Pygmies were the acknowledged masters of song and dance, and in ancient times they were brought to Egypt to entertain the pharaohs.

The languages spoken in black Africa belong mainly to three groups: the Khoi-San, the Niger-Congo, and the Sudanic. The Khoi-San languages, characterized by the famous clicks of the tongue, are spoken by the Bushmen and Hottentots. The Niger-Congo group, including Bantu, is a group of closely related languages spoken in the Congo region and the Guinea Coast. The Sudanic languages spoken in the northeastern region of black Africa consist of languages whose common origin is more conjecture than concrete fact. Most of the Bantu and many of the Sudanic languages are tone languages; that is, the pitch at which a syllable is spoken is relevant to the meaning of the word.

In present-day Africa Islam extends over much of the Hamitic and Negritic areas of the eastern coast, across the Mediterranean coastal region, and down through western Africa to the fringes of the Sahara. Wherever the practice of Islam appears, the local musical style is affected.

In black Africa the musical changes caused by the Muslim influence are often specific and easy to identify. Black Muslim singers ornament their lines with short, microtonal shakes and tend to use a tense, nasal voice quality. When voices and instruments are combined, the accompaniment is not the multiple drums or ostinatos on a melodic instrument, as found in central Africa, but rather a single or double drum or a bowed, stringed instrument played heterophonically. In general, the polyrhythms of black Africa seem to give way to single rhythmic lines wherever Islam has become dominant. In addition, the several harmonic and contrapuntal traditions of black Africa become less and less prominent under Muslim culture. Muslim music tends to be monophonic, although heterophony and drones are also often heard. Rhythm stems from the meters of poetry in this music, and rhythm patterns appear in all melodies, both vocal and instrumental. This is especially so in drum parts, which are almost as obligatory as they are in Indian music. Having to play in this fashion, drummers know things like "muffed" beats that are called *dum* and clear beats known as *tak*. There are also less muffed beats that are called *dim* and less clear beats that are called *tik*.

Polyphony is not as essential in Islamic music as it is in European music. It does exist, however, in three forms: heterophony, drones, and occasional consonances. The first is illustrated by what the Western world generally calls an ensemble, a combination of a number of different musical instruments and one or more singers. Drones are used in what is known as the *taqsim*, an improvised prelude that often precedes the beginning of a composition. Consonances are mainly ornaments in which two notes of constant value move about on the same beat. These usually are large intervals like the octave or the fourth.

At the terminals of the Saharan caravan routes there are many black African tribes that either maintain two separate musical traditions or show a definite mixture. The Wolofs of Senegal and Gambia, for example, show a mixture. For their secular dances they use cylindrical, single-headed drums in groups to produce African polyrhythms. On the other hand, when their holy men sing a Muslim *hasida* (hymn), a small kettledrum called a tabala is used along with an iron beater. Together they produce simple, single rhythms much more like the music of the rest of the Muslim world. The Wolof society has a class of professional entertainers called griots. The performances of these musicians reflect a strong Negro-Muslim mixture, for they sing praise songs, a common black African genre, with tense North African voices. They also tell stories to the accompaniment of a plucked, five-stringed halam. The narrative traditions that they use are as old as the camel caravan routes of pre-Muslim Africa. While the Muslim caravan narrators blow heterophonic accompaniments to their tales, the Wolofs play plucked, dronelike harmonies. Similar mixtures of style can be found all along the fringes of the Sahara.

In many ways the music of black Africa parallels folk music of Europe. On both continents there can be found religious and ceremonial music, social sounds, political songs, work songs, songs of allusion, and so on. The list seems endless. While both continents have a history of work songs, the work song in black Africa not only deals with the subject of labor, but is also accompanied by the rhythmic movements of the work, thereby making the task easier. In addition to music in the proper or accepted sense of the word, the use of musical sounds for signaling is also common in black Africa. The system of signaling is tied to the pitch structure of the languages.

The most striking thing about the forms of African music is their dependence on short units and, in many cases, on call-and-response techniques. Solo performance is common in Africa, but the most characteristic African music is performed by groups and gives occasion for the use of alternating performance techniques. This type of performance is more developed in Africa than anywhere else in the world, and it is this element that, perhaps more than any other, has been retained by the black culture in the New World.

To some extent African rhythms are more highly developed than the rhythms of other cultures. The more spectacular rhythmic complexity of black African music appears in the superimposition of several rhythmic structures (rhythmic polyphony) and is found in drumming. This rhythmic complexity is also present in the combination of several voices or, more frequently, in the combination of instruments with voices. The simultaneous use of various meters is widespread among black Africans. Rhythmic po lyphony of a rather complex type can be performed by a single person who may sing in one meter and drum in another. This superimposition of double and triple meters, called hemiola rhythm, is a basic ingredient of much black African rhythmic polyphony. There is a great deal of drumming in Africa, but in other ways the music is also dominated by a percussive quality. Individual tones in singing are attacked strongly, without legato, and generally the music is vigorously accented.

Another characteristic of black African music is its enormous variety of musical instruments. Far from being a land of just drums, black Africa is a land in which instruments and instrumental music play a role equal to that of the voice and vocal music. There is a great deal of music for solo instruments in all of Africa, and there are instrumental ensembles of unrelated instruments or of several instruments of the same type as well. These musical instruments are also used to accompany singers.

Four areas, some of which have been previously discussed in a different light, comprise the main body of African music. The Khoi-San musical region contains a good deal of music which is characterized by the presence of vocalization similar to yodeling. Eastern Africa has for centuries been somewhat under Islamic influence, though by no means to so great an extent as the northern part of Africa. Vertical fifths are more prominent here, and rhythmic structure is not as complex. Percussion instruments are also not as prominent. The central African musical area is distinguished by its great variety of instruments and musical styles, as well as by the polyphonic emphasis on the interval of the third. The main characteristics of the West Coast musical area are the metronome sense, the accompanying concept of "hot rhythm" or the simultaneous use of several meters, and the responsorial form of singing with an overlap between leader and chorus.

In light of this great diversity of styles, it can be assumed that the music of western Africa and certain parts of central Africa definitely was instrumental in asserting a strong influence on the early development of the blues. This music, with its tertial and quartal harmonies and parallelisms, can indeed take responsibility in part for the simple but intense melodic and harmonic features that early Afro-American musicians incorporated into their music. The areas that collectively comprised the Slave Belt were rich in a music that contained polyphony, harmony, and melodic phrases of a more complex nature than those found in other parts of black Africa, and the slaves who were transported from these areas were, as a matter of course, deeply rooted in this melodic and harmonic tradition.

From the evidence of recordings of African music from this area, it appears that the scale systems are diatonic in formula and are of three different major groups or schemes. These scales date back to the beginning of Africa's music history. There are the pentatonic scales (five tones), the heptatonic scales (seven tones), and, less frequently, the hexatonic scales (six tones).

Figure 1.1
Pentatonic Scale with Minor Thirds between the Third and Fourth and the Fifth and Sixth Degrees

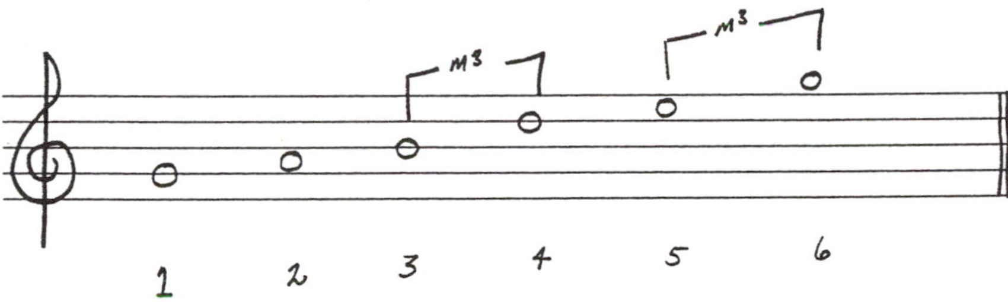

Figure 1.2
Pentatonic Scale with Minor Thirds between the Second and Third and the Fifth and Sixth Degrees

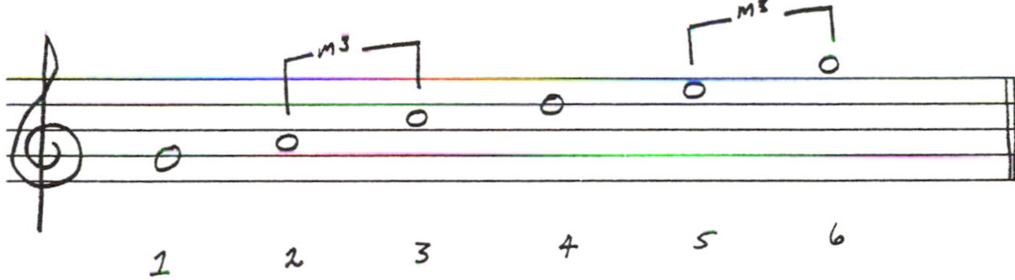

In addition to these, occasional short chromatic rows are also used. The pentatonic scales are, for the most part, anhemitonic in nature; that is, they do not incorporate half steps. Their construction is based entirely on major seconds and minor thirds, with the position of the minor thirds being the distinguishing factor in identifying the tone row. Two arrangements of these scales appear in figures 1.1 and 1.2. Note that while the minor third appears between the fifth and sixth scale degrees of both scales, in figure 1.1 there is a minor third between the third and fourth degrees, while in figure 1.2 a minor third appears between the second and third degrees.

The positions of the minor thirds in these scales are immensely important when comparing West African tonal organization with the melodic qualities of the blues. Blues scales are readily identified by the constant and peculiar appearance of the minor third. Figure 1.3 shows a heptatonic blues scale with the minor thirds between the first and third scale degrees and the fifth and seventh scale degrees. Keep in mind that the scale is neither major nor minor and should under no circumstances be referred to as such. Unlike the European tradition of tonal organization that consists of whole and half steps, the blues scale is built of half steps, whole steps, and one-and-one-

Figure 1.3
Heptatonic Blues Scale

Figure 1.4
C Major Scale

half steps. The major scale built on the same tonality in the European tradition shows little similarity in formula (figure 1.4).

Another scale that is of widespread use in West Africa is the heptatonic scale (seven tones). Similar to the European tradition of tonal progression, it contains whole and half steps but also incorporates two intervals that are a bit smaller than a minor third between the third and fourth degrees and the seventh and eighth degrees. The blues scale, particularly in its use by post–New Orleans jazz musicians, also contains a similarity to this tonal function. The notorious flatted fifth (C♭ [B♮] in the key of F) has a close physical and very strong psychological relationship to the raised fourth degree of the African heptatonic scale. Both scales show the raised fourth (or the flatted fifth) as well as the lowered seventh (E♭ in the key of F). In both, also, the raised fourth or the flatted fifth is generally approached from the note above, and the lowered seventh is approached either from above or below. Figure 1.5 is an example of an African heptatonic scale built on C.

The general contention is that the African slave, in his earliest musical adventures in America, simply retained his traditional vocal approach and altered, in most cases, the technique required to "play" the instruments he was presented with. That is, in order to best realize a certain degree of the

Figure 1.5
African Heptatonic Scale

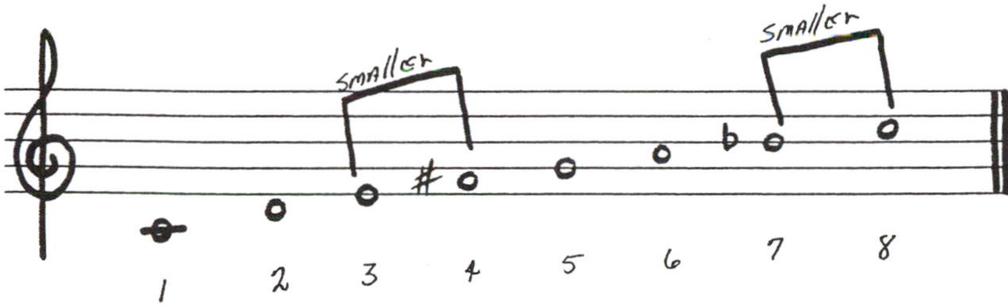

intensity and color his African musical psyche demanded, he unconsciously altered playing techniques and, in some cases, even musical instruments that were not tempered to his musical tradition. Tones that were available to his vocal styles sometimes could not be readily located on some of the instruments on which he first tried to make music. On brass and woodwind instruments, for instance, half valves, false fingerings, and extreme tunings were some of the tricks that were used to come to terms with the music. Stringed instruments were less problematic in this regard. A look into the history of the banjo will quickly relate it to African origins. The reason for this compatibility between stringed instruments and the Afro-American musical language is mainly embedded in the fact that strings are flexible to extremes unknown to other sound-producing materials. Even on conventional instruments, the ones with frets included, special tuning and finger placement can produce desired effects relating to tones that occur between those of the tonal mathematics of European music and are prominent in African music. Hence the banjo and guitar became popular instruments with early Afro-American blues practitioners. They were able to coax the sounds of home from those instruments, sounds that were still moving about the insides of their heads and caused a physical and psychological calm in an otherwise hostile atmosphere.

There are quite a few similarities as well as differences in the African, European, and Afro-American blues scales. Figure 1.6 contains four scales arranged in score to show the similarities and differences in relation to intervallic measurement.

The diagram in figure 1.7 outlines these similarities and differences in mathematical form using numbered scale degrees. Column 1 indicates the two scales that are being analyzed in each of lines A, B, C, D, and E. Column 2 shows the similarities in steps between each note of each of the two scales involved. For example, in line C (African pentatonic 1 and blues scale) similarities in intervallic measurement occur between notes 1 and 2 and also between notes 5 and 6 of both scales. The distance is one whole step in each instance. There is also a similarity between scale degrees 6 and 8 of

Figure 1.6
Musical Contrasts between African, European, and Blues Scales

both scales, that of a step and a half. Column 3 shows the scale degrees with differences in intervals, and column 4 gives the sizes of these different intervals.

African music, in contrast to European music, is not harmonically complicated in structure, although harmony does exist. In the form known as polyphony it is a very well developed factor of the African musical heritage. While the European verticalizations are extremely sophisticated in structure, the African harmonic elements are comparatively simple in that they incorporate, for the most part, two- or three-voice movements of the octave, fifth, fourth, and third. African harmony is not based on a system of block chords as in European music. It arises out of the horizontal process and, therefore, is closely associated with scales and melodic movements. Because of this horizontal (polyphonic) approach, much parallelism exists in the music. There are parallel thirds, fourths, fifths, and, in rare cases, sixths. Other intervals are seldom used. This is exactly the case in early forms of the blues.

Figure 1.8 shows a melodic line (bottom) and its harmonic accompaniment line, which contain expanses of the third, fourth, fifth, and octave. Keep in mind that this is but one example of many variations of African polyphony. Figure 1.9 shows three bars of a blues line with a typical harmony line on the top.

In addition to, and also in accompaniment of, Africa's rich rhythmic and vocal tradition, its music's melodic character, supported by stringed instruments of various timbres, asserted a strong influence on the birth and development of the blues. The traditional approach to playing the strings survived in the early Afro-American's technique on Western-made musical instruments such as the guitar and banjo, and the discipline of polyphonic

Figure 1.7
Mathematical Contrasts between African, European, and Blues Scales

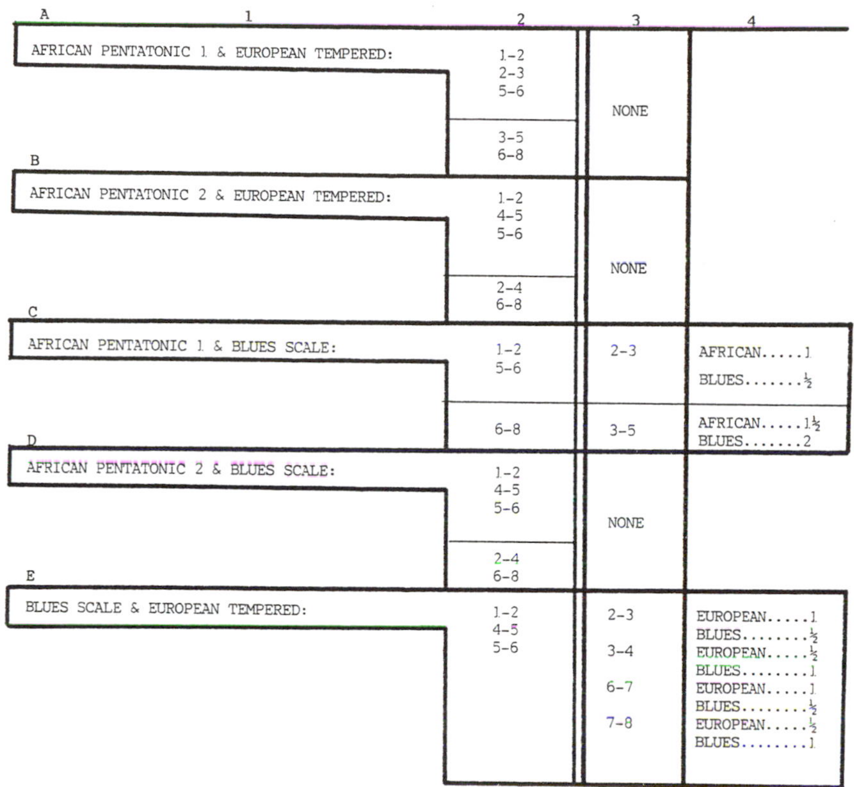

	1	2	3	4
A	AFRICAN PENTATONIC 1 & EUROPEAN TEMPERED:	1-2 2-3 5-6	NONE	
		3-5 6-8		
B	AFRICAN PENTATONIC 2 & EUROPEAN TEMPERED:	1-2 4-5 5-6	NONE	
		2-4 6-8		
C	AFRICAN PENTATONIC 1 & BLUES SCALE:	1-2 5-6	2-3	AFRICAN.....1 BLUES.......½
		6-8	3-5	AFRICAN.....1½ BLUES.......2
D	AFRICAN PENTATONIC 2 & BLUES SCALE:	1-2 4-5 5-6	NONE	
		2-4 6-8		
E	BLUES SCALE & EUROPEAN TEMPERED:	1-2 4-5 5-6	2-3 3-4 6-7 7-8	EUROPEAN.....1 BLUES........½ EUROPEAN.....½ BLUES........1 EUROPEAN.....1 BLUES........½ EUROPEAN.....½ BLUES........1

Figure 1.8
Twelve-bar Blues Harmony (Two Voices)

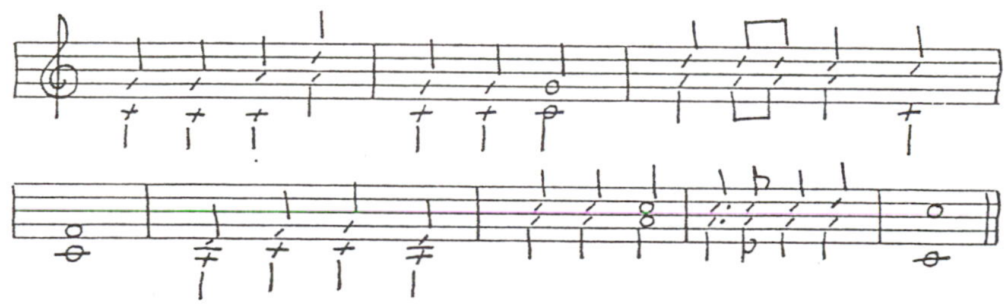

Figure 1.9
Blues Phrase with Melody on Bottom and Harmony Line on Top

lines and harmonies of the minor third, perfect fourth, and perfect fifth readily became basic elements of the blues language.

BIBLIOGRAPHY

Akpabot, Samuel E. *Ibibio Music in Nigerian Culture*. East Lansing: Michigan State University Press, 1975.

Anene, J. C. *Southern Nigeria in Transition, 1885–1906*. Cambridge: Cambridge University Press, 1966.

Arkell, A. J. *A History of the Sudan from the Earliest Times to 1821*. London: University of London, Athlome Press, 1961.

Arom, Simha. *African Polyphony and Polyrhythm: Musical Structure and Methodology*. Cambridge: Cambridge University Press, 1991.

Bebey, Francis. *African Music: A People's Art*. New York: L. Hill, 1975.

Bender, Wolfgang. *Sweet Mother: Modern African Music*. Chicago: University of Chicago Press, 1991.

Borill, E. W. *The Golden Trade of the Moors*. London: Oxford University Press, 1968.

Brandel, Rose. *The Music of Central Africa*. New York: Da Capo Press, 1983.

Chernoff, John Miller. *African Rhythm and African Sensibility: Aesthetics and Social Action in African Musical Idioms*. Chicago: University of Chicago Press, 1979.

Clark, John Desmond. *The Prehistory of South Africa*. New York: Penguin Books, 1959.

Cole, Sonia. *The Prehistory of East Africa*. New York: Penguin Books, 1954.

Curtin, Philip D. *African History*. New York: Macmillan, 1964.

Davidson, Basil. *Africa in History*. New York: Macmillan, 1968.

———. *The African Past*. Boston: Little, Brown and Company, 1964.

———. *Black Mother*. Boston: Little, Brown and Company, 1961.

Djedje, Jacqueline C., and William G. Carter, eds. *African Musicology: Current Trends*. Vol. 1. Atlanta: African Studies Association, 1989.

Drimmer, Melvin, ed. *Black History: A Reappraisal.* Garden City, N.Y.: Doubleday, 1968.

Fage, J. D. *An Introduction to the History of West Africa.* 3d ed. Cambridge: Cambridge University Press, 1962.

Freeman-Grenville, G.S.P. *The Medieval History of the Coast of Tanganyika.* London: Oxford University Press, 1962.

Graham, Ronnie. *The Da Capo Guide to Contemporary African Music.* New York: Da Capo Press, 1988.

Gray, John. *African Music: A Bibliographical Guide to the Traditional, Popular, Art, and Liturgical Musics of Sub-Saharan Africa.* Westport, Conn.: Greenwood Press, 1991.

Herskovits, Melville. *The Human Factor in Changing Africa.* New York: Alfred A. Knopf, 1962.

Hodgkin, Thomas. *Nigerian Perspectives.* 2d ed. London: Oxford University Press, 1975.

Jackson, Irene V., ed. *More Than Drumming: Essays on African and Afro-Latin American Music and Musicians.* Westport, Conn.: Greenwood Press, 1985.

Keil, Charles. *The Tiv Song: The Sociology of Art in a Classless Society.* Chicago: University of Chicago Press, 1979.

Latourette, K. S. *A History of the Expansion of Christianity.* The First Five Centuries, vol. 1. New York: Harper and Row, 1937.

Nettl, Bruno. *Folk and Traditional Music of the Western Continents.* Englewood Cliffs, N.J.: Prentice-Hall, 1965.

Nketia, Joseph H. *The Music of Africa.* New York: W. W. Norton, 1974.

Norborg, Ake. *A Handbook of Musical and Other Sound-Producing Instruments from Namibia and Botswana.* Philadelphia: Coronet Books, 1987.

Oliver, Roland. *The Dawn of African History.* 2d ed. London: Oxford University Press, 1968.

Rotberg, Robert I. *A Political History of Tropical Africa.* New York: Harcourt, Brace and World, 1965.

Shinnie, Margaret. *Ancient African Kingdoms.* New York: New American Library, 1970.

Southern, Eileen. *Biographical Dictionary of Afro-American and African Musicians.* Westport, Conn.: Greenwood Press, 1982.

Stapleton, Chris, and Chris May. *African Rock: The Pop Music of a Continent.* New York: Dutton, 1990.

Stone, Ruth M. *Dried Millet Breaking: Time, Words, and Song in the Wol Epic of the Kpelle.* Bloomington: Indiana University Press, 1988.

Trimingham, J. S. *A History of Islam in West Africa.* London: Oxford University Press, 1962.

Vansina, Jan. *Kingdoms of the Savanna.* Madison: University of Wisconsin Press, 1965.

Walker, Wyatt. *Somebody's Calling My Name.* Valley Forge, Penn.: Judson Press, 1979.

2

THE NEW WORLD

When the Portuguese first made contact with western Africa at the beginning of the fifteenth century, they found a number of well-established kingdoms along the Guinea Coast and at the mouth of the Congo River. There were great cities with elaborate palaces and regal courts administered with pomp and ceremony. Slavery was essentially an institution of the state and the kings. Furthermore, the number of slaves in Africa was not very great, and protection was provided in law as well as in tradition.

When the Portuguese established trading relations with these kingdoms, one of the first items of commerce was slaves. The African kings saw nothing wrong in selling slaves, and the Portuguese saw nothing wrong in buying them. By 1444 there was a thriving market for African slaves in Portugal. In fact, when Columbus reached America some fifty years later, there were provinces in Portugal where Africans outnumberd Europeans.

The discovery of America by Columbus in 1492 unleashed waves of both greed and idealism in Europe. Unfortunately, greed frequently motivated the actions taken by Europeans in the New World. The islands of the Caribbean, for example, proved to be ideal for the cultivation of sugarcane and other subtropical produce. For farming of this sort to be lucrative, an enormous amount of labor was needed. Though the first colonizers tried to enslave the Indian inhabitants of their new possessions, they failed. The Indians' cultural experience had been so different from that of their Spanish and Portuguese masters that they were totally incapable of adjusting. There were, for example, reports of Indians who simply sat down and died for no apparent reason. Those Indians who were forced to work in the mines and on the plantations of the Caribbean islands died in huge numbers both from oppressive labor and from European diseases to which they lacked a natural resistance.

Faced with the unsuitability of the Indians as a labor force, the colonizers turned to Africans for slaves. The fact that Africans were better able to withstand the conditions of forced labor is indicative not of a lack of courage to resist captivity, for their resistance was universally known and feared, but of their own cultural background and ability to adapt. African culture was not as different from European culture as that of the American Indians. The Africans did not, of course, submit to slavery gently, but they did not perish under it as did the Indians. The Africans were familiar with slavery as an institution and, to a degree, knew how to behave as slaves. Certainly they knew how to survive as slaves.

Thus the limelight centered on the Africans who, for a small amount of money, could be bought for life instead of for a few years, as was the case with indentured servants. The Africans presented an unlimited labor source; they required no governmental protection and were so visible by the color of their skin that they could run but not hide, at least not for long. The Africans were brought to America for no other reason but to serve. Their suffering began on the shores of their homelands and continued on the slave ships, where they perished in great numbers. Their suffering grew in the New World on the plantations of the Caribbean islands and of South and North America, which only half of the forty million blacks taken from Africa lived to see.

During its first century this commerce—which brought thousands of Africans to the New World and which later flowed northward to the English colonies—was almost exclusively limited to the Portuguese possessions in the Americas. Trade with the Americas opened formally in 1517, twenty-five years after Columbus's discoveries in the New World. Slavery, however, is known to have existed prior to that year in the Western Hemisphere in a less formal fashion.

From the middle of the sixteenth century to the beginning of the nineteenth century, England dominated the slave trade. At the height of the trade, in the eighteenth century, an estimated three-quarters of the English ships were involved in importing slaves. American ships from New England, however, were involved in the slave trade on a somewhat smaller scale as early as 1700.

The actual acquisition of slaves along the West African coast was an elaborate process. Permanent trading stations were established. Treaties were made with the African kings. Complicated bargaining sessions and exchanges between station officials and African officials were arranged. Finally, the slaves—war captives, criminals, political prisoners, and some people who were simply kidnapped—had to be brought from the interior. Ships frequently had to make several stops along the coast in order to acquire a full cargo for the trip to America. All of this demanded organization, discipline, and cooperation from both buyer and seller.

The slave trade flourished for over four hundred years. Never before in history had it been possible to accumulate so much capital in so short a period of time. The wealth that went to the operators of the trade was often reinvested in the mines, mills, and factories of Europe. Though it is difficult to determine the precise extent to which the slave trade spurred the industrial revolution in Europe, most historians agree that the role of the slave trade was critical. This trade reached a peak in the second half of the eighteenth century, and it has been conservatively estimated that fourteen million Africans were imported into the New World by the late nineteenth century, when the slave traffic ended. For every African who reached the American shores alive, four died either in the slave raids, during the marches from the interior, or on board the ships. Accounts of slave deaths due to overcrowding, disease, suicide, beating, mass murder, revolt, and malnutrition are well known. Over a period of some four hundred years Africa lost more than sixty million people through this type of genocide.

The slave trade, nevertheless, in its historical context was only one aspect of one of the cruelest periods of world history. In the seventeenth and eighteenth centuries life everywhere was cheap. Laws were harsh and inhumane. During this period public hangings were probably the most popular spectator sport in all the civilized states of Europe and America. According to eyewitness reports, literally thousands of people gathered to watch the frequent hangings. Entire families—men, women, and children—witnessed the death throes of the condemned. If the life of a slave was considered almost nothing, so was that of a free man, no matter what his color.

The various stages in the development of the slave trade had a decisive influence on the area of Africa from which the slaves were taken, as well as the area where they were placed in America. It was once thought that slaves came from all over Africa and that only the weak and inferior were captured and sold into slavery. Under such conditions African customs could hardly have survived in America. The majority of slaves came from the western coast of Africa, especially the Niger Delta, Senegal, the Congo, and near the Gulf of Guinea. One of the strongest and most well known of these West African areas was Ashanti (Ghana), whose magnificent coasts along Accra, Cape Coast, Elmina, and Tema became frequent ports of call. Many parts of Africa remained untouched, however, and certain distant locations supplied only a small number of slaves, since the long journey prevented large numbers from surviving the ordeal of the march.

Certain patterns evolved with the slave trade. As the search for slaves moved down the western coast of Africa from around Dakar all the way to the Congo, first Portuguese traders, then the Dutch, the English, and the French dominated the trade. Each European power supplied its own colonies in the New World with slaves from Africa, and the planters in each of the colonies came to prefer the tribesmen supplied by their own country. Spain, a partial exception, tended to buy from anyone who would sell, and England tended to sell slaves to anyone who would buy. Colonial preferences, nevertheless, became generally fixed. Brazilian planters, who were supplied at an early date with Senegalese slaves by Portuguese traders, preferred Senegalese slaves thereafter. In the same fashion English planters came to prefer Ashanti slaves; Spanish planters came to prefer the Yorubas; French planters came to prefer Dahomeans.

Slavery became concentrated in the Southern states mainly because of the economic importance of cotton and the consequent need of a labor force to cultivate and harvest the crop. Even though slaves were also kept in Northern states, they were not nearly as numerous there. Therefore, the majority of the earliest musical endeavors by the Africans in North America emanated from the South. While the North American colonists reflected the cultures of their European mother countries, the slaves exhibited totally different musical and religious traditions. Much of what an African exhibited regarding his traditions depended, among other things, on whether he was sold to a British-Protestant or to a Latin-Catholic colony.

The French, Spanish, and Portuguese planters of the Caribbean islands and South America did not seem to care what a slave thought or did in his spare time so long as it did not interfere with production. Perhaps this attitude was influenced by centuries of civilized interchange between the Mediterranean countries and North Africa, where the survival of slavery in itself was less important than the persistence of a long tradition of slave law that had come down through the Justinian Code, Spanish law, and the traditions of the Catholic church, where men were considered equal. Spanish and Portuguese law governing colonies in the Americas even encouraged the master to release his slaves and the slave to achieve freedom on his own.

With a British planter, however, a slave was likely to change his ways more quickly, discarding his own traditions and adopting those of the British. The reason for this stems from the fact that the British did not specialize in large plantations, and each slave owner possessed fewer slaves than the Spanish, Portuguese, or French. Because of the smaller number, a slave could come to know his master more easily. Sometimes he was used as a house servant and, watching his master, became ashamed of his own customs, which the English believed to be savage and barbaric. Wanting to improve his condition, he frequently made a point of concealing his own traditions, which, in many cases, he carried on underground. Under British West Indian and United States laws the slave could not hope for manumission. This route, if not entirely blocked, was made difficult by numerous impediments. The bias in favor of keeping the slave in bondage was in definite contrast with the other governing system present in the New World. Just as the approval of manumission was perhaps the most characteristic and significant feature of the Latin American slave system, opposition to manumission and denial of any opportunities to achieve it were the primary aspect of slavery in the British West Indies and the colonies of North America.

Because slave owners were suspicious and fearful of insurrections, which had occurred on both ship and land, slaves were often forced to sing songs while working to lessen the opportunities for planning other such incidents. Their songs and music, often molded in the context of the inhumane experiences of slavery, helped them to tolerate the often-oppressive conditions under which they worked. Music relieved the burden of their spiritual and physical problems and at times served as a lead for the slaves to entertain themselves. The early slave music consisted of the expression of many human passions rooted in oppression. Work songs, blues, and spirituals are some examples of their music that echoed despair as well as jubilation and optimistic yearning for a place, anywhere, without the conditions of slavery. These songs, born out of the duties and hardships of bondage, served them in work, in worship, and in play. On many plantations slaves were also involved in developing an entertainment medium that would later gain great popularity in the form of the minstrel shows that toured the United States during much of the nineteenth century.

Decades of abolitionist movements passed, a bloody and divisive civil war was fought, and a reconstruction plan was undertaken. But attitudes were hard to change. If anything, the country's attitude toward black people grew even more perverse. Jim Crow became the law of the land, and white racists killed many blacks who did not adhere to it.

How the Africans brought to America as slaves and their descendents were able to overcome the considerable odds against them and develop a culture that is universally acclaimed today is a fascinating story. Though slave owners tried to destroy all vestiges of the African past in their slaves, much of it survived. Especially important to the development of black culture was the survival of an oral tradition of storytelling, a tradition that was not merely a form of entertainment but a method of expressing and preserving the history, music, and philosophy of the people generation after generation. Another important vestige of the black man's past was a profound appreciation of music as an integral part of life with implications far beyond that of simple entertainment.

The South was a rural and raw land during much of early American history, and musical entertainment was a luxury that both blacks and whites cherished. For that reason many slave owners encouraged the Saturday night holiday and after-hours playing, dancing, and singing for their slaves. Some planters even hired their slaves out to neighbors, creating a sort of performing circuit among the plantations.

Fortunately, the genius of the black man could not be oppressed by the racial atmosphere that existed in America between 1876 and the start of World War I. In St. Louis, Memphis, and especially New Orleans blacks were alive and well despite Jim Crow, night riders, and "separate but equal" societies. This was the period when jazz and ragtime were being created by black musicians and singers in the brothels of Storyville and in the honky-tonks of St. Louis and Memphis. In the fields of the South where most blacks spent a good deal of their lives, a new type of song had developed, a moaning, downhearted sound that rose up from the heavy burdens of slave life. It was somewhat related to the spirituals but had a different texture and could only be described as "the blues."

It seems that the African, after having spent years under the influence of the North American South, both as a slave and freedman, would develop certain traits that would become identifiable in his art. Indeed, the movement from field hollers to work songs to the spirituals paved a musical path of development that ran up to and through the blues as well as to other more popular forms of contemporary black American music. After all, the structure of the work songs and the emotional qualities of the spirituals are direct influences on the blues phenomenon. Although some consider it feasible to relate the blues to the spirituals in a generic way, it seems clear that only the approach to melody and harmony show bits of relationship. The cosmetics of psychological play at means and end do not meet on a common ground. Only the emotional qualities come close, but on their own completely separate terms. The diagram in figure 2.1 is a geographical development plot of the blues from its early pre-American roots to its present various divisions.

After the abolition of slavery in the United States, blacks were, wholly in the interest of continued economic gain, given the choice either to remain on the farms and plantations or to leave and search out a livelihood elsewhere. Most chose to gravitate toward the latter and set out penniless into a little-caring world, but with the feeling that being free was surely the root of all success. Others stayed on to sharecrop under a system that they knew little of and that was ultimately responsible for keeping them socially and economically just a hairline above their former status as slaves.

No matter what the decision was, this new lifestyle proved to be different and extremely difficult for the ex-slave. New problems began to arise. Blacks suddenly encountered the intricacies of personal gain, free love, and many other elements of everyday community life that had previously been foreign to them. For a people who were descendants of those who embraced music as a life agent, a functional art of everyday, this change brought considerable need for a new musical form of expression and relief. The work songs and field hollers were hardly still effective. They served another purpose and could not give vent to these new experiences and the passions they influenced. It was about this time that the first strains of the blues started to surface. No one knows exactly what the sound of the blues was like at its beginning, but it is apparent that musically it grew out of the African's tonal tradition and the lyrics related to the new experiences of a free life.

Figure 2.1
Geographical Development of the Blues

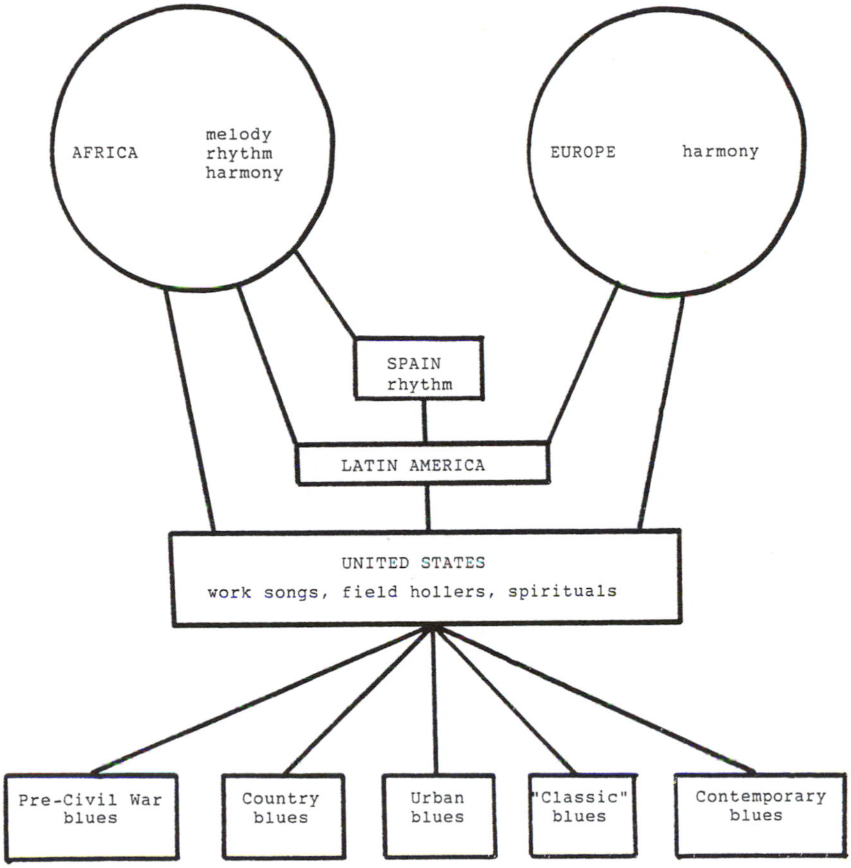

The blues' eventual development into a twelve-bar structure with its simple, blunt, effective I-IV-V chord progression was caused by a need for solid structural logic. In the beginning the music was totally melodic and unmeasured. It consisted mainly of lyrics and linear accompaniment figures, and since the music was performed by only one musician, little regard was given to bar measurement. The performer had total control of beginning, development, and end. When musicians began playing the blues together as a group, though, the need for structure arose. There had to be a definite design relating to melodic/harmonic content and musical direction to determine where the music and musicians were at any given time in a piece.

Figure 2.2 is an illustration of the twelve-bar scheme. Note the call-and-response–like interplay between the vocal and instrumental responsorial improvisations that is reminiscent of the work song. Occasional exceptions to this twelve-bar sequence occur. Blues tunes may run eight bars, sixteen

Figure 2.2
Twelve-bar Blues Form

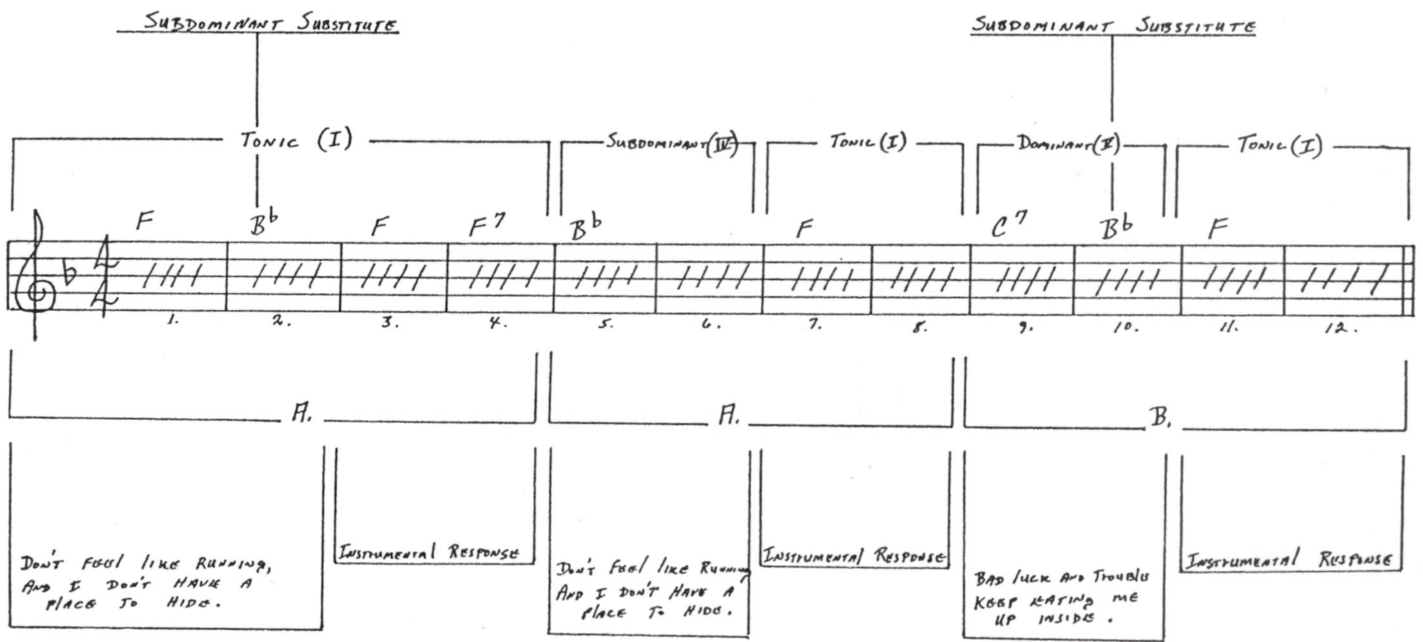

bars, thirty-two bars, or, in the jazz avant-garde, thirteen or twenty-one bars, but the most popular blues renditions are in the twelve-bar style.

The date of the first blues will probably never be known. The more researchers learn, the earlier it seems to have been. African songs of ridicule, pity, and sorrow were probably the source of this music. While spirituals might have been sung by slaves who received a convert's rather secondhand picture of Christianity, the blues songs were more likely to have been shaped by the slaves of the field and their descendents, who remained closer to their African traditions. This accounts in one way for the fact that the blues will not cover up reality with the idea of a future utopia, as do the spirituals, but instead come to grips with life and its frustrations, hardships, and unfavorable personal encounters. The natures of the two song types say much about the attitudes of those who created them.

The significance of the blues as perhaps the most authentic musical documentation of black attitudes for a great number of years leads one to expect that careful records were kept detailing its development. Yet quite the opposite is true. The blues, a music that blacks kept close to themselves, was not written at all until it was examined in the later part of this century by white intellectuals. Part of the secret of the blues' survival might lie in the fact that it remained a part of black culture and was never presented to whites for acceptance, even after the advent of popular recordings around 1971. Blues records were sold as "race" records. They were released through outlets in black communities and made available only on special order to others who might happen to know about them. The survival of the blues in spite of any efforts to discredit black music as a whole parallels the survival of the blacks themselves.

When black minstrel shows became common during the latter part of the nineteenth century, they attracted many talented youngsters hungry for a touch of adventure in show business. One of these young men was W. C. Handy, who joined Mahara's Minstrels in 1896 when he was twenty-three years old. A minister's son who became a musician despite the protests of his father, Handy taught himself how to play the cornet and studied the theory of music from books to become a good-enough musician to qualify for the job of bandmaster. Though he is often referred to as the man who invented the blues, this is not the case. The blues existed as an old form long before 1909, when Handy composed a political campaign song that he called "Mr. Crump" and that was published in 1912 as "Memphis Blues." Among the old musicians the blues continued to thrive in their country style, but it was Handy who began a tradition of composition in the twelve-bar style that could be played by others, thereby leading to its popularization.

BIBLIOGRAPHY

Abrahams, Roger D. *Afro-American Folktales: Stories from Black Traditions in the New World*. New York: Pantheon Books, 1985.

Bancroft, George. *History of the United States from the Discovery of the American Continent*. 10 vols. Boston: Little, Brown and Company, 1866–75.

Beard, Charles A., and William C. Bagley. *The History of the American People*. New York: Macmillan, 1933.

Billingsley, Andrew. *Climbing Jacob's Ladder: The Enduring Legacy of African-American Families*. New York: Simon and Schuster, 1992.

Bond, Horace Mann. *The Education of the Negro in the American Social Order*. New York: Prentice-Hall, 1934.

Brawley, Benjamin. *The Negro in Literature and Art*. New York: Duffield and Company, 1921.

Burlin, Natalie Curtis. *Songs and Tales from the Dark Continent*. New York: G. Schirmer, 1920.

Butcher, Margaret Just. *The Negro in American Culture*. New York: New American Library, 1957.

Couch, W. T. *Culture in the South*. Chapel Hill: University of North Carolina Press, 1934.

Cunard, Nancy. *Negro Anthology*. London: Wishart and Company, 1934.

Dabney, Virginius. *Liberalism in the South*. Chapel Hill: University of North Carolina Press, 1932.

Dance, Daryl C. *Long Gone: The Mecklenberg Six and the Theme of Escape in Black Folklore*. Knoxville: University of Tennessee Press, 1987.

Davie, Maurice R. *Negroes in American Society*. New York: McGraw-Hill, 1949.

Davis, Ronald L. F. *Good and Faithful Labor: From Slavery to Sharecropping in the Natchez District, 1860–1890*. Westport, Conn.: Greenwood Press, 1982.

Drake, St. Clair. *Black Folk Here and There: An Essay in History and Anthropology*. 2 vols. Los Angeles: Center for Afro-American Studies, University of California, 1990.

Drimmer, Melvin, ed. *Black History: A Reappraisal*. Garden City, N.Y.: Doubleday, 1968.

Du Bois, W.E.B. *Black Reconstruction*. New York: Harcourt, Brace and Company, 1935.

Dundes, Alan, ed. *Mother Wit from the Laughing Barrel: Readings in the Interpretation of Afro-American Folklore*. Jackson: University Press of Mississippi, 1990.

Embree, Edwin R. *Brown America*. New York: Viking Press, 1931.

Faison, Edward, Jr. *African-American Folk Tales*. New York: Vantage Press, 1989.

Fisher, Miles M. *Negro Slave Songs in the United States*. Ithaca, N.Y.: Cornell University Press, 1953.

Fletcher, Tom. *100 Years of the Negro in Show Business*. New York: Burdge and Company, 1954.

Fry, Gladys-Marie. *Night Riders in Black Folk History*. Athens: University of Georgia Press, 1991.

Gutman, Herbert G. *The Black Family in Slavery and Freedom*. New York: Random House, 1977.

Johnson, Charles S. *The Negro in American Civilization*. New York: Henry Holt and Company, 1930.

———. *Shadow of the Plantation*. Chicago: University of Chicago Press, 1934.

Katz, Bernard, ed. *The Social Implications of Early Negro Music in the United States*. New York: Arno Press and the *New York Times*, 1979.

Krehbiel, Henry E. *Afro-American Folksongs: A Study in Racial and National Music*. New York: G. Schirmer, 1914.

Lang, Iain. *Jazz in Perspective: The Background of the Blues*. London: Hutchinson, 1947.

Lester, Julius. *Black Folktales*. New York: Grove Weidenfeld, 1991.

Levine, Lawrence W. *Black Culture and Black Consciousness: Afro-American Folk Thought from Slavery to Freedom*. London and New York: Oxford University Press, 1977.

Miller, Kelly. *Race Adjustment*. New York: Neale Publishing Company, 1909.

Nobles, Wade W. *Africanity and the Black Family: The Development of a Theoretical Model*. Institute for the Advanced Study of Black Family Life and Culture, 1985.

Parker, Matthew, and Lee N. June, eds. *The Black Family: Past, Present, and Future*. New York: Zondervan, 1991.

Pomerance, Alan. *Repeal of the Blues: How Black Entertainers Influenced the Civil Rights Movement*. New York: Carol Publishing Group, 1991.

Powdermaker, Hortense. *After Freedom*. New York: Viking Press, 1939.

Roach, Hildred. *Black American Music: Past and Present*. Boston: Crescendo Publishing Company, 1973.

Rublowsky, John. *Black Music in America*. New York: Basic Books, 1971.

Sampson, Henry T. *Ghost Walks: A Chronological History of Blacks in Show Business*. Metuchen, N.J.: Scarecrow Press, 1988.

Smith, Wallace C. *The Church in the Life of the Black Family*. Valley Forge, Penn.: Judson Press, 1985.

Spear, Allan H. *Black Chicago: The Making of a Ghetto*. Chicago: University of Chicago Press, 1967.

Stearns, Marshall. *The Story of Jazz*. New York: Oxford University Press, 1958.

Warmoth, Henry Clay. *War, Politics, and Reconstruction*. New York: Macmillan, 1930.

Weiner, Leo. *Africa and the Discovery of America*. 2 vols. Philadelphia: Innes and Sons, 1922.

Work, John W. *American Negro Songs*. New York: Howell, Soskin, 1940.

3

SOME HIGHLY MUSICAL PLACES

THE MISSISSIPPI DELTA

Mississippi, Louisiana, Texas, and Tennessee have each been credited at one time or another with spawning the blues. Today, scholars agree that the Mississippi Delta is the most likely birthplace, if any one place can be so designated. There is no doubt that the Delta area has produced the largest number of important bluesmen. Since the first blues developed in rural places offering extremely limited instrumental resources and an almost total lack of European musical tradition, the voice, as in all African music, was used as an instrument. Later the guitar and the harmonica were added as background and fill instruments, respectively. The resulting music, totally black in sound, began as a form of self-expression, a genre of self-amusement that only later promoted dancing and good times. While this music has its roots in the various forms of black music that preceded it, it is basically a post–Civil War development. In its earliest stage it was the expression of musicians who traveled the farms, lumber camps, and towns of the rural South.

Although efforts have been made by some to differentiate blues styles, in most cases these differences are tenuous and can easily cause confusion. Yet the blues—in the truest, unalloyed sense of the word—survived in three separate and distinct expressions that were emitted from three separate and distinct lifestyles. These areas of development are the rural, the urban, and the commercially popular style performed by women called the "classical blues," probably because of its polished presentation. Although distinguishing characteristics can be associated with these different expressions and more logically with the geographical areas of the South, where they developed, these characteristics, nevertheless, overlap to form one strong and vital area of black art.

The Mississippi Delta style is regarded as the most primitive of all blues offerings. The music of this area is characterized by uneven rhyming patterns, limited melody, lyrics that are almost spoken rather than sung, and a delivery that encompasses shouts, moans, groans, and even yodeling. The bottleneck guitar technique, which endorses constant repetition of melodic figures, a heavy sound, and rough intensity, is also accepted as an identifier of the Mississippi Delta style.

Any map of the Delta country of Mississippi will include the town of Cleveland. Just outside of this town, on the Dockery Plantation, Charley Patton*[1] grew up. He was the first of the Delta bluesmen to emerge from the anonymity of the blues tradition. He was born a bit more to the south, near Vicksburg, in the little town of Edwards in 1885. Being a small, frail man, he was not built for the backbreaking work in the fields, and because of his skill with the guitar and song he managed to avoid this type of "new slavery" throughout most of his life. He possessed a strong, very deep voice and a remarkable ability to compose songs from the raw materials of the life he lived. What made his music unique was the fairly easily recognized nuances that amplified his innovativeness. His music was his own. It belonged to him and not tradition. Charley Patton's songs always made reference to his own adventures and those of very close friends. These references were often quite specific, to say the least, and his songs were more closely related to ballads announcing an event or telling a story than were those of the other bluesmen who followed him. However, these balladlike blues songs were not actually ballads because they did not reflect the objectivity characteristic of that song type. The blues spirit was always present in his songs, the emotion, the story told from the heart. Patton, who was the first Mississippi Delta bluesman to gain prominence, worked well in this sort of transitional idiom.

Patton recorded a great deal before his death in 1934. In just five years, beginning in 1929, he cut approximately sixty sides for Vocalion and Paramount. These recordings included a large selection of the blues, some ballads, and a few religious songs. He would be only a legend today if it were not for this recorded legacy he gave to the world. Patton rarely left the Delta country except to make trips north to record in Richmond, Indiana, Chicago, and New York. His life was dedicated to endless rounds of nights spent in juke joints and at country dances and days at picnics and fish fries, a pattern followed by all itinerant bluesmen of that era.

Charley Patton is important as an innovator directly related to the kinds of music that preceded the blues. He is also just as important as a link to the music that followed him. He traveled with Eddie James "Son" House, Jr.,* who was younger, tutored an even younger musician named Chester

1. An asterisk following a person's name indicates that a biographical sketch is to be found in chapter 7.

Burnett,* who later made a big name for himself as Howlin' Wolf, and inspired Bukka White (Booker T. Washington White),* who as a kid used to follow him around their hometown of Cleveland, Mississippi. Although it would be erroneous to name Patton as the originator of the Delta blues style, he was the earliest practitioner to send that style outside the region by way of recordings.

In the late 1930s Mississippi remained much the way it had been during the earliest days of the blues. Trapped by poverty and segregation, over 70 percent of the black population worked as sharecroppers and tenants on the cotton plantations. But in the decade that followed over a million blacks left the South, and Mississippi lost half of its young adults. However, there was probably still more support for the blues in Mississippi than anywhere else. Blues was being played on the plantations, in shacks at house parties, on the streets, in joints and honky-tonks, in cotton centers like Yazoo City, Greenville, and Clarksdale, in Memphis, and across the river in Arkansas in towns like Helena and West Memphis.

Although the core of Mississippi Delta blues, with its rhythmic tension, almost speechlike vocalizing, blurred bottleneck guitar style, and overall feeling of anxiety, remained the same throughout this period, not all Mississippi blues was like this. There had always been the instrumental flexibility of musicians like the Chatmons, the polite delicacy of Skip James and his followers, and the haunting restraint of the genius of Tommy Johnson and others. The Mississippi Sheiks were being recorded constantly from 1930 to 1935, and the demanding Bo Carter kept new material on the market throughout the 1930s until 1940. Still, despite the variations, traditions of the old Delta blues continued.

In 1940 record producer Lester Melrose brought to the recording studios one of the most primitive-sounding Delta musicians he could find, Booker T. Washington White. At the peak of the jumping urban blues era, and at a time when swing bands and jitterbug music were sweeping the United States and the world, Bukka, as he was popularly known, recorded a series of traditionally pure Delta blues that was rich in themes of death, love, and imprisonment. He had been recorded before in 1930 and had even had a respectable hit with "Shake 'Em On Down," which he recorded in 1937. But for reasons not fully known he had been sent for a while to Parchman Farm, the notorious prison farm in Mississippi. He did get a chance to play his music there and even recorded a couple of songs for John A. Lomax, who was then with the Library of Congress. But by 1940 Bukka's blues style was slowly being superseded, and success did not last long for him.

When Charley Patton died in 1934, his blues style was already beginning to seem out of date. But his friends Son House and Willie Brown continued playing together well into the 1940s and kept the tradition going. Son House was especially influential. Like Charley Patton, bluesman Son House was torn by an inner conflict between leading the profane life of a bluesman and the sanctified life of a preacher. As a young man working in the cotton fields and performing other chores, including those of a rural preacher, Son House had become upset when he heard men singing the blues. Only after he moved to St. Louis to work at the Commonwealth Steel Plant did he become interested in making music. That desire to make music was sparked by a street musician playing a guitar with a small medicine bottle on his finger. The sounds House heard coming from the instrument struck a sympathetic chord in him that vibrated for years.

Through Patton, who was more than fifteen years older, House made a test recording for a Paramount Records scout. The test earned a recording date at the company's studios in Grafton, Wisconsin, in July 1930. "Preachin' the Blues" and "Dry Spell Blues" were the outcome of this session. When his playing buddy Willie Brown died suddenly in 1948, House took the death of his friend as a sign from heaven that he should put his instrument away. Though he was never successful in completely purging himself of the blues, he managed to avoid recording again until 1962, when Alan Lomax talked him into cutting a number of songs for the Library of Congress.

Because Son House had indeed been a preacher, his life as a blues singer reflected an unresolved conflict. To a large part of the black community the blues was still the Devil's music, the music of eroticism, immorality, whiskey drinking, and violence. It was an unequaled source of corruption. To many blacks salvation was to be found only in ridding oneself of the music's control. The blues and all that it represented were foreign to the standards a preacher was expected to uphold in a purely religious sense. Son House and many other blues singers constantly felt torn between enjoying the good times of nightlife and still believing that they would someday be able to turn their backs on that intruder into righteous living called the blues and return to the path of good.

House made his choice more than once. At times of feeling intense guilt, he would return to preaching, only to gravitate quickly toward the blues to satisfy his thirst for that kind of life. His singing always had the intensity of a backcountry preacher, and he would sometimes put down his guitar to sing an unaccompanied gospel song. Even in his blues he would refer to the subject of religion.

One of the musicians who learned from Son House was a young man named Robert Johnson* who has become a legendary figure among white blues enthusiasts. A gifted young artist, he was driven by his hunger for life and his passion for music to excesses that killed him when he was only twenty-four years old. Yet he left behind him a treasury of blues recordings, around thirty songs, which have been a great source of inspiration to musicians and collectors alike.

Johnson was born in Hazelhurst, Mississippi, sometime between 1910 and 1914. He grew up in the vicinity of Robinsonville, Mississippi, in the

Yazoo basin. Johnson was known to his contemporaries as both Robert Dodds and Robert Spencer, since his mother's husband, Charlie Dodds, had to change his name to Spencer and flee to Memphis because of a racial incident. Robert's mother, Julia Major, subsequently became intimate with a field hand named Noah Johnson, and Robert was born. As a young kid in short pants, he showed up one night in Robinsonville, Mississippi, at a juke joint where Son House and Willie Brown were playing and asked if he could join them. Although he played the harmonica with a great deal of facility, it turned out that what he really wanted was to have them teach him the guitar. Before they had a chance to do that, however, House and Brown had to move on to play another town farther down the river. When they returned a few months later, they found that Johnson had not only taught himself to play the guitar but had also become a bluesman of considerable local reputation.

Johnson did not remain in Robinsonville very long. In the next few years he was constantly on the move throughout the South. He traveled to Memphis and St. Louis early in his career. Later he played for a while in Helena, Arkansas, then down through the delta of Louisiana and west to Texas. Sometime during Johnson's period of rambling from place to place, a local record salesman of the American Record Corporation heard him and recommended him to producer Don Law, who had come south to record local artists for the Vocalion label. The sessions that Johnson recorded for Law in November 1936 in San Antonio, Texas, and in June 1937 in Dallas, Texas, are among the richest in the history of the blues. Not only did they result in a permanent record of his skill with the guitar and his extremely flexible vocal style, but they also established a treasury of original material from which the younger generation of bluesmen has drawn liberally.

Robert Johnson was a man of contradictions. Had he lived longer, he might have reconciled some of them and settled down to a longer and more productive career. On the one hand, he was shy; on the other, he could be extremely bold, especially in his way with women. Jealousy seems to have been the cause of his death. He died mysteriously and violently in Greenwood, Mississippi, on August 16, 1938. There is no real evidence pointing out how Johnson died, but rumor has it that a woman either stabbed or poisoned him in a fit of jealousy.

Robert Johnson stands at the crossroads of several musical traditions. Having taken much of his music directly from Son House and Willie Brown, he inherited strong elements of the Mississippi Delta blues tradition. At the same time, he also embraced traces of other musical influences as diverse as Leroy Carr,* Lonnie Johnson,* and Nehemiah "Skip" James.* After having taken what he wanted from them and from other forms of American music, he transformed his catch into his own personal expression. Whatever impression his brief life left on those who knew him, his music remained to inspire them and others who had no knowledge of him. Versions of songs that he recorded or that were associated with him have been made by such singers as Muddy Waters (McKinley Morganfield),* Howlin' Wolf, Junior Parker,* Elmore James,* Homesick James (John A. Williamson), Johnny Shines,* Sonny Boy Williamson (Rice Miller),* Big Joe Williams, Robert Lockwood Jr.,* Roosevelt Sykes,* the Rolling Stones, and innumerable other rock and soul musicians.

Johnson helped to prepare what had been a music purely of the country community for acceptance into the urban lifestyle. His style of guitar playing was easily adaptable to a band setting with amplified instruments. The bass line and chords could be carried by the bass and piano, while the electric guitar and harmonica played melodic figures and the drums maintained the rhythm. When Mississippians migrated to Chicago, the blues of the 1940s and 1950s clearly expressed the spirit of Robert Johnson's death and helped to modernize the old blues. The growth of local blues radio broadcasting in Arkansas and Mississippi played an important role in this movement.

Memphis, that hub of Southern musical activity, played an immensely important role in the development of the Delta blues. It was there, amidst the rubble of juice and gambling joints, house parties, fish fries, and Beale Street, that performers of all types of music were able to stay for a while, perform regularly, and make a fairly decent living. Memphis was host to hundreds of musicians, a large number of them being blues musicians. One of these men, William Christopher Handy, was responsible for transcribing the blues and introducing its form to the world, making available to all that phenomenon of African-American art. Although Handy's role in the performance of the blues was limited, his role as annotator was of extreme importance. He was the first composer to get a blues song published. "Memphis Blues" (originally called "Mr. Crump"), the melody of which he borrowed from the blues of the early 1900s, was published in 1912 after being turned down by several publishing houses because of its form. Up to that time the twelve-bar song had not been popular, and its unusual makeup almost failed to cause an interest in its being commercially exploited. The blues had been around for quite a while at this point, though, in New Orleans as early as the 1890s and a bit later in Memphis.

Memphis's place in the history of the blues can be directly attributed to Beale Street, that thoroughfare of black activity. Beale Street provided numerous places for the blues performer to make a living playing his music. There were gambling joints, short-order houses, theaters, nightclubs, saloons, and the street, where a musician could usually make more money than in the clubs by just sitting around and playing for coins. Almost everyone who is someone in blues history played in Memphis and on Beale Street at one time or another. Walter "Furry" Lewis* lived on Beale Street. Gus Cannon; Jim Jackson; Will Shade and his Memphis Jug Band; Memphis Minnie Douglas;* Jim Turner, the violinist who, with his stories of Beale Street, was partially responsible for W. C. Handy leaving Florence, Alabama, and heading out to Memphis; "Little Brother" Montgomery (Eurreal W. Montgomery);* Roosevelt Sykes; Tampa Red (Hudson Whittaker);* and countless others played there. The entire atmosphere in Memphis was conducive to the way of the blues. Memphis Minnie, as well as many other women performers, played in the joints and on the street the same as the men did. They took an active role in the life of the street and influenced and were influenced by all of the surrounding vibes.

There were quite a few jug bands on Beale Street also. The Memphis Jug Band was one of the most popular. Will Shade, who played guitar, harmonica, jug, and bass, formed the unit in the mid–1920s and kept it together until well into the 1930s. The group included, at various times, Furry Lewis, Charlie Pierce, Ben Ramey, and Shade's wife, Jennie Mae Bofors. They performed in New Orleans, Chicago, and Atlanta as well as in and around Memphis and recorded for the Victor label in 1927. Furry Lewis led a jug band around 1917, and the Gus Cannon Jug Stompers lasted from 1908 to 1913.

Beale Street was at its zenith from around 1900 to around 1930, when, because of the combined onslaught of economic, social, and political change, it began to collapse at a drastically rapid tempo. The street did provide for its talented until the end, however, and stars like Riley "B. B." King* and Robert C. "Bobby" Bland,* who went to Memphis early in their careers to find fame and wealth, are now at the top of the blues field. By the 1950s Beale Street was all but dead. Stripped of its former glitter and high voltage by urban renewal, it is presently left with only vague memories of the lusty old days.

The Mississippi Delta, on the other hand, continues in its tradition of producing top-ranking bluesmen. Some of them remain at home to become popular there, while others migrate to cities like Chicago, Detroit, and Los Angeles and fall comfortably into the mainstream of blues and rhythm-and-blues society. These cities, especially Chicago, with Detroit running a close second, are centers of blues activity. Thanks for this should be given to the Delta bluesmen because the activity all started after the first exodus of Southern blacks to the North. The influence that the Delta bluesmen have on the ever-changing urban style is no less today than it was in the beginning. Although the Delta does not qualify as a center of the music industry in the areas of recording, publishing, and the like, it does qualify impeccably in the production of a root force, the human element that creates the music.

ARKANSAS AND "KING BISCUIT TIME"

When businessmen saw opportunities in advertising through radio broadcasts to reach the black market, they immediately went into it. This opened doors to new possibilities for the blues musicians. Through advertising certain products on the radio, a musician could not only reach a far wider audience and build up a reputation as a top bluesman, but he could also tell more people when and where he was going to play and pull a larger crowd and more money.

In the mid–1930s radio station KLCN in Blytheville, Arkansas, started employing a friend of Robert Johnson, guitarist Calvin Frazier, and a few other blues musicians. This move, quite innovative for the times, proved to be successful, although certain points (such as risqué lyrics) came under the scrutiny of the censors and had to be changed. The real breakthrough in blues radio came around 1941 when the white-owned radio station KFFA was established in Helena, Arkansas. The Interstate Grocery Company, owned by Max S. Moore, was producing King Biscuit flour at the time, and to advertise it to the black population in Helena, the company signed on two blues singers, Rice Miller, a harmonica player in his forties, and guitarist Robert Lockwood, Jr., whose mother had been one of Robert Johnson's girl friends. In order to cash in on the popularity of Chicago blues singer Sonny Boy Williamson, Miller was called Sonny Boy Williamson II, a name he forever after claimed to be his own. Broadcasting live five days a week around midday, "King Biscuit Time" was an absolute sensation. Sales of King Biscuit flour soared, and soon Sonny Boy white corn meal was on the market too. "King Biscuit Time" became an institution, and the band expanded, taking in at various times pianists Joe Willie "Pinetop" Perkins (Joe Willie Perkins) and Willie Love, drummer James "Peck" Curtis,* and guitarists Houston Stackhouse* and Joe Willie Wilkins. This band, known as the King Biscuit Boys, became extremely popular in the 1940s. It even went out on the road, playing for country dances and in front of grocery shops in a number of surrounding towns.

The success of "King Biscuit Time" encouraged more stations to get in on the act, and opportunities for blues musicians began to surface all over the place. The radio stations gave exposure to a large number of musicians who had hardly had a chance to work since the 1930s. Some of these men went on to make big names for themselves in the blues world, while others merely sank back into obscurity or gave up altogether.

In 1942 the success of King Biscuit flour spurred the Bright Star and Mother's Pride flour companies to compete. Using slide guitarist Robert Nighthawk to play the music, they secured their own radio spot, also on KFFA. Nighthawk had already made some records under various names, but these radio broadcasts soon made him one of the most popular musicians in the Delta.

Rice Miller frequently deserted the King Biscuit Boys and played for such stations as KNOE in Monroe, Louisiana, and KGHI in Little Rock, Arkansas, before moving on to team up with guitarist Elmore James. In the 1930s he and James had worked with Robert Johnson, and now they advertised Talaho tonic together in Mississippi over Yazoo City's WAZF and Greenville's WJPJ. KWEM in West Memphis, Arkansas, joined in when the success of Talaho tonic persuaded the vendors of Hadacol tonic to compete. In 1949 Howlin' Wolf began broadcasting on KWEM. He had a show that came on at three o'clock in the afternoon. Acting also as producer of the segment, he advertised everything from grain and household goods to tractors and plows.

West Memphis, Arkansas, soon developed into a jumping blues center. Just twenty minutes across the river from Memphis, Tennessee, it was a wide-open town with lots of vice, gambling, and nightclubs where blues musicians could hang out. Howlin' Wolf, Willie Love, Joe Hill (the Be-Bop Boy) Louis, Forest City Joe (Joe Pugh), B. B. King, Elmore James, and many others either played the nightspots in town or performed over KWEM.

Once the rise of "King Biscuit Time" had opened up the market, the most significant development in blues broadcasting was when WDIA in Memphis entered the field. In October 1948, risking the threats of white business sponsors, it put on its first all-black program, a thirty-minute disc jockey show. Its success was so great that WDIA turned its entire airtime to its potential audience of 1.25 million blacks. Styling itself "Mother Station of the Negroes," WDIA was instrumental in putting the South back on the blues map after many of the bluesmen had migrated to the North. The interest in field recordings returned. New radio stations were established in Memphis and other cities, and the South soon reasserted itself as the home of the blues.

In the late 1940s and early 1950s there was a sudden desire in the black ghettoes of America's large cities for the updated and amplified blues that had blossomed in the South. Some Delta men, like Muddy Waters, had settled in Chicago in the mid–1940s, and the South Side was already grooving to the electric sounds of funky, down-home blues. The recording industry was caught by surprise and looked to the South for more talent. It sought out musicians who had already established themselves as local stars on the smaller radio stations—people like Sonny Boy Williamson II (Rice Miller), Howlin' Wolf, and Elmore James.

For some, adapting to wider fame was extremely difficult. The man who had done so much to advance the rural blues, Sonny Boy Williamson II, was already nearly sixty years old when he had his few hit recordings in the 1950s. Behind him were years of paying his dues in roadhouses and juke joints, and he was out of touch with the times. He failed to accept the increasing demands of rhythm-and-blues musicians with whom he played. Miller was a strange man. Often remembered as a temperamental, tough, and embittered loner, he still had many friends and was an almost unrivaled influence as a harmonica player.

Today "King Biscuit Time" is a legend in the blues world. From the moment the first King Biscuit show was produced, an enormous sense of racial pride was born in being able to hear black performers on the radio in the South. Just a few minutes of advertising and music each day brought about a social and economic change that eventually triggered a better understanding between, as well as among, the races. "King Biscuit Time" continued long after Sonny Boy's death in 1965, and its spirit still lives today.

LOUISIANA

The French and Spanish colonial settlements in the South were mostly military establishments that were staffed at first by unmarried men. These men often took mistresses and sometimes wives from among the Indians and the blacks they governed. They fathered children of mixed blood and together with their offspring were contemptuously referred to as Creoles by those who stayed at home in Europe. The term *Creole*, meaning "of the colony," became a proud title when the colonies grew rich and the Creole families became more prominent than the Europeans who had scorned them. In Louisiana there were white Creoles and black Creoles, just as after the Acadians had established themselves in the southwestern part of the state, a shared culture resulted in both white Cajuns and black Creoles.

The children of white colonists and African slaves (octoroons and mulattos) in Louisiana, especially in New Orleans, were not ostracized to the same extent as their darker brothers. Instead they were assimilated. They rose in social and economic status and often, in the pleasure of living like Frenchmen or Spaniards, chose to forget their origins. Yet their African languages and the complex music and dance movements from Africa survived and flourished. New modes of speech developed. Creole, a West African linguistic adjustment to European contact, was given birth as a language.

The British-American pioneers in Louisiana, as well as in the rest of North America, expressed themselves musically mainly as ballad writers, hymn composers, and square dancers. The Creoles and their black brothers turned away from the British-American musical styles and went on to compose some of today's favorite American ballads. They also transformed the musically stiff, moralistic white man's folk hymns into the spiritual, a form of black expression unmatched for grandeur, emotion, and the joy of being alive and experiencing the world as it really is. Through all of this could be heard the notes of irony and sorrow, notes that were paving the way for a new direction in black music—the blues.

The roots of Cajun music, on the other hand, stretch back to northern France, to Picardy and Normandy, from which provinces came the settlers who colonized what is now known as Nova Scotia. They landed there in 1604, called it Acadia, and lived there until the conquest of French Canada by the British in the eighteenth century. Because of their refusal to swear allegiance to the British Crown, they were deported. Many finally arrived in Louisiana, the last remaining French colony in North America.

Coming to the port of New Orleans, they found, to their dismay, that it had fallen into Spanish hands. Sent into the wild interior of southern Louisiana, the Acadians settled on the prairies and along Bayou Lafourche, Bayou Teche, and Bayou Courtableau, traditional homes of the Attakapa and Chitimacha Indians. The United States government eventually bought Louisiana from the French, who by that time owned the colony again, and the Acadians became Americans. They have, however, always resisted Americanization and to this day, calling themselves Cajuns, are a distinct minority group found mostly in southwest Louisiana. Their language and their robust music have combined to keep their culture distinct and alive.

The sound of accordions and fiddles is the soul of Cajun music. The words of the songs are in the Cajuns' own patios French, and the mood of the music is distinctly rural. It is the music for the Saturday night dance when the Cajuns gather together in a local hall, house, or nightclub to drink, have fun, and dance. The music is distinctly European, with a heritage that goes back to the tunes and instruments available in northern France in the sixteenth and seventeenth centuries. At first, the accordion was not an integral part of Cajun music, but by the time the first recordings of Cajun music were made in the 1920s, it had become widely popular along the bayous.

In the first two decades of the twentieth century a musical exchange was taking place in southwest Louisiana that was to become the most creative era in the history of Cajun music. Newly improvised melodies and rhythms took the place of the earlier French folk musical forms of the Acadians when the accordion reached the hands (and heads) of musicians who played and sang the blues in French. In the hands of the Cajuns the accordion bore a definite European sound. When black musicians took up the instrument, the Cajun influence was blended with blues structures to produce a completely different accordion sound.

Perhaps the most outstanding musician to emerge from this cultural exchange between the Creoles and the Cajuns and to become famous in his own time was a small, French-speaking black man named Amede Ardoin.* Born a free man around 1899 in L'Anse Rouge (Eunice), Louisiana, Ardoin lived among the Cajuns and absorbed their Old World music. Being musically innovative and an accordion player of natural ability, he was the first person to incorporate a series of rhythmically complex melodic patterns that had never been previously played. His style embraced the use of a lyrical melody line executed over a rhythmically complicated countermelody within the framework of a I and V chord vamp of the bass tones. Amede's lyrical content dealt mainly with the pain women could cause a man, a common subject in the blues. He composed his own material, often altering the songs each time he played them. Amede made his living solely as a musician and was held in high esteem by the Cajuns, who often hired him to play for their house parties. Beginning in 1929, he recorded twenty-two songs for Bluebird and other record labels with a white fiddle player named Dennis McGee. Each of his songs is now regarded as a classic. Whether he played alone, with his nephew Alphonse "Bois-Sec" Ardoin* on triangle, or with Dennis McGee, he regularly filled dance halls with his energetic performances. Amede eventually became an alcoholic. He was also the victim of a severe beating at an outdoor fair in Crowley, Louisiana, that is thought to have resulted in some brain damage. According to musicians of the area, in the early part of 1940 he was committed to the Louisiana State Institution for the Mentally Ill in Pineville, Louisiana. A short time after, on November 3, 1942, he died.

The music of Amede's nephew, Alphonse "Bois-Sec" Ardoin, is quite popular in Cajun music circles. "Bois-Sec" was born in Duralde, Louisiana, in 1916 into a highly musical family. "Bois-Sec," which in English means "dry wood," is chief patriarch of the Ardoin family, which continues the family tradition of singing and playing the accordion. Along with Canray Fontenot* on fiddle, he continues to play today as he has done for over thirty-five years, though the band has changed from the traditional *'tit fer* (triangle) to include guitar, bass, and drums. Alphonse Ardoin's music is different from the zydeco beat of Clifton Chenier's* band. There is no saxophone, no rubboard, and there is a lot less of the rhythm-and-blues influence. His accordion style is much simpler than that of Chenier, and it works well with Fontenot's fiddle style.

Another black fiddle player is the legendary Joseph "Bebe" Carriere, who made his first violin at the age of twelve out of a cigar box. He and his brother Eraste "Dolon" Carriere, also a musician, lived in the Lawtell, Louisiana, area since their births in 1900 and 1908, respectively, to their deaths in the early 1980s. Eraste learned to play the accordion from his father, who played zydeco in the old-time Creole style. As a young man Joseph played in the Lawtell, Eunice, and Basile area with Amede Ardoin and other innovators of the zydeco sound. In the late 1970s he was still an incredible specimen of vitality and musical creativity and often played the old-time dances and early tunes of the area. A very good vocalist as well, he sings in a style closely associated with the blues.

Clifton Chenier, known the world over as the Zydeco King, was born on a farm near Opelousas, Louisiana, on June 25, 1925. He grew up listening to his father play the accordion at country dances and took up the instrument at a very early age. The music he learned from his father was a blend of traditional Cajun music, Delta blues, and rhythm-and-blues. As a youngster he helped his parents work in the cotton, rice, and corn fields, and in 1949 he followed his brother Cleveland, who plays the rubboard, to Lake Charles, where they worked in the oil fields and played music on weekends.

In that same year J. R. Fulbright, a Los Angeles talent scout, heard Clifton play at a country dance. He was so impressed that he continued to visit him periodically and in 1954 was finally able to drag Chenier into KAOK, a Lake Charles radio station, where he recorded "Clifton's Blues" and "Louisiana Stomp." They were released locally, and their success prompted Clifton to take a chance on a musical career. He went with Fulbright to Los Angeles. After trying Atlantic and several other labels and being turned down, he and Fulbright wound up at Specialty Records, where they recorded "Ay Tee Fee" (hey little girl) and "Boppin' the Rock." "Ay Tee Fee" was the local hit that opened the door to Chenier's ultimate worldwide popularity. Chenier played the piano accordion, not the traditional "French" or zydeco accordion, which is the small, concertina type that allows a musician to play in only two keys. He also played the harmonica, organ, and piano, and he was able to transfer the feeling of each to his accordion. He could bend blue notes on his instrument, and his voice was pure rhythm-and-blues. Sometimes moaning, sometimes shouting, he sang in Creole patois, French, and English.

The fact that black Creole blues is generally sung in French has led to an almost total ignorance about it and its origins, probably because few outsiders ever attempt to appreciate something foreign to their own understanding. Yet the pride that black Creoles have in their own music and its practitioners has always built a very strong market for their recordings. Though some regard it as a minority market, there has been an ever-increasing demand for this music in Canada and Europe, as well as in Louisiana, Texas, and California.

At its heart, black Creole blues is stimulating, emotional, and filled with inner tensions. It reveals without compromise the experiences common to all and offers the world a glimpse of an immensely rich culture that in spite of its size has influenced several areas of American music.

In addition to the zydeco element, Louisiana also boasts a strong tradition of rural and urban blues styling represented by musicians like Robert Pete Williams,* Huddie Ledbetter (Leadbelly),* Lonesome Sundown (Cornelius Green),* and the electric Professor Longhair (Roy Byrd).* Although at first hearing it may seem to be first cousin to the rural blues of the Mississippi Delta, Louisiana's country blues, as well as the other types, is of a tradition unlike any other.

The various types of Louisiana blues can be conveniently sectioned into four geographical areas, each having influence on the other, with certain elements common to the whole. These areas comprise all of north Louisiana, Baton Rouge and its surroundings, New Orleans and the lower Mississippi River valley, and southwest Louisiana. Of the four, the blues that was performed in north Louisiana by musicians like Huddie Leadbelly, Oscar Woods, and Stick Horse Hammond is more closely related to the blues of the Mississippi Delta in its style of one musician singing and accompanying himself in a basic melodic and harmonic fashion. Stylistic differences of this area from the Baton Rouge area are few.

In the New Orleans area, more than any place except the southwest section, there exists a strong rhythmic quality that is born from a combination of African and French-Caribbean origins. This rhythmic approach, coupled with the influence of some of that city's complicated harmonic standards that are innate in the jazz tradition, caused a blues quality like no other anywhere else in America. Rumbalike rhythms readily dominate a setting that consists of intricate jazz-influenced melodic and harmonic passages that follow the direction of raw, down-home vocals. The most widely known practitioner of this style of blues was Professor Longhair. He was a singer, piano player, and composer of some of New Orleans' best blues pieces.

Professor Longhair was born Roy Byrd in Bogalusa, Louisiana, on December 19, 1918. He was reared in New Orleans and became involved with music while very young. His mother played guitar and sang the blues and spirituals. He taught himself to play the guitar, and by the time he was a teenager, he had gained quite a bit of proficiency on the piano as well. Byrd did not start playing the piano professionally, however, until he was discharged from the army. It was at that time that he started working on his unique style of blues piano playing. Because of his small hands, he was unable to play all of the chords he desired when he began on the instrument, but he soon worked out a system of executing broken chord runs that he later described as "cross-chording," that is, playing the chords, substitutions, and fills in the arpeggio fashion. This approach enabled him to play in a highly syncopative manner that suggested rhythms of Latin and African flavor.

Professor Longhair's influence on the rhythm-and-blues of New Orleans has been likened to that of Jelly Roll Morton on the jazz of that city. He was successful at bringing together the intricate rhythmic statements of the Caribbean and the raw, soulful sounds of the Delta to form a unique brand of New Orleans blues. Perhaps best known for his "Mardi Gras in New Orleans," which he recorded in 1957, Professor Longhair was also the composer of many other hits, including "Big Chief" (1965) and "She Ain't Got No Hair" (1950).

Old-timers in New Orleans tell of hearing the blues long before jazz came about, and musicians of the stature of Jelly Roll Morton and Bunk Johnson readily spoke of the fact that the jazz pieces they first played were directly influenced by the blues in that they were constructed on the blues principles of melody, harmony, and the twelve-bar structure. It is an accepted fact that the first blues ever heard in New Orleans was probably performed by musicians working alone in a style not unlike that of the Mississippi Delta or other rural areas. Because of the fast-paced nature of music in New Orleans, the blues was never really able to survive in its original state, at least not for long. There were quite a few blues piano players in the city at the turn of the century, especially in Storyville, the section of New Orleans that was "reserved" especially for gambling, prostitution, and other shady activities. But it was the ragtime professors who played the best houses and made the most money.

Buddy Bolden,* cornet player and leader of the famed Eagle Band, the first jazz band in New Orleans, played the blues. The Eagle Band was probably the first group of musicians to play the blues at the turn of the century. Its music was a forerunner to the sounds that later became popular as jass and still later as jazz. In fact, Bolden's reputation as a musician was built on his blues playing.

The difference between New Orleans and other cities where the blues thrived was that the Crescent City, in addition to its relaxed social atmosphere, was musically intense enough to offer avenues of quick growth for the blues. These avenues led to jazz and to a closer, but not as intricate, relative, rhythm-and-blues. Professor Longhair grew up in this jungle of sounds.

During the 1950s New Orleans was the undisputed capital of blues and rhythm-and-blues recording in the deep South. Musicians came from all over to record and perform their music there. One of the true blues giants of the business at that time was a charismatic, often-explosive guitarist/singer who went by the name of Guitar Slim. Eddie Jones* (his christened name) was not originally from Louisiana. He was born in Greenwood, Mississippi, on December 10, 1926. He moved to New Orleans in the late 1940s and began recording for Imperial Records in 1953. Just about every song that he recorded throughout the 1950s was a hit. Unfortunately, Jones's life was cut drastically short by a game of Russian roulette in Houston, Texas, in 1959. But his short time in Louisiana was well spent, and through his recordings and frequent live appearances his influence on the blues of that state was matched by few. His electric guitar style, punctuated with sparse melodic figures, and his lyrics, which showcased uncanny originality, were more than a shot in the arm for the blues of Louisiana. Promising up-and-coming musicians as well as established performers played his songs and copied his guitar style almost note for note. In fact, his guitar accompaniment and solo on the hit "The Things That I Used to Do" are classics in the genre and are models for the young guitarist to this day.

While this musical gumbo was brewing in New Orleans, similar happenings, though on a smaller musical scale, were taking place a bit to the southwest. Blues recording was just beginning to take hold in places like Crowley through the efforts of Jay Miller and, to a lesser degree, in Lake Charles under the direction of Eddie Shuler. Unlike north Louisiana or even New Orleans, there is only a slight tradition of the itinerant lone bluesman in this area. Because the area is largely a Cajun-zydeco-jazz pocket of strong Haitian-French traditions, the blues did not really take hold there until the late 1940s. Even then it was not of the same fashion as that of other parts of the state. Young musicians, after they learned their instruments by listening to the popular blues and rhythm-and-blues recordings on radio, began to perform their renditions of current hits, usually note for note, and to compose pieces that were in the style of the hits. Out of this came some fairly popular material, and most of it was recorded in Crowley, Louisiana, a small town west of Baton Rouge.

Entrepreneur Jay Miller started to record the blues in Crowley in 1954, after his first blues artist, Lightnin' Slim (Otis Hicks),* had a sizable hit with the archaic-sounding "Bad Luck." Before that he had only recorded Cajun and country and western material. Lightnin' Slim was born in St. Louis, Missouri, in 1913. His family moved to St. Francisville, Louisiana, to farm in the late 1920s, and from there Hicks moved to Baton Rouge in 1946. He got involved in the blues scene there and played in his down-home fashion, mostly with just a drummer, until he met Miller in 1954. By 1958 Lightnin's records were selling throughout the South. In 1959 his "Rooster Blues" made the *Billboard* rhythm-and-blues chart, climbing up to number twenty-three. Lightnin' Slim and his music, which was influenced by the works of Blind Lemon Jefferson and Lightnin' Hopkins, made a great impression on the blues of Louisiana. His style influenced musicians throughout the state.

After Hicks's success with Jay Miller, many other good bluesmen headed for Crowley. Slim Harpo (James Moore)* had hits with "I'm a King Bee" (1957), "Rainin' in My Heart" (1961), and "Scratch My Back" (1966). Lonesome Sundown (Cornelius Green) connected with "Lost without Love," "I'm a Mojo Man," "I Stood By" (all recorded in 1957 or 1958), and "Lonesome Lonely Blues" (1962). Between 1956 and 1964 Lazy Lester (Leslie Johnson)* had a string of impressive recordings that included "Lester's Stomp," "They Call Me Lazy," "I'm a Lover, Not a Fighter," "I Hear You Knocking," "You Got Me Where You Want Me," and "Woah Now." Other artists who recorded for Miller included Guitar Gable (Gabriel Perrodin),* Carol Fran, Katie Webster),* Jay Nelson, Little Ray Campbell, Ernest "Tabby" Thomas,* Polka Dot Slim (Monroe Vincent),* Moses "Whispering" Smith,* Silas Hogan,* and Classie Ballou. Most of these later musicians were playing rhythm-and-blues, although with a strong down-home flavor.

A bit west of Crowley, in Lake Charles, Eddie Shuler of Goldband Records also recorded some blues material, but not with the same intensity as Jay Miller. His was mostly an offhanded approach, waiting for musicians to contact him first, then recording them and hoping for the best. His first venture with the blues came with James Freeman from Orange, Texas, who, after becoming quite popular around Lake Charles, suddenly retired from music in the mid–1950s. Then came Hop Wilson (Harding Wilson)* and his recording of "Chicken Stuff" in 1958. One of the things that made this recording unique was his use of the Hawaiian guitar. Weldon "Juke Boy" Bonner,* Tal Miller, Morris "Big" Chenier, Guitar Junior (Lee Baker), Big

Walter Price, Marcelle Dugas, Carol Fran, and Little Ray Campbell all recorded for Shuler.

New Orleans is Afro-French-Caribbean; southwest Louisiana is also Afro-French-Caribbean, and travel to and from the two places is easier by going through Baton Rouge, the state capital. Baton Rouge, however, shows few signs of this tradition. The blues music from this area of Louisiana is more closely related to that of the north of the state and the Mississippi Delta. When Harry Oster of Louisiana State University and Richard Allen of Tulane University of New Orleans, sponsored by the Louisiana Folklore Society, began recording old-time Baton Rouge–area bluesmen in 1959 in an effort to preserve the rapidly disappearing rural folk blues, one of their most rewarding stops was at the notorious Angola Prison. There they hoped to find undiluted renditions of early Louisiana blues for their work. To their dismay, however, they found that most of the inmates were more involved with the popular rhythm-and-blues tunes they heard on the radio and cared little about the old stuff. They did manage to round up a small number of bluesmen who played in the old-time gut-bucket style, however, and one of these men was Robert Pete Williams. Williams had been a professional blues musician since around 1935 and had developed a singing and playing style that was all his own. There was a crude rhythmic quality in his playing that made it impossible for any other musician to perform comfortably with him. In the fashion of the early bluesmen before him, his playing was highly modal, preferring single-note statements to chordal accompaniment. An album from that date was called *Angola Prisoner's Blues*, on which, some believe, Robert Pete Williams rendered the best work of his entire career. Through the merit of this recording, Williams soon became Louisiana's most sought-after exponent of the rural blues. He was paroled soon after and embarked on a succession of concert, club, and festival dates that lasted until his death in 1982. In addition to Robert Pete Williams, Oster and Allen also made recordings of Hogman Maxey, John Henry Jackson, Otis Webster, Guitar Welsh, and Jesse Butcher on the Angola session. On other sessions they recorded Smokey Babe, Butch Cage, Snooks Eaglin,* Willie Thomas, and Clarence Edwards.

The Baton Rouge rural blues style was also exploited widely by Jay Miller during the 1950s and early 1960s. Some of that city's most traditional blues stylists made the trip to Crowley to record. The blues in Louisiana is currently attracting some attention, albeit not as much as is deserved. Annual festivals around the state showcase blues talent, both traditional and contemporary, and the club scene is picking up sporadically, but the number of recordings is still very small. The ticket in Louisiana blues today is zydeco. It is gradually moving from a local position to one of worldwide proportion. The germ of Amede Ardoin that was taken up by Clifton Chenier is currently being spread by artists like Rockin' Dopsie (Alton Rubin),* the Sam Brothers Five, John Delafose, and Stanley "Buckwheat" Dural.* As jazz has brought universal attention to Louisiana, perhaps zydeco will also afford that special attraction. Its infectious dance beat has made it a favorite music of rock and rollers in various parts of the United States, Canada, and Europe. A list of the performers at almost any music festival in the 1990s, anywhere in the world, will more than likely include at least one zydeco band. While New Orleans, Baton Rouge, and north Louisiana still have their blues and rhythm-and-blues musicians who perform in Louisiana and Europe, southwest Louisiana has slipped almost entirely into zydeco.

In the early 1980s a new generation of blues-oriented musicians began to surface in southwest Louisiana. These young musicians came from two camps. Some of them were relatives of zydeco musicians and had cut their musical teeth on that music, and others started their training in various rhythm-and-blues bands throughout the region. As zydeco became more popular, these rhythm-and-blues bands began to switch over to that side. The result of this movement was an explosion of zydeco bands employing musicians of diverse technical abilities and musical orientations. Stanley "Buckwheat" Dural, Jr., is one of the most popular of the switchover musicians. He started out as a piano and organ player in area bands. He formed his own group while he was in his early twenties to play rhythm-and-blues dances throughout south Louisiana. His switchover to zydeco happened when he was hired by Clifton Chenier to play keyboards with his Red Hot Peppers Band. While Dural was with Chenier, he learned all that there was to know about zydeco. After getting the zydeco material down pat, he switched to keyboard accordion (the kind that Chenier played) and struck out on his own. He formed the zydeco Ils Sont Partis Band, a unit with a very strong rhythm-and-blues base, in the mid–1970s and scored with his first album, *One for the Road*, on Blues Unlimited Records. Clifton Chenier was responsible for blending the old Creole music with rhythm-and-blues to form the modern zydeco sound; Dural, his young prince, holds the banner for helping to develop a "third-stream" sound that consists of elements of Creole music, rhythm-and-blues, and soul.

Another young zydeco musician of note is alto saxophone/accordion player C. J. Chenier, the son of Clifton Chenier. C. J. was reared on the Creole sounds of his father and his uncle, rubboard player Cleveland Chenier. He started working in his father's band as a saxophone player because the nature of the accordion (soundwise) would not allow two of them to be played together in the same band. It was during this time, though, that he took time to learn to play the accordion. When his father died, he took over the band and continued to make advances in the music. His recordings include *Red Hot* (Slash 26263–4), *I Ain't No Playboy* (Slash 26788–4), and *Let Me in Your Heart* (Arhoolie C–1098).

The instrumentation in zydeco bands also went through some changes in the 1980s. The original instruments employed in Creole music ensembles were violin, accordion, and triangle or rubboard (played for rhythm). Under the influence of rhythm-and-blues the drums, electric guitar, and bass were added to the ensemble in the late 1960s. By the early 1980s a full-fledged zydeco band included accordion, saxophone, trumpet, keyboard, electric guitar, electric bass, rubboard, and drums. The violin and triangle were long gone from the scene. This combination of instruments gave zydeco a new dimension, but the basic elements of the music remained the accordion, the rubboard, and the Creole lyrics. This twist in instrumentation and dialect has given the blues new color. The following is a list of some of the more popular bluesmen from each of the four areas of Louisiana blues.

New Orleans

Professor Longhair
Tuts Washington
Sullivan Rock
Kid Stormy
Lizzie Miles
Cousin Joe Pleasant
Blue Lu Barker*
Esther Bigeou*
James Booker*
Richard Brown
Ann Cook
Fats Domino
Champion Jack Dupree*
Fird Eaglin
Henry Grey
Leon Gross
Edna Hicks
Charlie Jackson
James Johnson
Smiley Lewis*
Lemon Nash
Walter Fats Pichon
Tommy Ridgley
Blanche Thomas*
Irma Thomas

Baton Rouge

Robert Pete Williams
Lightnin' Slim
Buddy Guy
Silas Hogan
Little Walter Jacobs
Jimmy Anderson
Tabby Thomas
Matthew Jacobs*
Lazy Lester
Guitar Kelley*
Little Brother Montgomery
Slim Harpo
Raful Neal*
Bob Nelson
Rockin' Sidney Semien*
Cleve White*
Frank Murphy
Sylvester Buckley
Whispering Smith

North Louisiana

Oscar Woods
Country Jim
Margie Evans*
Guitar Grady

Southwest Louisiana

Clifton Chenier
Lonnie Brooks*
Rockin' Dopsie
Gatemouth Brown
Lonesome Sundown
Rick Williams
Joe Morris
Jay Nelson
Carol Fran
Guitar Gable
King Karl
Classie Ballou
Katie Webster
Joe James
Tal Miller
Morris Chenier
Guitar Junior
Ashton Savoy
Leroy Washington
Good Rockin' Bob
Skinny Dynamo
Charlie Morris
Little Ray Campbell
Sticks Herman
Joe Johnson
Al King
Sidney Maiden
Andrew McMahon
Luke Miles
Lafayette Thomas
Mighty Joe Young*
Huddie Leadbelly
Vernon Harrison

THE SOUTHEASTERN SEABOARD (THE CAROLINAS, GEORGIA, FLORIDA)

The southeastern seaboard, which includes North and South Carolina, Georgia, and Florida, is an area that seems to offer less in the way of blues than other places in the South and consequently has been given the least attention in works on the subject. The music of this area is much more danceable and incorporates a broad rhythmic concept that is influenced by both European and African folk traditions. In fact, a large part of the area's music consists of songs with origins that are directly linked to both traditions.

Pre–World War I rural music of the southeastern seaboard was a biracial concern. Both blacks and whites listened to, danced to, and played the same songs. There was also quite a bit of interaction between black and white musicians. They played together, performing the same material at functions of both races. In the prewar folk music of this area there was a common ground that was brought about by an uncommonly close social order. Musicians of this area did not have to deal with the same degree of ostracism as was imposed in Mississippi and other areas of the South. This is not to say that they were a part of a racially equal atmosphere, but there did exist a more defined musical interaction that led to a better understanding of each other as human beings. This, coupled with a common respect for the old songs and dances, brought about a casual cohesiveness.

The blues, when its form was first realized in that area, did not have as urgent a need to identify and separate itself as it did in other areas of the United States. Although it was later fortified and became an important part of the black experience in general, in the beginning it did not embrace the same amount of intensity, judgment, and general fire as in other areas. The racial blend and overall relaxed feeling that had taken nest in the rural dance forms also flourished in the blues. Instead of the edginess that identifies the blues in general, the blues of the southeastern seaboard projects a more melodic and gentle feeling.

This area has produced some influential bluesmen. Included among them are Peg Leg Howell (Joshua B. Howell), Blind Boy Fuller (Fulton Allen),* Sonny Terry,* Brownie McGhee,* Rev. Gary Davis,* J. C. Burris, Richard and William Trice, Blind James Weaver, Jesse Fuller,* Alden "Tarheel Slim" Bunn, Ray Charles, Pink Anderson, James "Kokomo" Arnold,* Charles "Baby" Tate, and Blind Willie Walker.

Blind Boy Fuller was born in 1908 in Wadesboro, North Carolina, one of ten brothers and sisters. His given name at birth was Fulton Allen. He learned to play the guitar in Rockingham, North Carolina, where his family moved when he was quite young. Fuller worked as a musician around Rockingham in his early teens, playing on the streets and for house parties. He went partially blind in 1926 and finally lost all sight around 1928, the year he set out as an itinerant bluesman. Fuller is perhaps the southeastern seaboard's best-known bluesman and by far the most recorded. He first went into the studio in 1935 and before his death in 1941 recorded around 135 tunes, most of them realizing considerable commercial success.

During the depression the tobacco towns of the southeastern seaboard were excellent places for street musicians, and Fuller made a good living playing his music around North Carolina. Protected from the bite of hard times by the continued sale of cigarettes, these towns were able to offer to musicians that bit of extra and much-needed money. Fuller worked for tips in Winston-Salem, North Carolina, and Danville, Virginia, before settling down in Durham, North Carolina, in 1929. From that time to 1934 he either worked alone or teamed up with harpist Sonny Terry, a washboard player called Bull City Red, or the blind Rev. Gary Davis on guitar, banjo, or harmonica. It was in Durham that he met J. B. Long, who at the time was selling race records and was also a sort of blues talent scout who arranged recording dates for record companies. Long became Fuller's manager and was responsible for the bulk of his recording activity until the time of his death.

Fuller's blues style was most representative of the easy-going, laid-back southeastern seaboard style. He played the tunes that were popular before his time, learning them from records and older musicians and incorporating their spirit into his original material. Through this process he created a vital blues style that was a great influence on the musicians who came after him. Fuller recorded for ARC from 1935 to 1938, for Decca in 1937, and for Vocalion in 1938. After a bit of inactivity that was caused by ill health, he recorded for Vocalion again in New York in 1940 and also for Okeh that same year. Fuller underwent a kidney operation in 1940, suffered complications later, and died at his home on February 13, 1941. His body is buried at Grove Hill Cemetery in Durham, North Carolina.

After Fuller's death the southeastern seaboard's blues continued in the same fashion. The migration of the 1930s and 1940s brought it to New York and New Jersey, but without causing much attention there. This was wholly due to the fact that East Coast blacks craved more in music than the old-style country blues had to offer. After all, that was part of what they had hoped to leave behind. The broad, modern temperament of jazz took no prisoners, and the new city folks took no time to look back. Fortunately, the style survived in some of its musicians. Guitarist Brownie McGhee and blind harmonica player Sonny Terry formed a partnership that lasted well over thirty years. Their worldwide popularity was purely the result of their continuing to play in the old rural fashion. But for the most part the musicians were born there, learned and perfected their art there, and then moved to cities like Chicago, Detroit, or Memphis to look for work. The towns of the Piedmont area were able to sustain, to a point, the early itinerant bluesman, but as the 1950s approached and rhythm-and-blues appeared, blues musicians were already moving toward greener pastures (like those that musicians in the Mississippi Delta had) or were changing their styles to accommodate the new dance craze. Up to the present day the fate of the southeastern seaboard's blues scene has not been unlike that of the Mississippi Delta. There are only a handful of blues musicians who choose to live there and play their music (with day jobs to support themselves, of course). Most musicians from the area, as in other parts of the United States, are either playing the more popular blues-influenced styles or are continuing in the pure blues format, but are based in larger cities like Chicago or Los Angeles.

TEXAS

In Texas in the 1920s there was blues music wherever black workers congregated. There was always a demand for singers and musicians in the farming areas of the state, but the hard times that came with the Great Depression of 1929 pushed many of the farmers and cotton workers into cities like Houston, Dallas, and Forth Worth. Although there was still employment for pianists in the old barrelhouses of the lumber camps in the piney woods of Texas, they increasingly looked for work in the nightclubs and juke joints in the large cities. Guitar and piano players often traveled the railroad lines, stopping off to play in the camps occupied by cotton pickers and oil-field workers, and then moving on to the honky-tonks in places like Port Arthur, Galveston, or Houston.

Compared with the threatening anxiety of life in Mississippi, Texas society was more varied, and opportunities for growth and independence were much greater there. Reflecting this societal change, the urgency and tension diminished in the blues of Texas musicians. There was a sense of ease in the singers' blurred voices and in the musicians' use of long, melodic phrases and embellishments. Overall, the blues that developed in Texas was characterized by a general feeling of calm and relaxation. Although the barrelhouse pianists were obliged to play fast boogies, their slow blues and shuffle rhythms portrayed a more controlled and contained emotional approach to the blues. When wartime job opportunities in the West Coast defense factories sucked workers out of Texas, this blues style was easily transported along with them. It not only continued to thrive undiluted well after the war had ended, but it also contributed to the growth of the highly sophisticated West Coast blues style that subsequently developed.

Huddie Ledbetter was the first bluesman of note to show up in Texas. He moved there from north Louisiana in 1909. The same music that was being played in Louisiana, Mississippi, and other parts of the South was in east Texas, too, in the form of breakdowns, ballads, and barrelhouse tunes, all of which were very popular at that time. The classical blues style was also taking shape and was following the same pattern of development, though somewhat retarded, as in other areas of the rural United States. The blues grew out of local circumstances. For some reason the Texas prisons, jails, and chain gangs—areas in which Ledbetter was certainly no stranger—were especially rich in providing the kind of music that helped immensely to deepen and extend the blues tradition in that state.

During the years that Ledbetter was living in Texas, he played and sang in the streets of Dallas with a bluesman, ten years his junior, named Lemon Jefferson.* Lemon Jefferson was born blind in 1897 in Couchman, Texas, and because of his musical genius and penchant for travel, all of the South came to know "Blind" Lemon Jefferson. He made his name one of the most famous in the blues world, working the tough street-corner affairs and going north to Chicago to record in April 1926. In Chicago he became the most prolific of all early blues recording artists. He recorded seventy-nine pieces for Paramount Records and two for Okeh before he died in 1930. He made money, but except for a car he bought and a chauffeur he kept on salary during the last years of his life, he squandered nearly all of it on good times and nightlife. Recording was Jefferson's life.

His best moments are on the eighty-one tracks he cut. He died just after a recording session in Chicago in the coldest part of winter. When he left the studio, his intention was to go directly to a party. He was to be picked up by his car, but for some reason the driver did not show up. Jefferson started out alone, convinced that he could make it on his own despite the snow. He was found the next morning frozen to death. Paramount Records shipped his body home, and Blind Lemon Jefferson, one of the great primitive talents in the blues, was buried beneath the warm Texas soil.

Another bluesman of note to emerge from Texas in the 1920s was Alger "Texas" Alexander.* He is about the only popular male blues singer who played no instrument. That being the case, he owed at least some of his early success to his accompanist, the great New Orleans–born and bred guitar player Lonnie Johnson. When Johnson left New Orleans just after World War I, Dallas was his first base of operations. While there, he hooked up with Alexander and helped to give a bit of polish to Alexander's style, which remained rather down-home throughout his career. When Johnson moved north and started to record, Alexander followed and began a modest recording career of his own with the Okeh label.

During the 1930s, when Alexander was back in Texas and down on his luck, he gave his cousin Sam "Lightnin'" Hopkins* his first professional experience as a musician. As Hopkins tells the story, Alexander was so desperate for an accompanist that he would carry a guitar around in case he would meet up with someone who could play it for him. Hopkins, as it happened, turned out to be that person. They began traveling together and even played in Houston for a while, but things did not go too well. It was the depression era, and times were especially tough in the Southwest. After a short while Hopkins decided to return to farming, which was his livelihood prior to his encounter with Texas Alexander.

He did not go back to Houston again until just after the war, and that time things went fairly well for him. He played temporarily with a barrelhouse pianist called "Thunder" Smith, and the two caught the attention of a talent scout from Aladdin Records on the West Coast. They received as a duo, and that was when Sam Hopkins became "Lightnin' " Hopkins, the name under which he has performed and recorded ever since.

Texas is also the producer of a fast blues piano style known as boogie-woogie. The up-tempo, rolling bass that gives this music an undercurrent of tremendous power is totally Texan in origin. Boogie-woogie piano playing, like other forms of Texas blues, originated in the lumber and turpentine camps and in the sportin' houses. In Dallas, Houston, and Galveston all black piano players played that way. The style was often referred to as a fast blues to differentiate it from the slow blues piano playing of St. Louis or New Orleans. Contrary to what has become almost popular belief, that style of playing was not originated by Mead Lux Lewis, Albert Ammons, or Clarence "Pine Top" Smith.* They were merely exponents of it.

The Texas barrelhouse piano style, on the other hand, was an intricate blend of medium-tempo blues and ragtime delivered with a strong left hand. It anticipated boogie-woogie by about a decade. Among those remembered as barrelhouse piano players are Robert Shaw, who has been recorded by Arhoolie Records, Frank Ridge, and R. L. McNeer. Pete Johnson,* the noted Kansas City traveling pianist, is considered a direct link between these Texas musicians and the exponents of the boogie-woogie style that he himself helped to perfect.

Overall, the Texas blues tradition has in most cases emphasized a somewhat lighter musical touch. Guitar players tend to be less concerned with chordal qualities, but place great emphasis on single-string melodic dexterity instead. A more relaxed vocal approach is evident. The musical accompaniment is sparse, leaving enough space for the vocalist to improvise freely. In a way, Texas and the surrounding states nurtured the blues idiom the most. During and after the war the most popular bluesmen from south Texas were Charles Brown,* Amos Milburn,* Andrew "Smokey" Hogg, Floyd Dixon,* Peppermint Harris (Harrison Nelson), Roy Brown,* T-Bone Walker,* Percy Mayfield,* Pee Wee Crayton (Connie C. Crayton),* and Lowell Fulson.* Other singers like Jimmy Witherspoon,* Joe Turner,* Eddie "Cleanhead" Vinson, and Wynonie Harris,* all carriers of the Kansas City shouting tradition, were also appearing in Texas, the South, and the Midwest at that time. Many of these blues artists had records that sold more than a million copies to an almost entirely black market, a market that came to be known as rhythm-and-blues.

The city of Houston became the capital of blues and rhythm-and-blues recording in Texas during the early 1950s when the music industry's economic power was beginning to develop in the hands of independent, small record companies. One of the most prolific of these companies was Peacock/Duke Records. The company, a one-man operation led by Don Roby, was started in 1949 and ran successfully for two decades. Its stable of artists included Clarence "Gatemouth" Brown,* who recorded Peacock's first release, Willie Mae "Big Mama" Thornton,* who recorded the original version of "Hound Dog" in 1952 (four years before Elvis Presley did it), and John Marshall "Johnny Ace" Alexander,* who scored big-time with hits like "My Song," "The Clock," "Please Forgive Me," and "Cross My Heart." Robert "Bobby" Bland was one of Roby's highest-profile singers and recorded more hits over a longer period of time than anyone else on his roster. As long as Peacock/Duke was in power, most of the company's artists made Houston their home and base of operations. When the record industry was once again moved into the hands of the majors, however, the musicians moved out also. What had once been an area of major rhythm-and-blues activity became just another stop on the road.

CHICAGO

Today Chicago, a city that stands apart from others with its own highly emotional style of blues playing, is the undisputed home of the blues. In the early years lovers of the music were fond of calling that blues style "urban blues" to distinguish it from the more primitive country blues that was played in the juke joints of the rural South. Today it is simply called Chicago blues, taking the name of the center of the urban style and the city where the blues was recorded the most.

Paramount Records in Chicago, with a gigantic mail-order and drummer trade in the South, was eager to record black musicians whose records the country and audience would buy. The man in charge of the company's "race" recording operations in Chicago was J. Mayo Williams, a black man who brought Blind Lemon Jefferson up from Texas to cut records as early as 1926. After a brief and unsuccessful venture on his own, Williams joined Vocalion Records as a talent scout and began recording everyone from the old Memphis bluesman Jim Jackson (known for "Kansas City Blues") to Tampa Red and Georgia Tom Dorsey.* Later, when the English Decca company opened an American office in Chicago in 1934, it employed Williams as a scout, and for it he built up an immensely impressive roster of black talent in just a year's time.

Not surprisingly, the depression hit the record industry hard, and that part of the industry supplying black music was hit hardest of all. Paramount closed down. Field expeditions to various sections of the South for on-the-spot recordings, which had become standard procedure for some companies, were discontinued. Somehow Chicago held on, perhaps because there was a sort of resident blues nucleus in the city by this time. Many bluesmen who had gone to Chicago or had been brought up north to record on one or another of the various labels thriving at the time simply stayed around to play at South Side clubs while they waited for their next recording sessions. In these South Side bars the country blues style of the South was metamorphosed into what would later be called urban blues, a type of blues that was a little less personal and a bit more structured than its country cousin.

One of the originators of this urban style in Chicago was William Lee Conley Broonzy,* better known as "Big Bill" Broonzy. He was born in Scott, Mississippi, on June 26, 1893. He stated in his autobiography, *Big Bill Blues*, that he went to Chicago in 1920 and started playing for food at Saturday night house-rent parties. After playing throughout the city for a while, he was able to convince J. Mayo Williams that he was ready to record. Of the four sides he subsequently cut for Paramount Records, only one, "House Rent Stomp," was released in 1929 after a delay of some months. Consequently, his initial impact as a recording artist was not that great, but he remained available for all sorts of music jobs and stayed visible on the blues scene in Chicago. He continued to record, usually solo, but sometimes backing up other singers. In spite of the fact that his performances consisted mostly of traditional material, his recorded works were largely his own compositions. His early recordings presented him playing country blues in the old style; then gradually throughout the early 1930s a change became evident. He teamed up with a piano player named Joshua Altheimen, added rhythm and a reedman named Buster Bennett, and formed what came to be known as Big Bill Broonzy's Memphis Five. The music they played was in a kind of good-time style that mixed blues, jazz, and popular dance music. Through the 1930s Broonzy became more and more proficient as a guitarist. He was able to hold a strong, steady rhythm, and as a soloist he was fluent and to a moderate degree imaginative. Largely because of his skill on the guitar and his wide contacts among Chicago blues and jazz musicians, he became associated with Lester Melrose, a white blues entrepreneur and independent record producer who worked with both the Vocalion and Bluebird labels. Broonzy recorded for both labels under Melrose's auspices, and for Bluebird he also became a house musician, putting together groups to record behind such artists as Washboard Sam (Robert Brown)—Broonzy's half brother—and with a top-notch female vocalist named Lil Green* who sang popular material and jazz in addition to a lot of blues.

Lester Melrose, who produced many of Broonzy's recordings, played a vital role in shaping the urban blues style in Chicago. In the 1920s Melrose had been involved in jazz circles with such people as King Joe Oliver and the great Jelly Roll Morton and had had initial contact with the Gennette Record Company. In February 1934 he made initial contact with RCA Victor and Columbia Records, explaining the blues and rhythm-and-blues talent he had ready in Chicago. They responded at once, and from March 1934 to February 1951 Melrose recorded at least 90 percent of all rhythm-and-blues talent for these two labels. The roster of musicians whom Melrose handled at one time or another is staggering—Big Bill Broonzy, St. Louis Jimmy (James Oden), Memphis Minnie, Lil Green, Roosevelt Sykes, Tampa Red, Big Joe Williams, Washboard Sam, Arthur "Big Boy" Crudup,* Lonnie

Johnson, Leroy Carr, Victoria Spivey,* Sonny Boy Williamson (Rice Miller), and many others, including some of the biggest stars of the urban blues school.

By and large, the Chicago blues sound began to blossom with the Bluebird sessions of the 1930s and early 1940s. The talent presented on them was overwhelmingly impressive. They were all top-shelf musicians who were instrumental, each in his own way, in turning the country blues into an urban entity. These bluesmen who sang about big-city miseries, depression, unemployment, tough cops, and freezing winds sang their longing for the South not because it was better, but because it was home. In their hands the Chicago sound became a blues cry of exile made by those exiled from the bluest parts of the South. The party-time feeling of earlier blues tunes was dampened by a heavier beat and a more pronounced boogie pattern.

At the same time electric guitars were gradually being introduced, not with the same degree of amplification as employed during the rhythm-and-blues era, but with just enough to lift and sustain the sound above the other instruments. Just as greater musicianship and tighter organization had been required of the jazz groups accompanying the women blues vocalists known as "classic" blues singers, the Chicago blues bands also adopted a well-planned pattern with instrumental breaks for the guitarist or pianist to assume the lead or the saxophone or trumpet player to take a solo.

Not all blues performers in Chicago were using large ensembles, however. Pianist Roosevelt Sykes would often make his recordings with just a bass player and drummer, and Big Bill Broonzy sometimes did not even use a rhythm section. In such cases a general lightness of tone and mood resulted.

Departing from the ease and subdued temperament of the blues that went before, the emotional level of blues in Chicago in the late 1930s and early 1940s was beginning to pick up. By that time the city's black population had established its own cultural roots, and there began a new feeling of assertion in the music. Different instrumental combinations sprang up. Melodic and rhythm patterns changed, and off-beat accents became popular. Vocal acrobatics also added greatly to a new musical excitement. All of these elements generated a strong sense of social cohesion and power among blacks.

One of the most lasting influences on this music was a young man from Tennessee named John Lee "Sonny Boy" Williamson and sometimes known as Sonny Boy Number One. He created a bridge first between the rural blues of the South and the Chicago blues of 1930s, and then again between the Chicago blues of the 1930s and postwar electronics. Williamson was born in Jackson, Tennessee, in 1914. In his teens he played harmonica and worked a regular circuit with Homesick James (John A. Williamson) and Sleepy John Estes. He arrived in Chicago in the mid–1930s, and when he first began recording in 1937, his music still had a strong taste of the rural South. With his slightly mumbled way of singing and his mournfully expressive harmonica playing, he exemplified the country blues of his homeplace.

His playing incorporated all the melodic and rhythmic subtleties of the best rural blues, but it also added a new dimension to the music by making the voice and harmonica almost a single entity. Williamson later revolutionized modern blues by creating a frontline instrument out of the harmonica. This instrument had always played a part in the blues and jug bands, mostly as accompaniment. Sonny Boy changed its role. He was a lead man completely attached to his instrument, and he made the harp (harmonica) a focal point in his music. The interplay between instrumental riffs and voice was innovative, bringing him a rapid rise and widespread fame as a bluesman in Chicago. The intense drive in his playing and the peculiar expressiveness (caused by a slight speech impediment) in his vocal mannerisms caused him to become a dominant figure on the blues scene. Additionally, the combination of his own rural abrasiveness and his slick, modern accompaniment showed early signs of how the blues was to develop. In May 1940, backed by piano player Joshua Altheimer and drummer Fred Williams, he recorded the hit song "I Been Dealing with the Devil," and in 1941 the poignant "My Black Name Blues."

From his first recording date to his last, all of Sonny Boy's compositions were distinctive reflections of his own personality. Like many of the blues performers of his time, he was a heavy drinker and would easily get into trouble, but the memories of his contemporaries seem always to lean on his generosity and good nature. He and his wife Lacey Bell, to whom he often referred in his songs, were well known for their sincere friendliness and hospitality. Sonny Boy appeared always ready to lend a helping hand to young musicians by demonstrating his harp techniques or solving musical problems they may have had. His enormous popularity and influence in molding the modern Chicago blues make all the more tragic the brutal way in which his life ended. In 1948 Lacey Bell was found lying on the doorstep, stabbed in the head. Sonny Boy fell into a coma and died.

Big Maceo Merriweather* was a pianist who often played with Sonny Boy Williamson. At the height of his musical career in 1946, Merriweather suffered a stroke and was left partially paralyzed at the age of forty-one. But from the time he started recording in 1941, Big Maceo was one of the major contributors to the primitive back-home quality that was injected into the Chicago blues. He employed not even the slightest hints of the ragtime style played by early barrelhouse pianists. Instead, with all of his 245 pounds, he played thunderously and relentlessly. An excellent example of his piano style can be found in his recording of "Chicago Breakdown," a rhythmically thick instrumental that demonstrated his unflagging power.

Big Maceo was born in Atlanta, Georgia, on March 31, 1905. Although he lived in Detroit and Chicago, he never lost the rough, down-home sound that was starting to move into the core of Chicago blues in the 1930s. The most copied and best remembered of all his songs was the quiet and tough "Worried Life Blues," a work that has been recorded by some of the best rhythm-and-blues artists for more than a decade.

One of the greatest of all women blues singers in Chicago in the 1930s was an aggressive vocalist and guitar player from Louisiana who performed under the name of Memphis Minnie. Born Lizzie Douglas* in Algiers, Louisiana, in 1897, Memphis Minnie lived a life that was completely submerged in music. She even married a succession of blues musicians: Casey Bill Weldon during the 1920s, Kansas Joe McCoy from 1929 to 1935, and "Little Son Joe" Ernest Lawlars from 1939 to 1961. She started recording in 1929. Her guitar duets with Joe McCoy, coupled with an earthy voice that had more than enough authority and distinction, made her one of the big stars of the 1930s. Then, like other popular musicians of the day, she started using larger bands with an extra guitar or mandolin and, on occasion, trumpet and/or saxophone. She continued recording through the 1950s, but the peak of her popularity was during her famous Blue Monday parties at Ruby Lee Gatewood's Tavern, one of the most famous nightclubs in Chicago at the time with its good food and large ballroom.

Blues recording activity in Chicago, as well as in other parts of the country, can be conveniently divided into two distinct periods, prewar and postwar. Among the reasons for this schism is the fact that shellac restrictions went into force early in 1942 and hit blues record production hardest of all. Additionally, James C. Petrillo, president of the American Federation of Musicians, became disturbed with the impact of jukeboxes on the employment of musicians for live entertainment and called for a strike in the same year. It took two years to reach agreement on an arrangement for royalties, and during this time, from 1942 to 1944, no recording was done by member musicians. Although not all bluesmen were union musicians, the recording ban still cut short what little studio activity there was.

When the ban was finally lifted, some record companies made an effort to revive race recording activity within the limitations imposed by the shellac restrictions. However, the record companies made the mistake of trying to bring back the old favorite prewar bluesmen, and not much happened. By that time there were different musical happenings on the blues scene. Almost overnight a new musical era had begun and was rapidly taking a popular hold. The Bluebird label, on which the early urban blues had been heard back in the 1930s, was dropped by Victor in 1950, and for the most part the major companies got out of the blues recording business just as the music was going into this new phase. With the war over and the blues once again in full swing, records of the new Chicago sound began to surface in large numbers on small, independent, local labels, such as VJ, Ora Nelle, J.O.B., and others.

The Aristocrat label, started by the manager of a blues club where most of the popular Chicago musicians worked, was renamed Chess in 1950, the year Bluebird was discontinued. The new company became just as important as Bluebird had ever been. Its roster included top names like Howlin' Wolf, Little Walter (Marion Walter Jacobs),* Muddy Waters, and just about every other good blues musician in the city. In the 1950s, with Chuck Berry (Charles E. A. Berry)* and Bo Diddley (Ellas McDaniel)* under contract, Chess was one of the first companies to make records of a new sound that was called rhythm-and-blues.

The Chess brothers, Phil and Leonard, owned a club in Chicago called the Macambo Lounge. As nightclub owners, they ventured into the recording business more or less by accident. Once in the business, though, they stayed and worked hard at it. For instance, while other people who ran small, independent labels were satisfied to sell their records across the bar and at a few stores in Chicago, the Chess brothers took their products to distributors and placed them directly in record shops, especially throughout the South. Their hard work paid off, and they were soon running a national operation. In the late 1940s and throughout the 1950s they hit their peak as recorders of the blues. In 1963 they paid a million dollars for a radio station in Chicago and converted it into WVON, which soon became the top black station in the area. Also, in the 1960s there were a number of separate record labels added to the Chess blanket. Argo (a jazz label), Cadet, and Checker were all part of a very large rhythm-and-blues recording business. Chess was in large measure responsible for getting the Chicago blues out for the rest of the world to hear. It kept the black blues fans happy, and moving into the 1960s, it helped reach a whole new audience of young whites with the music.

Although the blues recordings made in Chicago in the 1930s, 1940s, and 1950s played an important role in offering the world that blues style that has been so influential in American music for the past two decades, none of it would have happened had there not been an abundance of blues talent on the streets of the city. Because of the mass migration of blacks into Chicago after the war and the many places for musicians to play, Chicago became the blues mecca of the world. By the end of the 1950s there were blues bars all over the south and west sides of the city. Loyal and enthusiastic blacks went to these clubs, danced to the music, and bought the records.

But as time progressed, that audience of enthusiastic blacks gradually began to diminish. Possibly the birth of soul music changed the attitude of former blues fans. Another era was coming into being, and people who had once been staunch patrons of the blues were beginning to gravitate toward the elastic, extended forms of the new black music. Throughout the decade that followed, blues clubs began to close down at an alarming rate. As they closed, competition for jobs became intense. Periods of inactivity for musicians became longer and longer. Most of the clubs that stayed open relied on jukeboxes to provide entertainment. Finally, though, those hearty enough to weather the storm of adversity were rewarded. Beginning in the late

1960s, America's large, young, white rock audience discovered blues in the music of B. B. King, Albert King, and Muddy Waters, and in the early 1970s top Chicago blues bands were getting bookings at colleges, universities, festivals, and rock clubs around the country. Once given this type of exposure, they were able to pull in and hold audiences from all around the world. Chicago once again became the blues capital of the world in the 1980s and has held on to that position to this day. Young blues musicians, black and white, migrate to Chicago from all points to gain the experience and exposure needed to become professional in their art. In the mid–1980s Chicago had a larger population of blues vocalists and musicians than any other city in the world. Its two major record companies, Delmark and Alligator, continue in the 1990s to release the best of the Chicago blues sound. James Cotton,* Carey Bell,* Koko Taylor,* Buddy Guy,* Eddy Clearwater,* and many other younger musicians are keeping up the tradition side by side with other older masters. The Chicago Local 10–208 of the American Federation of Musicians boasts one of the largest rolls of blues musicians in the United States—a who's who of urban blues. That city's two jazz festivals, the Jazzfest, which is held in August, and the Chicago Jazz Festival, which is held in September, feature Chicago blues musicians also. Maxwell Street's marketplace blues sessions have become even bigger and more popular in the 1990s. The blues in Chicago is stronger than it has ever been and is infused with an energy that will undoubtedly continue to fuel its blue flames for years to come.

BIBLIOGRAPHY

Asch, M., and A. Lomax. *The Leadbelly Songbook*. New York: Oak Publications, 1962.

Barker, Danny, and Jack V. Buerkle. *Bourbon Street Black*. New York: Oxford University Press, 1973.

Bastin, Bruce. *Red River Blues: The Blues Tradition in the Southeast*. Urbana: University of Illinois Press, 1986.

Berkow, Ira. *Maxwell Street: Survival in a Bazaar*. Garden City, N.Y.: Doubleday, 1977.

Berry, Chuck. *Chuck Berry: The Autobiography*. New York: Harmony Books, 1987.

Berry, Jason, Jonathan Foose, and Tad Jones. *Up from the Cradle of Jazz: New Orleans Music since World War II*. Athens: University of Georgia Press, 1986.

Beyer, Jimmy. *Baton Rouge Blues*. Baton Rouge, La.: Arts and Humanities Council of Greater Baton Rouge, 1980.

Blassingame, John W. *Black New Orleans: 1860–1880*. Chicago: University of Chicago Press, 1973.

Bogaert, Karel. *Blues Lexicon: Blues, Cajun, Boogie-Woogie, Gospel*. Antwerp: N. V. Scriptoria, 1971.

Bradford, Perry. *Born with the Blues*. New York: Oak Publications, 1965.

Broonzy, William Lee Conley, and Yannick Bruynoghe. *Big Bill Blues*. Paris: Ludd, 1987.

Brove, John. *South to Louisiana*. Gretna, La.: Pelican Publishing Co., 1983.

Charles, Ray, and David Ritz. *Brother Ray: Ray Charles' Own Story*. New York: Dial Press, 1978.

Charters, Samuel. *The Country Blues*. New York: Rinehart, 1959.

———. *Robert Johnson*. New York: Oak Publications, 1973.

———. *The Roots of the Blues: An African Search*. New York: Pedigree/Putnam, 1982.

Chernoff, John Miller. *African Rhythm and African Sensibility: Aesthetics and Social Action in African Musical Idioms*. Chicago: University of Chicago Press, 1979.

Cone, James H. *The Spirituals and the Blues: An Interpretation*. New York: Orbis Books, 1991.

Cook, Bruce. *Listen to the Blues*. New York: Charles Scribner's Sons, 1973.

Cuney-Hare, Maud. *Negro Musicians and Their Music*. New York: Da Capo Press, 1974.

Dance, Helen Oakley. *Stormy Monday: The T-Bone Walker Story*. Baton Rouge: Louisiana State University Press, 1987.

Davis, Ronald L. *A History of Music in American Life*. Vol. 1, *The Formative Years, 1620–1865*. Melbourne, Fla.: Krieger, 1982.

Dennison, S. *Scandalize My Name*. New York: Garland Publishing, 1982.

Epstein, Dena J. *Sinful Tunes and Spirituals: Black Folk Music to the Civil War*. Urbana: University of Illinois Press, 1981.

Evans, David. *Tommy Johnson*. London: Studio Vista, 1971.

Fahey, John. *Charley Patton*. London: Studio Vista, 1970.

Feather, Leonard. *The History of the Blues*. New York: Charles Hansen Books, 1972.

Ferris, William, Jr. *Blues from the Delta*. Garden City, N.Y.: Doubleday, 1978; New York: Da Capo Press, 1984.

Floyd, Samuel A., Jr., and Marsha J. Reisser. *Black Music in the United States: An Annotated Bibliography of Selected Reference and Research Materials*. Millwood, N.Y.: Kraus International Publications, 1983.

Garon, Paul. *The Devil's Son-in-Law: The Story of Peetie Wheatstraw and His Songs*. London: Studio Vista, 1971.

Garvin, Richard M., and Edmond G. Addeo. *The Midnight Special: The Legend of Leadbelly*. New York: B. Geis Associates, 1981.

Georgia Writers' Project. *Drums and Shadows: Survival Studies among the Georgia Coastal Negroes*. Athens: University of Georgia Press, 1940.

Gillett, Charlie. *The Sound of the City*. New York: Pantheon Books, 1983.

Groom, Bob. *The Blues Revival*. London: Studio Vista, 1971.

Guralnick, Peter. *Feel Like Going Home*. New York: Outerbridge and Dienstfrey, 1971.

Hamm, Charles. *Music in the New World*. New York: W. W. Norton, 1983.

Handy, William C. *Blues: An Anthology*. New York: Macmillan, 1972.

Harris, Sheldon. *Blues Who's Who*. New Rochelle, N.Y.: Arlington House, 1979.

Hart, Mary L., Brenda M. Eagles, and Lisa N. Howorth. *The Blues: A Bibliographical Guide*. New York: Garland Publishing Company, 1989.

Haskins, James. *The Cotton Club*. New York: New American Library, 1977.

Katz, Bernard, ed. *The Social Implications of Early Negro Music in the United States*. New York: Arno Press and the New York Times, 1979.

Kmen, Henry. *Music in New Orleans: The Formative Years, 1791–1841*. Baton Rouge: Louisiana State University Press, 1966.

Lang, Iain. *Background of the Blues*. Bexhill-on-Sea, England: Blues Unlimited, 1968.

Leadbitter, Mike. *Delta Country Blues*. London: Blues Unlimited, 1934.

Leadbitter, Mike, and Eddie Shuler. *From the Bayou*. Bexhill-on-Sea, England: Blues Unlimited, 1969.

Lee, George W. *Beale Street: Where the Blues Began*. College Park, Md.: McGrath, 1969.

McKee, Margaret, and Fred Chisenhall. *Beale Black and Blue*. Baton Rouge: Louisiana State University Press, 1989.

Moore, Carman. *Somebody's Angel Child: The Story of Bessie Smith*. New York: Thomas Y. Crowell Company, 1969.

Oakley, Giles. *The Devil's Music: A History of the Blues*. New York: Taplinger Publishing Co., 1977.

Odum, Howard W., and Guy B. Johnson. *The Negro and His Songs*. Chapel Hill: University of North Carolina Press, 1925.

———. *Negro Workaday Songs*. Chapel Hill: University of North Carolina Press, 1926.

Oliver, Paul. *Savannah Syncopators: African Retentions in the Blues*. London: Studio Vista, 1970.

———. *Blues Fell This Morning*. London: Cassell and Co., Ltd., 1960; New York: Horizon Books, 1962; Republished as *The Meaning of the Blues*. New York: Collier Books, 1963.

———. *Conversations with the Blues*. London: Cassell and Co., Ltd., 1965; New York: Horizon Books, 1966.

———. *Screening the Blues*. London: Cassell and Co., Ltd., 1968; New York: Oak Publications, 1970.

———. *The Story of the Blues*. London: Barrie and Jenkins, 1969; Philadelphia: Chilton Book Company, 1969; New York: Penguin Books, 1972.

Olsson, B. *Memphis Blues*. Edited by Paul Oliver. London: Studio Vista, 1970.

Oster, Harry. *Living Country Blues*. Detroit: Folklore Association, 1969.

Parrish, Lydia. *Slave Songs of the Georgia Sea Islands*. New York: Creative Age Press, 1942.

Rodney, J. *Bossmen: Bill Monroe and Muddy Waters*. New York: Dial Press, 1971.

Rowe, Mike. *Chicago Breakdown*. London: Eddison Press, 1973; New York: Drake Publishers, 1975.

Ruspoli, Mario, ed. and trans. *Blues, Poésie de l'Amérique Noire*. Paris: Publications Techniques et Artistiques, 1947.

Russell, T. *Blacks, Whites and Blues*. Edited by Paul Oliver. London: Studio Vista, 1970.

Saxon, Lyle, Edward Dreyer and Robert Tallant. *Gumbo Ya-Ya*. Boston: Houghton Mifflin, 1945.

Schuller, Gunter. *Early Jazz: Its Roots and Musical Development*. New York: Oxford University Press, 1968.

Shaw, Arnold. *The World of Soul.* New York: Paperback Library, 1971.

Shirley, Kay, ed. *The Book of the Blues.* New York: Crown Publishers, Inc. and Leeds Music Corp., 1963.

Sonnier, Austin M. *Bunk Johnson: The New Iberia Years.* New York: Crescendo Publishers, 1977.

Stearns, Marshall. *The Story of Jazz.* New York: Oxford University Press, 1956; London: Sidgwick and Jackson, Ltd., 1957; New York: Mentor Press, 1958.

Traum, H., ed. *Guitar Styles of Brownie McGhee.* New York: Oak Publications, 1971.

Wittke, Carl. *Tambo and Bones.* Durham: Duke University Press, 1930.

Zur, Heide K. G. *Deep South Piano: The Story of Little Brother Montgomery.* Paul Oliver, ed. London: Studio Vista, 1970.

4

THE CLASSIC ERA

Women have played an important role in the blues since its early development. As far back as 1902 Mamie Desdoumes was singing the blues in joints and cribs in the Tenderloin district of New Orleans. Pianist Jelly Roll Morton remembered her as a poor, blues-singing girl who used to play pretty passable piano around the dance halls of Perdido Street. When entrepreneurs Lulu White or Hattie Rogers would put the word out that Mamie was going to be singing in their place, men would come in droves and the establishment's profits would soar.

Women, however, seem to have played a lesser role than men in the early days of country blues. Usually the men were more able to move around, leaving their jobs to make a living on the road with music while the women were left behind to care for the children. Still, there were many women like Josie Bush, for instance, who lived in Drew, Mississippi, with Willie Brown, one of Charley Patton's constant musical buddies when Patton was at Dockery's Plantation. Josie could sing and play the blues just as well as Brown. During his career Patton frequently played with women, one of them being his last wife, Bertha Lee, with whom he recorded in 1934. But the pattern of rural life seems to have been such that women played a secondary part, mainly following the men who were regarded as the best entertainers for plantation dances and house parties.

In the urban areas women had always played a prominent role in the black church and served also as the main strength and backbone of many families. At this point in history many black families were forced to accept a female head because some men, unable to function properly under extreme social and economic pressures, had to take to the road to survive. The man's departure usually left the woman to face the problems of rearing a family on her own. Understandably, in the new, striving urban communities both in the North and in the South, some found in the women blues singers the stability of the maternal figure.

These women came to be known as the "classic" blues singers, a term very loosely applied to singers from the tent and vaudeville shows and those who worked with jazz bands. Many of them had warm, beautiful voices. While they had the moaning, down-home quality of Southern rural blues, their style had little of the overall inconsistencies of the male singers. They projected strength and power, and their style was more formal due in great part to their work with large, jazz-oriented bands.

The importance of these women singers in blues history is overwhelming and can hardly be overstated. They were the first big stars in the business, and the names of singers like Bessie Smith* and Gertrude "Ma" Rainey* have become symbols of America's contribution to popular culture. These women frequently worked with jazz bands that, in contrast to the general isolation of the male rural blues singers, provided a visible display of togetherness. To the struggling migrants who were desperately trying to create a new community in the cities, they and their bands represented the unity for which everyone was fighting.

Despite the black woman's importance as head of the family, she often had to deal with what has been referred to as the double jeopardy of being not only black but also female. Because American society historically has been not only white dominated but also male dominated, a caste structure of sorts was reflected in certain areas with dominance by white men, followed by white women, then black men, and black women at the very bottom. Often limited to the roles of mammy or prostitute by white society, black women were without doubt economically exploited, sexually assaulted, and constantly forced to accept abuse.

Even though black women were able to work more than white women, the types of work to which they had access were very often restricted by their own lack of education and expertise, as well as by prejudice against blacks and the prevailing male ideas of what women could do and were worth. Made to accept the lowest-paid jobs out of pure economic necessity, they often did the same work as men and were paid less for it. With black families constantly on the brink of economic disaster, the tensions and personal conflicts were enormous. Because black women could often get work while their husbands could not, they soon came to accept the notions that black men were lazy and irresponsible. Many black men, in turn, found refuge in the belief that males were superior to females, thereby leaving the black woman to rely only on her power and determination to succeed.

In 1920 blues songwriter and pianist Perry Bradford* persuaded the recording director of the newly established Okeh label to arrange a recording session for a talented Harlem singer named Mamie Smith.* Smith, a struggling thirty-year-old blues singer from Cincinnati, recorded "Crazy Blues" during the session and secured a place for herself in blues history. It made the unknown Miss Smith the favorite of all black singers of her time. In an era when a record was an expensive luxury, "Crazy Blues" sold 75,000 copies the first month. They sold for a dollar each. Miss Smith was a sensation everywhere she went. She played theaters throughout 1920 and 1921 singing to crowds that consistently filled the house. She even had her own orchestra, the Jazz Hounds, to travel with her throughout the nation. One of its members, saxophonist Coleman Hawkins, was only fifteen when he joined her troupe.

The success of Mamie Smith's records made other labels aware of a market for the blues in Northern cities as well as in the rural South. Until then the blues had developed slowly, being transmitted orally by country itinerant performers and directed only toward the blacks of the South. When the sales of Mamie Smith's Okeh discs of "Crazy Blues" continued to grow, other labels began a talent hunt for blues singers. In 1922 Paramount Records, owned by a Wisconsin furniture company that had begun recording in 1917 to sell phonographs, launched its 12,000 series of "race records." In the next five years, under the enterprising direction of J. Mayo Williams, Paramount recorded an impressive number of rural blues singers whose work might otherwise have been lost to posterity. Among them were Charley Patton, Son House, and Blind Lemon Jefferson. Later Gennett Records of Richmond, Indiana, also started moving its portable recording equipment throughout the South to record bluesmen.

There were other successful female blues singers when Mamie Smith was at the peak of her form, including other Smiths, most of whom were not related. Mamie was known as "Queen of the Blues." Bessie Smith became acknowledged as "Empress of the Blues" and the favorite of all musicians. Trixie Smith,* on the other hand, had no such royal title, but her recordings were very popular.

As Mamie Smith's flame began to diminish, Gertrude "Ma" Rainey came out of Georgia and became perhaps the nation's favorite blues singer. In one of Ma Rainey's touring troupes, Bessie Smith got her start and subsequently topped Ma Rainey in popularity on records.

Ma was the oldest of the early blues singers. Born Gertrude Pridgett in Columbus, Georgia, in 1886, she worked with the Rabbit Foot Minstrels, in which her husband, William "Pa" Rainey, was a featured entertainer. She did not begin to record until 1923. At that time, for Paramount Records with Lovie Austin's Serenaders, she recorded such classic blues numbers as "Barrelhouse Blues," "Boll Weevil Blues," and the unique "Ma Rainey's Mystery Record" with Tommy Ladnier on trumpet and Lovie Austin on piano.

The band with whom she appeared most often on stage was a jazz-influenced ensemble that played in the early New Orleans style. Its instruments included trumpet, tenor saxophone, trombone, piano, bass, and drums. At the piano was "Georgia Tom" Dorsey, who was later recognized as one of the great composers of gospel songs. Ma was billed as Madame Ma Rainey, the Mother of the Blues, and would begin her act by emerging from an oversized phonograph. Although she was short and wore long dresses to make herself look taller, her voice was a deep resounding contralto, and her matronly bosom provided all the room needed to project the tough, uninhibited, down-home material she sang in performance. Her career continued until 1933, when she retired and returned to Georgia. She died there in 1939.

Frank Walker, then head of Columbia Records, happened to hear a remarkable young girl singing in a Salem, Alabama, juke joint while there on a field trip through the South and was totally impressed with her. Later, when he returned to the Columbia studios, he sent pianist Clarence Williams, who rehearsed and coached artists for the company, to find her. She turned out to be Bessie Smith.

On February 17, 1923, with Clarence Williams at the piano, Bessie made her first recording, entitled "Down Hearted Blues." The song had been written the year before by Chicago's celebrated blues singer Alberta Hunter and her bandleader Lovie Austin. Released without much fanfare, the record outsold the top Columbia hits of that year by a ratio of almost eight to one, raising Miss Smith overnight to the rank of superstar singer.

Bessie, from Chattanooga, Tennessee, was eight years younger than Ma Rainey and possessed a more compelling voice. She toured with the Raineys throughout the Theater Owners Booking Association (TOBA) or the "Tough on Black Asses" circuit, as the black performers wryly referred to it. Her innate musical talent and magnificent voice impressed Ma Rainey so much that she persuaded Bessie to go on tour with the minstrels. This venture turned out to be a valuable form of apprenticeship for her but not a particularly rewarding one financially. For some time Bessie scuffled for a livelihood, singing in small tent shows like the Florida Cotton Blossoms and in nightclubs and carnivals throughout the South. In early 1923, however, she started a series of unforgettable recording sessions with hits like "Down Hearted Blues," "Keeps On Rainin,' " and " 'Tain't Nobody's Business If I Do." Her acceptance by America's black population was even greater than that of her mentor Ma Rainey, and her first records reportedly sold more than two million copies the first year. Soon after joining Columbia, she became a headliner in the top-ranking black vaudeville shows of the day. During 1924 to 1927, when she was at the top of her form, Bessie was the highest-paid black vaudeville entertainer of America, with a weekly paycheck as high as fifteen hundred dollars.

In the beginning of her fame Bessie concentrated almost exclusively on the blues, but as her career blossomed, she began to work with more commercially popular material and even ventured into gospel songs. Her rendition of this music encompassed a fever and passion that only the great Mahalia Jackson could come near.

On May 23, 1929, Bessie recorded one of the most popular discs of her entire career, a Jimmy Cox song called "Nobody Knows You When You're Down and Out." This song had great meaning for her because she had known hard times and, ironically, by 1929 her career was headed downhill.

After her initial acceptance as a blues singer, she had attempted to approach the white audience by recording popular songs. These recordings did not project in the manner intended. Instead of gaining a wider audience, she only succeeded in alienating some of her black following. Also, the onset of the depression had by this time weakened the appeal of the blues.

Bessie found adjusting to these situations very hard. Her manager, Frank Walker, helped restrain her penchant for conspicuous spending and had her save some of her money. He even compelled her to invest in a house. But Bessie and her husband, a Philadelphia policeman, decided that they could do without Walker and the percentage he took from her earnings. Soon she was alienating theater managers with irritating displays of temper that stemmed from her heavy drinking and by becoming involved in frequent brawls. Coupled with her unruly behavior, the economic state of the country by 1931 caused a considerable decline in demand for her records.

Her last recording date, November 24, 1933, involved an all-star group of musicians that included trumpeter Frankie Newton with Jack Teagarden on trombone, Chu Berry on tenor saxophone, Buck Washington, Billy Taylor, Bobby Johnson, and, on one song, Benny Goodman on clarinet. The session was produced for Columbia by John Hammond, a friend and associate of Frank Walker. Bessie was in top form, and "Gimmie a Pigfoot and a Bottle of Beer," "Do Your Duty," "Take Me for a Buggy Ride," and "I'm Down in the Dumps" rank among her best works.

Throughout her career Bessie had employed only the best available jazzmen on her record and club dates. Clarence Williams served as her pianist and coach, and he had enough insight and musical know-how to team her immensely powerful voice in the hundreds of songs she recorded throughout the 1920s with the likes of Fletcher Henderson, Louis Armstrong, Don Redman, outstanding composer Buster Bailey, Coleman Hawkins, Tommy Ladnier, and James P. Johnson, who later became known as the father of the stride piano style.

But the end came tragically for Bessie. On Sunday morning, September 26, 1937, while traveling down a highway near Clarksdale, Mississippi, she crashed into the back of a lorry. The wreck left her terribly mutilated, with one arm almost torn from her body. A great deal has been published about what happened after the crash, and many conflicting stories have resulted. One story is that Bessie bled to death on the highway since no hospital in the area would take in a black woman. Another is that she died from exposure in a hospital ward while waiting for medical attention. Still another version maintains that while a passing doctor was trying to lift her into his car, the automobile was demolished by oncoming traffic. An ambulance arrived later and took her to the Negro ward of the G. T. Thomas Hospital in Clarksdale, where she died of injuries within a few hours. Whichever version one chooses to accept makes little difference. The tragic fact remains that one of America's greatest black female performers died much too soon, and the world of black music lost one of its finest singers.

At the peak of her career Bessie Smith transformed the classic blues style into a fresh and intriguing form of expression. With her natural genius for music, she took the vaudeville style, the rural blues, and jazz elements and combined them to form a new and distinct sound, a completely original art form.

In addition to Mamie, Ma, and Bessie, there were many other outstanding proponents of the classic blues style who made their mark, including a few more Smiths—Trixie, Laura, and Clara*—all unrelated.

Trixie Smith's big reputation among blues fans seems to be based on the results of two recording sessions. The Louis Armstrong session took place in 1925 and included the popular "Railroad Man Blues" and "The World's Jazz Crazy and So Am I." The Sidney Bechet session with Charlie Shavers was recorded in 1938, with "Freight Train Blues" and other very good songs coming out of that session. Trixie was a tremendously impressive singer who owed much to vaudeville.

Clara Smith, unlike Bessie and Trixie Smith, lived a life that is shrouded in mystery. This enigma may be the result of years of neglect on the part of collectors, historians, and critics, most of whom are simply not familiar with her work. The lack of information on Clara Smith is unfortunate because she was a fascinating singer who left behind her on records an almost complete history of her artistic progression. Her first recordings were made in 1923 and her last in 1932.

Clara's personal history is so obscure that even her birth place is uncertain. Some sources claim it was Spartanburg, South Carolina, in 1894 and this probably comes the closest. Her life before she went into music is completely undocumented, and not until she was in her mid-twenties did any knowledge about her surface. By 1918 she was a headline attraction on the TOBA circuit, and in 1921 she was a sensation at the Dream Theater in Columbus, Georgia. Her life followed the general pattern of most women blues singers. She made appearances at the Lyric Theater in New Orleans, at the Bijou in Nashville, and in 1923 at the Booker T. Washington Theater in St. Louis. In the same year she made her first records for Columbia, "Every Woman's Blues" and "I've Got Everything a Good Woman Needs," accompanied by Fletcher Henderson on piano. In October of the same year Clara achieved a personal triumph by recording a couple of duets with Bessie Smith. Bessie's jealously and contempt for other women blues singers is widely known, and her consent to record with Clara proves the respect she must have held for her. Together they did "Far Away Blues" and "I'm Going Back to My Use-to-Be" with Fletcher Henderson on piano. They later got together for another recording date in 1925.

Clara recorded two excellent songs with Don Redman on clarinet and Fletcher Henderson on piano on April 10, 1924. "Cold Weather Papa" and "Warhorse Mama," two slow blues pieces, show the immense strides she had taken in a very short time. A week later she was back at the Columbia studios with Henderson and guitarist Charlie Dixon to sing "Mean Papa Turn Your Key" and "West Indian Blues." More recordings followed at regular intervals, including some outstanding sessions with Louis Armstrong.

In her mature years Clara was undoubtedly a very good singer. Her voice was a bit less dynamic than Bessie Smith's, and she was much closer to the vaudeville style, although she later proved to be comfortable working in the blues tradition. At very slow tempos no other woman singer could come close to her, and she could and did compete with the best. In 1935 in Detroit, Michigan, where she had been living in retirement, Clara Smith had a fatal heart attack and died—like so many others—a forgotten woman.

The number of women blues singers seems unlimited. The great Ida Cox,* for instance, recorded as early as 1923 and as recently as 1961. Rosa Henderson,* Maggie Jones,* Viola McCoy,* Hannah Sylvester,* Katie Crippen, Edna Hicks, Faye Barnes, Isabella Washington, and Bessie Brown all recorded with the popular Fletcher Henderson Orchestra in the 1920s. Louis Armstrong, while still very young, recorded some of his most creative accompaniments with such vocalists as Bessie Smith, Trixie Smith, Margaret Johnson, Alberta Hunter,* Sippie Wallace,* Ma Rainey, Virginia Liston,* Victoria Spivey,* Blanche Calloway, Bertha "Chippie" Hill,* and Clara Smith.

In an advertisement by Black Swan Records, Ida Cox was called "The Uncrowned Queen of the Blues." Born in Toccoa, Georgia, in 1896, she died in Knoxville, Tennessee, in 1967. In her early years she traveled with both the Rabbit Foot Minstrels and its major competitor, Silas Green from New Orleans. Her road work began when she was only fourteen years old. She was married for a while to piano player Jesse Crump from Paris, Texas, who was seventeen years younger and who also served as her accompanist. On her recordings for Black Swan, she was accompanied by Lovie Austin on piano, the Pruett twins on guitar and banjo, or by her own band, the Blues Serenaders. Ida Cox left an indelible impression on the blues world with the amount of feeling she poured into her songs. She never once sacrificed the true feeling of the blues to the prettiness of vaudeville showmanship.

Bertha "Chippie" Hill was born in Charleston, South Carolina, in 1905. She made her debut in Harlem, sang and danced with Ma Rainey's troupe, and performed with King Oliver at the Palladium Dance Hall in Chicago. During 1925 and 1926 she recorded with Louis Armstrong and other jazz musicians and recorded the first disc of one of the most popular of all blues songs, Richard M. Jones's "Trouble in Mind." Bertha, who participated in a memorial concert for Bessie Smith at New York's Town Hall in 1948, was also killed in an auto accident two years later by a hit-and-run driver. Terribly injured, she died in a Harlem hospital on Sunday, May 7, 1950. Her style of singing was tough. She lacked a certain finesse on the more subtle, melodic pieces, but on songs with a "hot" flavor she was often at the top of her element.

Florence Mills was said to be the most beautiful and feminine of all the black women singers. She apparently did not record, but the way she sang is well remembered by musicians of her time. The great Duke Ellington supposedly had her in mind when he composed the hauntingly beautiful "Sophisticated Lady." For most of her brief career she was a star on Broadway and in numerous Harlem shows. Unfortunately, her life was short, and with her death, the world was robbed of her warm, sensuous singing style since it was never documented.

One of the many women blues singers born in New Orleans around the turn of the century was Lizzie Miles,* a Creole woman who possessed a large voice and a vigorous style of singing. Her repertoire included everything from vaudeville tunes, popular material, and Creole songs sung in Creole French to the more down-home types of rural blues. She sang with all of the best jazz musicians of New Orleans and recorded extensively in America as well as in Europe. She died of a heart attack in New Orleans while visiting the Lofton Catholic Old Folks Home on March 17, 1963.

While Lizzie Miles was a sensation in Paris, Alberta Hunter of Memphis, Tennessee, became the first American blues singer to perform in London, England. The year was 1926, and she was twenty-nine years old. There, at the Drury Lane, she played the role of "Queenie" in the first touring production of *Show Boat* that featured Paul Robeson. In 1922 she cut "Down Hearted Blues," which became her first successful recording until Bessie Smith came along and recorded the same song.

A far more sophisticated performer than Ma, Lizzie, Bessie, Ida Cox, and the other Smiths, Alberta was the first to sing "A Good Man Is Hard to Find," which she personally taught to Sophie Tucker. Later at the old Panama Cafe on Chicago's South Side she introduced the evergreen "Someday Sweetheart." Before World War II Alberta sang in twenty-five countries, and while the war was going on she performed in Europe and the South Pacific under the auspices of the USO. She was also the star of her own radio show in New York City from 1938 to 1940. She retired from singing and acting for a brief period in the 1960s to become a nurse. Eventually she worked at the Goldwater Memorial Hospital on Welfare Island. In her later years, however, she returned to show business, the only business for which she had a true love.

Julia Lee,* sister of Kansas City bandleader George E. Lee, was singing with her father's string trio at the age of four. She started playing piano at ten and in her teens was active as a singer/pianist at house-rent parties and amateur shows. Most of her professional engagements were in and around Kansas City. Although she did a short stint at the Three Deuces in Chicago, she would never stray far from home for too long a time. In 1944 she cut her first records in Kansas City for Capitol. She had a few good sellers in her short recording career, but her sudden death in December 1958 left the blues world considering how much more effective her singing might have been had she recorded as a younger woman.

The list of popular female blues singers of the classic blues tradition continues with a fine shouter who went by the name of Bricktop and with Victoria Spivey, a grand lady of song. Bricktop became famous as the owner of a Paris nightclub, while Victoria Spivey accounted for several of the most often recorded blues of that time. The popular "Black Snake Blues," "Bloodhound Blues," and "Dirty T. B. Blues" afforded her worldwide stardom.

There were many other female blues singers, such as Edmonia Henderson,* Virginia Liston, Monetta Moore, Mary Johnson, Julia Jones, Ann Cook,* Annie Turner, Ada Brown, Lela Bolden, Rosetta Crawford, Hattie McDaniel, Mae Scott, Helen Baxter, Mary Bradford, and Alice Moore. The list is endless. The need that existed for black female singers in the 1920s and the 1930s was truly a great one. No other musical era in the history of the world has given women such honor.

BIBLIOGRAPHY

Albertson, Chris. *Bessie*. New York: Stein and Day, 1972.

Bogle, Donald. *Brown Sugar: Eighty Years of America's Black Female Superstars*. New York: Harmony Books, 1980.

Bradford, Perry. *Born with the Blues*. New York: Oak Publications, 1965.

Butler, J. *Gender Trouble*. New York: Routledge, 1990.

Chilton, John. *Billie's Blues: Billie Holiday's Story, 1933–1959*. New York: Stein and Day, 1975.

Collier, James L. *The Making of Jazz*. New York: Dell, 1978.

Dexter, Dave. *The Jazz Story*. Englewood Cliffs, N.J.: Prentice-Hall, 1964.

Feather, Leonard. *The History of the Blues*. New York: Charles Hansen Books, 1972.

Gleason, Ralph J. *Celebrating the Duke and Louis, Bessie, Billie, Bird, Carmen, Miles, Dizzy, and Other Heroes*. New York: Dell, 1976.

Handy, William C., and Abbe Niles. *A Treasury of the Blues*. New York: C. Boni, 1949.

Harris, Sheldon. *Blues Who's Who*. New Rochelle, N.Y.: Arlington House, 1979.

Haskins, James. *The Cotton Club*. New York: New American Library, 1977.
Holiday, Billie, and William Dufty. *Lady Sings the Blues*. Garden City, N.Y.: Doubleday, 1956.
Horne, Lena, and Richard Schickel. *Lena*. Garden City, N.Y.: Doubleday, 1965.
Jones, Hettie. *Big Star Fallin' Mama: Five Women in Black Music*. New York: Viking Press, 1974.
Lewis, David. *When Harlem Was in Vogue*. New York: Oxford University Press, 1979.
Lieb, Sandra. *Mother of the Blues: A Study of Ma Rainey*. Amherst: University of Massachusetts Press, 1981.
McKee, Margaret, and Fred Chisenhall. *Beale Black and Blue*. Baton Rouge: Louisiana State University Press, 1989.
Moore, Carman. *Somebody's Angel Child: The Story of Bessie Smith*. New York: Thomas Y. Crowell Company, 1969.
Oakley, Giles. *The Devil's Music: A History of the Blues*. New York: Horizon, 1977.
Oliver, Paul. *Bessie Smith*. London: Cassell and Company, 1960.
Placksin, Sally. *American Women in Jazz*. New York: Wideview Books, 1982.
Roach, Hildred. *Black American Music: Past and Present*. Boston: Crescendo Publishing Company, 1973.
Schuller, Gunther. *Early Jazz: Its Roots and Musical Development*. New York: Oxford University Press, 1968.
Spelman, E. *Inessential Woman*. Boston: Beacon Press, 1988.
Stewart-Baxter, Derrick. *Ma Rainey and the Classic Blues Singers*. New York: Stein and Day, 1970.
Surge, Frank. *Singers of the Blues*. Minneapolis: Lerner Publications, 1969.
Taylor, Frank C., with Gerald Cook. *Alberta Hunter: A Celebration in Blues*. New York: McGraw-Hill, 1987.
Wallace, Michele. *Black Macho and the Myth of the Superwoman*. New York: Warner Books, 1980.
Waters, Ethel, and Charles Samuels. *His Eye Is on the Sparrow*. New York: Jove Publications, 1978.

5

HOODOO (VOODOO) AND THE BLUES

Africans believe in a supreme God who is the world's creator, who does not come in direct contact with man, but who can be reached at any time through the spirits of their ancestors. Their belief in one Supreme Being does not exclude the concept of many gods. Between this Supreme Being and man they recognize the many gods of the spirits, gods of the animals, plants, and minerals. Believed to have been created by the Supreme Being, these gods are also thought to possess certain like attributes in terms of power, thus explaining why some African societies worship the moon, the sun, and even certain trees. God is the creator of both good and evil in African religious belief. The African sees no wrong in worshipping certain objects as long as the supremacy of his God is acknowledged.

The African also believes that man is divided into two parts, body and spirit. While the body may perish, the spirit is immortal. Death does not eliminate members from family participation because the souls of the departed persons can be called upon for help anytime the living members are in trouble, just as the living may help the dead and should live to please them. Spirits may even get angry and do harm, so members of the living family are wise to take care that no displeasure comes to their ancestors. Nor should any decision be made without consulting them.

Since family ties are very strong, the African is willing to take care of relatives until they are able to care for themselves. A marriage is not just an affair between two individuals but between two families. Children belong to the community and can be disciplined by any respectable member of the community.

Africans are very fond of symbols, which have come to embody their beliefs; they dislike emptiness. Fetishism is therefore common, and witchcraft and sorcery are viewed not only as devices but as a way of life for many. The concept of accident is outside their realm of understanding, for every event has a cause and can be explained. Magic is used as a protective device, and many magical charms are personal and are worn on the body or hung over the entrance of the house. Rings, bracelets, necklaces, and many other decorations have magical as well as ornamental purposes. Even texts from the Koran and the Bible are used as protective amulets.

Religion is practiced at home as a family affair rather than as a group function in a church. God, perceived as being everywhere, does not need a special house for communal worship, and no one should try to confine him to a single place. Because of their fondness for symbols, Africans are connected to their faith by images, and each family has a special place in its house where the spirits can be invoked. Anyone may offer sacrifices, but elderly persons have priority since they are highly respected members of the family and community. An African priest may be of either sex, but in matters of fetishism women are often more effective than men.

African religion was not founded by a prophet or any other "man of God." Its basis is nature. It does not have a Bible or code of regulations, yet it is still a unified religion, full of understanding and tolerance. Nature, man, and the gods should never be separated.

The transportation of Africans, along with their religion, to the soil of San Domingo by Spanish slavers marked the beginning of a new form of worship called voodoo. In taking these people from Africa and casting them rather mercilessly on foreign soil and cultures, the traders and planters did not realize that these slaves would keep an unbreakable faith in their gods, in their spirits, and in their ancestors. Those men who were in search of an easy fortune failed to realize that the African slaves already had a way of life that they would neither forget nor give up easily. The behavior of many of the slaves in San Domingo gives evidence that the process of acculturation did not work out very well. Even those slaves who were conscious of their function had to deal with the hostilities of planters preoccupied with making money. The planters' belief was that whenever a slave was converted to the Christian faith, he could then benefit from certain Christian privileges. As far as they could see, that was not at all good for their empires. Though they preached obedience and acceptance, the missionaries became suspect. Planters created regulations prohibiting the building of churches on their plantations. The slaves had to go to church in town and could only leave the plantations to do so on Sundays. Of course, they could not worship in the same church as their masters. There was a separate place for them with their own priests. Later the planters began to complain about the idea of sending the slaves to attend church services on Sundays. They considered it a mistake for, first of all, it afforded the slaves the opportunity to escape, and second, planters considered it a waste of time and a loss of money. To pacify the complaining planters, the colonial administrators drew up a law making Sunday a market day and requested that slaves go back immediately after services to the plantations and the business of their masters.

Because of such actions, the slaves developed the habit of forming their own assemblies where they met as often as possible. Taking their small amount of Christian knowledge and coupling it with their own African beliefs, they gave birth to a new religion in which the holy names and symbols of Catholicism were combined with African idols and gods. The result came to be known as voodoo.

Many of the *loas* (voodoo gods) are identified with Catholic saints. For example, Saint Peter, who, according to Catholic belief, is the keeper of the gate, becomes Pap Legba, the master of the crossroads. The Blessed Virgin Mary becomes Erzulie Freda, the sensuous goddess who symbolizes all feminine grace and beauty. God is personified as Damballah, the Great Master (Gran Met La). Damballah comes in the form of a serpent and is sometimes shown swallowing his tail to symbolize that he is self-created without beginning or end.

The angels in Catholicism and the *zanges* in voodoo fulfill the same duties. They are God's spokesmen. The Catholic doctrine of purgatory suggesting that the living can help the dead is also to be found in voodoo, where the living always show faithful care for the dead.

Saint James becomes Ogou Feray in voodoo ceremonies, and Saint George is Djab Linglesou. The high-spirited Saint John becomes Agau Lefan. All of these, borrowed from Catholicism for the voodoo ceremonies, hold the same virtues, power, and functions attributed to them by the Catholic faith.

The long Catholic ceremonies accompanied with gestures, songs, chants, and vestments, all giving the mass a mysterious air, are not absent in voodoo. Generally speaking, there is much in voodoo practice and ceremony that resembles Catholic practice and ceremony. The same Catholic theology that teaches that God can be invoked and come to dwell in the host during the consecration exists in similar fashion in voodoo. The spirits of the loas can be invoked from above or below the earth to dwell in the *Houmfort*. No voodoo ceremony is begun without the sign of the cross made by the *houngan* (voodoo priest), who does nothing without begging Damballah's permission. The litany is even recited at a service for the dead.

From this confusion of religious beliefs developed the Southern black arts of hoodoo, the name blacks prefer, with its practitioners centered in the French South, especially in Louisiana. There is no historical record of the introduction of voodoo in Louisiana, but it must have occurred soon after shipments of slaves came from the French colonies of Guadeloupe, St. Domingue, and Martinique—all areas in which the slaves were totally controlled by the practice of voodoo. Although the growth of the cult in New Orleans and south Louisiana was slow, in 1782 Governor Bernardo de Galvez prohibited any further importation of slaves from Martinique because of the potential menace they presented. Baron de Carondelet, who was governor of Louisiana from 1792 to 1797, similarly forbade the planters and slavers to import blacks from St. Domingue, partly because of their attraction to voodoo. In 1803 the Municipal Council refused to permit a cargo of St. Domingue slaves to be unloaded from a ship that had brought them to New Orleans for sale. However, the bans that had been raised against the St. Domingue blacks were lowered a few years after the Louisiana Purchase, and at least five thousand refugee blacks, free and slave, arrived in New Orleans between 1806 and 1810. With this influx, the development of voodoo was felt more strongly in the life of Louisiana. Thereafter, although slaves continued to form the great majority of voodoo worshippers, the priests were almost entirely Creoles.

In Louisiana today there are countless men and women who are versed in the lore of voodoo and hoodoo and practice their arts for both good and evil. These are the hoodoos, the root doctors, the traiteuses and traiteurs (treaters who cure sicknesses in both humans and animals) whose powers are believed to be extensive and who are consulted by anyone, black and white alike, with a problem and the will to believe. Those who devote their powers toward good often prepare their spells and offer their services free, while those whose abilities are put to more evil use charge fees relative to the task. Both are widely respected and feared. Traiteurs are often summoned at the birth of a child to ease the birth and to perform spells that help to insure a good and healthy life for the newcomer. Barren women purchase their charms so that they may conceive, and when death approaches, the traiteur is called to smooth the journey of the departed and safeguard the lives of those who remain. From roots, animal hair, rocks, and ashes they fabricate charms that will bring good luck and wealth, and good-luck dust is sprinkled on doorsteps to keep evil out of the house. Among the most potent charms that are used to bring about evil are high John the conqueror root, which must be gathered before September 21, and goofer (goober) dust, powdered earth gathered from the grave of a child, which will bring death to the victim when it is sprinkled around his bed. Many blues songs refer to this procedure.

Among Louisiana blacks the power of the gris-gris and mojo are greatly respected. Such charms are made with great care from personal fragments and natural objects. Hair and pieces of fingernails and toenails are considered especially effective. Combined with the bones of a black cat, bats, toads, special dirt, ashes, and feathers, they are tied into small bags or put into jars and either carried to exert their power upon the victim when contact is made or buried beneath his doorstep, or better yet, hidden under his bed.

The traditional center of voodoo and hoodoo in the United States is New Orleans, from which the fame of many of its voodoo queens and root doctors has spread worldwide. People who have strong faith in their abilities both for good and evil will travel long distances and pay large sums of money for their help. But the hoodoo does not always prove successful; for every spell there is an antidote or counterspell that can combat its effects if used in time. The victim who has not been able to provide a shield to stop the hoodoo usually succumbs to its powers.

The first hoodoo doctor of whom there is any record in New Orleans was huge and black with a tattooed face. He called himself Doctor John and worked his magic during the early and middle 1840s. He was a mind reader and a believer in astrology. He sold magic shells that he soaked for three days in the oil of snakes, frogs, and lizards. Wrapped in a strand of human hair and carried in the pocket, one of these shells provided protection against all evil.

About fifteen years after Doctor John had retired with a fortune, the number one hoodoo doctor in New Orleans was a slave who was called Washington by his master. Among the blacks he was known as Doctor Yah Yah. His favorite cure was a mixture of jimpsonweed, honey, and sulphur that was to be sipped from a jar that had been rubbed against a black cat with one white foot. In 1861 Doctor Yah Yah got into a bit of trouble because of his famous concoction. He was accused of trying to poison someone with it and was placed in jail. His master bailed him out and sent him to the country, where he worked as a field hand. No more was heard of him in New Orleans.

A few years later Doctor Jack became the Crescent City's most sought-after hoodoo doctor. He was especially noted for the potency of his love charms, which were in constant demand. The most powerful of these, and the most expensive, was a beef heart made to smell good with spices and perfumes, then wrapped in a piece of white crepe paper. The cost of this hoodoo was twenty dollars, and it was known to be infallible if left under a doorstep. Above the head of Doctor Jack's bed at his home on Treme Street hung a specially charmed beef heart. It is said that he often told his customers that he could not die until it fell to the floor. On June 7, 1869, the heart fell from the wall and Doctor Jack became ill. On June 10, 1869, he died, three days after the heart hit the floor.

One of Doctor Jack's contemporaries, whose career was interrupted by a long jail sentence in 1868, was an extraordinarily eccentric old black man known as Doctor Beauregard who had come to New Orleans from Kentucky. Doctor Beauregard's hair, when combed out, reached almost to his waist. Most of the time he wore it rolled and tied into many small pockets in which he carried his hoodoos. A hot owl's head offered him the power to perform his greatest feats.

These hoodoo doctors and the extremely popular and often-powerful voodoo queens who worked along with them appear to have been more or less on equal ground so far as the practice of the art was concerned. In matters affecting worship, however, the queens possessed complete authority. One of the earliest of the voodoo queens in New Orleans was a quadroon named Sanite Dede, who dominated the cult for more than ten years after Louisiana had become a part of the United States. She was a free woman from St. Domingue, and when she was not doing work in voodoo, she peddled sweetmeats in front of the Cabildo and around the Place d'Armes in New Orleans. She held her cult meetings in an old, abandoned brickyard on Dumaine Street.

Sanite Dede was succeeded by the now world-famous Marie Laveau, the most powerful of all the voodoo queens and the most feared as well. Marie Laveau was a free mulatto and was born in New Orleans around 1796. On August 4, 1819, when she was in her early twenties, she married Jacques Paris in a ceremony that was conducted by Pere Antoine. Paris died in 1826, and a year or so afterwards Marie started living with a mulatto named Christopher Galpion. She and Galpion had a daughter, also named Marie, who was born in February 1827. By profession Marie Laveau was a hairdresser, and as a lucrative sideline she acted as a procuress for white men, furnishing girls for their pleasure. She also served as a messenger in clandestine love affairs that took place among her white customers. She became a member of the voodoo cult soon after Jacques Paris died, and she literally took Sanite Dede's place as queen a few years later. Sanite Dede was, of course, by then an old woman without much fight left in her.

On June 7, 1869, Marie Laveau's followers held a meeting in their chapel on Lake Pontchartrain and decided that Marie was to be taken from her position of power. Grounds were simply that she was no longer capable of taking care of the duties of her high position. She was well past seventy then, and the same fate that struck Sanite Dede dealt a hard blow to her as well. Malvina Latour was chosen to be the new queen.

Malvina Latour was a mulatto whose brother became a member of the notorious "black-and-tan" legislature that governed Louisiana for several years during Reconstruction. She was about thirty years old when she was chosen queen of New Orleans voodoo. Word has it that her favorite costume was a dress of blue calico and white dots and a brilliantly colored handkerchief that she tied into a tignon on her head.

Malvina Latour was the head of voodooism in New Orleans for almost twenty years, but unfortunately she did not possess the power and compelling personality of Marie Laveau. During her stay in power the cult as an organization began to deteriorate. Rival queens appeared everywhere and formed their own groups of followers. The hoodoo doctors began to assume the duties and privileges of priests and also formed groups over which they presided at ceremonies that were usually topped off with sexual orgies.

By the time Malvina Latour retired as queen in 1890, the word *voodoo* itself had been corrupted by the blacks to *hoodoo*. The cult had been divided into a number of small groups, each with its own priest or queen and its own ritual and ceremony.

In recent years, however, little has been heard of voodoo in the United

States. Because hoodoo is now an underground activity, the extent of its practice is not easily determined. Yet an enormous quantity of charms, magical dusts, and amulets is still being sold openly throughout the South. In greatest demand are the love potions and various powders and candles that are guaranteed to produce some specific favor. Novelty shops, rosary houses, and occult stores all advertise and sell power candles, easy-life lotions, special prayers, black cat's oil, love powders, goofer dust, and Catholic saints' pictures and statues as well. The original mixture of African beliefs and Catholicism still plays an active role in today's black lifestyles. Many traces of this can be found in the blues of all eras where blues musicians relied on hoodoo and have been influenced by its powers.

By the time the blues began to develop as an art form, voodoo had become known as hoodoo by blacks in America. The one thing that has always been common to both of these entities is their being able to cure certain pains. Hoodoo has always been used by black people in America to give relief to certain discomforts, including the blues. The blues is in itself both the discomfort and the relief. The Blues, as a feeling, can transport a person to the lowest levels of depression, but, as a music, it can reach down into the bowels of that depression and lift one to heights of exhilaration never before experienced by any other means. Black people in the early years of this century reached out to both hoodoo and the blues for salvation. The blues musician tried to find solutions to his problems; he did not look to God and the church. He had to look to his ancestry for help because his music and lifestyle were not accepted by the church. The blues, which has close musical ties with the music of the black church, was considered to be the Devil's music by that church. One could not ask God for help through music that is of the Devil, so the blues musician looked to hoodoo for help. Many blues songs are related to hoodoo in one way or another in their lyrics. Also, quite a few song titles mention various aspects that are related to hoodoo. Among them are the following:

Black Cats	"Black Cat Bone" (Lightnin' Hopkins)
	"Black Cat Bone" (Sonny Terry and Brownie McGhee)
	"Black Cat Bone Blues" (Bukka White)
	"Black Cat Cross My Trail" (Peter Chatman)
	"Black Cat Hoot Owl Blues" (Thomas Dorsey)
Goofer Dust	"Ashes in My Whiskey" (Walter Davis)
	"Ashes on My Pillow" (Oran Page)
Hoodoo	"Hoodoo, Hoodoo" (John Lee Williamson)
	"Hoodoo Blues" (Lightnin' Slim)
	"The Hoodoo Man" (Dave Alexander)
	"Hoodoo Man" (Amos "Junior" Wells)

	"Hoodoo Man" (John Lee Williamson)
	"Hoodoo Man Blues" (Victoria Spivey)
	"Hoodoo Party" (Tabby Thomas)
	"Hoodoo Woman" (Johnny Temple)
	"Hoodoo Woman Blues" (Cornelius Green)
Mojo	"Got My Mojo Working" (Muddy Waters)
	"Mojo Blues" (Walter Davis)
	"Mojo Hand" (Lightnin' Hopkins)
	"Mojo Hand" (Muddy Waters)
	"Mojo Hand Blues" (Ida Cox and Jesse Crump)
	"Mojo in My Hand" (L.C. Robinson)
Voodoo	"Voodoo Blues" (Otis Hicks)
	"Voodoo Child" (Jimi Hendrix)
	"Voodoo Woman" (Koko Taylor)

All people are influenced by their traditions. Voodoo, the black man's tradition, still has an influence, to varying degrees, on the lives of the black musician to this day. The blue note would not be a blue note had it not come from Africa, and voodoo would not be its sister had it not influenced the African way of life.

BIBLIOGRAPHY

Asbury, Herbert. *The French Quarter*. New York: Alfred A. Knopf, 1936.

Ashanti, Faheem C. *Rootwork and Voodoo in Mental Health*. Durham, N.C.: Tone Books, 1987.

Blagrove, Luanna C. *Voodoo Lost Arts and Sciences*. Berkeley, Calif.: Blagrove Publishing Company, 1988.

Bodin, Ron. *Voodoo, Past and Present*. Lafayette, La.: University of Southwestern Louisiana, Center for Louisiana Studies, 1990.

Brown, Karen M. *Mama Lola: A Vodou Priestess in Brooklyn*. Berkeley: University of California Press, 1991.

Courlander, Harold. *Haiti Singing*. Chapel Hill: University of North Carolina Press, 1939.

Evans-Pritchard, E. E. *Theories of Primitive Religion*. London: Oxford University Press, 1966.

Gillard, John T. *The Catholic Church and the American Negro*. Baltimore: Saint Joseph's Society Press, 1929.

Haskins, James. *Voodoo and Hoodoo*. Lanham, Md.: Scarborough House, 1990.

———. *Witchcraft, Mysticism, and Magic in the Black World*. Garden City, N.Y.: Doubleday, 1974.

Hurston, Zora Neale. *Tell My Horse: Voodoo and Life in Haiti and Jamaica*. Philadelphia: J. B. Lippincott Company, 1939.

King, Noel Q. *Religions of Africa*. New York: Harper and Row, 1970.

Kristos, Kyle. *Voodoo*. Philadelphia: J. B. Lippincott Company, 1976.

Martinez, Raymond J. *Mysterious Marie Laveau, Voodoo Queen, and Folk Tales along the Mississippi*. Jefferson, La.: Hope Publications, 1956.

Mbiti, J. S. *African Religions and Philosophy*. New York: Frederick Praeger, 1969.

Metraux, Alfred. *Voodoo in Haiti*. New York: Schocken Books, 1972.

Parrinder, Geoffrey. *West African Religion*. London: Epworth Press, 1969.

Tallant, Robert. *Voodoo in New Orleans*. New York: Collier Books, 1984.

———. *Voodoo Queen*. Gretna, La.: Pelican Publishing Company, 1983.

Weatherford, W. D. *American Churches and the Negro*. Boston: Christopher Publishing House, 1957.

Westermann, D. *Africa and Christianity*. London: Oxford University Press, 1937.

Woodson, Carter G. *The History of the Negro Church*. Washington, D.C.: Associated Publishers, 1921.

Yinger, J. Milton. *Religion, Society, and the Individual*. New York: Macmillan, 1957.

6

THE INFLUENCE OF THE BLUES

Just as the blues came out of gospel music and field songs, rhythm-and-blues came out of the blues (see figure 6.1). It started to surface around 1950 with the Chess recordings of Muddy Waters and Howlin' Wolf in Chicago. These new sounds, an extension of the blues with altered chords and progressions and up-tempo rhythms, spread across the United States and influenced other artists and songwriters. Soon songs like John Lee Hooker's* "Boogie Chillun' " and Elmore James's "Shake Your Moneymaker" were hot items on the market. "Juke," an instrumental by harmonica player Little Walter Jacobs, stayed on the rhythm-and-blues top-ten chart for fourteen weeks in 1952. Then along came Jimmy Reed,* who recorded "You Don't Have to Go" in 1955 for VJ Records. It topped the rhythm-and-blues charts. He immediately followed with a number of hits that included "Honest I Do," "Hush-Hush," and "Ain't That Lovin' You, Baby."

In Los Angeles Amos Milburn* and Charles Brown* were hitting the charts in the early 1950s with their up-tempo, jumpy blues for Aladdin Records. Aladdin also had a very big hit with Shirley and Lee's "Let the Good Times Roll" in 1956, one of rhythm-and-blues's biggest influences on rock and roll.

Antoine "Fats" Domino, the singer/piano player from New Orleans, signed with Lew Chudd's Imperial Records in 1949 and scored with a million seller on his first single, "Fat Man." From that point up to 1965 he had forty-three recordings that made *Billboard*'s charts, twenty-three gold records, and sales of more than sixty-five million records. Other recording companies who boasted big rhythm-and-blues names were King Records (the Ravens, Ivory Joe Hunter,* Wynonie Harris*) and Duke Records (Johnny Ace,* Bobby Bland).

Figure 6.1
The Blues Influence

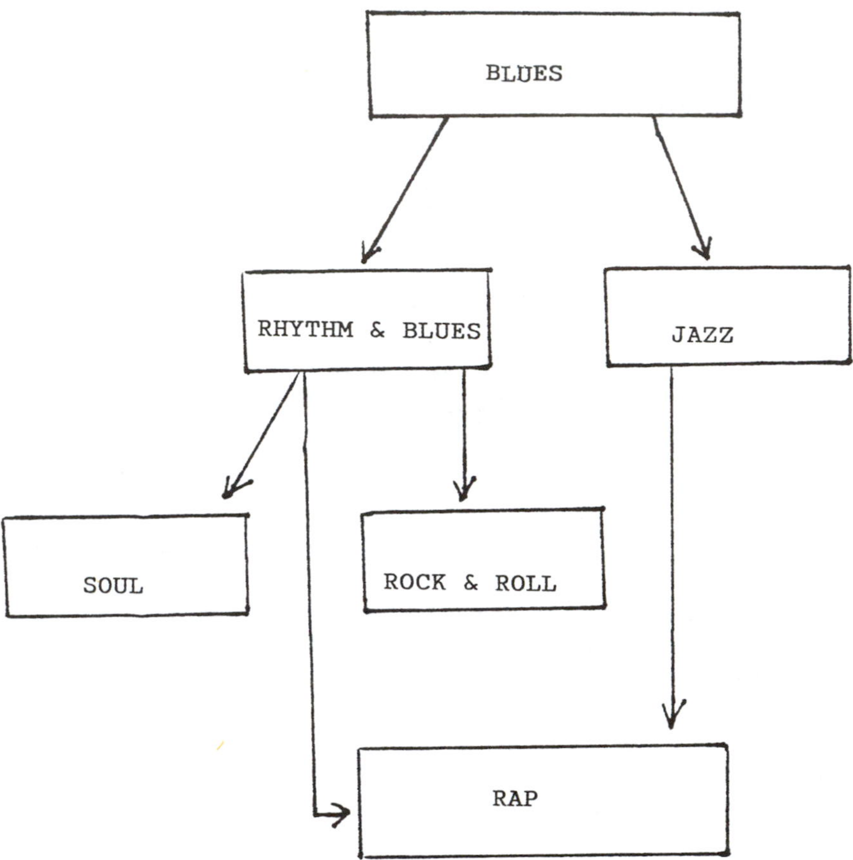

Also in the early 1950s, in cities like Detroit, New York, and Philadelphia, gospel-influenced rhythm-and-blues vocal groups started to be recorded and heard on the radio. The Dominoes, with Clyde McPhatter, recorded "Sixty Minute Man" in 1951. The Drifters, also with Clyde McPhatter, had a hit with "Money Honey" in 1953. The Teenagers, with thirteen-year-old Frankie Lymon, recorded "Why Do Fools Fall in Love?" for Gee Records in 1956. In a few months the song became a national hit. Other groups that had comparable success were the Ravens with "Bye, Bye Baby Blues," the Chords with "Sh-Boom," the Penguins with "Earth Angel," and the Monotones with "Book of Love."

By the mid–1950s the term *rock and roll*, which at first had been used generally to describe rhythm-and-blues artists, began to be used more specifically to describe a more frantic, hard-driving version of rhythm-and-blues music. Two practitioners of this style were Little Richard* (Richard

Penniman) and Charles Edward Anderson "Chuck" Berry,* two pioneers of rock and roll music. Little Richard started singing in a Baptist church choir as a preteenager. His first recordings, which were on the Camden label, were made in 1951 and were in the rhythm-and-blues styles of Fats Domino and Little Walter. Somewhere around 1953, however, he started to change his style of singing and performing. He began singing original material at very fast tempos while he played the piano standing up, beating on the keys with his fists, elbows, and the heels of his feet. He signed with the Speciality label and made his first recordings for it in 1955. "Tutti Frutti," his first big hit, sold two hundred thousand copies in two weeks. From 1955 to 1959 he recorded hit after hit and set a standard for the new music. "Lucille," "Jenny," "Long Tall Sally," "Keep A-Knockin'," "Slippin' and Slidin'," "Good Golly Miss Molly," and "Rip It Up" were just a few from his long lists of hits.

Chuck Berry started playing rhythm-and-blues in St. Louis, Missouri, in the early 1950s. Before that he played the blues. He was influenced by country and western music also. His idol, though, was bluesman Muddy Waters. In 1955 he moved to Chicago, where he hoped to hook up with Waters and other giants of the blues and rhythm-and-blues who lived there. He eventually did get to meet Waters and through him was offered a recording contract by Leonard Chess, owner of Chess Records. He recorded "Maybellene" (an original song that was influenced by both country and western music and the blues). Within a few weeks of its release "Maybellene" began getting national air play and soon became one of his biggest hits. Many others followed, including "Roll Over Beethoven," "Johnny B. Goode," "Rock and Roll Music," and "Sweet Little Sixteen."

At first only blacks bought rhythm-and-blues records, but as the 1950s started to unfold, more and more whites became aware of and interested in the music and started buying the records also. By the mid–1950s rhythm-and-blues music, now also called rock and roll, started its ascent to popularity among the young white audiences. They bought and listened to the recordings of Little Richard, Fats Domino, and Chuck Berry. Concerts and dances by these and other rock and roll artists that were originally attended only by blacks started to admit white teenagers. There was always a section of the room roped off for them so that they could enjoy the music and copy the movements of the black dancers. Rock and roll music, and its influence on American youth of all colors, grew vigorously in the 1950s, although it was given a beating by white society. No one, it seemed, wanted the music to touch the white youth. Rock and roll music was accused of being imbecilic, desperate, and generally lacking in good taste. Most executives of large record companies like Columbia, Capitol, RCA, and Decca were also prone to this point of view. But the fact that the small rock and roll–oriented independent companies were an economic threat to their business caused them to take measures to insure their control of this new trend. By the late

1950s they had started recording white artists who covered the black rock and roll material. One of the first of these artists was singer Pat Boone, who did watered-down versions of songs by Little Richard, Ivory Joe Hunter, Fats Domino, Etta James,* and T-Bone Walker. Boone achieved phenomenal success with these recordings of songs that had already been made popular by black artists. Other white "cover" artists followed in rapid succession throughout the late 1950s. By 1960 the rhythm-and-blues musicians who had started the trend were no longer on the record charts. The white cover artists were getting the air play, selling the records, and making the money.

During the 1960s two different types of blues-influenced music began to surface: soul music and psychedelic blues. Rock and roll still thrived, but by now mostly under the hands of white artists. The new soul music of James Brown, Aretha Franklin, Ray Charles, and other black artists took the world by storm. This music, which was an offshoot of the rhythm-and-blues of the 1950s, was a totally black entity. It was not until the end of the 1960s that a few white artists chose to venture into that area of music. The reason for this was that soul did not pertain just to the music. It also identified a black spirit and lifestyle.

James Brown, known as Soul Brother Number One, had been performing rhythm-and-blues before it became soul music. His first record, "Please, Please, Please," was made in 1956 and became a rhythm-and-blues hit. In 1958 he hit with "Try Me," and in 1960 with "Think." By 1962, when he recorded the legendary album *Live at the Apollo*, Brown was a household name in black America. He saw the beginning of the British musical invasion and realized that to survive, he would have to shift direction and concentrate on both black and white markets. To gain more control over his work, he also formed his own publishing company and record-production company in the mid–1960s. In 1965 "Papa's Got a Brand New Bag" was a million-seller. A string of other million-sellers followed during the rest of the 1960s, through the 1970s, and into the early 1980s. After a few years of inactivity caused by personal problems, Brown returned to the scene in the 1990s, doing guest appearances at concerts and on television shows. Most of his new energy, however, is currently directed to the business side of his music.

Aretha Franklin (Lady Soul) was born in Memphis, Tennessee, on March 25, 1942. She grew up singing in the church, and by the age of fourteen she was touring nationwide with her father, the Reverend C. L. Franklin, who recorded gospel music and sermons for Chess Records. Her signing on with Atlantic Records in 1966, a few years after her switch to ryhthm-and-blues, opened the doors of the world of soul to her. Her gospel-influenced, bluesy delivery afforded her hit after hit in the late 1960s. Songs like "Respect," "Natural Woman," "Chain of Fools," and many others quickly climbed the charts. Around 1969, though, she retired from music for personal reasons. She returned in the late 1970s. The 1980s and early 1990s saw a change in her recordings. She had begun to use large string orchestras as background accompaniment to her songs. Gone was the funky soul sound of the small band, but she still carried the blues-drenched soul in her voice.

Other soul singers of the 1960s included Wilson Pickett* ("In the Midnight Hour," 1965), Percy Sledge ("When a Man Loves a Woman," 1966), Sam Moore and Dave Prater ("Hold On, I'm Coming," 1966), and Otis Redding ("Respect," 1966). There were, of course, many others who saturated the market with their music.

Also, in the mid–1960s, apart from the soul explosion, there was another musical explosion of just as great a force. This new sound was a combination of the razor-edged guitar style of the past rock and roll British and white American musicians and the urban blues stylings of John Lee Hooker, Muddy Waters, and Howlin' Wolf. This music became known as psychedelic blues. One musician has been held responsible for bridging the gap between these two styles: Jimi Hendrix. His introduction to music, as a young beginner, was the electric blues sounds of Chicago. When he was discharged from the army in 1961, he moved to Nashville and worked as a professional musician with local blues bands. Later he worked with B. B. King, Little Richard, and James Brown. In 1964 he moved to New York City and played soul music for a little over a year. By 1966 he was in Europe working with his own group that he called the Experience. By this time he was just beginning to formulate his own style of stage presence using influences of blues and soul musicians with whom he had worked earlier. He recorded his first album, *Are You Experienced?*, in 1967. It opened the door to white audiences in both Europe and America. For the next three years he was totally consumed by success. He recorded material for over twenty-six albums, was the subject of film footage, and performed constantly in various venues in the United States and Europe. Although his innovations afforded him much visibility and influence, he was still not accepted by the black youth. They dismissed his music early on as having little rhythm and not being soulful enough to dance to. In an attempt to change this, he put together a new group (Band of Gypsies) in 1969, using black musicians. His health had already started to decline by then, though, and in 1970 he died.

A string of other Hendrix-styled guitarists hit the scene in the late 1960s—Eric Clapton, John Mayall, and Jeff Beck, to name a few. They were all influenced by and played the songs composed by black urban bluesmen like T-Bone Walker, Muddy Waters, Willie Dixon,* and Sonny Boy Williamson (Rice Miller). It was also a time that brought about a return (or turn) to the blues by white pop artists. These were not like the cover artists of the 1950s. They were sincere, serious musicians and singers who took care to give credit to their influences and performed the blues for the blues' sake and not the money. Some of the most popular of these artists were Janis Joplin, who was heavily influenced by Bessie Smith and bought a headstone for her unmarked grave; Johnny Winter,* who recorded the songs of Muddy

Waters, Sonny Boy Williamson, and Howlin' Wolf; Steve Miller, who worked as a backup musician for bluesmen like Jimmy Reed, James Cotton, and Howlin' Wolf; and Mike Bloomfield, who led a Chicago-based blues band.

Most of the popular music that surfaced in the 1970s was blues influenced to one degree or another. There was also an increased interest in the older blues musicians. Their popularity, slowly growing, was now beginning to cross over to a larger white audience. They were given more opportunities to survive as professional musicians because of this. B. B. King, for example, who had previously been popular only in black communities of America, was beginning to be known throughout the world. In the 1980s he suddenly became very popular with white audiences who were attracted to the purity and warmth of blues music. His jam-packed touring schedule took him to white venues throughout America and Europe. He was also getting more work at black venues that for over twenty years had all but locked their doors to the blues. The 1980s were good years for other blues musicians also. Those who had withstood the hard times that resulted from not being able to work steadily were celebrated with a rebirth of their music. This was a crossover period for the blues. A new generation of white musicians had developed a love for the blues because of the rock and roll to which they had been introduced a few years before. Musicians like Stevie Ray Vaughan* from Texas and Dr. John (Mac Rebennack) from New Orleans had started taking the blues to new heights in the white world. Some of the more established black blues artists started to employ more white musicians in their bands. John Lee Hooker, who is still going strong in the 1990s, works mostly with white musicians. So do Gatemouth Brown and Etta James. The young white blues audience began to grow quickly because of this exchange. Middle-aged blacks, who were nurtured on the blues but broke away from the music in the 1960s and 1970s, began readdressing the blues as their music in the late 1980s. This change in attitude by these blacks was prompted, it seems, by two things: (1) the decline of rhythm-and-blues activity and (2) the arrival of rap. The only comfortable way to go was back to the roots.

The crossover that the large record companies started in the late 1950s has finally come full circle in the 1990s, this time with more authenticity because white musicians really understand and feel the blues as much as the black bluesmen they work with. The blues, as a form of popular music, has traveled from a completely black entity in its beginning, through a period of being almost totally ignored, and finally to a time of acceptance by both blacks and whites. The circle is unbroken.

BIBLIOGRAPHY

Balliett, Whitney. *American Singers.* New York: Oxford University Press, 1979.

Bane, Michael. *Who's Who in Rock.* New York: Facts on File, 1981.

Baugh, John. *Black Street Speech*. Austin: University of Texas Press, 1983.
Berry, Chuck. *Chuck Berry: The Autobiography*. New York: Harmony Books, 1987.
Berry, Jason, Jonathan Foose, and Tad Jones. *Up from the Cradle of Jazz: New Orleans Music since World World II*. Athens: University of Georgia Press, 1986.
Broven, John. *Rhythm and Blues in New Orleans*. Gretna, La.: Pelican Publishing Company, 1978.
Charles, Ray, and David Ritz. *Brother Ray: Ray Charles' Own Story*. New York: Dial Press, 1978.
Clark, Dick. *Rock, Roll, and Remember*. New York: Popular Library, 1978.
Dalton, David. *The Rolling Stones*. New York: Knopf, 1981.
Davies, Hunter. *The Beatles*. New York: McGraw-Hill, 1968.
Davis, Jerome. *Talking Heads*. New York: Vintage Press, 1986.
Fox, Ted. *Showtime at the Apollo*. New York: Holt, Rinehart, and Winston, 1983.
Garland, Phyl. *The Sound of Soul*. Chicago: Henry Regnery, 1969.
George, Nelson. *The Death of Rhythm and Blues*. New York: Pantheon Books, 1988.
Goldrosen, John. *The Buddy Holly Story*. New York: Putnam Books, 1979.
Govenar, Alan, and Benny Joseph. *The Early Years of Rhythm and Blues: Focus on Houston*. Houston, Tex.: Rice University Press, 1990.
Hager, Steven. *Hip Hop: The Illustrated History of Break Dancing, Rap Music, and Graffiti*. New York: St. Martin's Press, 1984.
Haralambos, Michael. *Right On: From Blues to Soul in Black America*. New York: Da Capo Press, 1979.
Henderson, David. *Jimi Hendrix: Voodoo Child of the Aquarian Age*. Garden City, N.Y.: Doubleday, 1978.
Hopkins, Jerry. *Elvis: A Biography*. New York: Warner Books, 1971.
Jones, Quincy. *Listen Up: The Lives of Quincy Jones*. New York: Warner Books, 1990.
Lazell, Barry, ed. *Rock Movers and Shakers*. New York: Billboard, 1989.
Marsh, Dave. *Before I Get Old: The Story of the Who*. New York: St. Martin's Press, 1983.
Meltzer, Richard. *The Aesthetics of Rock*. New York: Da Capo Press, 1987.
Middleton, Richard. *Pop Music and the Blues: A Study of the Relationship and Its Significance*. London: Victor Gollancz, 1972.
Nite, Norm N. *Rock On*. 3 vols. New York: Thomas Y. Crowell, 1974.
Scaduto, Anthony. *Bob Dylan*. New York: New American Library, 1979.
Shaw, Arnold. *The Rock Revolution*. London: Collier Books, 1969.
Swenson, John. *Bill Haley: The Daddy of Rock and Roll*. New York: Stein and Day, 1984.
Taraborrelli, J. Randy. *Motown*. Garden City, N.Y.: Doubleday, 1986.
Turner, Tina, with Kurt Loder. *I, Tina*. New York: Avon Books, 1987.
Welch, Chris. *Hendrix*. New York: Flash, 1973.
White, Charles. *The Life and Times of Little Richard: The Quasar of Rock*. New York: Harmony Books, 1984.
Wilson, Mary. *Dreamgirl: My Life as a Supreme*. New York: St. Martin's Press, 1986.
Wood, Graham. *An A-Z of Rock and Roll*. London: Studio Vista, 1971.

Part II

EXPONENTS AND REFERENCE MATERIALS

7

THE MUSICIANS

ACE, JOHNNY. *See* Alexander, John Marshall, Jr.

ALCORN, OLIVER (Clarinet, saxophone). Born: New Orleans, Louisiana–August 3, 1910; died: Chicago, Illinois–March 18, 1981.

Oliver Alcorn came from a family of famous jazz musicians. During the 1920s and 1930s he performed in bands led by Clarence Desdundes and George McCullum, Jr., in New Orleans. He moved to Chicago in the 1940s and spent the rest of his professional life performing with Lee Collins, Natty Dominique, Lonnie Johnson, Little Brother Montgomery, and others.

ALEXANDER, ALGER "TEXAS" (Vocal). Born: Leona, Texas–ca. 1900; died: Houston, Texas–ca. 1954.

Alger Alexander was born in Leona, Texas, around 1900 and died in Texas around 1954. Just after World War I, he worked with New Orleans guitarist Lonnie Johnson in Dallas, Texas. He worked as an itinerant blues singer and made records from 1927 to 1934. He worked with King Joe Oliver in New York City in 1928. He was imprisoned for murder in the 1940s. He sang with his cousin Lightnin' Hopkins on Houston's streets in the early 1950s and recorded in Houston, Texas, in 1950. His style was based on work songs, shouts, and field hollers. A fuller description of him can be found in chapter 3.

RECORDINGS

Texas Alexander, Vol. 1. Matchbox 206
Texas Alexander, Vol. 2. Matchbox 214
Texas Alexander, Vol. 3. Matchbox 220
Texas Troublesome Blues. Agram 2009

ALEXANDER, DAVE (Piano, drums, vocal). Born: Shreveport, Louisiana–May 10, 1938.

Dave Alexander began teaching himself piano while he was in his mid-teens and was soon playing in nightclubs around his hometown. In 1957 he moved to Oakland, California, and joined forced with the likes of Lowell Fulson, Jimmy McCracklin, and L. C. Robinson. He was house pianist at the Ann Arbor Blues Festival in 1970 and also appeared at the Berkeley Blues Festival that same year. He recorded three songs for World Pacific Records, then moved on to Arhoolie, where he has two albums, *The Rattler* and *Dave Alexander*.

RECORDINGS
Dave Alexander. Arhoolie C–207
The Rattler. Arhoolie 1067

ALEXANDER, JOHN MARSHALL "JOHNNY ACE," JR. (Piano, vocal). Born: Memphis, Tennessee–June 9, 1929; died: Houston, Texas–December 24, 1954.

Johnny Ace began recording for Don Robey on his Duke label in 1952. "My Song" became the number one rhythm-and-blues hit of that year. "Cross My Heart," "The Clock," and "Please Forgive Me" followed in rapid succession. He was more of a pop balladeer than a bluesman and sang most of his songs in a slow tempo. He died at the height of his career in a game of Russian roulette. Reverend Moore, formerly Memphis singer Gatemouth Moore, delivered the funeral eulogy.

RECORDINGS
Johnny Ace Memorial Album. MCA 27014
A Memorial to Johnny Ace. Ace CH–40

ALIX, LIZA MAE (Vocal). Born: Chicago, Illinois–August 31, 1904; died: unknown.

Mae Alix worked as a cabaret artist in Chicago for many years. In 1922 she played the Edelweiss Club with Jimmie Noone, a bit later the Sunset Cafe with Carroll Dickerson, and then the Dreamland Cabaret in a duo with Ollie Powers. She was sometimes billed as the "Queen of the Splits." She toured Europe in the late 1920s, and in 1926 she recorded with Louis Armstrong and his Hot Five. In 1931–32 she moved on to Connie's Inn Revue, and in early 1935, before returning to Chicago, she worked the Harlem Opera House in New York City. Back in Chicago, she played the "It" Club, the Panama Club, and others before returning to New York City and the Mimo Club in the early 1940s. A long spell of poor health caused her to retire from full-time performance, and in the 1940s she was forced to move back to Chicago.

ALLEN, FULTON "BLIND BOY FULLER" (Guitar). Born: Wadesboro, North Carolina–1908; died: Durham, North Carolina–February 13, 1941.

Fulton Allen played music around Rockingham, North Carolina, through the mid–1920s. He went completely blind in 1928. He worked as an itinerant musician (mostly in North Carolina) from 1928 to the time of his illness in 1940. He recorded for the ARC label in New York City in 1935 and 1938. Allen also recorded for Decca Records in 1937, for Vocalion Records in 1938, 1939, and 1940, and for Okeh Records in 1940. A fuller description of him can be found in chapter 3.

RECORDINGS

East Coast Piedmont Styles. Columbia/Legacy CT–46777
1935–1940. Blues Classics BC–11
Truckin' My Blues Away. Yazoo CD–1060

ALLISON, LUTHER (Guitar, harmonica, vocal). Born: Mayflower, Arkansas–August 17, 1939.

After practicing and listening to his brother and other Chicago musicians for three or four years, Luther Allison formed his own band, the Four Jivers, around 1958. For five years during the 1960s he worked regularly in clubs on Chicago's West Side. In the early 1970s he spent most of his time touring in the Midwest. His albums included *Love Me Mama* and two tracks on *Sweet Home Chicago* on Delmark Records and *Bad News Is Coming* on the Motown label.

The 1980s were very productive years for Allison. He has become one of Chicago's most recorded blues musicians, both on his own dates and as backup guitarist for other artists. He has continued to perform throughout the United States and Europe during the early 1990s.

RECORDINGS

Life Is a Bitch. Encore Enc131C
Live in Paris. Buddah 82469–2
Love Me Mama. Delmark 625
Love Me Papa. Black and Blue 33.524
Power Wire Blues. Charly CRB1105
Rich Man. Charly CRB1227

ARCENEAUX, FERNEST (Accordion, vocal). Born: Lafayette, Louisiana–August 27, 1940.

Billed as the new "Prince of the Accordion," Fernest Arceneaux carries on the Clifton Chenier tradition. His style, unlike that of most of the other zydeco performers, is cool and a bit laid back. In 1979 Blues Unlimited Records released *Fernest and the Thunders*, one of the best examples of his approach to the music.

The 1980s and 1990s have been good years for Arceneaux. He is one of the pillars of the modern zydeco sound and a great influence on the many young musicians who are involved in the music industry. Each year finds him playing festivals and club dates throughout Europe and the United States.

RECORDINGS

Fernest and the Thunders. Blues Unlimited 5005
Zydeco Stomp. JSP CD220

ARDOIN, ALPHONSE "BOIS-SEC" (Accordion). Born: Duralde, Louisiana–November 16, 1916.

Alphonse Ardoin played triangle with his uncle, Amede Ardoin, in the mid–1930s. One of the few remaining practitioners of the prezydeco style or Creole blues, Ardoin performed throughout southwest Louisiana for over fifty years. He also worked with violinist Canray Fontenot for many years and continues to do so occasionally. He performed little during the late 1980s and early 1990s because of poor health. A fuller description of him can be found in chapter 3.

FILM

Drywood. Kay Jazz Video KJ067. 37 minutes, color.

ARDOIN, AMEDE (Accordion, vocal). Born: L'Anse Rouge (Eunice), Louisiana–1899; died: Pineville, Louisiana–November 3, 1942.

The father of zydeco blues and Cajun music, Amede Ardoin began playing his music at house parties around St. Landry Parish while in his teens. Between 1929 and 1934 he recorded roughly two dozen songs for RCA, Bluebird, and Vocalion Records, some with Cajun fiddle player Dennis McGee and the remainder alone. Some of his songs are "Les Blues de Voyage," "Les Blues de Crowley," and "La Valse de Amities." A fuller description of him can be found in chapter 3.

RECORDINGS

Amede Ardoin. Old Timey 124
Original Recordings, 1929–38. Arhoolie 1091

ARNOLD, JAMES "KOKOMO" (Guitar, vocal). Born: Lovejoy, Texas–February 15, 1901; died: Chicago, Illinois–November 8, 1968.

James Arnold acquired his nickname from the Old Original Kokomo Blues. He mostly worked outside of music in New York and Chicago. He recorded two sides for the Victor label in Memphis under the name Gitfiddle Jim. He did additional recordings for Decca in New York and Chicago in 1934–38. He is highly regarded by critics and collectors. He made a comeback in Chicago at the height of the folk-blues revival.

RECORDINGS

Bottleneck Guitar. Yazoo 1049
"Kokomo" Arnold and Peetie Wheatstraw. Blues Classics BC–4
Master of the Bottleneck Guitar. Document 512

AUSTIN, LOVIE. *See* Calhoun, Cora.

AVERY, JOSEPH "KID" (Trombone). Born: Waggaman, Louisiana–October 3, 1892; died: Waggaman, Louisiana–December 9, 1955.

Joseph Avery was one of the early jazz musicians who were heavily influenced by the blues. He played in the Tulane Orchestra in New Orleans from 1915 to 1922. He worked with Evan Thomas's Black Eagles and also the Yelping Hounds in Crowley, Louisiana, for a time. He recorded in 1954 for Southland Records. He popularized the old blues riff that early musicians knew as "Holler Blues."

BAILEY, DEFORD (Harmonica, guitar, bones, mandolin). Born: Rome, Tennessee–1900; died: unknown.

Deford Bailey played mostly in his hometown until he moved to Nashville in 1922. On December 10, 1927, opening night of the Grand Ole Opry, he appeared on the bill with his train imitation. He stayed with the Opry until 1941. On October 2, 1928, Victor Records went to Nashville to record Bailey. This was the first major recording session to be held in that city. Although Bailey was a very fine musician, he chose to earn a living from various day jobs from the late 1940s to the time of his death.

RECORDING

Harmonica Showcase. Matchbox 218

BARKER, LOUISE "BLUE LU" (Vocal). Born: New Orleans, Louisiana–November 13, 1913.

Blue Lu Barker is perhaps the best blues singer New Orleans has ever produced. Besides exerting a strong influence on Billie Holiday, she made records like "New Orleans Blues" and "Don't You Make Me High" in its original and best version. She is the wife of legendary New Orleans guitarist Danny Barker. During the 1980s she made infrequent brief appearances at the New Orleans Jazz and Heritage Festival. Poor health has kept her from performing since the late 1980s.

RECORDING

New Orleans Blues, 1923/1940. EPM 997550.

BASS, FONTELLA (Piano, vocal). Born: St. Louis, Missouri–July 3, 1949.

Fontella Bass was trained in gospel music. She worked with Little Milton during the early 1960s. She recorded her first hit single, "Rescue Me," in 1965. Her switch from the blues to a milder commercial set of material did not work, and she soon thereafter dropped from the charts. She was not very active during the 1980s and early 1990s.

RECORDING

Rescued: The Best of Fontella Bass. Chess CHD–9335

BATTS, WILL (Violin, mandolin, guitar, vocal). Born: Michigan (Benton County), Mississippi–January 24, 1904; died: Memphis, Tennessee–February 18, 1956.

One of the top musicians in the Memphis area, Will Batts has been hailed as one of the all-time great fiddlers for his accompaniments when playing with Jack Kelly's Jug Busters and others. He recorded with the Beale Street Sheiks for Victor Records in Memphis in 1929 and with Jack Kelly for Banner/Vocalion in New York City in 1933. He recorded under his own name on the Vocalion label in 1933 and again for Flyright Records with the Will Batts Novelty Band in 1954. His South Memphis Jug Band performed from 1934 to the early 1950s.

BELL, CAREY (Harmonica, guitar, bass, vocal). Born: Macon, Georgia–November 14, 1936.

Carey Bell taught himself to play the harmonica around 1944. He worked in and out of music in Meridian, Mississippi, from 1950 to 1955 and moved to Chicago in 1956. He toured with Earl Hooker's Band in 1968 and recorded with Hooker for Arhoolie Records that same year. These two also toured Europe in 1969. Later Bell toured Europe with Jimmy Dawkins in 1970. During the 1970s, 1980s, and early 1990s he continued to tour Europe and the United States.

RECORDING

Blues Harp. Delmark DC–622

BERRY, CHARLES EDWARD ANDERSON "CHUCK" (Guitar, piano, saxophone, vocal). Born: San Jose, California–January 15, 1926.

Chuck Berry, master of the guitar, piano, and saxophone, claims to have been influenced heavily by Charlie Christian, T-Bone Walker, and Muddy Waters. Berry recorded his first big hit, "Maybellene," on the Chess label. Berry's style embodies elements of rhythm-and-blues, pop, country and western, and basic down-to-earth blues. Some of his hits are "School Days," "Almost Grown," "Rock and Roll Music," "Roll Over Beethoven," and the ever-popular "Johnny B. Goode." Further description of him can be found in chapter 6.

RECORDINGS

The Best of. Hollywood HCD–100
Golden Hits. Mercury 826256–2
The London Chuck Berry Sessions. Chess CHD–9295
New Juke Box Hits. Chess CHD–9171
Two Great Guitars (with Bo Diddley). Chess CHC-9170
21 Greatest Hits. Zeta ZET–520

BOOK

Berry, Chuck. *Chuck Berry: The Autobiography*. New York: Harmony Books, 1987.

FILM
Chuck Berry: Rock and Roll Music. BMG Video 791146, color.

BIG MACEO. *See* Merriweather, Major.

BIG MAYBELLE. *See* Smith, Mabel.

BIGEOU, ESTHER (Vocal). Born: New Orleans, Louisiana–ca. 1895; died: New Orleans, Louisiana–ca. 1936.

Known as the Creole Songbird, Esther Bigeou sang and recorded with the A. J. Piron Orchestra in the 1930s. She worked with Peter Bocage for a while. She toured with the Theater Owners' Booking Association (TOBA) vaudeville circuit and appeared in the *Broadway Rastus Revue* and the *Darktown Follies Revue.* She recorded on the Okeh label in New York in 1921 and 1926, but retired from music in 1930.

BISHOP, ELVIN (Guitar). Born: Tulsa, Oklahoma–October 21, 1942.

Elvin Bishop performed as a sideman for Magic Sam, Junior Wells, and Hound Dog Taylor while living in Chicago. He joined Paul Butterfield's band in 1965. He recorded with his own group for Bill Graham's Fillmore label in 1969. He did a good deal of work until the end of the 1970s, but not much was heard from him after that.

RECORDINGS
The Best of. Epic PE–33693
Big Fun. Alligator 4767
Don't Let the Bossman Get You Down. Alligator ALCD–4791
Let It Flow. Polygram 839–142–4
Sure Feels Good. Polydor 314–513307–2

BLACK ACE. *See* Turner, B. K.

BLACKWELL, FRANCIS HILLMAN "SCRAPPER" (Guitar, piano, vocal). Born: Syracuse, South Carolina–February 21, 1903; died: Indianapolis, Indiana–October 7, 1962.

Francis Blackwell was a self-taught blues guitarist of infinite taste and dramatic appeal. He teamed up with pianist Leroy Carr in 1928, and together they wrote much of his repertoire. Blackwell was a prolific recording artist, and his work can be heard on Vocalion, Gennett, Champion, Bluebird, Bluesville, Seventy-Seven, and Prestige Records. When Leroy Carr died in 1935, Blackwell retired from music and until the mid–1950s did very little playing. When he did return to music, his performing was concentrated around the Indianapolis area.

RECORDINGS
Blues That Made Me Cry. Agram 2008
Mr. Scrapper's Blues. Ace CH255
The Virtuoso Guitar of Scrapper Blackwell. Yazoo 1019

BLAND, ROBERT CALVIN "BOBBY" (Vocal, guitar, saxophone). Born: Rosemark, Tennessee–January 27, 1930.

Both Bobby Bland and Johnny Ace worked with Adolph Duncan's band in 1949. Bland served as valet and chauffeur for both B. B. King and Roscoe Gordon. He cut his first recordings for the Bihari brothers' Modern Records in Los Angeles. He signed with Duke Records of Houston, Texas, in 1954 and has since recorded an astonishingly large number of hits for that company. A few of them are "I Smell Trouble" and "Farther on up the Road" (1955), "Ain't That Lovin' You," "Turn Around," "Lead Me On," "Yield Not to Temptation," and "I Pity the Fool" (1961), "That's the Way Love Is" (1963), and "Call on Me" and "I'll Take Care of You" (1968). Although Bland's choice of material in the 1970s, 1980s and 1990s has leaned toward love ballads, his style is still deeply embedded in the blues. His recordings with B. B. King for the MCA label in the mid–1980s are exceptional, portraying him as the master of the blues that he is.

RECORDINGS
Ain't Nothing You Can Do. MCA 27040
After All. Malaco MAL–7439–C
The Best of Bobby Bland, Vol. 1. MCA MCAD–31219
The Best of Bobby Bland, Vol. 2. MCA MCAC–27045
Blues, Chicken, Friends, and Relatives. Ace CH–222
Blues in the Night. Ace CH132
Blues You Can Use. Malaco MAL–7444–CD
Call on Me. MCA 27042
Dreamer. Beat Goes On BGOCD63
First Class Blues. Malaco MAL–5000-CD
Here's the Man. MCA MCAC–27038
Here We Go Again. MCA 883
His California Album. Beat Goes On BGOCD64
I Feel Good, I Feel Fine. MCA MCAC–27073
Introspective of Early Years. MCA MCAC2–4172
Midnight Run. Malaco MAL–7450–CD
Reflections in Blue. MCA MCAC–27043
The Soulful Side of Bobby Bland. Kent KENT–044
Soul of the Man. MCA 27041
Tell Mr. Bland. MCA 884
Together Again (with B. B. King). MCAC–27012
Together for the First Time, Live (with B. B. King). MCA 2–4160
Touch of the Blues. Mobile Fidelity MFCD–10–00770
Two Steps from the Blues. MCA MCAC–27036
Woke Up Screaming. Ace CH–41

BLIND BLAKE. *See* Phelps, Arthur.

BLIND BOY FULLER. *See* Allen, Fulton.

BLIND CHARLIE. *See* Hays, Charles.

BLOOMFIELD, MICHAEL (Guitar). Born: Chicago, Illinois–July 28, 1944; died: San Francisco, California–February 15, 1981.

Michael Bloomfield learned to play the guitar from such legendary blues greats in Chicago as Muddy Waters, Albert King, and others. He joined the Paul Butterfield Band in 1965. Later he recorded with Bob Dylan. He chose to keep a low profile but worked constantly doing gigs, film soundtracks, and studio recordings. He died of a drug overdose.

RECORDINGS

Gospel Guitar Duets (with Woody Harris). Kicking Mule KC164
If You Love These Blues. Kicking Mule KC166
I'm with You Always. Demon Fiend 92
Junko Partner. Intermedia QS–5068
Triumvirate. Edsel 228

BO DIDDLEY. *See* McDaniel, Ellas.

BOIS-SEC. *See* Ardoin, Alphonse.

BOLDEN, CHARLES "BUDDY" (Cornet). Born: New Orleans, Louisiana–September 6, 1877; died: Jackson, Louisiana–November 4, 1931.

Considered to be the first jazz musician, Buddy Bolden created a music that was a combination of the blues and ragtime. This music was very popular in New Orleans honky-tonks. He was the leader of the Eagle Band, a six-piece group that was to become the prototype of a New Orleans jazz ensemble. "Funky Butt," an early New Orleans blues song credited to Bolden, is still performed by blues and jazz musicians today.

BONNER, WELDON H. PHILIP "JUKE BOY" (Guitar, harmonica, drums, vocal). Born: Bellville, Texas–March 22, 1932; died: Houston, Texas–June 29, 1978.

For most of his life in the music business, Houston blues singer Juke Boy Bonner never ventured far from his hometown for any long period of time. In 1969 he toured England, France, Denmark, and most of Western Europe with Clifton Chenier. The following year he played at the Ann Arbor Blues and Jazz Festival and the Berkeley Blues Festival.

RECORDINGS

Going Back to the Country. Arhoolie 1036
Legacy of the Blues, Vol. 5. GNP 10015
One Man Trio. Fulbright 548

The Struggle. Arhoolie 1045
They Call Me "Juke Boy." Ace CHD269

BOOGIE JAKE. *See* Jacobs, Matthew.

BOOKER, JAMES (Piano). Born: New Orleans, Louisiana–December 17, 1939; died: New Orleans, Louisiana–November 8, 1983.

James Booker was one of New Orleans' most popular blues pianists. He played with Aretha Franklin, B. B. King, Joe Tex, Shirley and Lee, Junior Parker, Lionel Hampton, Charles Brown, T-Bone Walker, Wilson Pickett, and a host of other top-shelf rhythm-and-blues artists. His recording career began in 1954 with sides on the Imperial label. He later recorded for Chess, Ace, Peacock, Stax, Amiga (Germany), Island, and numerous other companies as sideman to major performers.

RECORDINGS
Classified. Rounder 2036
King of the New Orleans Keyboard. Junco Partner JP1
New Orleans Piano Wizard: Live! Rounder 2027

BOYD, EDWARD R. "EDDIE" (Piano, guitar, vocal). Born: Stovall, Mississippi–November 25, 1914.

A prolific composer, Eddie Boyd was one of Chicago's most popular blues figures in the early and mid–1950s. His piano playing is solidly based in the styles of Leroy Carr, Roosevelt Sykes, and Sunnyland Slim, incorporating a very strong rhythmic pulse and melodic lines of high musical intelligence. He taught himself to play the piano and guitar in the late 1920s and worked around Mississippi and Tennessee in the early 1930s. He settled in Memphis, Tennessee, in 1936 and worked as a soloist in Beale Street dives until 1940. He moved to Chicago in 1941 and began a prosperous career playing and recording with some of that city's finest musicians. From 1945 to 1965 he was recorded as both leader and sideman on more than two dozen labels. In the mid–1960s he decided to settle in Europe and has lived there ever since, first in France, then in Finland. His compositional output includes more than 120 songs that have been recorded both in the United States and Europe. Boyd was still active musically in the 1980s, playing in festivals throughout Europe.

RECORDINGS
Eddie Boyd and His Blues Band. Crosscut 1002
Five Long Years. L & R 42005
Lover's Playground. Stockholm RJ204
Ratting and Running Around. Crown Prince 400

BRADFORD, PERRY (Piano, vocal, producer). Born: Montgomery, Alabama–February 14, 1895; died: New York, New York–April 20, 1970.

By 1906 Perry Bradford was working with minstrel shows. He joined Allen's New Orleans Minstrels in 1907 but later left to work as a solo pianist. He toured the theater circuits for several years, playing in Chicago in 1909 and New York City in 1910. In 1920, after having established himself as a producer, publisher, and songwriter, he persuaded Okeh Records to let singer Mamie Smith record his "Crazy Blues." It became a big hit and initiated the so-called race recording business. Throughout the 1920s Bradford was involved in numerous recording dates that included such musicians as Louis Armstrong, James P. Johnson, and Willie "The Lion" Smith. Before losing his publishing business and most of his money during the depression, Bradford composed and published hundreds of songs, the most durable of which was "It's Right Here for You." In 1965 he published his autobiography, *Born with the Blues.*

BOOK

Bradford, Perry. *Born with the Blues.* New York: Oak Publications, 1965.

BROOKS, LONNIE (Guitar, vocal). Born: Dubuisson, Louisiana–December 18, 1933.

Lonnie Brooks worked small gigs around Port Arthur, Texas, in the early 1950s. He worked with Clifton Chenier in 1955. He recorded with his own band for Goldband Records in Lake Charles, Louisiana, in 1957. He moved to Chicago in 1959, hooked up with Jimmy Reed in 1960, and recorded and toured with him that same year. He has spent most of his professional career working out of Chicago, performing much club work and at festivals throughout the United States and Europe. He recorded often into the 1990s on labels like Chess, Capitol, and Alligator.

RECORDINGS

Bayou Lightning. Alligator ALCD–4714
Hot Shot. Alligator AL–4731
Live from Chicago. Alligator ALCD–4759
Satisfaction Guaranteed. Alligator ALCD–4799
Sweet Home Chicago. Evidence ECD–26001–2
Turn on the Night. Alligator ALCD–4721
Wound Up Tight. Alligator ALCD–4751

BROONZY, WILLIAM LEE CONLEY "BIG BILL" (Guitar, vocal). Born: Scott, Mississippi–June 26, 1893; died: Chicago, Illinois–August 15, 1958.

One of twenty-one children, William Broonzy spent the first forty years of his life on a farm in Arkansas. The relationship of his life as a farmer to the virile, simple style of his music is unquestionable. He recorded for Paramount Records in 1929. His first big disc was on the Bluebird label in 1934. The songs included "Take Your Hands off Her" and "The Sun Gonna

Shine in My Back Door Someday." In 1939 he finally yielded to repeated invitations to go to New York. There he did one Carnegie Hall concert and spent the rest of his time at the home of Huddie Ledbetter. On his second visit to New York in 1946 he made no public appearances at all. During the early 1940s he served as accompanist to Lil Green. He wrote "My Mellow Man," "Country Boy Blues," and "Keep Your Hands on Your Heart" for her. From 1925 to 1952 Broonzy recorded 260 blues songs. His death was caused by lung cancer. A fuller description of him can be found in chapter 3.

RECORDINGS

Big Bill Blues. Portrait Masters RJ44089
Big Bill Broonzy, 1927–1932. Matchbox 1004
Big Bill Broonzy and Washboard Sam. Chess 9251
Do That Guitar Rag. Yazoo 1035
Feeling Low Down. GNP Crescendo 10004
The Young Big Bill Broonzy. Yazoo 1011

BOOK

Broonzy, William Lee Conley, and Yannick Bruynoghe. *Big Bill Blues.* Paris: Ludd, 1987.

FILM

Big Bill Broonzy. TCB Releasing. 18 minutes, black and white.

BROWN, CHARLES (Piano, organ, vocal). Born: Texas City, Texas–1920.

Charles Brown's vocal style, which consists of a laid-back delivery and gospel-like frills, was a considerable influence on Johnny Ace, Ray Charles, Amos Milburn, Roy Milton, and many others. He is credited with having started the "cool school" of singing that became popular on the West Coast in the 1950s. Some of his most popular songs are "Driftin' Blue," "Merry Christmas Baby," "I Want to Go Home," and "Please Come Home for Christmas."

RECORDINGS

I'm Gonna Push On. Stockholm RJ200
One More for the Road. Alligator 4771
Please Come Home for Christmas. Gusto 5019
Racetrack Blues. Route 66 KIX17
Sail On. Jukebox Lil1106
Sunny Road. Route 66 KIX5

BROWN, CLARENCE "GATEMOUTH" (Harmonica, guitar, violin, vocal, drums, bass). Born: Vinton, Louisiana–April 18, 1924.

Born into a musical family, Clarence Brown started playing guitar and violin at a very early age. He made his professional debut as a drummer and singer at fifteen and got his big break when his idol, T-Bone Walker, became ill and asked Brown to replace him on his show. For the past twenty years he has worked and recorded steadily in Houston, Texas. In 1972 he toured Europe with the American Blues Festival, and in 1976 he played in Africa. In fact, the 1970s marked a sharp turning point in his career and the new worldwide acceptance that was offered. This provided enough work for him to survive on his music alone. He continued to enjoy his success in the 1980s by working and recording prolifically in both Europe and America. In 1988 Rounder Records released the very popular *Texas Swing* CD, and in 1992 *No Looking Back* on Alligator Records hit the market. Although Brown is in his late sixties, he tours and performs at a pace that would easily tire a man half his age.

RECORDINGS

Alright Again. Rounder 2028
Atomic Energy. Blues Boy BB305
Hot Times Tonight. P-Vine PCD2109
No Looking Back. Alligator ALCD–4804
Okie Dokie Stomp. Black and Blue 33.550
One More Mile. Rounder 2034
The Original Peacock Recordings. Rounder CD–2039
Pressure Cooker. Alligator 4745
Real Life. Rounder 2054
Sings Christmas Songs. King KLP–775
Standing My Ground. Alligator ALCD–4779
Texas Swing. Rounder CD–11527

FILM

Clarence Gatemouth Brown. Phoenix Films. 58 Minutes, color.

BROWN, IDA (Vocal). Born: Kansas City, Kansas–May 1, 1889; died: Kansas City, Kansas–March 31, 1950.

Even when the craze for women blues singers was at its height, Ida Brown was seldom recorded. Her first session was with Benny Moten in September 1923. On March 10, 1926, she again went into the studio, this time with a band that included Albert Nicholas, Barney Bigard, Johnny St. Cyr, and Louis Russell. In May 1926 she recorded her last session with pianist Porter Grainger accompanying her. Her theatrical career consisted of work with Bill "Bojangles" Robinson in the Broadway hit *Brown Buddies* and with Fats Waller in the film *Stormy Weather* in the 1940s. After that, she dropped from sight completely and was never heard of again.

BROWN, J. T. (Vocal). Born: unknown; died: Chicago, Illinois–November 24, 1969.

J. T. Brown recorded under his own name and as Nature Boy Brown for Meteor, States, and Atomic-H Records. He also worked and recorded as a sideman with Little Walter, Washboard Sam, Muddy Waters, Elmore James, and Roosevelt Sykes. His best-known composition is "Short Dress Woman," which he wrote for Muddy Waters.

RECORDINGS
Rockin' with J. T.. Crazy Kat 7420
Windy City Boogie. Pearl PL9

BROWN, OTHUM (Guitar, vocal). Born: unknown; died: New York, New York–1973.

Othum Brown was associated with John Lee "Sonny Boy" Williamson for a while in the early 1940s. In 1947 he recorded with Little Walter for Ora Nelle Records in Chicago and not long afterwards disappeared from the blues scene.

BROWN, ROY JAMES (Piano, vocal). Born: New Orleans, Louisiana–September 10, 1925.

Roy Brown is a blues shouter in the Wynonie Harris vein. Though the former professional boxer has traveled throughout the United States, he continues to make California his home. In 1947 he made his first recording on the Gold Star label in Galveston, Texas, and has since recorded on Deluxe, King, Imperial, Home of the Blues, Connies, Summit, Friendship, Mercury True-Love, Gert, Blues Way, Mobile, and DRA Records. Brown has not been very active in music for the past several years, but his recordings are still being released.

RECORDINGS
The Blues Way Session. Charly CRB1199
Good Rockin' Tonight. Route 66 KIX6
Hard Luck Blues. King 5036X
I Feel That Young Man's Rhythm. Route 66 KIX26
Laughing But Crying. Route 66 KIX2
Saturday Night. Mr. R & B 104

BROWN, RUTH (Vocal). Born: Portsmouth, Virginia–January 30, 1928.

Ruth Brown's first hit was the rhythm-and-blues single "Mama, He Treats Your Daughter Mean," recorded in December 1952. During the mid–1960s Brown worked the Playboy Club circuit for three and a half years. For a number of years she worked as a teacher in a preschool program in Deer Park, New York. During that time she worked only occasionally in clubs. In 1975–76 she played the role of Mahalia Jackson in the Hollywood production of *Selma*. Her albums included *Black Is Brown and Brown Is Beautiful* (Kent), *Ruth Brown '65* (Mainstream), *Big Band South of Thad Jones/Mel Lewis Featuring Miss Ruth Brown* (Solid State), and *The Real Ruth Brown* (Cobblestone). After moving into a sort of limbo, she had a comeback in the tremendously successful Broadway revue *Black and Blue.*

RECORDINGS
Blues on Broadway. Fantasy 9662
Fine and Mellow. Fantasy FCD–9663
Have a Good Time. Fantasy FCD–9661–2

Help a Good Girl Go Bad. Dcc Jazz DJC–602
Miss Rhythm. Atlantic 82061–2

BROWN, WILLIE LEE (Guitar). Born: Clarksdale, Mississippi–August 6, 1900; died: Tunica, Mississippi–December 30, 1952.

From the time he began playing music around 1916 to the time he stopped around 1941, Willie Brown spent most of his time performing around Mississippi with Robert Johnson, Son House, Tommy Johnson, and Charley Patton. He recorded for the Library of Congress label in 1941. He spent most of the 1940s in Rochester, New York, working outside of music. Around 1950 he moved back to Mississippi, where he worked as a farmer until his death.

BUCKWHEAT. *See* Dural, Stanley, Jr.

BURLESON, HATTIE (Vocal). Born: Texas–date unknown; died: unknown.

A blues singer in the classical mold, Hattie had only one known recording session, which took place in Dallas, Texas, in November 1928. The band that accompanied her included trumpeter Don Albert.

BURNETT, CHESTER "HOWLIN' WOLF" (Guitar, vocal, harmonica). Born: West Point, Mississippi–June 10, 1910; died: Hines, Illinois–January 10, 1976.

Born on a cotton plantation, Chester Burnett became interested in music in his teens, but he did not become a full-time professional until he was almost forty. While Charley Patton gave him a start in the blues, he also learned from Robert Johnson and Rice Miller. His boyhood idol was Jimmie Rodgers, who set the model for his best efforts at yodeling. When he discovered that his voice was too low for yodeling, he adopted a form of growling that eventually led to his being nicknamed Howlin' Wolf. In the late 1940s he formed his own band in West Memphis, Arkansas. It included James Cotton, then thirteen, and Little Junior Parker. In 1951 Burnett recorded "Moanin' at Midnight" and "How Many More Tears?" for Chess Records. "Sitting on Top of the World" was recorded on the Chess label in 1957. He remained active in music from the late 1940s until 1975, when he became ill and was forced to stop.

RECORDINGS
Cadillac Daddy. Rounder SS28
Change My Way. Chess CH93001
The Chess Box. Chess CHCD3–9332
Chicago—26 Golden Years. Chess CHC–9183
His Greatest Sides, Vol. 1. Chess CHC–9107
I'm the Wolf. Vogue VG–670412
The London Howlin' Wolf Sessions. Chess CHD–9297

Moanin' in the Moonlight. Chess CHD5908
Muddy and the Wolf (with Muddy Waters). Chess CHD–9100
The Real Folk Blues. Chess 9273
Ridin' in the Moonlight. Ace CH52

BUTTERFIELD, PAUL (Harmonica, vocal). Born: Chicago, Illinois–December 17, 1942; died: Los Angeles, California–May 3, 1987.

Paul Butterfield played with such Chicago blues greats as Muddy Waters, Buddy Guy, Howlin' Wolf, Otis Rush, Magic Sam, and Little Walter. He recorded his first LP in 1965 on Elektra Records. He worked constantly and recorded profusely from the mid–1960s until the time of his death.

RECORDINGS

East-West. Edsel 212
It All Comes Back. Rhino 70878
North-South. Rhino 70880
An Offer You Can't Refuse. Red Lightnin' 008
The Paul Butterfield Blues Band. Elektra 7294–2
Paul Butterfield's Better Days. Rhino 70877
Put It in Your Ear. Rhino 70879
The Resurrection of Pigboy Crabshaw. Elektra 74015–2

BYRD, ROY "PROFESSOR LONGHAIR" (Piano, vocal, guitar, drums). Born: Bogalusa, Louisiana–December 19, 1918; died: New Orleans, Louisiana–January 30, 1980.

Roy Byrd began working professionally as a pianist upon his discharge from the army. Most of his hits date from the late 1940s and early 1950s. In 1949 he took over Dave Bartholomew's job at the Caldonia Inn and recorded his first sides for Star Talent and Atlantic Records. He acquired the nickname "Professor Longhair" while working at the Caldonia Inn. He recorded as Roy Byrd for Mercury and Atlantic Records and became Professor Longhair again for his second series of Atlantic sessions in 1953. His recording of "Big Chief" was a regional hit in 1965. Known as the Father of Rock and Roll, Byrd has been a heavy influence on the likes of Mac Rebennack (Dr. John), Huey "Piano" Smith, Fats Domino, and Alan Toussaint. A fuller description of him can be found in chapter 3.

RECORDINGS

The Complete London Session. JSP202
Crawfish Fiesta. Alligator 4718
Houseparty New Orleans Style. Rounder CD2057
The Last Mardi Gras. Atlantic SD–2–4001
Mardi Gras in Baton Rouge. Rhino/Bearsville R4–70736
Mardi Gras in New Orleans. Krazy Kat 7408
Mardi Gras in New Orleans. Nighthawk NHCD108
New Orleans Piano: Blues Originals, Vol. 2. Atlantic 7225–2
Rock n' Roll Gumbo. Dancing Cat 3006

CADILLAC BABY. *See* Eatmon, Narvel.

CALHOUN, CORA "LOVIE AUSTIN" (Piano). Born: Chattanooga, Tennessee–September 19, 1887; died: Chicago, Illinois–July 1972.

Cora Calhoun studied piano at Knoxville College and Roger Williams University in Nashville before embarking upon her career as a professional musician. In 1923 she played on Ma Rainey's and Ida Cox's first records on the Paramount label. During the next few years she recorded and played with singers such as Edmonia Henderson, Ethel Waters, Edna Hicks, Priscilla Stewart, and Alberta Hunter. She also played at Jimmy Payne's dancing school at the Penthouse Studios in Chicago for many years beginning in the late 1940s.

CAMPBELL, "LITTLE" MILTON (Guitar, vocal). Born: Inverness, Mississippi–September 7, 1934.

Milton Campbell was fifteen years old when he left home to play with Eddie Cusic's band. He also worked with Sonny Boy Williamson (Rice Miller), Willie Love, and Joe Willie Wilkins for about a year and a half in Mississippi. Milton's first record was on the Sun label in 1953. Since then he has been recorded on Meteor, Bobbin, Chess, and Stax, with the single "We're Gonna' Make It" and the Stax LP *Waiting for Little Milton* being his biggest hits. He has been relatively inactive since 1980.

RECORDINGS

Annie Mae's Cafe. Malaco 7435
Blues n' Soul. Stax 8518
Grits Ain't Groceries. Stax 8529
I Will Survive. Malaco 7427
Little Milton Sings Big Blues. Chess 9265
Raise a Little Sand. Red Lightnin' 0011
The Sun Masters. Rounder SS35

CARR, LEROY (Piano, vocal). Born: Nashville, Tennessee–March 27, 1905; died: Indianapolis, Indiana–April 29, 1935.

Leroy Carr is credited with completely transforming the blues singing style. Possessing a soft, mellow voice, he brought sophistication to the blues. During his career he reportedly recorded over one hundred songs, all blues. He moved to Chicago in 1928 and recorded his first disc for the Vocalion label during that year. He was accompanied on most of his recordings by Scrapper Blackwell, whose single-string guitar style is regarded as a forerunner of Charlie Christian's artistry. His "How Long, How Long Blues" was an instantaneous hit and has since been recorded by a long line of black blues artists.

RECORDINGS

Blues before Sunrise. Portrait Masters RJ44122
Great Piano-Guitar Duets. Old Tramp 1204
Leroy Carr. Collectors Classics CC38
Naptown Blues. Yazoo 1036
1929–1934. Document 543
Singin' the Blues. Biograph BLP C–9

CARTER, WILLIAM "BOM-BAY" (Guitar, harmonica, vocal, bass). Born: Chicago, Illinois–June 23, 1950.

The son of Dan Richmond, who played guitar and harmonica around Chicago in the 1940s and 1950s, William Carter has toured extensively with J. B. Hutto's band and has recorded behind Hutto, Lee Jackson, and Johnny Young. He has a 45 record out under his own name on C. J. Records where he is backed by his own band, Blues Unlimited. Carter spent the 1970s, 1980s, and early 1990s performing in Chicago with his own band as well as playing as a sideman with other blues artists. Occasionally he performed in tours and at festivals in the United States and Europe.

CHARITY, PERNELL (Guitar, kazoo, vocal). Born: Waverly, Virginia–November 20, 1920.

Charity Pernell worked as a partner with guitar player Sam Jones in the late 1930s and early 1940s. The team lasted until around 1944, when Jones gave up the blues for religion. In 1947 Pernell did a six-month stint in New York City, and from 1958 to 1969 he was completely inactive musically. He recorded for Trix Records in the early 1970s. He dropped from the blues scene in the mid–1970s and was not heard from again.

CHATMAN, PETER "MEMPHIS SLIM" (Piano, vocal, organ, bass). Born: Memphis, Tennessee–September 13, 1915.

Composer of the great blues standard "Everyday I Have the Blues," Memphis Slim is one of the longest-lived recording artists in the blues field. He made his first recording in 1949 on the Miracle label and was still doing work in the studios in the late 1960s. His recordings were released on King, Peacock, Premium, Argo, Mercury, Chess, United Artists, VJ, Folkways, Verve, Collector, Storyville, Xtra, Bluesville, Candid, Fontana, Agorilla, and Polydor. Despite all his recordings with these companies, he never really had a solid hit. After a fruitless effort to survive in the United States, he moved to Paris, France, where he still resides. In the early 1960s he recorded material for the albums *Steady Rolling Blues*, released in 1961, and *Dialog in Boogie*, released on January 14, 1980.

RECORDINGS

All Kinds of Blues. Fantasy/OBC OBC–507
The Blues Is Everywhere. Charly CRB1030
Blue This Evening. Black Lion BLCD–760155

Dialog in Boogie. Zeta ZET–711
I Guess I'm a Fool. Vogue VG–670408
Legacy of the Blues, Vol. 7. GNP Crescendo GNPO–10017
Life Is Like That. Charly CD249
Memphis Blues. Milan 73138–35618–2
Memphis Slim Story. Esperance ESPCD 1909
Memphis Slim U.S.A. Candid 9024
Parisian Blues. EmArcy 834658–2
Raining the Blues. Fantasy FCD–24705–2
The Real Folk Blues. Chess CHD9270
Real Honky Tonk. Folkways 3535
Steady Rolling Blues. Fantasy/OBC OBCCD–523–2

CHATMON, ARMENTER "BO CARTER." Born: Bolton, Mississippi–March 21, 1893; died: Memphis, Tennessee–September 21, 1964.

Chatmon was from a musical family. His mother, father, and four brothers all played music. He formed a family string band around 1917. Through most of the 1920s he played for tips and kept a job outside of music. He recorded for the Brunswick label in 1928 and 1929. He toured with the Mississippi Sheiks from 1930 to 1935, traveling throughout the south and recording for Okeh, Paramount, and Bluebird records. He recorded with his brothers on the Bluebird label in 1938 and again in 1940. He retired from music in the early 1940s.

RECORDINGS
Banana in Your Fruit Basket. Yazoo CD–1064
Greatest Hits (1930–1940). Yazoo 1014

CHATMON, SAM (Guitar, vocal, banjo, mandolin, harmonica). Born: Bolton, Mississippi–January 10, 1897; died: Hollandale, Mississippi–February 2, 1983.

Sam Chatmon was the oldest surviving member of the musically famed Chatmon family of Mississippi. Like his brothers Lonnie and Bo Chatmon, he was a member of the legendary Mississippi Sheiks. For a while he traveled throughout the South with them, but he elected to settle down in Hollandale, Mississippi, rather than live the life of an itinerant musician. In his later years Sam appeared at festivals and concert dates throughout the United States, proving himself to be one of the best of the old-time blues musicians.

RECORDINGS
Sam Chatmon and His Barbecue Boys. Flying Fish 202
Sam Chatmon's Advice. Rounder 2018

FILM
Sam Chatmon: Sitting on Top of the World. Mississippi Authority for Educational Television. 28 Minutes, color.

CHAVIS, WILSON "BOOZOO" (Accordion, vocal). Born: Lake Charles, Louisiana–October 23, 1930.

Wilson Chavis has been playing zydeco music for over thirty years. In 1954 he had one of the first zydeco hits, "Paper in My Shoe," on the Folk Star label. It was later leased to Imperial and sold over 100,000 copies. He plays a down-to-earth, no-nonsense, energy-packed style of music.

RECORDINGS

Boozoo Zydeco. Maison de Soul 1021
Louisiana Zydeco Music. Maison de Soul 1017
The Lake Charles Atomic Bomb. Rounder 2097
Zydeco Homebrew. Maison de Soul 1028
Zydeco Live! From Richard's Club, Lawtell, La. Rounder 2069

CHEATHAM, JEAN EVANS (Piano, vocal). Born: Akron, Ohio–date unknown.

Jeannie Cheatham started her music studies at age five in Akron, Ohio. As a piano player she accompanied Dinah Washington, Al Hibblen, Jimmy Witherspoon, and others. She married jazz trombonist Jimmy Cheatham. She appeared on PBS Television's *Three Generations of the Blues* in 1983 with Sippie Wallace and Big Mama Thornton. She recorded *Sweet Baby Blues* on the Concord Jazz label in 1985.

CHENIER, CLIFTON (Accordion, vocal, harmonica, piano, organ). Born: Opelousas, Louisiana–June 25, 1925; died: Lafayette, Louisiana–December 12, 1987.

Clifton Chenier grew up listening to his father play accordion at house parties and dances and started playing the instrument himself at a very early age. In 1949 he and his brother Cleveland moved to Lake Charles, Louisiana, where they worked day jobs and played music at night and on weekends. In 1954 J. R. Fulbright, a Los Angeles talent scout, took Chenier into KAOK, a Lake Charles radio station, where he recorded "Clifton's Blues" and "Louisiana Stomp." He later recorded "Boppin' the Rock" and "Ay Tee Fee" for the Specialty label. Known as the Zydeco King, Chenier played a kind of blues that is performed by French-speaking blacks in southwest Louisiana and Texas. It is a highly rhythmic, danceable kind of music, played on accordion, guitar, bass, washboard, and drums. For the last twenty years of his life Chenier added a rock and roll beat to his music and was successful in making it popular throughout the South and California. A number of his albums were released on Arhoolie Records. He was nominated for Grammies in 1979 and 1980. He was the subject of the film *Hot Pepper* by Les Blank of Flower Films. A fuller description of him can be found in chapter 3.

RECORDINGS

Bayou Soul. Maison de Soul 1002
Black Snake Blues. Arhoolie 1038
Bon Ton Roulet. Arhoolie 1031
Boogie 'n Zydeco. Maison de Soul 1003
Classic Clifton. Arhoolie 1082
Clifton Chenier and Rockin' Dopsie. Flyright CD17
The King of Zydeco. Arhoolie 1086
Sings the Blues. Arhoolie 1097

FILMS

Hot Pepper. Kay Jazz Video KJ006. 54 minutes, color.
The King of Zydeco. Arhoolie Video ARV401. 55 minutes, color.

CLAYTON, PETER JOE "DOC" (Vocal). Born: Georgia–April 19, 1898; died: Chicago, Illinois–January 7, 1947.

Doc Clayton's intense style of singing was a big influence on Jimmy Witherspoon, B. B. King, and Joe Williams. He did most of his work in and around the Chicago area from the mid–1930s to the time of his death. Before that, he worked bars and dance halls in St. Louis, Missouri, where he was raised. He recorded for Bluebird in 1941 and 1942 and for Victor in 1946. All of the sessions took place in Chicago.

CLEARWATER, EDDY (Guitar, vocal). Born: Macon, Mississippi–January 10, 1935.

Eddy Clearwater got his first guitar from Reverend Houston Harrington, his uncle, when he was thirteen years old. He started playing church music and did not get into the blues until around 1952, after he moved to Chicago. He did most of his recording between 1956 and 1969 for labels like Atomic-H, Federal, U.S.A., and Versa. *Flimdoozie* was released by Rooster Blues Records in 1987; *A Real Good Time, Live!* was released on Rooster Blues in 1991; and *Help Yourself* was released on the Blind Pig label in 1992.

RECORDINGS

The Chief. Rooster Blues 2615
Flimdoozie. Rooster Blues 2622
Help Yourself. Blind Pig OP–74792
A Real Good Time, Live! Rooster Blues R–72625

FILM

Eddy Clearwater. Gerry Chodkowski. 60 Minutes, black and white.

COBBS, WILLIE (Harmonica). Born: Monroe, Arkansas–July 15, 1940.

Willie Cobbs got exposure as an actor in the movie *Mississippi Masala* and had two songs on the soundtrack. He also appeared with Cybil Shepherd and Moses Gunn on Turner Broadcasting's *Memphis*. His "You Don't Love Me" was recorded by the Allman Brothers, Albert King, and Sonny and Cher. Cobbs has been recorded on Rooster Blues Records. He has frequently worked at other jobs outside of music and has no recordings currently on the national blues market.

COLLINS, ALBERT (Guitar, vocal). Born: Leona, Texas–October 3, 1932.

Albert Collins moved with his family to Houston, Texas, in 1939, and for the first few years of his career he played almost entirely in that city. He made his first recordings there in 1958 on the Kangaroo label. In 1968 he moved to California and settled in Los Angeles the following year. He has since recorded on Blue Thumb, Tumbleweed, Flyright, Red Lightnin', Imperial, Hall, and Great Scott Records. Along with other bluesmen of his generation, Collins still records, plays nightspots, and tours throughout the United States and Europe.

RECORDINGS

The Cool Sound Of. Crosscut 1011
Frostbite. Alligator 4719
Frozen Alive. Alligator 4725
Jump the Blues Away. Verve 841 287–1
Live in Japan. Alligator 4733
Showdown. Alligator 4743

COLLINS, LOUIS "MR. BO" (Guitar, vocal). Born: Indianola, Mississippi–April 7, 1932.

Louis Collins started playing guitar when he was eleven years old. He moved to Chicago in 1946, then to Detroit in 1950, where he started playing music professionally in 1956. He formed his own band in 1958, and between 1966 and 1971 he was under contract with producer Diamond Jim Riley, for whom he recorded about ten singles on the Big D and Diamond Jim labels. Aside from the single "Plenty Fire Below," which he released on his own Gold Top Label, there have been no recent records of Collins's work. Outside of Detroit he is known only to a handful of blues lovers.

CONLEY, CHARLES (Guitar, vocal). Born: Curtain Bottom, Texas–1928.

Charles Conley learned to play the guitar from Lil Son Jackson in West Dallas, Texas. Working mostly as a solo guitarist, he traveled throughout west Texas playing juke joints and roadhouses. In 1954 he moved to Los Angeles, where he played with Little Walker, Little B. B., Al Simmons, and Guitar Slim Green. Because of personal problems he was forced to stop playing music in 1957 and did not return to the scene again until 1973. His return was short-lived. He soon thereafter returned to obscurity and was not heard from again.

COOK, ANN (Vocal). Born: St. Francisville, Louisiana–May 10, 1903; died: New Orleans, Louisiana–September 29, 1962.

Ann Cook was at the height of her singing career between 1917 and 1924. She worked many of the bars and houses in the Storyville section of New Orleans, including Countess Willie Piazza's Place. In 1927 she recorded with Louis Dumaine for the Victor label and again with Wooden Joe Nicholas for the American Music label in 1949. From the 1930s until the time of her death she worked mostly outside of music to make a living.

COPELAND, MARTHA (Vocal). Born: unknown; died: unknown.

A very fine singer who never achieved the fame she deserved, Martha Copeland did most of her recording for the Columbia and RCA labels. Some of her more popular songs were Victoria Spivey's "Black Snake Blues," "Soul and Body,"and "Sorrow Valley Blues."

RECORDINGS

The Complete Recordings, Vol. 1. Blues Documents 2071
The Complete Recordings, Vol. 2. Blues Documents 2072

COTTON, JAMES (Harmonica, vocal, guitar, drums). Born: Tunica, Mississippi–July 1, 1935.

James Cotton worked twelve and a half years with the Muddy Waters band. He cut his first sides for the Sun Label in Memphis in 1954. He lived with Sonny Boy Williamson (Rice Miller) for a while and became a mascot for the bluesman's band. In the summer of 1967 he signed up with the Verve/Forecast label and has since proven to be more than capable as a bluesman both on records and in performances.

RECORDINGS

Cut You Loose. Vanguard VMD 79283
Dealing with the Devil. Intermedia QS–5006
High Compression. Alligator ALCD–4737
James Cotton Live. Antone's 0007
Live from Chicago. Alligator 4746
Take Me Back. Blind Pig 2587
Two Sides of the Blues. Intermedia QS–5011

COUSIN JOE. *See* Joseph, Pleasant.

COX, IDA (Vocal). Born: Toccoa, Georgia–February 25, 1896; died: Knoxville, Tennessee–November 10, 1967.

The first of the Paramount blues artists, Ida Cox recorded her first records in June 1923, six months before Ma Rainey. This stage of her recording career lasted until her final session for Paramount in October 1929. Jesse Crump was her regular accompanist for many years, but she also worked with King Oliver and Tommy Ladnier. She was one of the few classic blues singers to work constantly throughout the 1930s. In 1939 she started to record again, this time with an all-star band that included Oran "Hot Lips" Page, James P. Johnson, and J. C. Higginbotham. In 1940 she recorded with Cliff Jackson and Henry "Red" Allen before retiring from the blues scene. In 1961, as a very old woman, she made her last studio date after much persuasion. Roy Eldridge, Sammy Price, and Coleman Hawkins appeared in that session. Further description of her can be found in chapter 4.

RECORDINGS
Ida Cox. Collectors Classics CC56
Ida Cox and Bertha "Chippie" Hill. Queen Disc 048
Wild Women Don't Have the Blues. Rosetta 1304

CRAYTON, CONNIE CURTIS "PEE WEE" (Guitar, trumpet, vocal). Born: Rockdale, Texas–December 18, 1914.

Ever since the mid–1940s Pee Wee Crayton has worked out of the Los Angeles area. A flashy guitarist and singer, he combined the blues with the more popular rhythm-and-blues style with much success. His association with Ivory Joe Hunter, Red Callender, Johnny Otis, and Gatemouth Brown showcased his versatility as a musician. Some of the labels he has recorded on include Pacific, 4-Star, Aladdin, Hollywood, Imperial, VJ, Fox, Smash, Epic, Vanguard, Blues, Spectrum, and Pablo. Clayton was not involved in any musical activity during the 1980s and early 1990s.

RECORDINGS
After Hours Boogie. Blues Boy BB307
Make Room for Pee Wee. Murray Brothers 1005
Rocking down on Central Avenue. Ace CHA–61
Things I Used to Do. Vanguard VMD–6566

CREACH, "PAPA" JOHN (Violin, vocal). Born: Beaver Falls, Pennsylvania–May 17, 1917.

Papa John Creach was schooled in the jazz and blues music of the 1930s and 1940s. His violin style is deeply rooted in the soul of Kansas City shout, the intricateness of jazz saxophonist Charlie Parker, and the down-home singularity of the Delta blues. He is perhaps best known for his work with the popular rock groups Jefferson Airplane and Hot Tuna. He was 50 years old when he joined Jefferson Airplane in 1967, and his popularity rose steadily, affording him the luxury of several well-received albums. Creach dropped from musical sight in the mid–1970s.

FILM
Papa John Creach: Setting the Record Straight. Kay Jazz Video KJ083. 58 minutes, color.

CRIPPLE CLARENCE. *See* Lofton, Clarence.

CRUDUP, ARTHUR "BIG BOY" (Guitar, vocal). Born: Forest, Mississippi–August 24, 1905; died: Nassawadox, Virginia–March 28, 1974.

Arthur moved to Chicago in the mid–1930s and began to record in 1944. He became one of the most prolific blues recording artists of the decade and also one of the first to accompany himself on the amplified guitar. He composed many blues hits, including "I'm All Shook Up" (recorded by Elvis Presley), "Black Pony Blues," "That's All Right," and "Mean Old Frisco

Blues." He was rediscovered in the mid–1960s and played and recorded regularly up to the time of his death.

RECORDING

Previously Unissued 1960–62 Recordings. Krazy Kat 7410

FILM

Born in the Blues. WETA-TV, Washington, D.C. 29 Minutes, color.

CURTIS, JAMES "PECK" (Drums, jug, rubboard). Born: Benoit, Mississippi–March 7, 1912; died: Helena, Arkansas–November 1, 1970.

James Curtis started playing music when he was twenty years old in various traveling shows that worked throughout the South. During the 1930s he worked with Howlin' Wolf at local dances in West Memphis, Arkansas. His association with Sonny Boy Williamson (Rice Miller) lasted through the 1940s, with their most publicized appearances being on "King Biscuit Time" on radio station KFFA in Helena, Arkansas. During the 1950s and 1960s he worked mostly with guitarist Houston Stackhouse throughout the Mississippi Delta. He recorded on the Modern label in 1952 and with Houston Stackhouse for Testament Records in 1967.

DARBY, THEODORE "TEDDY" (Guitar, vocal, piano). Born: Henderson, Kentucky–March 2, 1906; died: unknown.

Theodore Darby moved to St. Louis in the 1920s and started learning to play the guitar in a workhouse there. In 1927 he lost his eyesight, and in 1929 he made his first sides for Paramount Records, "My Leona Blues" and "Lawdy Lawdy." He also recorded for Victor, Bluebird, Vocalion, and Decca Records.

DAVENPORT, JOHN "LITTLE WILLIE JOHN" (Vocals). Born: Detroit, Michigan–1938; died: Walla Walla, Washington–June 1968.

Little Willie John had a national hit on the rhythm-and-blues charts in 1956 with "Fever," the song that two years later became a national pop hit for Peggie Lee. In 1958 he scored another hit with "Talk to Me, Talk to Me," and in 1960 "Sleep" also made the charts. He was an extremely versatile musician with an affection not only for the blues but for popular and jazz material as well. In May 1966 he was sent to prison for a manslaughter he committed in Seattle. He was in the Washington State Penitentiary in Walla Walla when he died of pneumonia.

RECORDINGS

15 Original Greatest Hits. Deluxe DCD–7837
Mister Little Willie John. King KCD–603
Sure Things. King KCD–739
Talk to Me. King KL5–596

DAVIS, REV. GARY (Guitar, harmonica, vocal, banjo, piano). Born: Laurens, South Carolina–April 30, 1896; died: Hammonton, New Jersey–May 5, 1972.

Gary Davis was born on a small farm in Laurens County, South Carolina, where he was blinded as a young child. After having played with a number of country blues bands, he was ordained a minister in 1933. In 1935 he went to New York and recorded as "Blind" Gary for Perfect Records and accompanied "Blind Boy" Fuller on studio dates. In the early 1940s he settled in New York and worked as a street preacher and singer. He was not heard from again until the mid–1950s, when he made a number of albums for Folk-Lyric, Prestige, and Vanguard Records and appeared at the Newport Folk Festival.

RECORDINGS

Children of Zion. Heritage 308
From Blues to Gospel. Biograph BCD–123
Gospel, Blues, and Street Songs. Fantasy/OBC OBC–524
Pure Religion and Bad Company. Smithsonian/Folkways CDSF–40035
Ragtime Guitar. Heritage 309
Reverend Gary Davis. Heritage CD02
The Singing Reverend. Stinson 56
Sun Is Going Down. Folkways 3542
When I Die I'll Live Again. Fantasy 24704

FILMS

Blind Gary Davis. University of California. 12 minutes, black and white.
Rev. Gary Davis. Seattle Folklore Society. 26 minutes, black and white.
Rev. Gary Davis and Sonny Terry: Masters of the Country Blues. Yazoo Video 000501. 60 minutes, color.

DAVIS, "BLIND" JOHN HENRY (Piano, vocal). Born: Hattiesburg, Mississippi–December 7, 1913; died: unknown.

John Henry Davis began playing professionally in Chicago speakeasies in 1930 at the age of seventeen and continued to perform his irresistible combination of boogie, blues, jazz, and ragtime for the rest of his life. He recorded and performed with an astonishing array of other blues and jazz stars, including John Lee "Sonny Boy" Williamson, Tampa Red, Big Bill Broonzy, and Sidney Bechet. For a decade he worked for the RCA Bluebird label as a house pianist and later toured Europe eight times.

RECORDINGS

Blind John Davis. L & R 42056
In Memoriam. Document DL505
Stomping on a Saturday Night. Alligator 4709
You Better Cut That Out. Red Beans 008

DAWKINS, JAMES HENRY "JIMMY" (Guitar, vocal). Born: Tihula, Mississippi–October 24, 1936.

James Dawkins got his first guitar in 1952, moved to Chicago in 1955, and began playing music professionally shortly after that. After a brief stint with harmonica player Lester Hinton's band, he formed his own group and worked the streets as well as many noted Chicago blues bars. In Orange, France, on November 27, 1971, he was awarded the Grand Prix of the Hot Club of France for being the best jazz/blues guitarist and having the best record of the year, *Fast Fingers*. Regarded as one of the urban blues giants of the 1980s and early 1990s, Dawkins makes Chicago his base of operation. His third CD, *All for Business*, was released on Delmark Records in 1991, and *Kant Sheck Dees Bluze*, on Earwig Records, hit the shops in 1992.

RECORDINGS
All for Business. Delmark DS–634
Blisterstring. Delmark 641
Fast Fingers. Delmark 623
Feel the Blues. JSP CD206
Kant Sheck Dees Bluze. Earwig 4920CD

DECOU, WALTER (Piano). Born: New Orleans, Louisiana–1890; died: New Orleans–December 12, 1966.

Walter Decou played banjo in various Storyville locations as a teenager. He was the leader of his own small bands during the 1920s, playing jazz and blues at honky-tonks in New Orleans. He recorded with orchestra leader Sam Morgan in 1927 and with trumpet pioneer Bunk Johnson. Morgan spent much of his time playing in blues/jazz bands in the small towns west of New Orleans.

RECORDING
Bunk Johnson and His Superior Jazz Band. Good Time Jazz M12048

DIDDLEY, BO. *See* McDaniel, Ellas.

DIXON, FLOYD (Piano, vocal). Born: Marshall, Texas–February 8, 1929.

With his very first recording, "Dallas Blues," Floyd Dixon achieved national prominence. He also had several big hits from 1949 to 1952 on Aladdin, Atlantic, and Chess. His smooth delivery and piano style enabled him to be listed with Ray Charles, Roy Brown, and Amos Milburn on the national rhythm-and-blues charts and on tours throughout the United States. Dixon was a very important influence on the California blues scene. He was at his musical peak in the 1950s. Gradually he dropped from national attention and was not heard from in the 1980s or early 1990s.

RECORDINGS
Empty Stocking Blues. Route 66 KIX27
Houston. Route 66 KIX11
Marshall Texas Is My Home. Specialty SPCD–7011–2
Opportunity Blues. Route 66 KIX1

DIXON, MARY (Vocal). Born: Texas–date unknown; died: unknown.

Dixon spent some time in New York City during 1928–29, where she did five recording sessions that produced ten songs. A number of these were released on Columbia and Vocalion Records.

DIXON, WILLIE JAMES (Bass, composer). Born: Vicksburg, Mississippi–July 1, 1915; died: Chicago, Illinois–1993.

Willie Dixon lived in the Vicksburg area until the age of eleven, when he moved north to Chicago to live with a sister. At the age of fourteen he returned home to Vicksburg, only to leave again in three years, heeding the call of the Windy City, where he lived for the rest of his life.

His early writings were school poems that he eventually set to music. His first actual song was titled "Somebody Tell That Woman," later recorded as "Big Boat up the River" by Peter, Paul, and Mary. This tune was first recorded by one of Willie's original groups, the Four Jumps of Jive, in 1939. However, this was not Dixon's first taste of show business. Under the name of James Dixon he was crowned Golden Glove heavyweight champion in Chicago in 1937.

Prior to discovering that his compositions were in demand by recording artists, Dixon sold many of his songs to other musicians in the 1930s at the rate of fifteen to twenty dollars each, outright and with no royalties. His first big-selling tune was "Signifying Monkey," which sold about 40,000 copies. It was recorded by one of Dixon's early groups, the Big Three Trio, on the Bullet record label in the early 1940s. Next came the Muddy Waters hit "I'm Your Hoochie Coochie Man" (Chess Records, early 1954), which sold in excess of 75,000 copies during its initial release period. This tune, along with "The Seventh Son," which helped launch the career of Johnny Rivers; "My Babe," which has been recorded by Elvis Presley, Peggy Lee, Peter, Paul, and Mary, Nancy Wilson, Nina Simone, Peter and Gordon, and many other top artists; and "I Just Want to Make Love to You," recorded by Muddy Waters, the Rolling Stones, Otis Redding, Fog Hat, and others, were considered by Dixon to be his all-time best-sellers, totaling profits well into the millions.

In 1974 Ovation Records released the LP *Willie Dixon—Catalyst*, which included four standards, "My Babe," "I Just Want to Make Love to You," "Bring It On Home," and "Wang Dang Doodle," plus six brand new Willie Dixon classics. In 1989 Chess Records released *The Chess Box*, a Willie Dixon songbook of thirty-six songs performed by Dixon and other legendary Chess artists. In 1990 Columbia released *The Big Three Trio* in its Roots and Blues series.

RECORDINGS

The Big Three Trio. Columbia C–46216
The Chess Box. Chess CHD2–16500
Ginger Ale Afternoon. Varese Sarabande CD52354–2

Hidden Charms. Capitol CI–90595
I Am the Blues. Columbia PCT–09987
Willie's Blues. Fantasy/OBC OBC–501
Willie Dixon and His Chicago Blues Band. Spivey 1016

BOOK

Dixon, Willie, and Don Snowden. *I Am the Blues: The Willie Dixon Story.* London: Quartet Books, 1989.

DORSEY, THOMAS A. "GEORGIA TOM" (Guitar, piano, vocal). Born: Villa Rica, Georgia–July 1, 1899; died: Chicago, Illinois–January 23, 1993.

Thomas Dorsey's first experience in music was in Atlanta, Georgia, where he sang in a church choir at the age of six. He learned to read music from Atlanta's theater pianists around 1910 and launched himself on a distinguished career as a jazz/blues musician that lasted until the early 1930s. During that time he performed and/or recorded with Will Walker's Whispering Syncopators, Ma Rainey, Tampa Red, the Hokum Jug Band, Memphis Minnie, and others. In 1930 he formed the Thomas A. Dorsey Gospel Songs Music Publishing Company and became active as a composer of gospel music from that point on. He was the composer of a large number of blues and gospel songs as well as the author of three books: *Inspirational Thoughts* (1934), *My Ups and Downs* (1938), and *Dorsey's Book of Poems* (1941).

RECORDING

Come on Mama, Do That Dance. Yazoo 1041

DOUGLAS, K. C. (Guitar, vocal). Born: Sharon, Mississippi–November 21, 1913; died: Berkeley, California–October 18, 1975.

After playing music around his home state of Mississippi, K. C. Douglas moved to California in 1945 and recorded for Cook, Down Town, and Bluesville Records. He then dropped out of sight and was not heard from again until the early 1970s, when he recorded for Arhoolie Records. He later made two appearances at the San Francisco Blues Festival and one at the Western Bicentennial Folk Festival.

RECORDINGS

Big Road Blues. Ace CH254
The Country Boy. Arhoolie 1073
K. C.'s Blues. Fantasy/OBC OBC–533
Mercury Boogie. Oldie Blues 2812

DOUGLAS, LIZZIE "MEMPHIS MINNIE" (Guitar, vocal, banjo). Born: Algiers, Louisiana–June 3, 1897; died: Memphis, Tennessee–August 6, 1973.

Minnie Douglas's father bought her a banjo when she was still very young, and within two weeks she was playing at house parties. By the time she was fifteen, she had switched to guitar and was working on Memphis streets and at Handy Park. In 1929 a Columbia Records talent scout discovered her singing in a Beale Street barber shop, took her to New York City, and recorded her under the name Memphis Minnie. She recorded prolifically from 1929 to 1954 for over half a dozen companies. Her most exciting sessions were the duets she performed with her second husband "Kansas" Joe McCoy. She moved back to Memphis in 1957 and performed there occasionally until 1960, when she retired from music completely. A fuller description of her can be found in chapter 3.

RECORDINGS
Hoodoo Lady (1935–1937). Columbia/Legacy CK–46755
I Ain't No Bad Gal. Portrait Masters RK–44072
Memphis Minnie. Blue Classics C–215
Memphis Minnie, Vol. 2. Earl BD617
Moanin' the Blues. MCA 1370
My Girlish Days. Travelin' Man 803

DUPREE, WILLIAM T. "CHAMPION JACK" (Piano, guitar, vocal). Born: New Orleans, Louisiana–July 4, 1910; died: France–1991.

William Dupree learned to play piano while he was in the Colored Waifs Home for Boys in New Orleans. He frequently played with Chris Kelly, Papa Celestine, and Kid Rena in the 1920s. From 1932 to 1940 he worked as a professional boxer. During the 1940s and mid–1950s he was back into music and working mostly out of New York City. During this period and the years to follow he accumulated an impressive amount of recordings under his own name and with other blues and jazz greats. He moved to Europe in the 1960s and continued to perform and record all over the continent until his death.

RECORDINGS
Champion Jack Dupree. EPM Musique FDC5504
The Death of Louis. Vogue 600096
Jackson Blues. Travelin' Man 807
The Joe Davis Sessions. Flyright CD22
Sings the Blues. King KCD735

DURAL, STANLEY, JR., "BUCKWHEAT" (Accordion, keyboards, vocal). Born: Lafayette, Louisiana–November 14, 1947.

Stanley Dural played with Little Richard, Clarence "Gatemouth" Brown, and Barbara Lynn in the 1960s. Soon thereafter he formed his own band, called the Hitchhikers, and made local records. His biggest seller, "Miss Hard to Get," was released on Soul Unlimited in 1972. After he played in Clifton Chenier's Band, he turned to zydeco. He is considered a major zydeco performer. A fuller description of him can be found in chapter 3.

RECORDINGS
Buckwheat's Zydeco Party. Rounder 11528
Ils Sont Partis. Blues Unlimited 5022
On a Night Like This. Island 422–842739–1
100 Percent Fortified Zydeco. Black Top 1024
People's Choice. Blues Unlimited 5017
Take It Easy, Baby. Blues Unlimited 5009
Taking It Home. Island 90961
Turning Point. Rounder 2045
Waitin' for My Ya Ya. Rounder 2051
Where There's Smoke, There's Fire. Island 842 925–1

DURHAM, BUDDY (Guitar). Born: Ashburn, Georgia–1915; died: unknown.

Buddy Durham did not start playing guitar until he was twenty-one years old and did most of his playing around the state of Georgia. He was a nephew of Lightnin' Hopkins. In 1973 he recorded for Flyright Records in Albany, New York.

DUSKIN, JOE (Piano, vocal). Born: Birmingham, Alabama–February 10, 1921.

Joe Duskin is a pianist set in the mold of Pete Johnson, Albert Ammons, and Meade Lux Lewis. After playing in Cincinnati and New York City, he got out of music for quite a few years, only to return in the late 1960s. Duskin retired from music again in the early 1970s.

RECORDINGS
Cincinnati Stomp. Arhoolie 1080
Don't Mess with the Boogie Man. Special Delivery 1017

EAGLIN, FIRD "SNOOKS" (Guitar, vocal). Born: New Orleans, Louisiana–January 21, 1936.

When Fird Eaglin was less than two years old, he suffered the loss of his sight due to a brain tumor. For many years he played the streets of New Orleans in the tradition of the first recorded generation of blind, itinerant bluesmen like Blind Boy Fuller, Lemon Jefferson, and Willie McTell. Never venturing far from the city, Eaglin was regularly seen with Professor Longhair's band. He has also worked the annual New Orleans Jazz and Heritage Festival for a number of years. Starting in 1952, Eaglin recorded for Folkways, Folk-Lyric, Imperial, Prestige/Bluesville, Storyville, Heritage, and Sonet Records.

RECORDINGS
Baby, You Can Get Your Gun. Black Top 1037
Blues from New Orleans, Vol. 2. Storyville 140
Portraits in Blues, Vol. 1. Storyville SLP–146
Possum up a Simmon Tree. Arhoolie 2014

EATMON, NARVEL "CADILLAC BABY" (Songwriter, producer). Born: Cayuga, Mississippi–1914; died: unknown.

Narvel Eatmon became professionally involved in the blues in 1935 when he opened his own nightclub, Cadillac Baby's Show Lounge in Chicago. He worked as a disc jockey for radio station WOPA for a while, and in 1955 he started his own record company, Bea and Baby Records. For over twenty years Eatmon recorded and represented such artists as Little Walter, L. C. McKinley, Hound Dog Taylor, Bobby Saxton, Eddie Boyd, Little Mack, Detroit Junior, and many others.

ESTES, "SLEEPY" JOHN ADAMS (Guitar, vocal). Born: Ripley, Tennessee–January 25, 1899; died: Brownsville, Tennessee–June 5, 1977.

Even though he lived and played music in total obscurity for nearly two decades, John Estes' performing longevity is almost unequalled among bluesmen today. He first recorded his high, cracked vocal style of "crying the blues" in the early 1920s and did not record again until the 1960s for Delmark Records. He and harmonica player Hammie Nixon worked as partners beginning in 1934 and can be heard on the Delmark sides as well as on an LP issued by Japan's Trio Records. Some of Estes' more familiar blues songs are "Broke and Hungary," "Someday Baby," "Rats in My Kitchen," and "You Oughtn't Say That."

RECORDINGS

The Blues of Sleepy John Estes, Vol. 1. Swaggie 1219
Broke and Hungry. Delmark 608
Brownsville Blues. Delmark 613
Electric Sleep. Delmark 619
In Europe. Delmark 611
Recorded Live. Wolf 120.913

FILM

Sleepy John Estes. Televista Projects. 60 minutes, black and white.

EVANS, MARGIE (Vocal). Born: Shreveport, Louisiana–July 17, 1940.

Margie Evans sang in her family church in Shreveport as a child. She moved to Los Angeles in 1957, where she has lived since. She frequently worked in nightclubs, at festivals, and on studio recordings. She also performed on many European and Far East tours with people such as Johnny Otis and Willie Dixon and also toured Europe on her own. She recorded on Epic, Yambo, and Buddah Records. Later she worked on radio and television shows around the Los Angeles area. She spent the late 1970s, 1980s, and early 1990s dividing her performance time between the West Coast and Europe.

RECORDINGS

Another Blues Day. L & R 42060
Mistreated Woman. L & R 42050

FONTENOT, CANRAY (Violin). Born: Eunice, Louisiana–ca. 1915.

Canray Fontenot comes from a musical family. He started laying the violin in his early teens. As a young man he played house parties with Amede Ardoin around the Eunice-Crowley, Louisiana, area. He performed with Alphonse "Bois-Sec" Ardoin for over thirty-five years. He played in Europe and at festivals in Canada, Washington, D.C., and Louisiana from the early 1980s to the early 1990s. He also performed at the Festival International in Lafayette, Louisiana, in 1993. His CD *Louisiana Hot Sauce Creole Style* was issued on Arhoolie Records in June 1992.

RECORDINGS

Cajun Fiddle Styles, Vol. 1 (with the Carrere Brothers). Arhoolie 5031
Louisiana Hot Sauce. Arhoolie CD–381

FILM

Drywood. Kay Jazz Video KJ067. 37 minutes, color.

FORHAND, "ELDER" ASA (Guitar, vocal). Born: Columbus, Georgia–August 9, 1890; died: Memphis, Tennessee–May 9, 1972.

Also known as Acey Forhand, A. C. Forhans, and U. C. Forham, Asa Forhand was a left-handed guitarist who played music in Memphis for over forty years. At the time of his death, he had been blind for sixty-eight years.

FORHAND, FRANCES (Piano, organ). Born: New Orleans, Louisiana–July 5, 1920.

Frances Forhand met and married Asa in Memphis when she was sixteen years old. She is also blind and worked with her husband around Memphis. Along with her husband in his later years, she was active in the Church of God in Christ.

FORTESCUE, JOHN HENRY "GUITAR SHORTY" (Guitar, vocal). Born: Belhaven, North Carolina–January 24, 1923; died: Rocky Mount, North Carolina–May 6, 1976.

John Fortescue learned to play the guitar from an uncle. His on-off career produced recordings for Cobra Records in 1957 and Pull Records in 1959. In 1971 and again in 1972–73 he recorded for the Flyright label. An album called *Alone in His Field* was produced by Pete Lowry of Trix.

FRAZIER, CALVIN H. (Guitar). Born: Osceola, Arkansas–February 16, 1915; died: Detroit, Michigan–September 23, 1972.

Frazier played with Robert Johnson in Osceola, Arkansas, throughout the early 1930s. He performed frequently on radio station KLCN in Blytheville, Arkansas, in the mid–1930s. In the late 1930s he moved to Detroit, Michigan. He recorded for the Library of Congress there in 1938. He worked with blues bands in Detroit throughout the 1940s and 1950s. He recorded on the Savoy label in 1951, and the JVB label in 1958. He worked mostly outside of music through the late 1950s and 1960s. His last recording was on Barrelhouse records in Chicago in 1972.

FREDRICKS, HENRY. *See* Mahal, Taj.

FROST, FRANK OTIS (Guitar, harmonica, vocal, piano). Born: Augusta, Arkansas–April 1936.

Frank Frost began playing music in St. Louis in 1951. He met Sonny Boy Williamson in 1959 and played with him until 1960. He played on Williamson's Chess recording, "The Goat," and on the "King Biscuit Time" radio show with Sonny Boy and drummer Sam Carr. Frost's first record, including "Jelly Roll King" and "Crawlback," was made in 1963 on Phillips International. In 1966 he recorded for Jewel Records with his regular sideman Sam Carr and Jack Johnson, as well as with Chip Young on bass and Oscar Williams on harmonica. The 1970s, 1980s, and early 1990s all held good years for Frank Frost as a professional bluesman. During that time he performed at clubs and blues festivals in the United States, Canada, and Europe. Also, his recordings are constantly on the market.

RECORDINGS

Harp and Soul. P-Vine PCD2135
Hey Boss Man! P-Vine PLP360
The Jelly Roll Kings Rockin' the Juke Joint Down. Earwig LPS–4901
Midnight Prowler. Earwig CD–4914
Ride with Your Daddy Tonight. Charly CRB1103

FULLER, JESSE (Guitar, harmonica, kazoo, vocal, washboard). Born: Jonesboro, Georgia–March 12, 1896; died: Oakland, California–January 29, 1976.

Jesse Fuller lived with a number of relatives until he ran away from home at a very early age. He joined a circus and made his way to California in the 1920s. In the late 1940s he began to play small clubs and house parties and made his first records for the World Song label. Most of Fuller's professional work took place in and around California's Bay Area.

RECORDINGS

Folk Songs, Spirituals, and Blues. Good Time Jazz 10031
Frisco Bound. Arhoolie 2009
The Lone Cat. Fantasy/OBC OBC–526
Move on down the Line. Topic 134

FILM

Jesse Fuller: Lone Cat. Seattle Folklore Society. 26 minutes, black and white.

FULSON, LOWELL (Guitar, vocal). Born: Tulsa, Oklahoma–March 1921.

Lowell Fulson recorded over fifty songs for Bob Geddins's Big Town and Gilt Edge Labels. They were later leased to Jack Lauderdale and Swing Time Records. Of the sides issued, "Old Time Shuffle," "Blue Shadows," and

"Everyday I Have the Blues" were best-sellers. In 1952 he recorded four sides for Aladdin Records in New Orleans. From around 1953 to 1964 he was under contract with Checker Records. He also recorded for Kent Records in Los Angeles in 1964, but has not been very active in recent years.

RECORDINGS

Baby, Won't You Jump with Me? Crown Prince IG407–408
The Blues Got Me Down. Diving Duck DD4306
It's a Good Day. Rounder 2088
Reconsider Baby. Chess (United Kingdom) CDRED15
So Many Tears. Chess (France) 670403
Think Twice Before You Speak. JSP CD207

GABRIEL, CLARENCE (Guitar, banjo, piano). Born: New Orleans, Louisiana–June 3, 1905; died: New Orleans, Louisiana–1973.

Clarence Gabriel worked with jazz trumpeter Louis Dumaine in New Orleans venues in the late 1920s. He toured with the Sam Morgan Orchestra and worked small clubs in New Orleans during the depression. He was not engaged in much activity after 1950.

GALLOWAY, CHARLIE (Guitar). Born: New Orleans, Louisiana–during the Civil War; died: New Orleans, Louisiana–1916.

Charlie Galloway played guitar and sang on the streets of New Orleans for tips during the mid–1880s. Although he was a victim of polio, he was a very skilled guitarist. He led his own ragtime band in the 1890s and worked frequently with cornetist Buddy Bolden's Eagle Band.

GARLOW, CLARENCE JOSEPH "BON TON" (Accordion, violin, guitar, vocal). Born: Welsh, Louisiana–February 27, 1911; died: Unknown.

Clarence Garlow learned to play the violin at eight years of age and began playing in his father's band soon afterward. His first recording was done on the Macy label in Houston, Texas, in 1949. During the 1950s he recorded for a number of small independent labels in Texas and Louisiana. Although his style of playing was closer to that of rhythm-and-blues, his biggest hit on records was "Bon Ton Roule," a zydeco staple. During the 1960s, Garlow worked mostly as host of his own radio show and owner of his own record company and a few other other nonmusic businesses.

RECORDING

Clarence Garlow, 1951–1958. Flyright 586

GARY, TOMMY (Harmonica). Born: Brownsville, Tennessee–January 9, 1919; died: Memphis, Tennessee–July 31, 1975.

When Tommy Gary was twelve years old, Sleepy John Estes took him to Memphis and used him as an accompanist until Hammie Nixon came along. In the 1920s he played with Son Borum, and the 1930s found him playing with Robert Wilkins. In 1969 Gary appeared with Estes on the Blue Thumb album *Memphis Swamp Jam* and a bit later on *The Memphis Blues Again, Vol. 2* for Adelphi Records. In 1971 he accompanied Estes and Yank Rachell at the Smithsonian Folk Festival in Washington, D.C.

GEORGIA TOM. *See* Dorsey, Thomas A.

GIBSON, CLEOTHUS "CLEO" (Vocal). Born: unknown; died: unknown.

Cleo Gibson started in show business as a member of the vaudeville duo of Gibson and Gibson. She presumably got a recording date because of her amazing resemblance to Bessie Smith, and after cutting only two songs she dropped from the scene completely. Sidemen of the session included trumpeter Henry Mason and pianist Neal Montgomery.

GLENN, LLOYD (Piano). Born: San Antonio, Texas–November 22, 1909; died: unknown.

Lloyd Glenn made his debut with Millard McNeil's Melody Boys at the age of nineteen. After working with Terrence Holder, he joined Boots and His Buddies, a band led by drummer Clifford "Boots" Douglas and considered one of the best in Texas. He made his recording debut with trumpeter Don Albert in 1937. In the early 1940s he moved to California, where he led his own groups, worked for a short while with Kid Ory, and recorded prolifically. Glenn was as much at home in jazz as he was in the blues.

RECORDINGS

After Hours. Oldie Blues 8002
Texas Man. Jukebox Lil608

GLINN, LILLIAN (Vocal). Born: Dallas, Texas–date unknown; died: unknown.

Lillian Glinn was a blues singer of much refinement who recorded on location in Dallas, New Orleans, and Atlanta. Her best-known songs are "Black Man Blues," "Atlanta Blues," "Shake It Down," and "Shreveport Blues."

RECORDING

Lillian Glinn and Mae Glover. Blues Documents 2009

GOREED, JOSEPH "JOE WILLIAMS" (Vocal, piano). Born: Cordele, Georgia–December 12, 1918.

Brought up in Chicago, Joe Williams worked with clarinetist Jimmy Noone, Andy Kirk, Lionel Hampton, and Coleman Hawkins's big band. In the early 1940s he toured with pianist Albert Ammons and Pete Johnson. Although he is closely associated with the blues, his most popular recording being "Everyday I Have the Blues" as recorded with Count Basie in 1952, Joe Williams has a current repertoire containing more popular material. He was active musically into the 1990s, though not totally as a blues performer.

RECORDINGS

Ballad and Blues Masters. Verve 314–511354–2
Chains of Love. Jass J–C–6
Everyday I Have the Blues. Savoy Jazz SJL–1140

GRAY, HENRY (Piano, vocal). Born: Kenner, Louisiana–January 19, 1925. Known primarily as a singer for the past thirty years, Henry Gray broke into the music world when he worked as piano player for Howlin' Wolf in Chicago. Currently he plays nightclubs in Baton Rouge, Lafayette, and occasionally other areas of southwestern Louisiana. A professional lyricist, he has received much recognition from fellow musicians for his songs "How Can You Do It?," "Grave Bounce," and "Going Down Slow."

RECORDING

Lucky Man. Blind Pig 2788

GREEN, CORNELIUS "LONESOME SUNDOWN" (Guitar, vocal). Born: Donaldsonville, Louisiana–December 12, 1928.

Cornelius Green taught himself to play the piano as a teenager. In 1948, when he was twenty years old, he moved to New Orleans. While doing various day jobs there, he taught himself how to play the guitar. In 1953 he was living in Port Arthur, Texas, where he performed occasional gigs with local musicians. Clifton Chenier heard him play and hired him. He worked with Chenier until 1955, when he left Chenier's band and moved to Opelousas, Louisiana. He did his first recording in 1956 on Excello Records in Crowley, Louisiana. In 1965 he left the music business to devote his life to religion. He returned to the blues in 1977 by way of a series of recordings that were released on Joliet Records. He did not experience much activity through the 1980s or early 1990s.

RECORDINGS

Been Gone Too Long. Hightone HCD–8031
Been So Long. Joliet 6002
Bought Me a Ticket. Flyright 529
Lonesome Sundown. Excello 8012

GREEN, LILLIAN "LIL" (Vocal). Born: Mississippi–December 22, 1919; died: Chicago, Illinois–April 14, 1954.

Lillian Green had a slightly nasal voice (very strong in the high register), a superb sense of timing, and accurate intonation. She recorded fifty songs for the Bluebird/Victor label during her brief career as a singer. Most of her records had Big Bill Broonzy on guitar and Simeon Henry, her regular accompanist, on piano. The one record that afforded her great success was her own composition called "Romance in the Dark." It is still a popular song today with many singers. During the height of her career she worked places like the Club Delisa and the Regal Theater in Chicago and the Apollo Theater in New York City.

RECORDING

Chicago, 1940–47. Rosetta RR1310

GREEN, NORMAN G. "GUITAR SLIM" (Guitar, vocal). Born: Bryan, Texas–July 25, 1907; died: Los Angeles, California–September 28, 1975.

Norman Green lived in Oklahoma and Las Vegas before moving to California in 1947. He recorded for several Los Angeles–based labels in the early 1950s and a few years later cut the album *Stone Down Blues* for Kent Records under the production of Johnny Otis. He remained active in music around the Los Angeles area until the early 1970s.

GRIFFITH, SHIRLEY (Guitar). Born: Brandon, Mississippi–April 26, 1908; died: Indianapolis, Indiana–June 18, 1974.

Shirley Griffith learned most of his music from Tommy Johnson in Jackson, Mississippi, and later from Leroy Carr and Scrapper Blackwell in Indianapolis in 1928. His only recordings were two 1961 Prestige/Bluesville albums and a recent Blue Goose LP, *Mississippi Blues.* In 1969 he appeared at the Ann Arbor Blues Festival and at the Midwest Blues Festival in South Bend, Indiana. Working with Yank Rachell and J. T. Adams, he was active in music up to the time of his death.

GUESNON, "CREOLE" GEORGE (Guitar, banjo). Born: New Orleans, Louisiana–May 25, 1907; died: New Orleans, Louisiana–May 5, 1968.

George Guesnon started working in New Orleans nightspots shortly before the depression. He toured with bandleader Sam Morgan during the early 1930s. He recorded in New York for Decca Records. He returned to New Orleans in 1946. In the mid–1950s he performed with clarinet player George Lewis's band.

GUITAR GABLE. *See* Perrodin, Gabriel.

GUITAR SHORTY. *See* Fortescue, John Henry.

GUITAR SLIM. *See* Green, Norman G.

GUITAR SLIM. *See* Jones, Eddie.

GUITAR SLIM. *See* Stephens, James.

GUY, GEORGE "BUDDY" (Guitar, vocal). Born: Lettsworth, Louisiana–July 30, 1936.

Although George Guy has been heavily influenced by Mance Lipscomb and Sam "Lightnin' " Hopkins, he also leans toward B. B. King. He met and became associated with Junior Wells at Theresa's in Chicago in 1958. In 1968 he recorded his debut album for Vanguard, *A Man and the Blues*. In the summer of 1969 Guy became the first American bluesman to tour central and eastern Africa. He has always been a popular figure around his home base of Chicago.

RECORDINGS

Breaking Out. JSP CD215
Drinkin' TNT n' Smokin' Dynamite. Blind Pig 1182
In the Beginning. Red Lightnin' 001
A Man and the Blues. Vanguard 79272
This Is Buddy Guy. Vanguard 79290

HAMMOND, JOHN PAUL (Guitar, vocal). Born: New York City–November 13, 1942.

John Hammond is a blues guitar player and singer who studied slide guitar in the mid–1950s. He performed at the Newport Folk Festival in 1963. His first album was recorded by Vanguard Records. He worked on the soundtrack of Dustin Hoffman's film *Little Big Man* in 1970. He recorded on various labels, including Vanguard, Columbia, Atlantic, and Spindrift.

RECORDINGS

The Best of John Hammond. Vanguard VSD 11/12
Frogs for Snakes. Rounder 3060
Live. Rounder 3074
Mileage. Rounder 3042
Spoonful. Edsel 129

FILM

John Hammond: From Bessie to Springsteen. SMV Video 490572. Color.

HARNEY, RICHARD "HACKSAW" (Guitar, piano). Born: Money, Mississippi–July 16, 1902; died: Jackson, Mississippi–December 25, 1973.

Richard Harney was half of the Pet and Can guitar duo that recorded behind Pearl Dickson and Walter Rhodes for Columbia Records in 1927. In the mid–1940s he made guitars and ran a music store in Clarksdale, Mississippi. In later years he made his living by tuning and repairing pianos. In the early 1970s he recorded on the Adelphi label and made appearances in Boston and Chicago in 1972.

HARRINGTON, REV. HOUSTON H. (Guitar, violin). Born: Macon, Mississippi–March 3, 1924.

Houston Harrington's recording activities began in his hometown in the late 1940s. He owned the only record-cutting machine in the area and consequently made a number of recordings of local talent, including the Salt and Pepper Shakers (Preston Spiller, violin; Percy Spiller, mandolin;

Doc Spiller, guitar), which was the best band around that part of the country. After moving to Chicago, he quickly established himself as an auditioning service for labels like United, Cobra, Chess, VJ, and a few others. Through his service he made demonstration discs of people like Chuck Berry, Otis Spann, Phil Upchurch, Magic Sam, and the Staple Singers. On his own label, Atomic-H, he issued singles by Mighty Joe Young, Jimmy Rogers, Jo Jo Williams, Baby Blount, Tall Paul Hawkins, Bill Ace and his Rocking Aces, and Eddy Clearwater. During the 1960s Atomic-H lapsed into inactivity; nothing happened until Harrington revived the label with a series of spiritual recordings, only to move back into inactivity after a short while.

HARRIS, DON "SUGARCANE" (Violin, piano, guitar, harmonica). Born: Pasadena, California–June 18, 1938.

Don Harris studied classical violin for ten years. He started playing music professionally in the late 1950s and has since worked and recorded with some of the best rhythm-and-blues and rock musicians in the United States and Europe. He has recorded under his own name for the Specialty, Eldo, Epic, and MPS labels and with Little Richard on VJ, Frank Zappa on Bizzarre, Johnny Otis on Epic, and John Mayall on Polydor. He worked out of Los Angeles, California, but has not been active since the early 1980s.

HARRIS, HOMER (Piano, vocal). Born: Drew, Mississippi–May 6, 1916.

Homer Harris moved from Mississippi to Chicago, where he became interested in music, in 1943. Usually teaming up with Jimmy "Beale Street" Clark, he began performing in 1944 and appeared at major Chicago clubs with people like Memphis Slim, Little Walter, Big Maceo, Roosevelt Sykes, Elmore James, and many others. He retired from music in 1956.

HARRIS, JAMES D. "SHAKEY JAKE" (Harmonica, vocal). Born: Earle, Arkansas–April 12, 1921.

James Harris started playing the blues under the inspiration of John Lee "Sonny Boy" Williamson. In the late 1940s he began to work in Chicago, first as a sideman with people like Little Walter and Muddy Waters and later, in 1952, with his own band. Unfortunately, music was secondary in Harris's lifestyle; his number one endeavor was gambling.

HARRIS, WYNONIE (Piano, vocal, drums). Born: Omaha, Nebraska–August 24, 1915; died: Los Angeles, California–June 14, 1969.

Wynonie Harris was at the peak of his career in the late 1940s and early 1950s. Some of his best recordings from this period include "Quiet Whiskey," "Grandma Plays the Numbers," and "All She Wants to Do Is Rock." He died almost unnoticed.

RECORDINGS
Good Rockin' Blues. Gusto 5040x
Here Comes the Blues. Official 6024
Mr. Blues Is Coming to Town. Route 66 KIX3
Oh Babe! Route 66 KIX20
Playful Baby. Route 66 KIX30

HAWKINS, JALACY J. "SCREAMIN' JAY" (Piano, saxophone, vocal). Born: Cleveland, Ohio–July 18, 1929.

Known as a wild blues singer, Jalacy Hawkins is influenced by the stylings of Jimmy Rushing, Louis Jordon, and the powerful Wynonie Harris. He went into music full-time after a short stint as a professional boxer. He toured and recorded with Tiny Grimes and Fats Domino in the 1950s and made quite a few recordings under his own name for Grand (1954), Okeh (1956), Red Top (1958), Roulette (1963), Planet (1965), Decca (1967), Philips (1969), Hot Line (1973), and RCA Victor (1974). In 1983 he recorded the album *Real Life* for the EPM label. His other recent releases include CDs on Rhino (1990, 1992) and Bizarre (1991).

RECORDINGS
Black Music for White People. Bizarre R2–70556
Cow Fingers & Mosquito Pie. Epic EK–47933
Feast of the Mau Mau. Edsel EDCD252
Live and Crazy. Evidence ECD–26003–2
The Night and Day of Screamin' Jay. 52° Rue Est RECD–9023
Real Life. EPM FDC–5509
Spellbound. Bear Family BCD 15530
Voodoo Jive. Rhino R2–70947

HAYS, CHARLES "BLIND CHARLIE" (Guitar, banjo, violin, vocal). Born: New Orleans, Louisiana–1885; died: New Orleans, Louisiana–February 1949.

Charles Hays played the blues on the streets of New Orleans as a teenager. Later he worked with Bunk Johnson. Although quite a few of his performances were by himself, he also worked with trumpeter Louis Dumaine's band and was with Peter Bocage's outfit in 1948.

HEGAMIN, LUCILLE NELSON (Vocal). Born: Macon, Georgia–November 29, 1894; died: New York City–March 1, 1970.

Lucille Hegamin did her first professional work with one of the early Leonard Harper road shows. She moved to Chicago in 1914 and for the next four years proceeded to make a name for herself. She played popular places like the Mineral Cafe (with Dan Paris on piano), Charlie Letts', and the Sherman Blackwell with her husband, Bill Hegamin, accompanying her on piano. In 1918 on Fourth and Central she acquired the name "The Blues Singer Supreme." She moved to New York in 1919 and started her recording career there. On April 30, 1920, she sang at the Happy Rhone's All Star Show and made such an impression that she was asked back to do two more shows. "Arkansas Blues" became a smash hit in June 1921, and in November of that year she was booked at the Shuffle Inn on 131st and 7th Avenue. Her success there gained her a starring role in the famous *Shuffle Along* revue. She recorded extensively on Arto, Paramount, Plaza, Cameo, Columbia, and numerous other labels, including some recent issues for Spivey and Prestige/Bluesville. In 1923 she toured the country in a musical comedy called *Creole Follies*. January 1925 saw her back in New York as a main attraction at the Cotton Club. Her popularity can be measured by the fact that she recorded "Arkansas Blues" for twelve different labels in 1921. She retired from music in 1930 and did not record again until 1961–62.

RECORDING
Alberta Hunter/Lucille Hegamin: The 20s and 30s. Jass J-CD–6

HENDERSON, EDMONIA (Vocal). Born: c. 1900; died: unknown.

"Brown Skin Man," the record that made Edmonia Henderson famous, and "Traveling Blues" were recorded with Lovie Austin and her Blues Serenaders. These are good examples of Edmonia's style. She also recorded some blues with pianist Jelly Roll Morton.

HENDERSON, KATHERINE (Vocal). Born: St. Louis, Missouri–June 23, 1909; died: unknown.

When Katherine Henderson was six years old, she traveled to Australia and New Zealand with the Josephine Gassman Phina and Company Show. She settled in New York City in 1921 and began acting. Among the shows she worked on were *Bottomland* in 1927 and *Keep Shufflin'* in 1929. She also recorded with Clarence Williams's Blue Five for Brunswick Records in 1927.

HENDERSON, ROSA (Vocal). Born: Henderson, Kentucky–November 24, 1896; died: New York City–April 6, 1968.

Rosa Henderson did her first recordings for Victor in 1923 and her last one eight years later for Columbia. During that period she also recorded for a number of other labels, including Vocalion, Ajax, Edison, and Paramount, under such pseudonyms as Josephine Thomas, Sarah Johnson, and Mamie Harris. Her accompanists included Fletcher Henderson, Coleman Hawkins, Charlie Green, James P. Johnson, and countless others. She left the profession in the late 1920s but played occasional engagements during the 1930s. She worked for many years in a New York department store.

HENRY, OSCAR "CHICKEN" (Trombone, piano). Born: New Orleans, Louisiana–June 8, 1888; died: New Orleans, Louisiana–1960s.

Oscar Henry began his professional career by playing at Hattie Rogers's Bordello in New Orleans in 1906. He studied music at Straight University. He switched to playing trombone in 1931. He played with the WPA Brass Band in New Orleans during the depression and worked with Avery "Kid" Howard and other area bands after the depression. He played with the Eureka Brass Band around 1959 and performed at Preservation Hall in New Orleans in the 1960s.

HICKS, OTIS "LIGHTNIN' SLIM" (Guitar, vocal). Born: St. Louis, Missouri–March 13, 1913; died: Detroit, Michigan–July 27, 1974.

Born near St. Louis and raised in Louisiana, Otis Hicks made his first recordings for Jay Miller on the Feature label in Crowley, Louisiana, in 1954. He stayed with Feature for about ten years, recorded more than sixty sides, and became quite popular in Southern blues circles. Only one of his records, "Rooster Blues," recorded in 1959, made the *Billboard* rhythm-and-blues charts. Hicks left Louisiana in the mid–1960s, got a nonmusical job in Detroit, and was not heard from professionally until about 1970. Beginning in 1972, he toured Europe five times, had two LPs issued on the Excello label, and recorded for Big Bear, the English agency that was responsible for his European tours.

RECORDINGS

Bell Ringer. Excello 8004
The Early Years. Flyright 524
London Gumbo. Excello 8023
Rolling Stone. Flyright CD08
Rooster Blues. Excello 8000
We Gotta Rock Tonight. Flyright 612

HIGGENBOTHAM, ROBERT "TOMMY TUCKER" (Piano, vocal). Born: Springfield, Ohio–March 5, 1933.

Tommy Tucker, as Robert Higgenbotham is known professionally, studied clarinet and piano formally and can also play organ, bass, and drums. When he was seventeen, he started playing with a singing group called the Dusters. He stayed with the group until 1959 and backed it on recordings for Arc and Hudson Records in 1955. In 1962 he recorded six tracks under his own name for Atlantic Records, and in 1964 he taped his hit "Hi-Heel Sneakers" for Checker. In 1964 he went on tour with Ray Charles, and in October and November 1965 he played a thirty-nine-day tour of Europe. He worked as leader of his own band as well as a sideman in various blues and rhythm-and-blues groups throughout the 1970s and 1980s.

RECORDINGS
Mother Trucker. Red Lightnin' 0022
Rocks in My Pillow. Red Lightnin' 0037

HILL, BERTHA "CHIPPIE" (Vocal). Born: Charleston, South Carolina–March 15, 1905; died: New York City–May 7, 1950.

Bertha Hill's family moved to New York City when she was about thirteen years old. She got her first big break there at a nightspot called Leroy's. After several years in New York City, she moved to Chicago, where she did her first session for Okeh Records on November 9, 1925, with Richard Jones on piano and Louis Armstrong on trumpet. She shared the bill with King Oliver at the Palladium Dance Hall for a while with much success. In the late 1920s she decided to retire from music and was not heard from again until 1946, when she recorded for Rudi Blesh's Circle label. In 1948 she appeared at the Paris Jazz Festival. On May 7, 1950, during the height of her comeback, she was killed by a hit-and-run driver. Further description of her can be found in chapter 4.

RECORDING
Ida Cox and Bertha "Chippie" Hill. Queen Disc 048

HILLERY, MABLE (Vocal). Born: La Grange, Georgia–July 22, 1929; died: New York City–April 26, 1976.

Mable Hillery's early life was deeply rooted in the blues and spirituals. In the early 1960s she joined the Georgia Asa Island Singers and later performed on her own in the Southern Folk Festival tours and at various other festivals and concerts.

HITE, MATTIE (Vocal). Born: New York City–ca. 1890; died: New York City–ca. 1935.

A singer of some extremely risqué songs, Mattie Hite was best known for a very fine version of "St. James Infirmary." She recorded with Fletcher Henderson on the Pathe label in 1923 and with Cliff Jackson for Columbia Records in 1930. Some of the revues she appeared in were *Hot Feet* (1928), *Tip-Top Review (1928)*, *Chocolate Blonds* (1929), *The Temple of Jazz* (1929), *Desires of 1930* (1930), and *That Gets It* (1932).

HOGAN, SILAS (Guitar, harmonica, vocal). Born: Westover, Louisiana–September 15, 1911.

Silas Hogan is a Louisiana blues musician who has been influenced by Robert Pete Williams and Lightnin' Slim. Although his career as a bluesman has been on and off, he has managed to make a few recordings for the Excello label in Crowley, Louisiana, and for Reynaud-Flyright in Opelousas, Louisiana. He also recorded with Guitar Kelly for Arhoolie/Excello in Baton Rouge in 1970.

RECORDINGS
The Godfather. Blues Southwest BSW003
I'm a Free Hearted Man. Flyright 595
Trouble. Excello 8019

HOLMES, LEROY (Guitar). Born: Woodbine, Florida–April 8, 1921.

Both Leroy Holmes's mother and father were guitar players. He started playing music professionally in 1938 and worked regularly until 1945, when he quit music to find work with a more stable future.

HOMESICK JAMES. *See* Williamson, John A.

HONEYDRIPPER, THE. *See* Sykes, Roosevelt.

HOOKER, EARL "ZEBEDEE" (Guitar, vocal, harmonica, piano). Born: Clarksdale, Mississippi–January 15, 1930; died: Chicago, Illinois–April 21, 1970.

Earl Hooker was a cousin of John Lee Hooker and Joe Hinton. He began playing guitar in 1945, went to Memphis in 1949, and joined and toured with Ike Turner. He later settled in Chicago, where he worked with Junior Wells and Muddy Waters. In 1965 he performed in Paris with Joe Hinton, and in that same year he was featured on a television special by the Beatles. Hooker's first hit record was "Blue Guitar" on the Ace label. He also had releases on Blue Thumb, Cuca, Bluesway, and Arhoolie. In 1969 he toured Europe with the American Folk Blues Festival.

RECORDINGS
Blue Guitar. P-Vine PCD2124
His First and Last Recordings. Arhoolie 1066
Two Bugs and a Roach. Arhoolie 1044 and C/CD324

HOOKER, JOHN LEE (Guitar, vocal). Born: Clarksdale, Mississippi–August 22, 1917.

John Lee Hooker grew up in Memphis, worked in Cincinnati, and matured in Detroit. He did not begin recording until after World War II. He learned to play guitar from his stepfather, who came from Shreveport, Louisiana, and whose home was visited by Blind Lemon Jefferson, Charley Patton, and Blind Blake when Hooker was a boy. Like most Delta bluesmen, he used open tuning (G chord): D, G, D, G, B, D. He cut his first recordings in November 1948 for Modern Records at Detroit's United Sound studios. There was such a demand for Hooker in that year that he recorded for many labels under many different names. On Modern Records he remained John Lee Hooker for five consecutive years. He was "Texas Sam" during most of those years on the King label. On Regent he was "Birmingham Sam" in 1949. In 1949 and 1959 he was "Johnny Williams" on the Staff label. He maintained this name during 1952 and 1953 on Gotham. He appeared as "John Lee Booker" on Chance, Acorn, Deluxe, Gone, and Rockin' in 1951. On Gone and Rockin' he was also known as "The Boogie Man." After 1953 he began recording for labels other than Modern as John Lee Hooker, with the VJ label of Chicago serving as home base from 1958 to 1963. Records by him can be found on Chess, Specialty, Atco, Prestige, Impulse, Riverside, Vanguard, Verve-Folkways, and Bluesway.

RECORDINGS

Alone. Specialty SPC–2125
The Best of. Suite Beat D2012
Black Snake. Fantasy F–24722
Boogie Chillun. Charly CD4
The Cream. Tomato R2–70388
Get Back Home. Evidence ECD–26004–2
House of the Blues. Chess 9258
House Rent Boogie. Charly CD62
I'm in the Mood. CSI Classics–40125
Let's Make It. Charly CD120
Mad Man Blues. Chess CHC2–92507
Never Get out of These Blues Alive. MCA MCAD–31361
Plays and Sings the Blues. Chess 9199
Sings Blues. King KLP–727
That's My Story. Fantasy/OBC OBCCD–538–2

FILM

John Lee Hooker. Seattle Folklore Society. 25 minutes, black and white.

HOPKINS, JOEL (Guitar, vocal). Born: Centerville, Texas–January 3, 1904; died: Galveston, Texas–February 15, 1975.

Joel Hopkins is an older brother of Sam "Lightnin' " Hopkins. He started playing guitar when he was nine years old. After working as a medicine-show back-end wing dancer, he met up with Blind Lemon Jefferson in 1922. The two traveled together for a number of years, playing mostly country house parties. He recorded with Lightnin' Hopkins for Gold Star Records (1947) and for Arhoolie in 1964 and 1965. He also did a recording date for Candid Records in 1959, but was mostly inactive as a musician from the late 1960s to his death.

HOPKINS, SAM "LIGHTNIN' " (Guitar, vocal, piano). Born: Centerville, Texas–March 15, 1912.

Sam Hopkins moved to Houston, Texas, at the end of World War II and worked there as an accompanist to Texas Alexander for a while. Along with piano player "Thunder" Smith, he went to Hollywood for a recording session on the Aladdin label in November 1946. In 1947 he began recording for a small Houston, Texas, label called Gold Star Records. The sides that were released on this label were instrumental in establishing his reputation as a blues artist. For the past twenty-five years Hopkins has recorded hundreds of sides, many for independent rhythm-and-blues labels like Time, Herald, Jax, RPM, Ace, and Kent.

RECORDINGS

Ball n' Chain (with "Big Mama" Thornton). Arhoolie CD–305
Blues in My Bottle. Fantasy OBC OBC–506
Flash Lightnin'. Diving Duck 4307
The Gold Star Sessions, Vol. 1. Arhoolie C/CD 337
Lightnin' Hopkins. Arhoolie C–201
Mojo Hand. Collectables 5111
Move On Out. Charly 1147
Soul Blues. Prestige 7377
Texas Bluesman. Arhoolie 1034

FILMS

The Blues According to. Kay Jazz Video KJ053. 47 minutes, color.
Lightnin' Hopkins. Seattle Folklore Society. 25 minutes, black and white.
Mance Lipscomb and Lightnin' Hopkins: Masters of the Country Blues. Yazoo Video 000502. 60 minutes, color.
A Program of Songs. University of Washington Press. 8 minutes, black and white.
Sam Lightnin' Hopkins. Indiana University. 30 minutes, color.

HORTON, "BIG" WALTER (Harmonica). Born: Horn Lake, Mississippi–April 6, 1917.

Walter Horton mastered the harmonica while still a child. By 1930 he was good enough to record with the legendary Memphis Jug Band. Soon he was traveling throughout the Delta, playing at an endless series of fish fries, parties, and roadhouses. His first recordings were made on Memphis's Sun Records. Later in Chicago he replaced Junior Wells in Muddy Waters's band. After working with Waters for about a year, he quite and went out on his own. He recorded both as sideman and leader for Chess Records, and with the Chicago Blues All-Stars he toured Europe and recorded on a number of European and American labels.

RECORDINGS

Big Walter Horton. Alligator 4702
Chicago Blues (with Johnny Young). Arhoolie 1037
Harmonica Genius. Black Magic 9010
Little Boy Blue. JSP208
Mouth Harp Maestro. Ace CHCD252
The Soul of Blues Harmonica. Chess 9268

HOUSE, EDDIE JAMES, JR., "SON" (Guitar, vocal). Born: Riverton, Mississippi–March 21, 1902; died: unknown.

Son House was constantly tormented by an inner conflict between the impious life of the blues and the consecrated life of the preacher. He recorded for Paramount Records in Grafton, Wisconsin, in July 1930, moved to

Rochester, New York, in the early 1940s, and later worked as a railroad porter for about twelve years. When his playing buddy Willie Brown died in 1948, he took this as a sign to put his guitar away and give up his life as a bluesman. He did not record again until 1962, when Alan Lomax persuaded him to cut a batch for the Library of Congress. A fuller description of him can be found in chapter 3.

RECORDINGS
The Complete Library of Congress Sessions. Travelin' Man CD02
Death Letter. Edsel ED167
Father of the Delta Blues. Columbia CAT–48867
The Legondary 1941–2 Recordings. Folklyric 9002
Real Delta Blues. Blue Goose 2016
Son House and Blind Lemon Jefferson. Biograph 12040
Son House in Concert. Kicking Mule SG–202

FILM
Son House. Seattle Folklore Society. 25 minutes, black and white.
Son House and Bukka White: Masters of the Country Blues. Yazoo Video 00500. 60 minutes, color.

HOUSTON, EDWARD WILSON "BEE" (Guitar, vocal). Born: San Antonio, Texas–April 19, 1938.

Bee Houston's first professional job was in a backup band for Henderson Glass in San Anselmo, Texas. There he was able to play with people like Bobby Bland, Amos Milburn, Charles Brown, Little Willie John, and T-Bone Walker. Leaving Texas, he traveled to New Mexico, where he backed up Brook Benton for a while. In the mid–1960s he moved to Los Angeles and started working with Big Mama Thornton, first as a sideman, then as leader of the band. With Thornton he played the Monterey Jazz Festival in 1968 and recorded several albums. In 1971 he recorded an LP under his own name for Arhoolie Records. He continued to make Los Angeles his home base throughout the 1970s and 1980s. He has had many performances and much studio work as a sideman and has played festivals on the West Coast and Europe.

RECORDING
Bee Houston. Arhoolie 1050

HOWARD, MAXINE (Vocal). Born: unknown.

Maxine Howard is a young blues shouter in the tradition of Koko Taylor and her school of singers. Most of her musical accomplishments were made in Europe.

RECORDING
Blues Shoes with No Strings. Line CD900840

HOWARD, ROSETTA (Vocal). Born: Chicago, Illinois–1914; died: Chicago, Illinois–1974.

Rosetta Howard made a name for herself with an excellent blues band led by Charlie and Joe McCoy (the McCoy brothers). On her own, she recorded "Rosetta Blues" and "If You're a Viper"; the latter is a humorous song about smoking pot. She began singing professionally in 1932 and worked in Chicago with Herb Morand and Odell Rand during the mid–1930s. In 1937 and 1938 she played New York with them. During the latter part of 1938 and most of 1939 she worked with Eddie Smith's band in Chicago. During the 1940s she did mostly solo work.

RECORDING

With the Harlem Hamfats and the Harlem Blues Serenaders. Earl Archives 620

HOWLIN' WOLF. *See* Burnett, Chester.

HUFF, LUTHER (Mandolin, guitar). Born: Fannin, Mississippi–December 5, 1910; died: Detroit, Michigan–November 18, 1973.

When Luther Huff was fifteen, he and his brothers played at picnics and other affairs throughout the Delta. He was drafted into the army in 1942, and while he was in Liege, Belgium, he cut two songs on metal discs in 1944. A few weeks later he was taken to a studio, where he recorded "E.T.P. Blues" and "Sorry I Can't Come Home." Huff moved to Detroit in 1947, and other than a recording session for the Jackson-based Trumpet label in 1951, he lived in obscurity for most of the last twenty-six years of his life.

HUNTER, ALBERTA (Vocal). Born: Memphis, Tennessee–April 1, 1897; died: unknown.

Alberta Hunter was one of the earliest women singers to record. Her work can be found on Paramount and Prestige Records under her own name as well as the name Josephine Beatty. "Down Hearted Blues," recorded in 1922, was her first success, though Bessie Smith later outshone her with the same song. In 1939 she costarred with Ethel Waters in the Broadway musical *Mamba's Daughter*. During World War II she was decorated for traveling all over the world to entertain troops. In 1952 she worked in Britain with Snub Mosley. A bit later she toured Canada and played long residencies in Chicago. In 1954–55 she understudied in the Broadway show *Mrs. Patterson*. She left the music profession for a brief period in the 1960s. During the 1970s she appeared on numerous television shows and at festivals in Europe and the United States. Further description of her can be found in chapter 4.

RECORDINGS

Amtrak Blues. Columbia PC36430
The Glory of Alberta Hunter. Columbia FC37691
Look for the Silver Lining. Columbia FC38970
Young Alberta Hunter. Jass CD6

BOOK

Taylor, Frank C., with Gerald Cook. *Alberta Hunter: A Celebration in Blues*. New York: McGraw-Hill, 1987.

FILM

Alberta Hunter. Kultur 1270. 60 minutes, color.

HUNTER, IVORY JOE (Piano, vocal). Born: Kirbyville, Texas–1911; died: Memphis, Tennessee–November 8, 1974.

Known in his early years as "Rambling Fingers," Ivory Joe Hunter began playing professionally at local dances on the radio and singing in church choirs at the age of thirteen. He had his own radio show on KFDM in Beaumont, Texas, and in 1944 he wrote and recorded "Blues at Sunrise" on his own label, Ivory Records. In 1946 he signed with King Records, where his biggest hit was "Guess Who." In 1950 he recorded "I Need You So" and "I Almost Lost My Mind" on MGM Records. By 1956 Hunter had signed with Atlantic, where his biggest hit was the blues ballad "Since I Met You, Baby." During his career Hunter composed close to two thousand songs. In his last years he recorded country and western material; his last LP was issued on the Paramount label in 1974.

RECORDINGS

The Artistry of Ivory Joe Hunter. Bulldog 1016
I Had a Girl. Route 66 KIX25
I'm Coming Down with the Blues. Home Cooking HCS112
Jumping at the Dew Drop Inn. Route 66 KIX15
Seventh Street Boogie. Route 66 KIX4
16 of His Greatest Hits. King KCD–605
This Is Ivory Joe Hunter. Ace CH–97

HURT, "MISSISSIPPI" JOHN (Guitar, vocal). Born: Teoc, Mississippi–July 3, 1893; died: Grenada, Mississippi–November 2, 1966.

John Hurt went to New York in 1928 and recorded a number of blues songs. He then returned to Mississippi and disappeared in the cotton fields for thirty-five years. In March and April 1963 he cut thirteen sides for the Piedmont label in Washington, D.C. By September 1963 he had embarked on a concert tour that covered most of New England. He appeared at Newport in 1964 and was recorded live by Vanguard Records. Only three years after starting his career anew, he died of a heart attack in Grenada, Mississippi.

RECORDINGS
Avalon Blues. Flyright CD06
The Candy Man. Intermedia QSC–5042
The Immortal. Vanguard VMD–79248
In Concert. Kicking Mule SG–201
Last Sessions. Vanguard VMD79327
Monday Morning Blues. Flyright 553
1928 Sessions. Yazoo 1065
Satisfied. Intermedia QSC–5007
Today. Vanguard 79220

HUTTO, JOSEPH BENJAMIN (Guitar, vocal, piano, drums). Born: Blackville, South Carolina–April 26, 1926.

J. B. Hutto moved to Chicago in 1941. By the age of twenty he was playing drums with Johnny Ferguson's Twisters, but after hearing Big Bill Broonzy, he decided that he preferred guitar. He began to teach himself, picking up his slide guitar style from the grand master of them all, Elmore James. Since forming the Hawks, he has played Chicago's West and South Side clubs and was a regular at Turner's Blue Lounge for ten years. Charlie Musselwhite introduced J. B. to white audiences in 1965. Later that same year J. B. recorded for Vanguard Records. He cut his first records for Chance in 1954 and has since made six albums featuring his own compositions.

RECORDINGS
Hawk Squat. Delmark 617
J. B. Hutto and the Hawks. Testament 2213
Slideslinger. Varrick CVR 003
Slidewinder. Delmark DD–636
Slippin' and Slidin'. Varrick CVR 006

IRONING BOARD SAM. *See* Moore, Sammie.

JACKSON, ARTHUR "PEG-LEG SAM" (Harmonica, vocal). Born: Jonesville, South Carolina–December 18, 1911; died: Jonesville, South Carolina–October 27, 1977.

Peg-Leg Sam Jackson was a carnival/medicine-show musician/dancer/singer for most of his performing career. He lost the lower part of his right leg in a train accident while hoboing across the United States around 1921 and thus was called "Peg-Leg Sam." He recorded with the Chief Thundercloud Medicine Show in 1972 (Trix), with Ruff Johnson in 1972 (Trix), and with Louisiana Red in 1975 (Blue Labor). The mid–1970s were an off-again, on-again period for Jackson due to poor health.

RECORDING
Joshua. Tomato 2696650–2

JACKSON, BENJAMIN CLARENCE "BULL MOOSE" (Vocal, saxophone, violin). Born: Cleveland, Ohio–1919.

Benjamin Jackson's first professional work was with the Harlem Hotshots. He later worked with Lucky Millinder, who organized the Bearcats to back him up on the King recordings. He scored a best-seller in 1946 by providing an answer to a Millinder hit, "Who Threw the Whiskey in the Well?" Jackson was a natural comic and was at his best in novelty tunes like "Sneaky Pete" and "I Want a Bow-legged Woman." "I Love You, Yes, I Do" and "Little Girl, Don't Cry" became mild hits. His nickname, Bullmoose, had more relevance to his physical makeup than to his voice, which was a high baritone. He settled in Philadelphia, Pennsylvania, around 1960 in order to work outside the music business.

RECORDINGS

Big Fat Mamas Are Back in Style. Route 66 KIX14
Moosemania. Bogus 0214851
Moose on the Loose. Saxophonograph BP506

JACKSON, JOHN (Guitar, banjo, vocal). Born: Woodville, Virginia–February 25, 1924.

John Jackson started playing music when he was four years old, duplicating his father's playing on an old flat-top guitar. For a number of years he played house parties, but becoming disillusioned, he dropped from the music scene for almost ten years. His association with geologist Church Perdue marked a turning point in his life. Through Perdue's influence Jackson realized a rebirth of interest in his music and went on to play festivals and concerts, including a tour of Latin America and Europe. He was not heard from in the 1980s.

RECORDINGS

Deep in the Bottom. Rounder 2032
John Jackson. Arhoolie C–221
John Jackson in Europe. Arhoolie 1047
Step It Up and Go. Rounder 2019

FILM

John Jackson: An American Songster. Rhapsody Films. 30 minutes, color.
A Musical Portrait. Kay Jazz Video KJ076. 30 minutes, color.

JACKSON, MELVIN "LIL SON" (Guitar, vocal). Born: Barry, Texas–August 16, 1915; died: Dallas, Texas–May 30, 1976.

Lil Son Jackson did not think seriously of becoming a professional musician until after World War II. In 1948 he made his first recordings for Bill Quinn of Gold Star Records. He was under contract with Imperial from 1950 to 1953, at which time he retired from music to go back to work as a mechanic. Though he recorded again in 1960 for Arhoolie Records and in 1963 for producer Roy Ames, Jackson remained inactive in music during the last years of his life.

RECORDING

Blues Come to Texas. Arhoolie 1004

JACKSON, WILLIAM "NEW ORLEANS WILLIE" (Vocal). Born: New Orleans, Louisiana–1895; died: New Orleans, Louisiana–unknown.

William Jackson was a very popular jazz/blues singer around New Orleans in the 1920s. He recorded fourteen sides with pianists Clarence Williams, Steve Lewis, and Buddy Christian serving as accompanists. He did not perform much after 1950.

JACOBS, MARION WALTER "LITTLE WALTER" (Harmonica, guitar, vocal). Born: Marksville, Louisiana–May 1, 1930; died: Chicago, Illinois–February 15, 1968.

Little Walter Jacobs moved to Chicago in 1947 while still in his teens. He worked with Muddy Waters until 1952, when he recorded an instrumental song called "Juke" for Checker Records. The song became a big hit, and on the strength of it Walter left Waters and formed his own band, the Jukes, with Louis Mayers on guitar, Dave Mayers on bass, and Fred Below on drums. Walter was at the height of his career in the mid–1950s, touring the United States and recording a string of hit singles. As his popularity died, work became scarce, and by the 1960s, he was only playing occasionally as a sideman with other musicians.

RECORDINGS

The Best of Little Walter. Chess 9192
The Blues World of Little Walter. Delmark 648
Boss Blues Harmonica. Chess 2–92503
Hate to See You Go. Chess 9321

JACOBS, MATTHEW "BOOGIE JAKE" (Piano, guitar). Born: Marksville, Louisiana–1929.

Boogie Jake Jacobs started playing professionally in the early 1950s. He moved to Baton Rouge in 1956 and started working with drummer Joe Hudson. He recorded with Slim Harpo in Crowley, Louisiana, in 1957 and did his own record session in Crowley that same year. In 1959 he recorded for Minit Records in New Orleans. He formed his own five-piece band in 1959 and toured the South for three years. He worked sporadically during the mid- and late 1960s. He retired from music in the early 1970s.

JAMES, ELMORE (Guitar, vocal). Born: Richland, Mississippi–January 27, 1918; died: Chicago, Illinois–May 24, 1963.

Elmore James was active as a professional musician for more than thirty years and was one of the most prominent and influential bluesmen of his era. His innovativeness was responsible, in part, for the harmonic development of the Mississippi Delta blues. Though he traveled extensively, most of his work was concentrated around the Mississippi Delta and Chicago. Some of the record labels for which he recorded were Trumpet, Meteor, Checker, Flair, Atlantic, Chief, Fire, and Chess.

RECORDINGS

The Best of Elmore James and His Broom Dusters. Ace CH31
Dust My Broom. Tomato R2–70389
Golden Classics. Collectables COLCD–5112
King of the Slide Guitar. Capricorn 42006
Let's Cut It. Ace CDCH–192
The Original Meteor and Flair Sides. Ace CH112
Red Hot Blues. Intermedia QSC–5034
Street Talkin'! (with Jimmy Reed and Eddie Taylor). Muse MCD–5087

JAMES, ETTA (Vocal). Born: Los Angeles, California–1938.

Etta James started singing at a very early age in the church. Later she was influenced by the classic blues singers. She was discovered by Johnny Otis in the early 1950s. She had a hit in 1955 with "Roll with Me, Henry." She performed regularly until the 1970s. After that time she was forced to retire from the music business because of a drug problem. She came back into the business in the 1980s, singing the blues mainly on the East Coast and in Europe.

RECORDINGS

At Last! Chess CHD–9266
Come a Little Closer. Chess CHC–91509
Etta, Red Hot 'n' Live. Intermedia QSCD–5014
Etta James/Martha Reeves. Dominion 885–2
Good Rockin' Mama. Ace CHC–803
Her Greatest Sides. Chess CHC–9110
R 'n' B Queen. Crown GEMC–005
Second Time Around. Chess CHD–9287
Seven Year Itch. Island 422–842655
Sticking to My Guns. Island 442–842926–1
The Sweetest Peaches. Chess CHC2–6028
Tell Mama. Chess CHD–9269
Tuff Lover. Ace CH–73

JAMES, NEHEMIAH "SKIP" (Guitar, piano, vocal). Born: Bentonia, Mississippi–June 9, 1902; died: University of Pennsylvania Hospital, Philadelphia–October 3, 1969.

Skip James began playing guitar in 1912 and was active as a professional musician until 1932. He recorded for Paramount in 1930. After a brief hiatus he resumed his career in 1938 and traveled for a few years with a gospel group. In 1964 he appeared at the Newport Folk Festival, and he toured Europe in 1967.

RECORDINGS

Devil Got My Woman. Vanguard VMD 79273
Greatest of the Delta Blues Singers. Biograph BCD–122
Skip James: The Complete 1931 Session. Yazoo 1072
Today! Vanguard VMD 79219

JEFFERSON, BONNIE (Guitar, vocal). Born: Shoal Creek, Arkansas–June 28, 1919.

By the time Bonnie Jefferson was ten years old, she was singing all over the state of Arkansas in a church choir. Inspired by Mamie Scott, a prominent female guitarist-vocalist of the time, Bonnie took up the guitar in the early 1930s. She was active in music until 1949, when she gave it up to be a housewife and did not play again until the early 1970s. She performed sporadically from 1971 to 1973; then she dropped from the scene again.

JEFFERSON, "BLIND" LEMON (Guitar, vocal). Born: Couchman, Texas–July 1897; died: Chicago, Illinois–February 1930.

By the time Lemon Jefferson was fourteen, he had mastered the guitar and was singing on the streets of Wortham, Texas. At twenty he left his parents' farm and traveled to Dallas, where he earned money performing as a novelty wrestler. He met and joined forces for a short while with Leadbelly during this period in Dallas. He recorded for Paramount in April 1926 and wound up making seventy-nine blues records for that company in the four years of his active recording career. In February 1930, as a result of his blindness and perhaps drunkenness, he was found dead in the snow one morning after a recording session at Paramount's Chicago studios. His guitar was found beside his frozen body. He is buried in an unmarked grave between his mother and sister in a field outside Wortham, Texas. A fuller description of him can be found in chapter 3.

RECORDINGS

Black Snake Moan. Milestone 2013
Blind Lemon Jefferson. Milestone MCD–47022–2
Golden Classics: Penitentiary Blues. Collectables COLCD–5194
The Immortal Blind Lemon Jefferson. M–2004
King of the Country Blues. Yazoo CD–1069

JEFFERY, ROBERT (Piano, guitar, vocal). Born: Tulsa, Oklahoma–January 14, 1915; died: San Diego–July 20, 1976.

Robert Jeffery came from a musical family and was quite small when his mother started him playing piano. He met T-Bone Walker (his cousin) in 1936 and worked with him for a while playing mostly house parties. During the war Jeffery moved to San Diego and teamed up with Tom Shaw for a number of years. After he started working at Camp Pendleton, music became a weekend profession until his last years.

JESSE JAMES. *See* Richard, James.

JOHNSON, ALONZO "LONNIE" (Guitar, piano, violin, vocal). Born: New Orleans, Louisiana–February 8, 1900; died: Toronto, Canada–June 16, 1970.

Alonzo Johnson studied guitar and violin as a child in his native New Orleans. During World War I he formed an act with his brother James and later played in vaudeville, working in London in 1919. His stint with Charlie Creath's band led to his settling in St. Louis, where from 1925 to 1932 he was one of the most popular artists on the Okeh label. During this period he recorded with Louis Armstrong, McKinney's Cotton Pickers, and Duke Ellington. From 1932 to 1937 Johnson made Cleveland, Ohio, his home, doing radio work and a short stint with Putney Dandridge. In 1937 he recorded for Decca and in 1939 for Bluebird. In 1940 he was in Chicago with Johnny Dodds and Jimmie Noone. "Tomorrow Night," one of the biggest hits of his career, was recorded on the King label in the late 1940s. He toured England in 1952 and was not heard from after that until 1960, when he began to record again. After working in New York and with the American Blues Festival in Europe, Johnson settled in Toronto, where he became a popular figure on the local blues and jazz scene. He never fully recuperated from injuries that resulted from being struck by a car in Toronto in 1969 and was found dead in his apartment several months later. His repertoire included ballads and pop tunes as well as the blues.

RECORDINGS

Blues and Ballads. Fantasy/OBC OBCCD–531–2
Eddie Lang and Lonnie Johnson. Swaggie 1229
Idle Hours (with Victoria Spivey). Fantasy/OBC OBC–518–2
Lonnie Johnson Sings 24 Twelve Bar Blues. King KLS–958
Losing Game. Fantasy/OBC OBCCD–543–2
Mr. Johnson's Blues. Mamlish 3807
Steppin' on the Blues. Columbia C46221
Swingin' with Lonnie. Storyville 4042

JOHNSON, HERMAN E. (Guitar, vocal). Born: Louisiana–1910.

Although Herman Johnson has been playing since 1927, he was not discovered and recorded until 1960 by Harry Oster. Twelve years later Arhoolie Records issued an LP of these recordings, *Louisiana Country Blues.* He retired from music completely in the early 1960s and was not heard from again.

RECORDING

Louisiana Country Blues. Arhoolie 1060

JOHNSON, LESLIE "LAZY LESTER" (Harmonica, guitar, drums, vocal). Born: Torras, Louisiana–June 20, 1933.

Influenced by Chicago bluesmen Jimmy Reed and Little Walter, Leslie Johnson was a self-taught musician. He first recorded in 1957 with Lightnin' Slim. From around 1957 to around 1965 he worked steadily in the recording studio, making his own records and playing behind other artists. He joined Lightnin' Slim's band in 1965–66. He then worked outside of music until 1970. In the early 1970s he moved to Chicago and continued to work in music, playing the blues at blues clubs and the blues festivals in the United States and Europe. Although there has been a recent interest in Louisiana blues, this curiosity extends more to the recordings than performances. Leslie Johnson, like so many of his blues-playing compatriots, has had to make a living outside of music since the 1970s.

RECORDINGS

Harp and Soul. Alligator 4768
Poor Boy Blues. Flyright 544
Lazy Lester. Excello 8006
Lazy Lester. Flyright FLYCD07
They Call Me Lazy. Flyright 526

JOHNSON, NOON (Tuba, bazooka, guitar). Born: New Orleans, Louisiana–August 24, 1903; died: New Orleans, Louisiana–September 18, 1969.

Noon Johnson played on the streets of Storyville for tips as a young boy. He mostly led his own trio, performing in various New Orleans honky-tonks. He was a master at playing the blues on an assortment of his uniquely designed bazookas. He played with the Tuxedo Brass Band.

JOHNSON, OLLIE "DINK" (Piano, vocal, drums). Born: Biloxi, Mississippi–October 28, 1892; died: Portland, Oregon–November 29, 1954.

"Dink" Johnson started his music career in New Orleans honky-tonks. He played drums with the Creole Orchestra in California and with his brother-in-law, Jelly Roll Morton. He also worked as a pianist with Freddie Keppard and George Baquet. He recorded for the American Music label. He spent a great part of his career playing piano and singing the blues in California.

JOHNSON, PETE (Piano). Born: Kansas City, Missouri–March 24, 1904; died: Buffalo, New York–March 23, 1967.

Pete Johnson played drums in his high school band, and in 1922 he started playing the piano. A few years later he met singer "Big Joe" Turner, who was then working as a bartender. They teamed up and were discovered by John Hammond, who presented them at his Spirituals to Swing concert in 1938. Johnson's recording career lasted from 1938 to 1946. In the late 1930s and early 1940s he did a long stint at the Cafe Society in New York.

The late 1940s found him at Central Plaza. In 1958 he played the Newport Jazz Festival and was later stricken with a heart attack from which he never fully recovered. His final public appearance was at John Hammond's Spirituals to Swing concert at Carnegie Hall on January 15, 1967.

RECORDINGS

Boogie Woogie Mood. MCA 1333
Master of Blues and Boogie Woogie. Oldie Blues 2801
Master of Blues and Boogie Woogie, Vol 2. Oldie Blues 2806
Master of Blues and Boogie Woogie, Vol. 3. Oldie Blues 2823
Pete's Blues. Savoy SJC414

BOOK

Mauerer, Hans J. *The Pete Johnson Story.* Frankfurt, Germany: Hans J. Mauerer, 1965.

JOHNSON, ROBERT (Guitar, harmonica, vocal). Born: Hazelhurst, Mississippi–ca. 1910–14; died: Greenwood, Mississippi–August 16, 1938.

Despite Robert Johnson's impact on the Muddy Waters generation, he was only about twenty-four years old when he was murdered. He avidly studied the work of Son House when he first began to play the guitar and soon became the idol of his time. From 1933 to 1935 he traveled with Walter Horton and Johnny Shines, and in November 1936 Don Law recorded him for the American Recording Corporation in San Antonio, Texas. A few months later, in June 1937, Law recorded him in Dallas, this time for Vocalion Records. The facts of Johnson's death are not clear. Rumor has it that he was stabbed or poisoned by a woman in a fit of jealousy. A fuller description of him can be found in chapter 3.

RECORDINGS

The Complete Recordings. Columbia C2K–46222
King of the Delta Blues Singers, Vol. 2. Columbia PCT–30034
Thesaurus of Classic Jazz. Columbia PCT–01654

BOOK

Charters, Samuel. *Robert Johnson.* New York: Oak Publications, 1973.

JOHNSON, TOMMY (Guitar, kazoo). Born: Terry, Mississippi–c. 1896; died: Crystal Springs, Mississippi–November 1, 1956.

Johnson started playing the guitar around 1910, after his family moved to Crystal Springs, Mississippi. From around 1916 to 1956 most of his work as a performing musician was done in Mississippi and Louisiana, sometimes solo, often with Willie Brown and Charley Patton. He recorded for Victor Records in 1928 and for Paramount in 1930. He suffered a fatal heart attack in 1956.

JONES, EDDIE "GUITAR SLIM" (Guitar, vocal). Born: Greenwood, Mississippi–December 10, 1926; died: Houston, Texas–February 7, 1959.

Eddie Jones started his career as a gospel singer. He turned to the blues early in life, and after becoming a sensation in the nightclubs of New Orleans, he made his first recordings there on October 26, 1953, for the Specialty label. He was not only a great performer, but one of the most original lyricists ever to work in the blues form. His "The Things That I Used To Do" was the best-selling record of 1954, placing number one on the *Billboard* rhythm-and-blues charts for six consecutive weeks. His life was tragically short; he was killed in a game of Russian roulette at the age of thirty-two. A fuller description of him can be found in chapter 3.

RECORDINGS

The Atco Sessions. Atlantic 81760–1
Battle of the Blues (with Earl King). Ace CHD189
Red Cadillacs and Crazy Chicks. Sundown 709–08
Sufferin' Mind. Specialty SPCD–7007
The Things That I Used to Do. Ace CHD110
The Things That I Used to Do. Specialty SPC–2120

JONES, FLOYD (Guitar, vocal). Born: Marianna, Arkansas–July 21, 1917.

Floyd Jones began recording in 1947 and eventually became a familiar figure around Chicago's South Side. In 1953 he wrote and recorded "On the Road," a song that became a favorite of Canned Heat in the early 1970s.

RECORDINGS

Elmore James, John Brim, Floyd Jones. Chess (France) 600119
Masters of the Modern Blues, Vol. 3. Testament 2214

FILM

Dark Roads. Gerry Chodkowski. 30 minutes, black and white.

JONES, MAGGIE (Vocal). Born: Hillsboro, Texas–ca. 1900; died: unknown.

By the time Maggie Jones was twenty, she was performing in the East as Faye Barnes (her maiden name). She made her first records under this name and later recorded as Maggie Jones for Paramount, Black Swan, Path/Perfect, and Columbia (for which she made thirty-four records). Around 1930 she drifted away from the music scene and was never heard of again.

JONES, RICHARD MYKNEE (Piano). Born: Donaldsonville, Louisiana–June 13, 1889; died: Chicago, Illinois–December 9, 1945.

Richard Jones started his music career as a pianist in New Orleans. He was a "professor" at some of the higher-class Basin Street bordellos as a teenager. At thirteen he played alto horn in a brass band. He led his own group at various Storyville honky-tonks from 1910 to 1920. Trumpeter King Joe Oliver worked in his band. He worked as an administrator for the Clarence Williams Publishing Company in 1919. In Chicago in 1925 he was "race" recording director for Okeh Records. He worked for Decca Records in an administrative position in the late 1930s. From around 1940 until his death he worked mostly as an arranger/composer. His many songs included "Trouble in Mind" and "Riverside Blues."

JONES, SAM (Guitar, vocal). Born: Waverly, Virginia–October 15, 1922.

Sam Jones began playing guitar when he was ten years old. He teamed up with Charity Pernell in the late 1930s and worked with him until 1944, when he abandoned the blues for the church. He then formed a band that specialized in gospel music and has played mainly around Virginia, North Carolina, and Washington, D.C.

JORDAN, LOUIS (Alto sax, vocal). Born: Brinkley, Arkansas–July 8, 1908; died: Los Angeles, California–February 4, 1975.

Louis Jordan's brand of happy, swinging jump blues made him a major figure in the early years of rhythm-and-blues. He learned music from his father and made his professional debut with the Rabbit Foot Minstrels in the late 1920s. He worked in Philadelphia in 1930 and a few years later was in New York with Chick Webb. Webb got him a date with Decca Records, and soon Jordan and his combo, the Tympany Five, were national hit makers. His association with Decca lasted until 1951. In 1953 he moved to Aladdin Records, then later to Mercury, Tangerine, and other labels. Some of his hits were "Saturday Night Fish Fry," "Choo Choo Choo Boogie," "Ain't Nobody Here But Us Chickens," and "Gonna Move on the Outskirts of Town." His last recordings were on Johnny Otis's Blues Spectrum label and the French Black and Blue Records.

RECORDINGS

And His Tympany Five. Circle LP53
Beat Petite and Gone. Krazy Kat 7414
The Best of Louis Jordan. MCA MCAD4079
Cole Slaw. Jukebox Lil605
G.I. Jive. Jukebox Lil602
Greatest Hits, Vol. 2. MCA 1337
I Believe in Music. Black and Blue 59.052–2
Live Jive. A Touch of Magic Atom 4
Look Out Sister. Krazy Kat 7415
Rock and Roll Call. Bear Family BFX 15257
Rockin' and Jivin'. Bear Family BFX 15207
Somebody Done Hoodooed the Hoodoo Man. Jukebox Lil691
The V-Discs. Official 6061

FILMS

Louis Jordan: Five Guys Named Moe. Jazz Classics Video JCVC 2004. 56 minutes, black and white.
Louis Jordan: 1941–1945. Jazz Classics Video JCVC 105. Black and white.

JOSEPH, PLEASANT "COUSIN JOE" (Piano, guitar, vocal). Born: Wallace, Louisiana–December 21, 1907; died: unknown.

Cousin Joe received most of his formative training in the nightspots of New Orleans. After going to New York to replace one of the Ink Spots (a gig that never materialized), he was heard and recorded by Leonard Feather. While he was in New York, he either worked or recorded with Billy Holiday, Mezz Mezzrow, Leonard Feather, Sammy Price, Dickey Wells, Pete Brown, and Sidney Bechet. His recordings can be found on King, Gotham, Savoy, Signature, Imperial, Decca, and DeLuxe Records. In 1964 he toured Europe with George Wein and in 1971 did another five-week tour that included France, Belgium, Spain, and Switzerland. Though still based in New Orleans, Cousin Joe played club dates and festivals all over Europe and America during the 1970s and 1980s.

RECORDINGS

Bad Luck Blues. Black and Blue 33.549
In His Prime. Oldie Blues 8008
Relaxin' in New Orleans. Great Southern GS 11011

K-DOE, ERNIE (ERNEST KADOR, JR.) (Vocal). Born: New Orleans, Louisiana–February 22, 1936.

Ernie K-Doe sang with gospel groups, the Moonglows, the Flamingos, and the Blue Diamonds. He made solo records on Specialty, Herald, and Minit. His song "Mother-in-Law," which was produced by Allen Toussaint, was a number one hit in 1961 both on rhythm-and-blues and popular charts. After a handful of singles on small labels, he settled in New Orleans to work outside of music, although he still performed at local venues on occasion. His music has been a part-time endeavor during the 1980s and early 1990s.

KELLEY, ARTHUR "GUITAR" (Guitar, vocal). Born: Clinton, Louisiana–November 14, 1924.

Arthur Kelley's guitar-playing and singing style are deeply rooted in the traditional Louisiana blues genre. He was playing the guitar by the time he was fourteen years old and worked frequently with Lightnin' Slim and Silas Hogan. He has been based in the Baton Rouge area all of his life and recorded there for Arhoolie/Excello in 1970.

KENNER, CHRIS (Vocal). Born: New Orleans, Louisiana–1930; died: New Orleans, Louisiana–1976.

Chris Kenner never quite made it into the big time, although two of his songs, "I Like It Like That" and "Land of a Thousand Dances," were national successes. Locally he had hits with "Something You Got," "Packin' Up," and "Sick And Tired." His last years were filled with problems, some related to health, and he was unable to do much performing or recording.

RECORDINGS
Golden Classics: I Like It Like That. Collectables COLCD–5166
I Like It Like That. Charly CD230.

KIMBALL, JEANNETTE (Piano). Born: New Orleans, Louisiana–December 18, 1908; died: ca. 1985

Jeannette Kimball's entire musical career was spent in New Orleans, most of it as a pianist in trumpeter Oscar "Papa" Celestin's band. She recorded with Papa Celestin in 1926 and again in 1954 for Southland Records. She experienced sporadic activity during the 1960s and 1970s. She worked with the New Orleans Band in 1982.

KING, ALBERT (Guitar, vocal). Born: Indianola, Mississippi–April 25, 1923; died: Memphis, Tennessee–December 21, 1992.

Albert King claimed to be a cousin of B. B. King. He taught himself to play guitar by listening to recordings of T-Bone Walker and Blind Lemon Jefferson. In December 1953 he made his first records in Chicago on the Parrot label. For three years, from 1959 to early 1962, he recorded on the Bobbin label in St. Louis. He also did quite a bit of work for King Records in 1962 and Coun-tree Records in 1965. The year 1966 marked the beginning of a long and fruitful association with Stax Records of Memphis, Tennessee. For the rest of his life he enjoyed the glamour of exposure due to steady and lucrative dates. His hit records include "Born under a Bad Sign," "Laundromat Blues," and "Crosscut Saw."

RECORDINGS
Albert King. Tomato 269625–2
Albert Live. Charly CD136
The Best of Albert King. Stax CD60–005
King of the Blues Guitar. Atlantic 8213–2
Live Wire/Blues Power. Stax SCD–4128
New Orleans Heat. Tomato 269633–2
Truckload of Lovin'. Tomato 269631–2

KING, B. B. *See* King, Riley B.

KING, EARL (Guitar). Born: New Orleans, Louisiana–February 7, 1934.

One of the master singer/songwriter/guitarists from the New Orleans area, Earl King has written for or worked with just about everyone on the city's music scene. Some of the hit songs he recorded himself include "Those Lonely, Lonely Nights," "Trick Bag," and "Mama and Papa." King continues to be a mainstay in New Orleans blues venues and spends much time working and recording songs for other singers.

RECORDINGS
Glazed. Black Top 1035
Let the Good Times Roll. Ace CH–15
Sexual Telepathy. Black Top CD–BT–1052
Street Parade. Charly CD232

KING, FREDDIE (Guitar, vocal). Born: Gilmer, Texas–September 30, 1934; died: Dallas, Texas–December 28, 1976.

Freddie King cut his first two sides in Chicago in 1956. From 1969 until his switch to the Cotillion label (when the spelling of his first name changed from "Freddy" to "Freddie"), he recorded for Federal in Cincinnati. His first album on the Cotillion label, *Freddie King Is a Blues Master*, was produced by saxist King Curtis.

RECORDINGS
The Best of Freddie King. Shelter SRZ–8010
Freddie King Sings. Modern Blues MBLP 722
Getting Ready. Shelter CD8003
Just Pickin'. Modern Blues MBXLCD–721
Larger Than Life. Polydor 831816–1
Let's Hideaway and Dance Away. King KCD–773
1934–76. Polydor 831817–1
17 Original Great Hits. Deluxe CDC–7845

KING, RILEY B. "B. B." (Guitar, vocal). Born: Indianola, Mississippi–November 16, 1925.

From the time Riley King's mother died, when he was only eight years old, to his fourteenth year, when his father found him and insisted that he live with an aunt, King supported himself as would an adult. He worked in the cotton fields and attended school only when the weather was not fit to work the crops. He earned fifteen dollars a month, and by the time he was twelve he owned a mule and a plow. King learned to play guitar by watching a cousin, a preacher who used that instrument in his church. He became the "Beale Street Blues Boy" during his three-and-a-half-year stint with radio station WDIA in Memphis. In 1945 he recorded his first four sides on the Bullet label.

In 1946 he switched to RPM Records and stayed with them for twelve years. In 1952 he recorded "Three O'Clock Blues" and "You Know I Love You." "Please Love Me" made the top ten in 1953. "Everyday I Have the Blues," recorded in 1955, also made the charts. He cut the song again in 1959 with a Kansas City–type big band employing the electric bass in place of the large, cumbersome acoustical one. That year he also did an album of gospel songs backed by the Charioteers vocal group and a church rhythm section. In 1960 he had three records that were top sellers: "Sweet Sixteen," "Partin' Time," and "I Got a Right to Love My Baby." In March 1962 he cut his first of more than fifty songs for ABC/Bluesway. The album *Live at the Regal*, recorded in 1964, is considered the most representative of his genius.

The entire 1970s were good years for King. He played most of the major festivals, had a number of hit albums on the market (including two double-record sets with Bobby Bland), and was continually featured in top clubs in both the United States and Europe. In the 1980s his career continued to accelerate. He was the subject of feature articles in major music magazines and performed an average of three hundred days a year, which was more than he had ever done in his career before then. A few of his album releases in the 1980s were *The Best of, Vol. 1*, *Blues n' Jazz/The Electric B. B.* (1987), *Indianola Mississippi Seeds* (1989), *King of the Blues* (1989), *Six Silver Strings* (1985), and *Spotlight on Lucille* (1987).

The 1990s find him going stronger than ever. He continues to average three hundred performances a year, and the output of his recorded work is staggering. Some of the albums that have been released so far include *The Best of B. B. King, Vol. 1* (1991), *Live at the Regal* (1991), *Live at San Quentin* (1990), *Lucille* (1992), *There Is Always One More Time* (1991), and *To Know You Is to Love You* (1991).

RECORDINGS

Across the Tracks. Ace CHD–230
Ambassador of the Blues. Crown GEMC–001
Back in the Alley. MCA MCAD–27010
The Best of B. B. King. Ace OH–30
The Best of B. B. King. MCA MCAD–31040
Blues Is King. MCA MCA31368
Blues n' Jazz. MCA MCAC–27119
Blues n' Jazz/The Electric B. B. MCA MCAD–5881
Completely Well. MCA MCAD–31039
Do the Boogie! Ace CDCH916
Great Moments. MCA 2–4424
Guess Who. MCA MCAC–10351
Indianola Mississippi Seeds. MCA MCAC–10351
In London. BGO BGOCD42
King of the Blues Guitar. Ace CH–152
Live and Well. MCA MCAC–27008
Live at the Apollo. GRP GRD–9637
Live at Cook County Jail. MCA MCAD–31080
Live at Newport (with Muddy Waters and Big Mama Thornton). Intermedia QSC–5022
Live at the Regal. Mobile Fidelity UDCD–01
Live at San Quentin. MCA 6455
Love Me Tender. MCA 886
Lucille. MCA MCAD–10518
The Memphis Masters. Ace CH–50
Midnight Believer. MCA MCAD–27011
One Nighter Blues. Ace CHD–201

Rock Me Baby. Ace CH–119
Six Silver Strings. MCA MCAD–5616
Spotlight on Lucille. Ace CH–30
Spotlight on Lucille. Flair V21Y–86231
There Is Always One More Time. MCA MCAD–10295
There Must Be a Better World Somewhere. MCA MCAD–27034
Together Again (with Bobby Bland). MCA MCAC–27012
Together for the First Time, Live (with Bobby Bland). MCA2–4160
To Know You Is to Love You. MCA MCAD–10414

BOOK

Sawyer, Charles. *The Arrival of B. B. King: The Authorized Biography*. Garden City, N.Y.: Doubleday, 1980.

FILMS

Blues Master. DCI Music Video. 3 vols. 65 to 85 minutes each, color.
Live in Africa, 1974. BMG Video 791010. Color.

KNOWLING, RANSOM (Bass). Born: New Orleans, Louisiana—1911; died: Chicago, Illinois—October 22, 1968.

Ransom Knowling worked with Sidney Desvignes's band on the Strekfus Line steamers and made his first recording in 1928. He moved to Chicago in 1938, and there he worked and recorded with such blues greats as Washboard Sam, Tampa Red, Big Bill Broonzy, Big Joe Williams, Arthur Crudup (with whom he made his last recording date for Delmark Records in July 1968), and many others. He was also a regular with the Harlem Hamfats and singer Lil Green's band. In 1964 he toured Europe with a blues package.

LACY, REV. RUBIN (Guitar, mandolin, vocal). Born: Pelahatchie, Mississippi—January 2, 1901; died: Bakersfield, California—1972.

In the 1920s Rubin Lacy moved to Jackson, Mississippi, and became one of the main figures on the blues scene there, playing with people like Tommy Johnson, Charlie McCoy, and Jimmie Rodgers. In 1927 he settled briefly in Yazoo City and then moved to Etta Bena and then to Greenwood. Under the production skills of record talent scout Ralph Lembo, Lacy recorded four blues songs for Columbia Records on December 9, 1927; none was issued. In March 1928 he and Lembo went to Chicago, where Lacy recorded "Mississippi Jail House Groan" and "Ham Hound Crave" for Paramount Records. Lacy continued to play in the Delta until 1932 when a near-fatal accident moved him to give up the blues and become a minister.

LATIMORE, BENNY (Piano, melodica, vocal). Born: Charleston, Tennessee—September 1939.

Benny Latimore's blues roots were firmly established during his early years in Tennessee. His style is smooth and sophisticated and embraces more than a touch of passion. He started singing while in college with a vocal group called the Neptunes. After dropping out of school, he started playing with Louie Brooks and stayed with him for two years. In 1961 he went on tour with Joe Henderson of "Snap Your Fingers" fame. He settled in Miami, Florida, in the mid–1960s and has had an uphill climb ever since. His recordings, "Let's Straighten It Out" and "There's a Red-Neck in the Soul Band," were nationwide hits in the early 1980s. He was not very active in the late 1980s and early 1990s.

RECORDINGS
Everyway But Wrong. Malaco MAL–7436–C
Good Time Man. Malaco MAL–7423–C
I'll Do Anything for You. Malaco MAL–7414–C
Singing in the Key of Love. Malaco MAL–7409–C
Slow Down. Malaco MAL–7443–CD

LAZY LESTER. *See* Johnson, Leslie.

LEADBELLY. *See* Ledbetter, Huddie William.

LEDBETTER, HUDDIE WILLIAM "LEADBELLY" (Guitar, mandolin, vocal). Born: Mooringsport, Louisiana–January 29, 1889; died: New York–December 6, 1949.

Leadbelly was seven years old when his uncle gave him his first instrument, a windjammer (accordion). He learned to play the guitar by listening to his father and two uncles. From 1918 to 1925 he did time in a Louisiana penitentiary for murder, and from February 1930 to August 1934 he was held in a Texas jail for attempted homicide. His first recording date was for Columbia Records in 1935. John Lomax arranged for him to make a series of recordings for the archives of the Library of Congress, and in 1941 he also did some recordings for Moe Asch on the Asch and Stinson labels. "Midnight Special" is considered one of his most moving and exciting compositions. He made numerous recordings for Asch, Capitol, Disc, Columbia, Folkways, Stinson, Musicraft, and Victor. More description of him can be found in Chapter 3.

RECORDINGS
Alabama Bound. RCA 9600–2
Defense Blues. Collectables COlCD–5196
Golden Classics. Collectables COlCD–5183
Huddie Ledbetter's Best. Capitol 92075.2
King of the 12-String Guitar. Columbia/Legacy CT–46776
Leadbelly. Columbia CK30035
Sings Folk Songs (with Woody Guthrie, Cisco Houston, and Sonny Terry). Smithsonian/Folkways CDSF–40010

BOOKS

Asch, M., and A. Lomax. *The Leadbelly Songbook*. New York: Oak Publications, 1962.

Garvin, Richard M., and Edmond G. Addeo. *The Midnight Special: The Legend of Leadbelly*. New York: Bernard Geis Associates, 1981.

FILM

Leadbelly: Three Songs. Film Images. 8 minutes, color.

LEE, JOHN ARTHUR (Guitar, vocal). Born: Mount Willing, Alabama–May 24, 1915; died: unknown.

By the time that John Lee was in his early teens, he was playing at Saturday night fish fries and dances in his hometown. In 1951 Ralph Bass of Federal Records recorded five tracks of his work; four were released without much success. Lee continued to play regularly until 1955, when he dropped from the music scene for about sixteen years. In 1973 he recorded for Rounder Records, and he appeared at the National Folk Festival at Wolftrap, Virginia, in August 1974.

RECORDING

Down at the Depot. Rounder 2010

LEE, JULIA (Piano). Born: Boonville, Missouri–October 13, 1903; died: Kansas City, Missouri–December 8, 1958.

Julia Lee began singing at the age of four and started taking piano lessons when she was nine years old. She also studied piano in college and started playing music professionally around 1920 in Kansas City, Missouri. She worked mostly out of that city throughout her career. Lee worked with the George E. Lee Novelty Singing Orchestra through the late 1920s and with jazz trumpeter Bunk Johnson in 1931. She worked as a single at Milton's Taproom from 1933 to 1948. In 1939 she performed with jazz drummer Baby Dodds and recorded with Jay McShann and his Kansas City Stompers for Capitol Records in 1944. In 1948 she did a command performance for President Harry Truman at the White House. Lee did frequent jobs outside Kansas City, performing and recording from 1948 to 1957. She suffered a fatal heart attack in 1958.

LEWIS, SMILEY (Piano, vocal). Born: Union, Louisiana–July 5, 1920; died: New Orleans, Louisiana–October 7, 1966.

Smiley Lewis was among the very best of the rhythm-and-blues singers of 1950s New Orleans. His recordings can be found on Deluxe, Imperial, Loma, Okeh, and Dot. Except for tours along the Gulf Coast, Lewis worked mainly in New Orleans, and his influence can still be heard there today.

RECORDINGS

Caledonia's Party. KC 103
Down Yonder. KC 104
Hook, Line, and Sinker. KC 102

New Orleans Bounce. Sequel NEXCD 130
Volume 1. KC CD01
Volume 2. KC CD02

LEWIS, STEVE (Piano). Born: New Orleans, Louisiana–March 19, 1896; died: New Orleans, Louisiana–1939.

Steve Lewis was an established Basin Street "professor" in the Storyville district of New Orleans. He did a vaudeville tour with Billy Mack's company in 1917. He joined the A. J. Piron Orchestra in 1918 and played the calliope on the riverboat SS *Capitol* around 1919. He composed "Purple Rose of Cairo," "Kiss Me, Sweet," and "Sud Bustin' Blues." Lewis recorded with A. J. Piron and made a piano roll of "Mama's Gone Goodbye." He also accompanied New Orleans Willie Jackson on sides for Columbia records in 1926.

LEWIS, WALTER "FURRY" (Guitar, harmonica, vocal). Born: Greenwood, Mississippi–March 6, 1893; died: unknown.

Walter "Furry" Lewis started playing the blues on a homemade guitar when he was six years old. He worked in medicine shows in the early 1900s. Lewis suffered the loss of his leg in a train accident in 1916. He performed in the Memphis area throughout the 1920s, recording for Vocalion Records in 1927. Lewis did further recordings on various labels, including Victor, Folkways, Prestige/Bluesville, Rounder, Sire–Blue Horizon, Adelphi, Ampex, and Biograph/Matchbox. He also appeared in a number of films, such as *The Blues* (1963), *Blues under the Skin* (1972), and *Out of the Blacks into the Blues* (1972). Lewis stayed active musically, playing festivals and concert dates up to the time of his death.

RECORDINGS
Done Changed My Mind. Ace CH260
In His Prime (1927–28). Yazoo CD–1050

FILM
Furry Lewis. Seattle Folklore Society. 25 minutes, black and white.

LIGHTFOOT, "PAPA" GEORGE (Harmonica, vocal). Born: Natchez, Mississippi–March 2, 1924; died: Natchez, Mississippi–November 28, 1971.

Popularly known as Papa George in his hometown, George Lightfoot did most of his recordings in the early 1950s for King, Savoy, Sultan, Imperial, Peacock, and other labels. He also toured with the Horace Heidt band in the early 1950s. His last public appearance of some substance was at the 1970 Ann Arbor Blues Festival, where he played with his old friend Big Joe Turner.

RECORDING
Natchez Trace. Crosscut CCR1001

LIGHTNIN' SLIM. *See* Hicks, Otis.

LIPSCOMB, MANCE (Guitar, vocal). Born: Navasota, Texas–April 9, 1895; died: Navasota, Texas–January 30, 1976.

The son of a fiddle player who had been born a slave, Mance Lipscomb spent most of his life in and around Navasota, where from the age of eleven he farmed lands as a sharecropper. At fourteen he took up the guitar, and within a few years he was playing at house parties, dances, and other types of entertainment in the Brazos Valley region. He was discovered and first recorded in 1960 by Mack McCormick and Arhoolie Records owner Chris Strachwitz, by whose company most of Lipscomb's recordings have been issued. Over the last decade and a half of his life, he appeared at numerous festivals, at club and concert dates, and on a forty-four-minute film, *A Well Spent Life,* by Les Blank.

RECORDINGS

Texas Blues. Arhoolie 1049
Texas Songster. Arhoolie CD306
Texas Songster and Sharecropper. Arhoolie 1001, 1023, 1026, 1033, 1069
You'll Never Find Another Man like Mance. Arhoolie 1077

FILMS

Mance Lipscomb. Seattle Folklore Society. 25 minutes, black and white.
Mance Lipscomb: A Well Spent Life. Kay Jazz Video 055. 44 minutes, color.
Mance Lipscomb and Lightnin' Hopkins: Masters of the Country Blues. Yazoo Video 000502. 60 minutes, color.

LISTON, VIRGINIA (Vocal). Born: ca. 1890; died: St. Louis, Missouri–June 1932.

Virginia Liston cut her first record on September 14, 1923, and her last on May 26, 1962. "Rolls Royce Papa" and "I'm Gonna Get a Man, That's All" contain excellent, down-home singing.

LITTLE BROTHER. *See* Montgomery, Eurreal Wilford.

LITTLE MILTON. *See* Campbell, Milton.

LITTLE RICHARD. *See* Penniman, Richard.

LITTLE WALTER. *See* Jacobs, Marion Walter.

LITTLE WILLIE JOHN. *See* Davenport, John.

LITTLEJOHN, JOHN (Guitar, vocal). Born: Lake, Mississippi–April 16, 1931; died: Chicago, Illinois—February 1, 1994.

Born John Funchess, Littlejohn taught himself to play the guitar when he was around nine years years old. He performed professionally around Mississippi throughout the 1940s. He recorded for Ace Records in New Orleans in 1951. He moved to Chicago around 1953 and worked mostly outside of the music industry until the early 1970s. He was very active musically in the 1970s, 1980s, and early 1990s. Even though he was based in Chicago, he played blues venues around the world. Littlejohn is among the new generation of Chicago blues musicians. In his work he has successfully incorporated the Delta bottleneck style with the complexities of modern harmony, creating a sound that is totally his own. He recorded his debut album, *John Littlejohn's Chicago Blues Stars,* for Arhoolie Records in the summer of 1969. The album was produced by Chris Strachwitz and Willie Dixon. Rooster Blues Records released *So-called Friends* in 1986, with Eddie Taylor and Lafayette Leake as sideman. In March 1992 Arhoolie Records reissued the *Chicago Blues Stars* album.

RECORDINGS

Chicago Blues. Arhoolie (Japan) PCD2107
Chicago Blues Stars. Arhoolie 1043
John Littlejohn's Blues. Wolf 120859CD
So-called Friends. Rooster Blues 2621

LOCKWOOD, ROBERT, JR. (Guitar, vocal). Born: Marvell, Arkansas–March 27, 1915.

Robert Lockwood was taught to play the guitar by Robert Johnson. He moved to Chicago early in his career, and after a few years of leading his own group he recorded for the Mercury label. He worked with Sonny Boy Williamson (Rice Miller) in 1936, 1944, and 1945. He later earned a living as a studio musician for Chess Records, working with the likes of Muddy Waters, Little Walter, and the Moonglows and on Freddie King's first session. *Steady Rollin' Man,* Lockwood's first LP, was released on Delmark Records and was placed on the market again in April 1988 on CD by the same company.

RECORDINGS

The Baddest New Guitar. P-Vine PCD2134
Dust My Broom (with Johnny Shines). Flyright 563
Hangin' On (with Johnny Shines). Rounder CS–2023
Mr. Blues Is Back to Stay (with Johnny Shines). Rounder 2026
Plays Robert and Robert. Black and Blue 33.740
Steady Rollin' Man. Delmark DC–630

LOFTON, "CRIPPLE" CLARENCE (Piano). Born: Kingsport, Tennessee–March 28, 1890; died: Chicago, Illinois–January 9, 1957.

Little is known of Clarence Lofton's personal history except that he spent most of his life in Chicago. During the 1920s and 1930s he ran a club called the Big Apple in that city. His most famous composition was "Strut That Thing," which was later called "I Don't Know."

RECORDINGS
Clarence's Blues. Oldie Blues 2817
Cripple Clarence Lofton/Meade Lux Lewis. Euphonic 1208
Cripple Clarence Lofton/Walter Davis. YAZLP 1025

LONDON, MELVIN R. (Songwriter, publisher, producer). Born: Mississippi–April 9, 1932; died: Chicago, Illinois–May 16, 1975.

One of Chicago's leading blues producers of the 1950s and 1960s, Mel London was responsible for some of the finest records ever made by Elmore James, Junior Wells, Earl Hooker, Lillian Offitt, and Magic Sam. His business ventures led to his owning five record labels (Chief, All Points, Mel, Age, and Mel-Lon), and some of his popular tunes are "Cut You A-Loose," "Messing with the Kid," "Little by Little," and "Will My Man Be Home Tonight?" In spite of his involvement in the music business, Mel spent his last years clerking and driving a truck for United Records Distributors and Ernie's One-Stop.

LONESOME SUNDOWN. *See* Green, Cornelius.

LOUISIANA RED. *See* Minter, Iverson.

LUANDREW, ALBERT "SUNNYLAND SLIM" (Piano, vocal). Born: Vance, Mississippi–September 5, 1907; died: unknown.

A key figure in the Chicago blues world for over three decades, "Sunnyland Slim" Luandrew's contribution to the blues piano tradition is an exceptional one. By the time he was in his teens, he was playing professionally at juke joints and taverns around Vance for fifty cents a night. He went on the road in 1923 and after two years decided to settle down in Memphis, Tennessee. He lived in Memphis from 1925 to 1942, working with the likes of "Memphis Minnie" McCoy, Big Walter Horton, Blind Boy Fuller, and Robert Johnson. In 1942 he moved to Chicago, where he made his first recordings as a featured vocalist for Victor Records in 1947. He continued to record during the 1940s and 1950s, establishing himself as one of the leading blues pianists of the postwar Chicago school and becoming part of a group that included Otis Spann, Jimmy Walker, and Johnny Jones. Sunnyland Slim was still active as a pianist in Chicago in the early 1980s.

RECORDINGS
Chicago Jump. Red Beans 007
Sad and Lonesome Blues. Storyville 4043
Slim's Shout. Prestige 7723
Sunnyland Slim. Flyright 566
Sunnyland Train. Red Beans 002
Travelin'. Black and Blue 33.743

FILM
Sunnyland Slim. Moviemakers Company. 12 minutes, color.

MABON, WILLIE (Piano, harmonica, vocal). Born: Hollywood, Tennessee–October 24, 1925.

Willie Mabon taught himself to play the piano when he was sixteen years old. It was not until 1942, after he had moved to Chicago with his parents, that he started taking formal music lessons. He formed his own band, the Blues Rockers, and worked in Chicago nightspots from 1947 to the early 1950s. His composition "I Don't Know" put him on the rhythm-and-blues map. He remained very busy playing and recording his smooth, sophisticated songs in and around Chicago through the 1950s and 1960s. The early and mid–1970s found him in Europe, where he performed regularly on stage and for recordings. In the late 1970s he was back in Chicago. Some of the record labels on which he can be found are Apollo, Chess, Aristocrat, Federal, Black and Blue (France), American (France), Mad, USA, Antilles, Sirens, Big Bear (England), and Esceha (West Germany). He was not active in the 1980s.

RECORDINGS
Chicago Blues Session. L & R 42003
I'm the Fixer. Flyright 580
The Seventh Son. Crown Prince 402
Willie Mabon. Chess 9189

MACON, JOHN WESLEY "MR. SHORTSTUFF" (Guitar, vocal). Born: Crawford, Mississippi–1923; died: Macon, Mississippi–December 28, 1973.

A cousin of Big Joe Williams, John Wesley Macon recorded for Spivey and Folkways/Xtra Records in 1964. He worked with Big Joe Williams sporadically from 1964 to the early 1970s.

MAGHETT, SAMUEL "MAGIC SAM" (Guitar, vocal). Born: Granada, Mississippi–February 14, 1937; died: Chicago, Illinois–December 1, 1969.

An excellent guitarist and singer, Sam Maghett learned to play the guitar in Granada, Mississippi, his hometown for a little over thirteen years. He turned professional in Chicago in 1955 and performed regularly in blues spots on the South and West sides from that time. His first recordings were made for the Cobra label in 1957–58. Throughout 1960–61 he worked with Chief Records. In the late 1960s he recorded two albums for the Delmark label, *West Side Soul* and *Black Magic.* He appeared in concerts, festivals, and clubs throughout the United States, and in October 1969 he toured Europe with the American Folk Blues Festival.

RECORDINGS
Black Magic. Delmark 620
Calling All Blues. Charly CRB 1134
The Late, Great Magic Sam. L & R 42014

Out of Bad Luck. P-Vine PCD 2123
West Side Soul. Delmark 615

MAGIC SAM. *See* Maghett, Samuel.

MAHAL, TAJ (HENRY FREDRICKS) (Harmonica, piano, vocal). Born: New York City–May 17, 1942.

Taj Mahal learned to play the guitar when he was fifteen years old. He performed around Boston during the mid–1960s. He moved to Los Angeles in 1965. He spent the remainder of the 1960s working around the Los Angeles area. Although he performed a good deal in Europe throughout the 1970s, 1980s, and early 1990s, he also worked often in the United States. He composed the soundtrack for the film *Sounder* in 1972. During this time he recorded for Columbia Records. Additionally, he worked as an actor, appearing in *Play It Again, Sam* (1975), *Sounder* (1972), and *Scott Joplin* (1976). He is currently still very active professionally as an actor, blues historian, movie-music composer, and musician. Although his talents are spread out in many different directions, he is still first of all a bluesman. His album releases in the 1990s have included CDs on Mobile Fidelity, Private Music, and Columbia/Legacy.

RECORDINGS

The Best of, Vol. 1. Columbia CK–36258
Big Blues. Essential ESMCD002
The Collection. Castle Communications CCSCD 180
Giant Step/Ole Folks at Home. Columbia CGT–00018
Happy to Be Just Like I Am. Mobile Fidelity MFCD–10–00765
Like Never Before. Private Music 2081–2–P
Mo' Roots. Columbia PCT–33051
Natch'l Blues. Columbia PCT–09698
OOOh So Good n' Blues. Columbia PCT–32600
The Real Thing. Columbia CGT–30619
Recycling the Blues and Other Stuff. Columbia PCT–31605
Taj's Blues. Columbia/Legacy CT–52465

FILM

That's All. PBS Video. 29 Minutes, color.

MARS, JOHNNY (Harmonica, vocal). Born: South Carolina–December 7, 1942.

Johnny Mars got his first harp at the age of twelve. He names Sonny Boy Williamson (Rice Miller), Junior Parker, Junior Wells, and Little Walter as his greatest influences. He recorded for Mercury in 1967, and between 1968 and 1971 he worked with his own group, the Blue Flames. He also toured with Magic Sam. In 1972 he decided to make his home in London, England, and recorded the album *Blues from Mars*, on the Polydor label while living there. Not much has been heard from Mars in the 1980s and the early 1990s.

MARTIN, SARA (Vocal). Born: Louisville, Kentucky–June 18, 1884; died: Louisville, Kentucky–May 24, 1955.

Sara Martin had a very big reputation throughout the 1920s. Although her recordings were a little less than exciting, on stage she was superb and was able to hold her audience in the palm of her hand. The records she made with King Joe Oliver did very well commercially. She also recorded with Clarence Williams, Fats Waller, and Sylvester Weaver. In the early 1920s she toured the TOBA circuit with W. C. Handy and Fats Waller. Some of the stage shows she was a part of included *Jump Steady* (1922), *Get Happy Follies* (1928), and *Sun-Tan Frolics* (1929).

RECORDING

1922–1928. Best of the Blues BOB19

MAYFIELD, PERCY (Piano, vocal). Born: Minden, Louisiana–August 12, 1920.

Percy Mayfield hit number one on the rhythm-and-blues charts in 1951 with his blues ballad, "Please Send Me Someone to Love," recorded for Art Rupe on the Specialty label. Other hits followed on Specialty, but by the mid–1960s he was best known as a songwriter. He recorded some high-quality blues albums for Tangerine Records in 1963 and RCA in 1970. Other labels he recorded on are Supreme, Specialty, Chess, Imperial, Cash, Victor, and Atlantic. His CD *Poet of the Blues* was released in August 1990 on the Specialty label.

RECORDINGS

The Best of. Specialty 2126
For Collectors Only. Specialty 7000
Hit the Road Again. Timeless STP170
Live. Winner Winner–445
My Heart Is Always Singing Sad Songs. Ace CHD–153
Please Send Me Someone to Love. Intermedia QSC–5010
Poet of the Blues. Specialty SPCD–7001

FILM

Poet Laureate of the Blues. Rhapsody Films. 30 minutes, color.

MAYS, CURLEY (Guitar, vocal). Born: Maxie, Louisiana–November 26, 1938.

Curley Mays was brought up in Beaumont, Texas, where, inspired by the success of his uncle, Gatemouth Brown, he started playing guitar at the age of fourteen. By 1958 he had moved to Dallas, where he worked with a number of big-name stars, including Jerry Butler. In 1959 he joined Etta James's band in Los Angeles and stayed with her until 1963. From 1963 to 1966 he worked with James Brown, Little Willie John, L. C. Robinson, and Tina Turner. He also played in Las Vegas and Montreal, Canada, during the 1970s. Mays is reported to have fronted his own band in San Antonio, Texas, during the 1980s. Little has been heard from him recently.

McCAIN, JERRY (Harmonica, guitar, trumpet, vocal). Born: Gadsden, Alabama–June 19, 1930.

Jerry McCain is an Alabama bluesman whose down-home music gained him local prominence during the 1960s. In spite of excellent recordings for a number of labels, including Excello, Rex, Okeh, RIC, Continental, Jewel, and Royal American, he has yet to receive nationwide acceptance. He had two albums released on the Wild Dog Blues label in the early 1900s, *Love Desperado* (June 1991) and *Struttin' My Stuff* (June 1992).

RECORDINGS

Blues 'n Stuff. Ichiban 1047
Choo Choo Rock. White Label 9966
Love Desperado. Wild Dog Blues ICH–9008
Struttin' My Stuff. Wild Dog Blues ICH–9020–CD

McCOY, VIOLA (Vocal, kazoo). Born: Memphis, Tennessee–ca. 1900; died: Albany, New York–ca. 1956.

Possessing a lovely contralto voice and exquisite diction, Viola McCoy was also gifted with a strong jazz influence. This led to her recording with the Fletcher Henderson Orchestra in 1927. She recorded prolifically for three years, and because of her high musical standards, she always made records of excellent quality. Some of the many revues and musical comedies in which she appeared were *Moonshine* (1922), *Frolickers* (1923), *Hidden Treasure* (1924), *Rarin' to Go* (1927), *Brownskin Brevities* (1928), *Hop Off* (1929), *At the Barbeque* (1930), *Sweet Papa Garbage* (1931), *Plenty of It* (1932), and *Walking on Air* (1934). From 1923 to 1926 she recorded for Gennett, Columbia, Pathe, Ajax, Brunswick, Cameo, and Banner Records.

McDANIEL, ELLAS "BO DIDDLEY" (Guitar, harmonica, vocal). Born: McComb, Mississippi–December 30, 1928.

Ellas McDaniel's first recording, "I'm a Man," was released on the Checker label. It was this song that skyrocketed him to fame on the "race" market. Some of his other hits included "Cops and Robbers," "Bo Meets the Monster," and "Hey! Bo Diddley." Because of the public's recent interest in the blues, McDaniel has enjoyed exposure throughout the United States and the world.

RECORDINGS
Bo Diddley. Chess CHC–9194
Bo Diddley/Go Bo Diddley. Chess CHD–5904
Bo Diddley Is a Gunslinger. Chess CHD–9285
The Chess Box. Chess CHD2–19502
Diddley Daddy. Chess CDRED2
Hey! Bo Diddley. Instant CDINS5038
His Greatest Sides, Vol. 1. Chess CHC–9106
In the Spotlight. Chess CHD–9264
London Sessions. Chess CDRED21
Oh Yeah! Chess CDRED31
Rare and Well Done. Chess CHD–9331
Super Blues (with Muddy Waters and Little Walter). Chess CHC–9168
The Super Blues Band (with Muddy Waters and Howlin' Wolf). Chess CHC–9169
Two Great Guitars (with Chuck Berry). Chess CHC–9170

McDOWELL, "MISSISSIPPI" FRED (Guitar, vocal). Born: Rossville, Tennessee–January 12, 1904; died: Memphis, Tennessee–July 3, 1972.

Fred McDowell made his first recordings in 1959 for Alan Lomax. He toured Europe in 1965 and 1969 and worked a number of clubs and festivals, including the Ann Arbor Blues Festival in 1969 and 1970. His song "You've Got to Move" was recorded by the Rolling Stones. His material included gospel as well as the blues, and his work may be heard on Atlantic, Arhoolie, Vanguard, Capitol, Prestige, and Testament Records.

RECORDINGS
Long Way from Home. Fantasy/OBC OBC–535
Mississippi Delta Blues. ARHCD304
Mississippi Fred McDowell. Heritage 302
Standing on the Burying Ground. Red Lightnin' 0053
With Blues Boys. Arhoolie 1046

FILM
Fred McDowell. Seattle Folklore Society. 15 minutes, black and white.

McGHEE, BROWNIE (Guitar, vocal, banjo, kazoo). Born: Knoxville, Tennessee–November 30, 1915.

Brownie McGhee's father, a guitarist and singer, taught him to play the guitar. McGhee has a lame right leg that is the result of an attack of polio in his early years. While he was in his teens, he formed a string band that featured two washboards. He teamed up with Leslie Riddles in Kingsport, Tennessee, in 1932 and performed with him until 1939. His first recordings were made in Chicago in 1938. In April 1939 he and Sonny Terry's paths crossed. They combined their talents to form the team of Brownie and Sonny, and as such they traveled and performed extensively. Together they played on Broadway in *Cat on a Hot Tin Roof* from 1955 to 1957 and in the road-show version in 1958. McGhee opened a school for guitarists and singers in Harlem known as the House of the Blues.

RECORDINGS

Back to New Orleans. Fantasy FCD 24708–2
Brownie McGhee & Sonny Terry. MCA MCAC–1369
Brownie McGhee & Sonny Terry. Smithsonian/Folkways CDSF–40011
Brownie's Blues. Fantasy/OBC OBCCD–505–2
Climbin' Up. Savoy SJL 1127
The Folkways Years, 1945–1959. Smithsonian/Folkways CDSF40034
Jumpin' the Blues. Savoy Jazz 5JK–1204
Just a Closer Walk with Thee (with Sonny Terry). Fantasy OBCCD–541–2
The 1958 London Sessions. Sequel NEXCD 120
Rainy Day. Tomato 269610–2
Sonny and Brownie. A & M 75021–0829–2

BOOK

Traum, H., ed. *Guitar Styles of Brownie McGhee*. New York: Oak Publications, 1971.

FILMS

Sonny Terry and Brownie McGhee. Seattle Folklore Society. 25 minutes, black and white.
Walter Brownie McGhee. Seattle Folklore Society. 25 minutes, black and white.

McKENZIE, ELIAS "MAC" (Violin, vocal). Born: Charleston, South Carolina–May 15, 1915.

Elias McKenzie started in show business as a dancer when he was eight years old. He worked a string of blues gigs until the late 1930s and early 1940s, when be became involved in the New York jazz scene, sitting in on violin with people like Monk (Thelonius Monk), Bird (Charlie Parker), and Diz (Dizzy Gillespie). He moved to Albany in the 1940s, and for twelve years he played many of the local blues clubs. In 1953 he gave up music to concentrate on a full-time job in another field and has not returned to music since.

McSHANN, JAY (Piano). Born: Muskogee, Oklahoma–January 12, 1909.

Jay McShann started playing piano at the age of twelve. He moved to Kansas City in the early 1930s and formed his own band there in 1937. Personnel included Charlie Parker, Gene Ramey, Gus Johnson, Al Hibbler, and Walter Brown. The band enjoyed its biggest years from 1941 to 1943. Blues singer Jimmy Witherspoon made his recording debut with McShann's band. McShann toured Europe in 1969 and appeared at Montreal's Man and His World Exposition and at the Monterey Jazz Festival in 1971. Currently McShann works as a single, playing for concerts and recordings mostly in Europe. He appeared at the Edinburgh Jazz Festival in Scotland in 1992.

RECORDINGS
Airmail Special. Sackville CD23040
At Cafe des Copains. Sackville SKCD2–2024
Blues from Kansas City. Decca Jazz GRD–614
Going to Kansas City. New World NW–358–2
Just a Lucky So-and-So. Sackville 3035
Kansas City Hustle. Sackville 3021
The Man from Muskogee. Sackville 3005
A Tribute to Fats Waller. Sackville 3019
Tuxedo Junction. Sackville 3025

FILM
Roosevelt Sykes: The Honeydripper plus Jay McShann. Kay Jazz Video KJ096. *Sykes*: 27 minutes, black and white; *McShann*: 30 minutes, color.

McTELL, WILLIE SAMUEL "BLIND WILLIE" (Accordion, guitar, violin, harmonica, vocal). Born: Thomson, Georgia–May 5, 1901; died: Milledgeville, Georgia–August 19, 1959.

Blind Willie McTell was one of the most visible blues singers of the 1920s and 1930s. His travels took him from Georgia to New York City, playing the streets, parks, work camps, and clubs all along the way. He recorded for Victor from 1927 to 1929, for Columbia from 1929 to 1931, for Okeh in 1931, and for Vocalion in 1933. In the early 1930s he frequently played with Blind Lemon Jefferson throughout the South. He also recorded for Decca (1935), the Library of Congress (1940), and Prestige/Bluesville (1956). From 1957 to the time of his death he was active as a preacher at Mt. Zion Baptist Church in Atlanta, Georgia.

RECORDINGS
Blind Willie McTell. MCA 1368
Doing that Atlanta Strut. Yazoo 1037
The Early Years. Yazoo 1005

MEMPHIS MINNIE. *See* Douglas, Lizzie.

MEMPHIS SLIM. *See* Chatman, Peter.

MERRIWEATHER, MAJOR "BIG MACEO" (Piano). Born: Atlanta, Georgia–March 31, 1905; died: Chicago, Illinois–February 26, 1953.

Major Merriweather taught himself to play the piano at age fifteen. He worked as a part-time musician around Atlanta, Georgia, in the early 1920s. He moved to Detroit, Michigan, in 1924 and worked both inside and outside of music until 1941. In 1941 he moved to Chicago, where he became more active in music. He recorded with Tampa Red for Bluebird Records in 1941–42 and again in 1945–46 and with Big Bill Broonzy on Columbia Records in 1945. He was partially paralyzed by a stroke in 1946, but continued to perform and record on piano with one hand until 1953, when he suffered a fatal heart attack. A fuller description of him can be found in chapter 3.

BOOK

Williams, Martin T. *The Art of Jazz*. London: Oxford University Press, 1959.

MILBURN, AMOS (Piano, vocal). Born: Houston, Texas–April 1, 1927.

Between 1945 and 1949 Amos Milburn recorded about one hundred blues titles for Aladdin Records. "Hold Me Baby" and "Chicken Shack Boogie" made the rhythm-and-blues charts. In 1951 he had a number one hit with "Bad, Bad Whiskey." This prompted him to record "One Scotch, One Bourbon, One Beer" and "Let Me Go Home Whiskey," both of which became fairly big hits. An album of his early material has been issued by Riverboard Records of France. He has not been very active since about 1970.

RECORDINGS

His Greatest Hits. Sequel NEXCD 132
Just One More Drink. Route 66 KIX7
Rock, Rock, Rock. Route 66 KIX21

MILES, ELIZABETH MARY PAJAUD LANDREAUX "LIZZIE" (Vocal). Born: New Orleans, Louisiana–March 31, 1895; died: New Orleans, Louisiana–March 17, 1963.

Lizzie Miles left New Orleans in 1909 with the Jones Brothers' Circus and for the next eight years traveled with circuses and minstrel shows. She became ill in 1918 and temporarily left the profession. Upon returning to music, she recorded with Jelly Roll Morton and Clarence Williams in New York in 1922. In New York City she played Herman's Inn in 1924 and the Capitol Place in 1926. In 1925 she visited Europe with Alexander Shargenski's troupe. She became ill in the 1930s and again retired from the profession. Upon her return she worked mostly in California. In 1952 she was featured at the Hangover Club in San Francisco and worked with Bob Scobey regularly from 1955 to 1957. She returned to New Orleans in the spring of 1957 and worked jobs with Freddie Kohlman and other stalwarts of that city. The year 1958 found her back in California with Joe Darensbourg. She also performed at the Monterey Jazz Festival in 1958 and 1959. In 1959 she retired from professional singing and devoted most of her time to church work.

MILLER, RICE "SONNY BOY WILLIAMSON" (Harmonica, vocal). Born: Mississippi–December 5, 1899; died: Helena, Arkansas–May 25, 1965.

Sonny Boy Number Two, as he is sometimes called, made his first recordings for Trumpet Records of Jackson, Mississippi, in 1951. Although his given name is Aleck, he is known mostly as either "Alex" Miller or "Rice" Miller. In 1955 he moved to Chicago and recorded regularly for

Chess Records with Muddy Waters, Willie Dixon, and Otis Spann. With the American Folk Blues Festival in 1963 Miller toured Europe, where he appeared on television and did some recording in Copenhagen. He made a second trip to England in 1964. After a short while he returned to "King Biscuit Time" in Helena, Arkansas, a program for which he had performed regularly since 1941.

RECORDINGS

The Chess Years. Charly Chess Box CD1
Down and Out Blues. Chess 9257
In Paris. GNP Crescendo 10003
Portraits in Blues, Vol. 2. Storyville SLP–4016
Real Folk Blues. Chess 9272

FILM

Sonny Boy Williamson II. TCB Releasing Ltd. 10 Minutes, black and white.

MILTON, ROY (Drums, vocal). Born: Wynnewood, Oklahoma–July 31, 1907; died: unknown.

Roy Milton moved from Oklahoma to California in 1934 and proceeded to make a name for himself as a rhythm-and-blues singer in the Charles Brown mold. In the late 1930s he formed his own band and has continually been featured in Los Angeles' top nightspots ever since. One of rhythm-and-blues' stronger pioneers, Milton formed and recorded on his own label in 1945. Later recordings were made on Hamp-Tone, Speciality, Dootone, King, Warwick, and Kent.

RECORDINGS

And His Solid Senders. Speciality SP–7004
Big Fat Mamas. Jukebox Lil616
Grandfather of R & B. Jukebox Lil600

MINOR, FRED (Banjo, guitar). Born: New Orleans, Louisiana–December 8, 1913; died: unknown.

Fred Minor was active in music beginning in the depression. He played with Paul Barbarin's band during the late 1950s and early 1960s. He also worked with Noon Johnson's Bazooka Trio in the mid–1960s.

MINTER, IVERSON "LOUISIANA RED" (Guitar, harmonica, vocal). Born: Vicksburg, Mississippi–March 23, 1936.

Iverson Minter spent most of his childhood with relatives and in an orphanage. His mother died of pneumonia one week after his birth, and his father was lynched by the Ku Klux Klan when Red was only five years old. In 1949 he recorded "Sweet Geneva" and "Gonna Play My Guitar" for Chess Records. Upon his discharge from the army in 1958, he worked with John Lee Hooker for about a year and a half in Detroit, Michigan. His work can be found on Chess, Checker, Atlas, Glover, and Roulette, on which he had his most successful record, "Red's Dream." In 1972 he recorded for Herb Abramson, who leased twelve tracks to Atco Records for the album *Louisiana Red Sings the Blues.*

RECORDINGS

Boy from Black Bayou. L & R 42055
Midnight Rambler. Tomato R2–70664
My Life. L & R 42061

MR. BO. *See* Collins, Louis.

MR. SHORTSTUFF. *See* Macon, John Wesley.

MITCHELL, EDNA (Piano, vocal). Born: New Orleans, Louisiana–unknown; died: New Orleans, Louisiana–unknown.

Edna Mitchell worked in the cabarets of New Orleans as a blues vocalist and piano player for many years. She played with Louis Armstrong in the early 1920s at Tom Anderson's Restaurant on Rampart Street.

MONETTE, JOHNNY "SHA-SHANT" (Bass, guitar, vocal). Born: Lafayette, Louisiana–March 9, 1939.

Johnny Monette started playing the blues when he was six years old. His first instrument was a homemade guitar that was made of a tin cooking-oil can and window-screen wire. His father was a piano player, his uncles played music also, and his brother Raymond Monette was a guitarist. He played in area blues bands throughout the 1950s and early 1960s. He was not engaged in much musical activity during the 1970s, but returned to more frequent playing in the late 1980s. Currently he is involved in playing bass in zydeco and blues bands.

MONETTE, RAYMOND "SHWANK" (Guitar). Born: Lafayette, Louisiana–December 13, 1936; died: Lafayette, Louisiana–January 4, 1977.

One of southwest Louisiana's most prolific blues guitarists, Raymond Monette played a wide range of music from rhythm-and-blues to zydeco. He taught himself to play the guitar when he was in his early teens. He later worked as a sideman with area musicians such as Guitar Gable, Carroll Fran, Rockin' Dopsie, Marcelle Dugas, and Rickey Williams. When Clifton Chenier formed his first big band, he hired Monette as his guitarist. Monette worked with Chenier's Red Hot Louisiana Band until the time of his death.

MONTGOMERY, EURREAL WILFORD "LITTLE BROTHER" (Piano, vocal). Born: Kentwood, Louisiana–April 18, 1906.

Eurreal Montgomery was playing piano professionally by the time he was eleven years old and while in his teens worked the barrelhouse circuit in New Orleans. During the 1930s and 1940s he played with several New

Orleans and Chicago jazz bands, including his own Southland Troubadours and a band led by Kid Ory. He recorded the blues under his own name as well as with Otis Rush, Little Willie Foster, and Magic Sam. He also worked as accompanist to a number of famous female blues singers.

RECORDINGS

At Home. Earwig CD–4918
Blues. Folkways 3527
Chicago Blues Session. Redita 133
Chicago—The Living Legends. Ace CH263
Church Songs. Folkways 31042
Farro Street Jive. Folkways 31014E

BOOK

Zur Heid, Karl. *Deep South Piano: The Story of Little Brother Montgomery*. London: Studio Vista, 1970.

MOORE, ALEXANDER H. "WHISTLING" (Piano, vocal). Born: Dallas, Texas–November 22, 1899; died: unknown.

Alexander Moore spent most of his life playing piano and working at odd jobs in Dallas, Texas. Although he recorded during the 1930s for Columbia and Decca Records, his career never got off the ground. This could have been partly because of his reluctance to go on the road. He started recording again in the late 1970s. One of his albums, *Wiggie Tail*, was released in 1988 on the Rounder label.

RECORDINGS

In Europe. Arhoolie 1048
Piano Blues. Arhoolie 1008
Wiggie Tail. Rounder CD–11559

MOORE, JAMES "SLIM HARPO" (Harmonica, vocal). Born: Lobdell, Louisiana–January 11, 1924; died: Baton Rouge, Louisiana–January 31, 1970.

James Moore's musical career was divided into two brief but active periods. From the mid–1940s to the early 1960s he was active in southwest Louisiana recording and performing solo as well as working as accompanist to Lightnin' Slim. During this period he recorded for Excello Records almost exclusively except for one date on Imperial in 1962. His second career in music started around 1966 and lasted until 1969. During this time he performed extensively in Chicago, Los Angeles, and New York City.

RECORDINGS

Blues Hangover. Flyright 520
Rainin' in My Heart. Excello 8003
Scratch My Back. Excello 8005
Slim Harpo Knew the Blues. Excello 8013

MOORE, SAMMIE "IRONING BOARD SAM" (Keyboards, vocal). Born: Rockhill, South Carolina–1939.

Sammie Moore played music in Miami, Florida; Memphis, Tennessee; Chicago; Los Angeles; and Waterloo, Iowa, before making New Orleans his home in 1974. He recorded singles for Atlantic, Holiday Inn, Styleton, and his own label, called Board. Although he recorded singles that are no longer on the market, there is no information available concerning any albums being released during the 1980s or early 1990s. He appeared at the New Orleans Jazz and Heritage Festival during the early 1980s.

MOORE, WHISTLING. *See* Moore, Alexander H.

MOORE, WILLIE (Guitar, vocal). Born: Kinston, North Carolina–April 22, 1913; died: Albany, New York–May 2, 1971.

After playing guitar for about five years, Willie Moore entered a blues contest in Kinston, North Carolina, and won the fifty-dollar first prize and a little gold guitar. This win led to his going to New York in 1937 and, along with Sonny Terry and Blind Boy Fuller, recording several sides for J. B. Long. After the session he returned to Kester until 1940, did some time in the army, and from 1945 to 1947 worked with Sticks McGhee (Brownie McGhee's brother). He moved to Albany in 1948 and remained there, working a day job and playing local bars until his death.

MORAND, HERB (Trumpet, vocal). Born: New Orleans, Louisiana–1905; died: New Orleans, Lousiana–February 22, 1952.

Half brother of blues vocalist Lizzie Miles, Herb Morand toured the Southwest with Nat Towles's Creole Harmony Kings in 1923. In 1924 he played a carnival in Merida, Yucatan, Mexico. He played with Cliff Jackson in New York in the mid–1920s and later with Chris Kelly in New Orleans. He recorded in Chicago with Frank Melrose and the Harlem Hamfats. He also worked with George Lewis in New Orleans in 1940s, but was not engaged in much activity after 1950.

MORGANFIELD, MCKINLEY "MUDDY WATERS" (Guitar, harmonica, vocal). Born: Rolling Fork, Mississippi–April 14, 1915; died: Downers Grove, Illinois–April 30, 1983.

Muddy Waters was twenty-six when Alan Lomax and John Work recorded him on Howard Stovall's plantation. They cut "Country Blues" and "I Be's Trouble" for the Library of Congress. In July and August 1942 he was again recorded at Stovall's, this time with Son Simms Four. By 1948 he had moved to Chicago, where he did a session for Columbia Records. During this time he worked with a trio known as the Headcutters, including harpist Little Walter and guitarist Jimmy Rogers. He recorded with Little Walter for the Aristocrat label in 1950 and with the Muddy Waters Blues

Band in 1953. Members of this band included Little Walter on harmonica, Otis Spann on piano, Jimmy Rogers on guitar, Elgar Edmonds on drums, and Big Crawford on bass. Waters was one of the giants of the Chicago school of the blues. He spent his entire music career, from 1948 to the time of his death in 1983, performing and recording all over the United States and the world.

RECORDINGS

At Newport. Chess HCD–31269
Baby, Please Don't Go. Vogue VG–670410
The Best of Muddy Waters. Chess 9255
Can't Get No Grindin'. Chess CHD–9319
Folk Singer. Chess CHC–9261
Good News. Syndicate Chapter 002
Hard Again. Blue Sky PZT–34449
I'm Ready. Blue Sky PZT–34928
King Bee. Columbia P237064
Live in Switzerland 1976, Vol. 1. Landscape L32–908
The London Muddy Waters Sessions. Chess CHD–9298
Muddy, Brass, and the Blues. Chess CHD–9286
Muddy and the Wolf (with Howlin' Wolf). Chess CHD–9100
Muddy "Mississippi" Waters Live. Blue Sky PZT–35712
Mud in Your Ear. Muse MCD6004
Rare and Unissued. Chess CHD–9180
The Real Folk Blues. Chess 9274
Rolling Stone. Chess CHC–9101
Sweet Home Chicago. Intermedia QSC–5071
The Warsaw Sessions, Vol. 1. Kicking Mule Pol–79
The Warsaw Sessions, Vol. 2. Kicking Mule Pol–80
They Call Me Muddy Waters. Chess CHD–9299
Trouble No More. Chess CHD–9291
"Unk" in Funk. Chess CHC–91513

BOOK

Rooney, Jim, *Bossmen: Bill Monroe and Muddy Waters*. New York: Dial Press, 1971.

FILM

Chicago Blues (starring Buddy Guy, Johnny Lewis, Floyd Jones, J. B. Hutto, Muddy Waters, and others). Kay Jazz Video KJ004. 50 minutes, color.

MORRIS, WILLIE, JR. (Guitar, harmonica, vocal). Born: Camden, Alabama–January 3, 1925.

Willie Morris started playing guitar and harmonica when he was ten years old. He moved to Mobile around 1940, and in 1950 he recorded some sides for Decca Records. After injuring his left hand in 1968, he gave up music completely.

MUDDY WATERS. *See* Morganfield, McKinley.

MURPHY, MATT (Guitar, bass). Born: Sunflower, Mississippi–ca. 1939 (unconfirmed).

In the 1950s Matt Murphy played guitar on Junior Parker's first recordings with the Blue Flames. He also worked with Memphis Slim in the late 1950s. After recording with Muddy Waters on Chess and with Lillian Offitt (playing bass) for Chief Records, Matt toured Europe in 1963 with Otis Spann, Lonnie Johnson, and Willie Dixon. Since returning from Europe, he has played mostly in and around Chicago with the Dynasonics, Bobby Buster, Jack McDuff, and James Cotton. He has also recorded with Willie Dixon, Albert King, and James Cotton. His CD *Way Down South* was released in September 1990 on Antone's Records.

RECORDING

Way Down South. Antone's ANT–0013

MUSSELWHITE, CHARLES DOUGLAS (Harmonica). Born: Kosciusko, Mississippi–January 31, 1944.

Considered to be the best living white blues harmonica player, Charles Musselwhite is of Choctaw Indian ancestry. He was raised in Memphis, where he started playing the harmonica at thirteen. He moved to Chicago in 1966 and worked with J. B. Hutto, Mike Bloomfield, Big Joe Williams, John Lee Hooker, and many others. He started recording for Vanguard in 1966 and recorded other albums on Arhoolie and Kicking Mule. Musselwhite has continued to be a staple on the Chicago blues scene in the 1990s. He is currently performing in nightspots, at festivals, and on television throughout the United States and Canada. He had four albums released during 1990 and 1991.

RECORDINGS

Ace of Harps. Alligator 4781
Cambridge Blues. Blue Horizon 005
Goin' Back down South. Arhoolie 1074
Harmonica According to Musselwhite. Kicking Mule KC–305
Mellow Dee. Crosscut CCR1013
Memphis, Tennessee. Crosscut 1008
Memphis Charlie. Arhoolie CD–303
Signature. Alligator ALCD–4801
Takin' My Time. Arhoolie 1056

MYERS, LOUIS (Guitar, harmonica, vocal). Born: Byhalia, Mississippi–September 18, 1929.

Louis Myers moved to Chicago in 1941 and has used that city as his base ever since. In addition to leading his own bands, he has also performed with Muddy Waters, Big Bill Broonzy, Little Walter, Otis Spann, Otis Rush,

Buddy Guy, Jimmy Rogers, Sunnyland Slim, Andrew Odum, and many others. Extremely popular in Chicago, he has also recorded with many of the great bluesmen of that city. He toured Europe and Japan frequently up through the 1990s.

RECORDING
I'm a Southern Man. Advent 2809

NEAL, KENNY (Guitar, vocal). Born: Baton Rouge, Louisiana–ca. 1957 (unconfirmed).

Son of the famed blues harmonica player Raful Neal, Kenny Neal is a good solid singer and guitar player, though he is still searching for his own voice. He spent some time in the 1980s living and playing the blues in Chicago. He performed quite a bit in the 1980s and early 1990s traveling throughout the United States and Europe, and made recordings that were released on compact disc in the late 1980s and early 1990s.

RECORDINGS
Big News from Baton Rouge. Alligator ALCD–4764
Devil Child. Alligator ALCD–4774
Walking on Fire. Alligator ALCD–4795

NEAL, RAFUL (Harmonica, vocal). Born: Chamberlin, Louisiana–1936.

Raful Neal was one of the first Baton Rouge blues musicians to record. In 1957 Whit Records released his "On the Dark Side Cryin' " and "Cryin' Blues." He did not return to the studio again until 1968, when he cut singles that leaned more toward soul than blues. None of his recordings was very successful. He played with his sons in the Neal Brother's Funk Band. He recorded material for an album for the Wild Dog Blues label in 1991. He is currently living in Baton Rouge, Louisiana, performing whenever work is possible.

RECORDINGS
I've Been Mistreated. Wild Dog Blues ICH–9004
Louisiana Legend. Alligator ALCD–4783

NEW ORLEANS WILLIE. *See* Jackson, William.

NIXON, ELMORE (Piano, vocal). Born: Crowley, Louisiana–November 17, 1933; died: Houston, Texas–1975.

A long-time figure on the Houston blues scene, Nixon worked and recorded with some of the best, including Hop Wilson, Lightnin' Hopkins, and Ivory Lee Semien. He recorded under his own name for Peacock, Sittin' In With, Luck 7, Savoy, Imperial/Post, and Mercury Records.

OTIS, JOHNNY (Piano, vibes, leader, composer). Born: Vallejo, California–December 28, 1921.

From 1956 to 1961 Johnny Otis hosted his own television show in Los Angeles. He is directly responsible for the early success of "Little" Esther Phillips. After a few years of almost total inactivity in music, he gradually returned to playing and record production in the late 1960s. In 1969 his album *Cold Shot* on the Kent label was an instant success. He has been traveling nationally with his show since 1970, often featuring his son Shuggie Otis. Some of his well-known compositions are "Every Beat of My Heart," "So Fine," "Dance with Me, Henry," and "Hand Jive." In 1971 he toured the Far East, then Europe in 1972 and Africa and Europe in 1974. He has performed in two movies, *Jukebox Rhythm* in 1958 and *Play Misty for Me* in 1971. In 1970 he and his group played the Monterey Jazz Festival, and in 1974 they performed at the Antibes Festival. He formed a New Johnny Otis Show in the 1980s and traveled intermittently with it. He is still active in the business aspects of the music industry.

RECORDINGS

The Capitol Years. Capitol 92858–2
Gee Baby. Jukebox Lil617
Good Lovin' Blues. Ace CDCH299
The New Johnny Otis Show. Alligator 4726
Snatch and Poontangs. Snatch 101

BOOK

Otis, Johnny. *Listen to the Lambs.* New York: W. W. Norton, 1968.

PARKER, HERMAN "JUNIOR" (Harmonica, vocal). Born: West Memphis, Arkansas–March 3, 1927; died: Blue Island, Illinois–November 18, 1971.

Herman Parker spent part of his life working in the cotton fields of Mississippi. He grew to love the blues by listening to Sonny Boy Williamson (Rice Miller) on the radio. By 1948 Junior had learned to play Williamson's songs on the harmonica and finally got to meet his idol in Clarksdale at a dance. Parker created such an impression that Williamson invited him to join his band. Under the superb tutorship of Sonny Boy, Parker soon flowered into a top-notch bluesman and fronted the band whenever Williamson left town for other jobs. In 1949 he toured the Midwest with Howlin' Wolf's band and also played regular gigs in Chicago. By 1951 he was fronting Wolf's band, and he made his first recordings for Modern Records in 1952 in Memphis, Tennessee. "Feelin' Good," recorded on Sam Phillips's Sun label in 1953, hit the top ten on the rhythm-and-blues charts that year. Don Robey brought him to Houston in 1954 for his first session on Duke Records. On the Duke label he recorded "The Next Time You See Me" in 1957; "That's All Right" in 1958; and his biggest hit, "Annie Get Your Yo-yo," in 1962. He left Duke in the mid–1960s and recorded for Minit,

Mercury, and Capitol. He is also credited with advancing the career of Bobby Bland.

RECORDINGS

The Best of. MCA 27046
Blues Consolidation. MCA 27037
Driving Wheel. MCA 27039

PATTON, CHARLEY (Guitar). Born: Edwards, Mississippi–1885; died: Indianola, Mississippi–April 28, 1934.

Charley Patton was the first Delta bluesman to gain national popularity. He spent most of his life as a professional but only performed in Mississippi. The music he played was directly related to the kinds of music that preceded the blues and also directly linked to the blues that followed him. From 1929 to the time of his death in 1934, he recorded approximately sixty sides for Vocalion and Paramount Records. A fuller description of him can be found in chapter 3.

RECORDINGS

Founder of the Delta Blues. Yazoo CD–1020
King of the Delta Blues. Yazoo CD–2001

BOOK

Fahey, John. *Charley Patton.* London: Studio Vista, 1970.

PEG-LEG SAM. *See* Jackson, Arthur.

PENN, SAMMY (Drums, vocal). Born: Morgan City, Louisiana–September 15, 1902; died: Florida–September 18, 1969.

Sammy Penn did his first professional work in the blues band of Jake Johnson in Morgan City. He moved to New Orleans in 1921. He worked with Kid Rena, Chris Kelly, and the Eureka Brass Band, and later with Kid Thomas's Band for a gig that lasted more than a quarter of a century. Having led his own group, Penn and His Five Pennies, in Chicago in the mid–1950s, he died while on tour with the Preservation Hall Jazz Band.

PENNIMAN, "LITTLE" RICHARD (Piano, vocal). Born: Macon, Georgia–December 25, 1935.

Little Richard recorded his first hit, "Tutti Frutti," on the Specialty label in 1955. By 1956 he had a string of hits, including "Rip It Up," "Slippin' and Slidin'," "Long Tall Sally," and "Ready Teddy." In 1957 he recorded "Keep A-Knockin'," "Send Me Some Lovin'," "Miss Ann," and "Jenny," all top-ten rhythm-and-blues best-sellers. The year 1958 brought a temporary halt to Little Richard's recording and touring endeavors. "Good Golly Miss Molly" of that year was his last hit. He retired from music and enrolled in a college in Alabama to study for the ministry. His time spent as a minister was short, however, and he soon started touring outside the

United States. Later he started recording again. His last hit on the now-defunct Specialty label was "Bama Lama Bama Loo," released in 1963. He returned to full-time ministry work in the mid–1970s and remained active in that capacity for a number of years. His last return to show business in the early 1980s proved to be a good move. He has since enjoyed more work than ever before in his career. The 1990s found him doing movies, commercials, and public appearances on television talk shows as well as selected performances in large venues throughout the world.

RECORDINGS

The Best. Dominion 784–2
Big Hits. GNP Crescendo 9033
Compact Command Performances. Motown 37463–9066–2
18 Greatest Hits. Rhino R2–75899
The Essential Little Richard. Specialty SPCD–2154
The Fabulous. Ace CDCHM 133
The Fabulous Little Richard. Specialty SPC–2104
The Formative Years. Bear Family BCD15448
The Georgia Peach. Specialty SPCD–7012
Greatest Hits, Live. Epic ER–40389
Greatest 17 Original Hits. Specialty SPC–2113
Here's Little Richard. Ace CH–128
His All Time Greats. Special Music Co. SMC–4908
His Biggest Hits. Specialty SPC–2111
His Greatest Recordings. Ace CHC–109
Little Richard. Specialty SPC–2103
Original. RCA-Camden CAN–420
Rock Legends (with Roy Orbison). RCA 9969–4–R
Shut Up! Rhino R4–70236
16 Great Hits. Zeta ZET–519
20 Greatest Hits. Deluxe DCD–7797
22 Classic Cuts. Ace CDCH–195

BOOK

White, Charles. *The Life and Times of Little Richard: The Quasar of Rock*. New York: Harmony Books, 1984.

PERRODIN, GABRIEL "GUITAR GABLE" (Guitar, vocal). Born: Bellevue, Louisiana–August 17, 1937.

Gabriel Perrodin started playing the guitar in 1953. His first recording, in 1956, resulted in a local hit called "Congo Mombo." A few months later he recorded "Guitar Rhumba" and "Irene," the latter becoming another local hit. During the next year Perrodin, along with his vocalist King Karl, recorded a string of mild hits. Apart from playing the local clubs and other venues, he was also active as a studio musician, backing up artists such as Bobby Charles, Lazy Lester, and Slim Harpo. He stopped recording in the late 1950s, and after a stint in the armed forces he returned to music, but as a sideman performing sporadically.

RECORDING
Cool, Calm, and Collected. Flyright 599

PERRYMAN, RUFUS "SPECKLED RED" (Piano, vocal). Born: Monroe, Louisiana–October 23, 1892; died: St. Louis, Missouri–January 2, 1973.

One of sixteen children, Rufus Perryman was raised in Detroit, Michigan, but moved back to Hampton, Georgia, around the time his brother William "Piano Red" Perryman was born. Their father, Henry Perryman, played passable blues piano for his own entertainment. Perryman did most of his professional work in sawmill camps and turpentine jukes. He was the author of "The Dirty Dozens," a popular dirty-talking insult song. His recordings can be found on the Vocalion, Brunswick, Bluebird, Folkways, Tone, and Storyville labels.

RECORDING
Speckled Red. Wolf 113

PERRYMAN, WILLIAM "PIANO RED" (Piano, vocal). Born: Hampton, Georgia–October 19, 1911; died: unknown.

William Perryman's approach to the piano was undoubtedly influenced by the style of his older brother, Rufus "Speckled Red" Perryman. A similar ragtime flavor can be found in the music of both men. William's first recordings were made in 1950, and "Rockin' with Red" was a hit during that year. "Dr. Feelgood," recorded in 1961, was also a mild hit for Perryman.

RECORDINGS
Dr. Feelgood. Oldie Blues 2821
Dr. Feelgood Alone. Arhoolie 1064
Music Is Medicine. L & R 42019
Percussive Piano. Euphonic 1212
Wildfire. Matchbox MB902

PHELPS, ARTHUR "BLIND BLAKE" (Guitar, vocal). Born: Jacksonville, Florida–ca. 1895; died: Chicago, Illinois–between 1932 and 1941.

There have been many conflicting reports regarding Blind Blake's birth and death dates. He is believed to have moved from Florida to Georgia at a very early age and to have worked around the state as a blind street musician until around 1920. In 1921 he played with guitarist Bill Williams at road camps near Bristol, Tennessee. He settled in Chicago in the mid-1920s, and from that point on into the early 1930s he recorded prolifically under his own name for Paramount Records and as accompanist to Ma Rainey and other popular blues figures. Around 1930 or 1931 he toured with the show *Happy Go Lucky.* Then he simply dropped out of sight.

RECORDINGS
The Accompanist, 1926–31. Wolf 133
Ragtime Guitar's Foremost Fingerpicker. Yazoo 1.68
The Remaining Titles. Matchbox 1003

PHILLIPS, "LITTLE" ESTHER (Piano, drums, vocal). Born: Galveston, Texas–December 23, 1935; died: 1984.

Esther Phillips's musical career had numerous ups and downs. She made her first recording for Johnny Otis in September 1949 when she was only thirteen years old. The title was "Double Crossing Blues," and it sold over a million copies. She stayed with Otis until 1954, when she joined Slide Hampton's band and toured with it for eight months. After her stay with Hampton she went out on her own, playing throughout the United States and making records for Savoy, Decca, Federal, Roulette, Lenox, and Atlantic. Personal problems and a heroin addiction hampered her career somewhat, but after a short hiatus she returned to the music world full blast in the early 1970s. Throughout the rest of the 1970s and the early 1980s she enjoyed the work and exposure associated with her being "rediscovered" by a younger audience. She recorded fine albums like *The Best of Esther Phillips* on Columbia and *Confessing the Blues* for Atlantic in the 1970s. Her final recording date, which produced *A Way to Say Goodbye,* was done on March 6, 1984, for Muse Records.

RECORDINGS

The Best of Esther Phillips. Columbia Jazz Contemporary Masters ZT–45483
The Complete Savoy Recordings. Savoy SJL 2258
Confessing the Blues. Atlantic 90670–4
From a Whisper to a Scream. CTI/CBS Associated ZK–40935
A Way to Say Goodbye. Muse MCD–5302
What a Difference a Day Makes. CBS Associated ZK–40710

PIANO RED. *See* Perryman, William.

PICKETT, WILSON (Vocal). Born: Prattville, Alabama–March 18, 1941.

Wilson Pickett started singing professionally in 1959 in Detroit, Michigan, where he was raised. He had a hit record in 1963 with his single "If You Need Me." In 1964 he signed with Atlantic Records and produced a string of rhythm-and-blues and soul hits in the 1960s, including "In the Midnight Hour," "Mustang Sally," "Funky Broadway," and "Hey Jude." He has not been heard of much in the late 1970s, 1980s, and early 1990s.

RECORDINGS

American Soul Man. Motown 37463–6244–4
The Best of. Atlantic 81283–4
A Man and a Half. Rhino R4–70287
Greatest Hits. Atlantic CS2–501

PIERCE, BILLIE GOODSON (Piano, vocal). Born: Marianna, Florida–June 8, 1907; died: New Orleans, Louisiana–September 29, 1974.

Billie Goodson Pierce, sister of Sadie Goodson, who played with Buddy Petit in 1931, learned to play piano as a child in Florida. On one occasion she played for Bessie Smith when she was sixteen years old. She moved to New Orleans in 1930 and played a few jobs for Sadie with Buddy Petit. During the depression she worked jobs at various clubs in the French Quarter with her husband, trumpeter Joseph "Dee Dee" Pierce, and clarinetist George Lewis. She and Dee Dee played Luthjen's for several years after the depression. She recorded for Alden Ashforth and David Wycoff in 1951. In the 1960s she and Dee Dee recorded for Atlantic, Riverside, and other small labels and began spending several months a year on the road. They appeared on major television talk shows, played the Fillmore East and West with John Mayall and the Grateful Dead, and toured overseas.

RECORDINGS

New Orleans Jazz. Arhoolie CD–346
New Orleans Jazz at the Kitty Halls. Arhoolie 1013
Vocal Blues and Cornet in the Classical Tradition. Fantasy/OBC OBC–534

PITCHFORD, LONNIE (Guitar, vocal). Born: Lexington, Mississippi–ca. 1955.

Lonnie Pitchford, like other blues greats before him, is a virtuoso on the one-string guitar, an instrument he has been playing since he was a child. He appeared at the Festival of American Folklife in Washington, D.C., in 1964 and at the New Orleans Jazz and Heritage Festival in 1976. He dropped from sight in the early 1980s.

POLKA DOT SLIM. *See* Vincent, Monroe.

PORK CHOP. *See* Smith, Jerome.

PROFESSOR LONGHAIR. *See* Byrd, Roy.

PRYOR, JAMES EDWARD "SNOOKY" (Harmonica, drums, vocal). Born: Lambert, Mississippi–September 15, 1921.

Snooky Pryor moved to Chicago in 1945 and formed his first band there the following year. Its members included Floyd Jones, Eddie Taylor, Homesick James, and Moody Jones. His first disc was made in 1947, and afterwards he recorded prolifically until 1962, when he retired from music, leaving most of his past work to be reissued on labels like Mamlish, Sunnyland, Buddah, Flyright, Blues Classics, and Muskadine. He returned to the blues world in 1972 by making his first public appearance at the Brown Shoe in Chicago's Old Town. On September 15 of that same year he recorded an album for Blues on Blues Records, and in 1973 he made a tour of Europe. He continued to perform through the 1980s and early 1990s, mostly at blues festivals. He recorded for Blind Pig Records in the late 1980s and for Antone's Records in 1991.

RECORDINGS

Real Fine Boogie. Flyright 565
Snooky. Blind Pig 2387
Snooky Pryor. Flyright CD20
Too Cool to Move. Antone's ANT–0017

RAINEY, GERTRUDE PRIDGETT "MA" (Vocal). Born: Columbus, Georgia–April 26, 1886; died: Columbus, Georgia–December 22, 1939.

Gertrude Rainey made her first public appearance at the age of twelve as part of *A Bunch of Blackberries*, a show playing at the Spring Opera House in Columbus, Georgia. She married William Rainey in 1904 and toured with the Rabbit Foot Minstrels and Tolliver's Circus. In the early 1920s she worked regularly with pianist Troy Snapps. After achieving success with her recordings, she formed and headed her own show, which featured the Georgia Jazz Band. This was a Dixie-style band that included trumpet, trombone, saxophone, drums, and Georgia Tom Dorsey–who was later recognized as one of the great writers of gospel songs–on piano. Except for a short retirement in Mexico, she did theater and tent-show tours throughout the 1920s. She shared the bill with Bessie Smith at a Fort Worth stock show early in the 1930s. After the death of her mother and sister in 1933, Ma retired and lived the rest of her life in Columbus, Georgia. Further description of her can be found in chapter 4.

RECORDINGS

Blues the World Forgot. Biograph 12001
Complete Recordings, Vol. 1. VJM VLP81
Complete Recordings, Vol. 2. VJM VLP82
Ma Rainey (with Louis Armstrong, Buster Bailey, and Georgia Tom Dorsey). Milestone MCD–47021–2
Ma Rainey's Black Bottom. Yazoo 1071
The Paramounts Chronologically 1923–1924, Vol. 1. Black Swan WHCD–12001
The Paramounts Chronologically 1924–1925, Vol. 2. Black Swan WHCD–12002
Queen of the Blues. Biograph 12032

BOOKS

Lieb, Sandra. *Mother of the Blues: A Study of Ma Rainey*. Amherst: University of Massachusetts Press, 1981.

Stewart-Baxter, Derrick. *Ma Rainey and the Classic Blues Singers*. New York: Stein and Day, 1970.

RAITT, BONNIE LYNN (Guitar, vocal). Born: Burbank, California–November 8, 1949.

Bonnie Raitt learned to play the guitar at nine years of age. She performed mostly folk music throughout the 1960s. She toured with Fred McDowell, Mississippi John Hurt, and others in the late 1960s. She began her recording career in 1971 on the Warner Brothers label. She worked mostly on the East Coast and in Europe throughout the 1970s, 1980s, and early 1990s.

She had hits with "Takin' My Time" (1974), "Streetlights" (1975), and "Home Plate" (1976). She was very active during the 1980s, getting national hits and receiving awards on into the 1990s.

RECORDINGS

Bonnie Raitt. Warner Bros. M5–1953
The Bonnie Raitt Collection. Warner Bros. 26242–4
Give It Up. Warner Bros. M5–2643
The Glow. Warner Bros. M5–3369
Green Light. Warner Bros. M5–3630
Luck of the Draw. Capitol C21Z–96111
Nick of Time. Capitol C21Z–91268

REED, DALTON (Vocal, piano, trumpet, trombone). Born: Cade, Louisiana–August 23, 1952.

Dalton Reed started singing in a church choir when he was in the third grade. He started playing with various local rhythm-and-blues bands while in high school in Lafayette, Louisiana. He later toured with zydeco artist Rockin' Sidney throughout Texas, Louisiana, and Alabama. In 1986 he formed his own record label (Sweet Daddy Records) and put out a 45 record that included "Givin' on in to Love" and "Strange Things." Both songs were written by Reed and did very well locally. His influences are Otis Redding, Ray Charles, and Sam Cooke. In 1992 Bullseye Records released his CD titled *Louisiana Soul Man.*

RECORDING

Louisiana Soul Man. Bullseye Blues CDBB–9506

REED, JIMMY (Guitar, harmonica, vocal). Born: Dunleith, Mississippi–September 6, 1925; died: Chicago, Illinois–August 29, 1976.

Guitarist and childhood friend Eddie Taylor taught Jimmy Reed the basics of the blues on a homemade cigar-box guitar. By his seventh year Jimmy was already on his way to mastering both the guitar and his second instrument, the harmonica. Upon leaving home at the age of fifteen he traveled north and supported himself with dozens of odd jobs for a number of years, all the while perfecting his instrumental technique and working on original material. He spent most of his career under the guidance of producer and songwriter Albert B. Smith, who wrote "Big Boss Man" and several other hits. In the early 1950s he moved to Chicago, where for three years he performed nightly for the most demanding of nightclub audiences and solidified his reputation in the blues world as a singer, guitarist, and harmonica player. Reed has recorded extensively over the years, and the better part of his work is still on the market. Some of his hits are "Honest I Do," "My First Plea," "Peepin' and Hidin'," "Little Rain," "You Don't Have to Go," and "Ain't That Lovin' You, Baby?"

RECORDINGS

The Best of. GNP Crescendo GNPD–0006
The Best of Jimmy Reed. VJ 1039
Big Boss Blues. Charly CD3
Compact Command Performances. Motown 37463–9065–2
Got Me Dizzy. Charly CRB 1028
Greatest Hits. Hollywood/IMG HT–445
Jimmy Reed. Flyright CD15
Rockin' with Reed. Charly CD61
Street Talkin'! (with Elmore James and Eddie Taylor). Muse MCD–5087
Upside Your Head. Charly CRB 1003

REED, MALINDA (Guitar, bass, congas, vocal). Born: Chicago, Illinois–January 29, 1953.

One of the few young women singing the blues today is Malinda Reed, daughter of famous artist Jimmy Reed. Malinda has been around studios and doing concerts with her father since she was five years old. She is now working mostly in Chicago as a professional musician and professional model. She was not engaged in much musical activity in the 1980s and early 1990s, but made sporadic appearances at blues festivals and nightspots in Chicago.

RICHARD, "JESSE" JAMES (Guitar, vocal). Born: Mississippi–December 10, 1926; died: Chicago, Illinois–September 1976.

James Richard did most of his professional playing in his home state of Mississippi. In 1947 and 1948 he performed on live radio broadcasts from Canton, Mississippi. In 1951 he left Mississippi for Muskegon, Michigan, and later Chicago. From that time on he hardly played at all.

RIDDLES, LESLIE (Guitar, mandolin). Born: Brunsville, North Carolina–June 13, 1905; died: unknown.

Leslie Riddles started playing guitar in 1913. During the 1920s he played music and worked at a cement plant in Kingsport, Tennessee. After getting hurt on the job in 1927, he moved back to North Carolina until 1939. During that year he returned to Kingsport and teamed up with Brownie McGhee until 1942. He also worked with white country musician A. P. Carter for three years, traveling around eastern Tennessee and Virginia. In 1942 he moved to Rochester, New York, and played occasionally with Jimmy Johnson and the Rochester Stars.

ROBINSON, FENTON (Guitar, vocal). Born: Greenwood, Mississippi–September 23, 1935.

Fenton Robinson broke onto the blues scene while still in his early twenties, competing side by side with giants such as B. B. King, Bobby Bland, and Junior Parker. In 1960 he moved to Chicago, where he landed a regular gig at the legendary Pepper's Lounge. He later got a recording contract and also toured the country with Charlie Musselwhite. His composition "Somebody Loan Me a Dime" sold 150,000 copies in Chicago alone and hundreds of thousands more in the "cover" version by Boz Scaggs and Duane Allman.

RECORDINGS

I Hear Some Blues Downstairs. Alligator 4710
The Mellow Blues Genius. P-Vine PLP 9001
Night Flight. Alligator 4736
Somebody Loan Me a Dime. Alligator ALCD–4705
Special Road. Black Magic CD9012

ROBINSON, LOUIS CHARLES "GOOD ROCKIN' " (Guitar, vocal, violin, harmonica). Born: Brenham, Texas–May 15, 1915; died: Berkeley, California–September 26, 1976.

Louis Charles Robinson moved from Texas to San Francisco in 1940. He and his brother A. C. Robinson (a harmonica and bass player) joined forces and formed the first of many Robinson groups that worked the West Coast through the years. In 1957 A. C. quit the blues to devote his time to the church and its music. L. C. continued to play harder than ever. Since the late 1960s he has recorded three albums and works almost constantly.

RECORDING

Ups and Downs. Arhoolie 1062

ROCKIN' DOPSIE. *See* Rubin, Alton.

ROCKIN' SIDNEY. *See* Semien, Sidney.

ROGERS, JIMMY LANE (Guitar, harmonica, vocal). Born: Ruleville, Mississippi–June 3, 1924.

Jimmy Rogers started playing music when he was thirteen years old and began playing professionally in Chicago at twenty-two. He worked with a great many big-name musicians, including Little Walter, John Lee Williams, Tampa Red, Muddy Waters (with whom he worked during most of his early career), Sonny Boy Williamson (Rice Miller), Robert Nighthawk, and Johnny Shines. His first recording, "Little Store Blues," was made in 1947 for the Ora-Nelle label. Rogers has been a staple on the Chicago blues scene for over thirty years. His latest CD, *Ludella,* was released by Antone's Records in June 1990.

RECORDINGS

Chicago Bound. Chess 9300
Jimmy Rogers. Chess 2–92505
Left Me with a Broken Heart. Vogue VG–670409
Ludella. Antone's ANT–0012CD
Sings the Blues. Shelter SR28016
That's All Right. Chess CDRED16

ROSS, CHARLES ISAIAH "DR." (Harmonica, guitar, vocal). Born: Tunica, Mississippi–October 21, 1925.

Dr. Ross is a country bluesman who grew up in and around Tunica, Mississippi. He made his first recordings in Memphis, Tennessee, when he was twenty-six years old. One of these, "Country Clown," was issued on Chess Records. An LP of his early recordings was also issued on Arhoolie Records.

RECORDING

His First Recordings. Arhoolie 1065

RUBIN, ALTON "ROCKIN' DOPSIE" (Accordion, vocal). Born: Lafayette, Louisiana–February 10, 1932; died: Opelousas, Louisiana–August 26, 1993.

Alton Rubin started playing music in his late teens and was influenced by Clifton Chenier. He started his recording career in 1968 with sides cut mostly on Blues Unlimited and Bon Temp Records. In 1976 he moved to Sonet Records and did quite a bit of work for that label with Sam Charters as producer.

RECORDINGS

Big Bad Zydeco. GNP Crescendo 2154
Clifton Chenier and Rockin' Dopsie. Flyright CD17
Crowned Prince of Zydeco. Maison de Soul 1020
French Style. Sonet 872
Good Rockin'. GNP Crescendo 2167
Hold On. GNP Crescendo 2156
Rockin' Dopsie. Flyright 592
Rockin' Dopsie and the Twisters. Rounder 6012
Saturday Night Zydeco. Maison de Soul CD104
Zy-De Blue. Sonet 761
Zy-De-Co-In'. Gazell GCCD3003

RUSH, OTIS (Vocal, guitar, harmonica, drums). Born: Philadelphia, Mississippi–April 29, 1934.

One of Chicago's most noted musicians, Otis Rush moved there in 1948 and started playing music professionally a year later. Since that time he has performed both as a sideman and feature act at just about every blues club in Chicago, as well as throughout the United States. A favorite at blues festivals throughout the world, he has recorded on Delmark, Cotillion, Chess, Cobra/Blue Horizon, Duke, Vanguard, Black and Blue, and many other labels. He continues to be in demand for worldwide tours, radio and television shows, club dates, and recording sessions.

RECORDINGS

Door to Door. Chess 9322
Groaning the Blues. Flyright 560
1956–58: His Cobra Recordings. Flyright FLYCD01

Otis Rush and Magic Sam. Flyright 562
Right Place, Wrong Time. Hightone 8007
So Many Roads. Delmark 643
Tops. Blind Pig 73188

RUSHING, JAMES ANDREW "JIMMY" (Piano, vocal). Born: Oklahoma City, Oklahoma–August 26, 1903; died: New York City–June 8, 1972.

Jimmy Rushing's earliest contact with music was on the violin. Later he was taught piano by a cousin. He studied music at Douglas High School in Oklahoma City and began to sing professionally while still in his teens. In 1932 he went to Los Angeles, where he played piano in after-hours clubs. When Walter Page formed his Blue Devils in 1927, Rushing joined the band and stayed through the leadership of both Page and Benny Moten. After Moten's death in 1935 he joined Count Basie's band at the Reno Club in Kansas City and remained as its featured vocalist until October 1948. From 1950 to 1952 he fronted his own band and then decided to work as a single, touring both the United States and Europe. In 1958 he was featured with Benny Goodman at the World's Fair in Brussels. He worked again with Goodman in 1961, and in 1964 he toured Australia and Japan with Eddie Condon. Rushing appeared at numerous jazz festivals, recorded prolifically, and in 1969 landed an acting role in the film *The Learning Tree*. In the early 1970s he worked regularly at the Half Note in New York City. Some of his best work can be found on Vanguard, Columbia, and RCA.

RECORDINGS
Five Feet of Soul. Fresh Sound FSR 642
Hold It Right There. Muse MR–5243
I Want a Little Girl. Official 3020
Kidney Stew. Black and Blue CD–233021
Old Kidney Stew Is Fine. Delmark CD–631
Sings the Blues. Muse MR–5310
You and Me That Used to Be. Bluebird 6460–2RB

SANTIAGO, BURNELL (Piano). Born: New Orleans, Louisiana–September 1915; died: New Orleans, Louisiana–January 6, 1944.

Originally from a New Orleans musical family, Burnell Santiago billed himself as the King of Boogie Woogie in the 1930s. He worked mainly as a soloist or in a trio with bass and guitar. He is considered by many musicians to be one of the finest jazz/blues pianists of his era.

SCHOOLBOY, CLEVE. *See* White, Cleve.

SEALS, FRANK "SON" (Guitar, vocal). Born: Osceola, Arkansas–August 13, 1942.

Frank Seals grew up listening to great bluesmen such as Sonny Boy Williamson (Rice Miller) and Robert Nighthawk, with whom he worked as a drummer at thirteen. He took up the guitar and at eighteen was already leading his own group, which played a Little Rock club for over four years. An old friend, Albert King, hired Seals in 1966 to play in his band as a drummer. A good example of his drumming can be heard on King's album *Live Wire/Bluespower*, which was recorded live at the Fillmore West. Seals moved to Chicago's South Side in 1971 and began jamming with people like Buddy Guy and Hound Dog Taylor. In a few short years he was able to get his own band together (the Son Seals Blues Band), tour the United States, and record for Alligator Records. During the 1980s Seals continued to make a name for himself recording, touring, and performing locally in Chicago. His latest CD, *Living in the Danger Zone,* was released by Alligator records in June 1991.

RECORDINGS

Bad Ax. Alligator 4738
Chicago Fire. Alligator 4720
Live and Burning. Alligator AL–4712
Living in the Danger Zone. Alligator ALCD–4798

FILM

Big City Blues. Rhapsody Films. 28 minutes, color.

SEMIEN, SIDNEY "ROCKIN' SIDNEY" (Multi-instrumentalist, vocal). Born: Lebeau, Louisiana–April 9, 1938.

Having started playing music professionally in his teens, Sidney Semien recorded his first single, "Make Me Understand," on the Carl label in 1957. For the next few years he recorded for Fame, Rod, and Jin Records without much success. He signed with Goldband Records in 1965 and gave a shot at recording soul music. It was not until the mid-1970s that he decided to enter the zydeco arena. With this new musical setup he recorded singles until the 1980s, though he scored a hit with his infectious "Don't Mess with My Toot Toot." This song was a commercial success and afforded Rockin' Sidney national attention.

RECORDINGS

Boogie, Blues 'n' Zydeco. Maison de Soul 1008
Creole: Talk of the Town. ZBC 102
Give Me a Good Time Woman. Maison de Soul 1007
A Holiday Celebration. ZBC 100
Hot Steppin'. ZBC 101
Joy to the South. Bally Hoo 2001
My Zydeco Shoes Got the Zydeco Blues. Maison de Soul 1009
Squeeze That Thing. ZBC 103
They Call Me Rockin'. Flyright 515

SHAKEY JAKE. *See* Harris, James D.

SHA-SHANT. *See* Monette, Johnny.

SHAW, THOMAS EDGAR (Guitar, harmonica, vocal). Born: Brenham, Texas–March 4, 1908; died: San Diego, California–February 24, 1977.

Thomas Shaw started to learn the guitar from a cousin named Willie Shaw, Jr., in 1917. He met Blind Lemon Jefferson in 1926 and followed him around, learning all he could about the blues. In 1934 he moved to San Diego and a year later got a job doing a fifteen-minute spot on radio station XEMO. Shaw worked sporadically until the early 1970s, when he recorded for Blue Goose, Advent, and Scott Records and played the San Diego State College Traditional Music and Blues Festival and the Cal Poly Folk Festival.

SHINES, JOHNNY (Guitar, vocal). Born: Frayser, Tennessee–April 26, 1915; died: Tuscaloosa, Alabama–April 20, 1992.

Johnny Shines began playing the blues in his mid-teens by studying the guitar styles of Lonnie Johnson, Blind Lemon Jefferson, Charley Patton, and Scrapper Blackwell. In 1934 he met Robert Johnson, and for two years the two traveled together throughout Mississippi and to St. Louis, Chicago, and New York. After Johnson's death in 1938, Shines traveled alone until he moved to Chicago in 1941. He recorded sporadically in the 1940s and 1950s, but it was not until 1965 that he really came to the attention of the blues public. Since that time he has recorded several albums and appeared in concerts and at festivals throughout the United States and Europe. He was the recipient of the 1989 Alabama Folk Heritage Award.

RECORDINGS

Dust My Broom (with Robert Lockwood, Jr.). Flyright 563
Hangin' On (with Robert Lockwood, Jr.). Rounder CS–2023
Hey, Ba-Ba-Re-Bop. Rounder CD202
Johnny Shines. Hightone HCD–8028
Johnny Shines. P-Vine PCD 2014
Mr. Blues Is Back to Stay. Rounder 2026
Recorded Live. Wolf 120.914
Too Wet to Plow. Tomato 269636–2
Traditional Delta Blues. Biograph BCD–121

FILM

Black and Blue. University of Alabama Television. 58 minutes, color.

SHWANK. *See* Monette, Raymond.

SIMON, JOE (Vocal). Born: Simmesport, Louisiana–September 2, 1943.

After beginning his recording career in 1960, Joe Simon had a million seller in 1969 with the single "The Chokin' Kind." In the 1970s he worked with Philadelphia producers Kenny Gamble and Leon Huff. This musical marriage resulted in two big hits, "Drowning in the Sea of Love" in 1971 and "The Power of Love" in 1972. Not much was heard from him in the 1980s and early 1990s.

RECORDINGS

Drowning in the Sea of Love. South Bound SEW–021
Get Down. South Bound SEW–013
Mood, Heart, and Soul/Today. South Bound SEW–971
The Sounds of Simon/Simon Country. South Bound SEW–954

SLIM HARPO. *See* Moore, James.

SMITH, ALBERT B. (Dancer, producer, vocal). Born: Mississippi–1924; died: Chicago, Illinois–February 7, 1974.

Albert Smith danced with jug bands and traveled with Silas Green's minstrel show in Mississippi before going to Chicago and becoming the leader of his own band in the 1950s and 1960s. It was as a producer, not a performer, that he made his mark on the blues world. He worked with VJ, Chance, United, ABC/Dunhill, Exodus, Blues on Blues, Bluesway, and other independent record companies for two decades prior to his death. Jimmy Reed spent most of his career under Smith's guidance; Smith wrote "Big Boss Man" and several other Reed hits. During Smith's career as a producer, he worked with such stars as T-Bone Walker, John Lee Hooker, Roosevelt Sykes, Jerry Butler, Big Joe Williams, the Dells, the Impressions, Betty Everett, and many others.

SMITH, BESSIE (Vocal). Born: Chattanooga, Tennessee–April 15, 1894; died: Clarksdale, Mississippi–September 26, 1937.

Bessie Smith made her professional debut at the Ivory Theater in Chattanooga, Tennessee, at the early age of nine. Her first recordings, "Down Hearted Blues" and "Gulf Coast Blues," were made on February 17, 1923. Like Gertrude "Ma" Rainey, she used some of the finest jazz musicians in her sessions from 1923 to her final recording date in 1933. The titles that she made with Louis Armstrong in the January 24, 1925, session are included in volume one of a two-volume set issued by Columbia Records. She also appeared in the film *St. Louis Blues*. The advent of the depression of 1929 caused her to fade into obscurity for a while, but in 1933 John Hammond brought her back to the studio with a band of star musicians that included Jack Teagarden, Benny Goodman, Chu Berry, and Frankie Newton. This was to be her last session. On the morning of September 26, 1937, she died from injuries that resulted from an auto accident. Throughout her career she was affectionately known as the Empress of the Blues. A fuller description of her can be found in chapter 4.

RECORDINGS

Any Woman's Blues. Columbia CGT–30126

Bessie Smith, Louis Armstrong, and Cab Calloway. Biograph M–3

The Collection. Columbia CJ44441

The Complete Recordings, Vol. 1: Empress of the Blues. Columbia/Legacy C2K–47091

The Complete Recordings, Vol. 2. Columbia/Legacy C2K–47471

Great Original Performances, 1925–33. BBC REB602

1925–1933. Hermes 6003

1923–1933. L'Art Vocal

Nobody's Blues But Mine. Columbia CGT–31093

St. Louis Blues. Buda 82465–2

BOOKS

Albertson, Chris. *Bessie*. New York: Stein and Day, 1972.

Brooks, Edward. *The Bessie Smith Companion*. New York: Da Capo Press, 1983.

Moore, Carman. *Somebody's Angel Child: The Story of Bessie Smith*. New York: Thomas Y. Crowell Company, 1969.

Oliver, Paul. *Bessie Smith*. London: Cassell and Company, 1960.

FILMS

Bessie Smith. Filmmakers Co-op/Canyon Cinema. 14 minutes, black and white.

Bessie Smith and Friends, 1929–1941. Jazz Classics Video JCVC–103. Black and white.

SMITH, CLARA (Vocal). Born: Spartanburg, South Carolina–1894; died: Detroit, Michigan–February 2, 1935.

Clara Smith's first recordings were made in 1923 and her last in 1932. By 1918 she was a headline attraction on the TOBA circuit. She made appearances at the Dream Theater in Columbus, Georgia; the Lyric in New Orleans; the Booker T. Washington Theater in St. Louis; and the Bijou in Nashville, Tennessee. In 1923 she cut her first records for Columbia. She recorded again for Columbia in 1925. On April 10, 1924, she participated in a recording session with Fletcher Henderson and Don Redman. A fuller description of her can be found in chapter 4.

RECORDING

Complete Recorded Works, 7 vols. Document 566 to 572

SMITH, CLARENCE "PINE TOP" (Piano, vocal). Born: Troy, Alabama–January 11, 1904; died: Chicago, Illinois–March 15, 1929.

"Pine Top" Smith played solo piano on the TOBA circuit and worked for a while as an accompanist to Ma Rainey. He settled in Chicago in the late 1920s and died accidently during a dance-hall brawl. Smith gained posthumous fame through his composition "Pine Top's Boogie Woogie," which he recorded in 1928.

RECORDING

Clarence "Pine Top" Smith and Romeo Nelson: Their Complete Recordings. Oldie Blues 2831

BOOK

Paparell, Frank. *Five Boogie Woogie Blues Piano Solos by "Pine Top" Smith*. New York: Leeds Music Corp., 1941.

SMITH, JEROME "PORK CHOP" (Drums). Born: December 26, 1895; died: unknown.

"Pork Chop" Smith worked with Sam Morgan and trumpeter Kid Rena in the 1920s. He moved to Chicago in the late 1920s and played with a number of jazz/blues bands, including those of Little Brother Montgomery and Lee Collins.

SMITH, MABEL "BIG MAYBELLE" (Piano, vocal). Born: Jackson, Tennessee–May 1, 1924; died: Cleveland, Ohio–January 23, 1972.

Big Maybelle Smith began her career in the early 1940s and achieved considerable popularity by making a number of hit records for the Okeh label. She was featured in the film *Jazz on a Summer's Day,* made at the Newport Jazz Festival in 1958. The latter part of her career consisted of a close association with religious music.

RECORDINGS

Big Maybelle. Savoy 1143
Blues, Candy, and Big Maybelle. Savoy Jazz ZDS–1168
The Okeh Sessions. Charly CD108
Roots of Rock n' Roll, Vol. 13: Blues and Early Soul. Savoy Jazz ZDS–1143

SMITH, MAMIE (Vocal). Born: Cincinnati, Ohio–May 26, 1883; died: New York City–October 30, 1946.

Mamie Smith was historically the most important of all black blues singers. Her pioneering work paved the way for other artists who were to come later. She did her first professional work as a member of a white act known as the Four Dancing Mitchells. In her teens she joined S. T. Whitney's Smart Set. In 1933 she moved to New York City and found plenty of work at places like the Gold Grabins, Percy Brown's, and Barron Wilkins'. She met composer-band leader-singer Perry Bradford in 1920 and with his incredible energy and ambition was able to land a recording contract with Okeh Records. She cut "That Thing Called Love" and "You Can't Keep a Good Man Down," both Bradford compositions, on February 14, 1920. This was the first recording ever made by a black blues singer. In August of that same year she returned to the studio and recorded two more Bradford tunes, "Crazy Blues" and "It's Right Here for You." In the first month of issue "Crazy Blues" sold 75,000 copies and became the high point in Mamie's career. For the next ten years she toured the country, playing all the best clubs and theaters, and recorded almost a hundred songs in a seven-year period. During the depression she was forced into retirement and did not appear again until around 1940, when she was featured in a number of short films, one of them being *Paradise in Harlem*. By this time her health was failing, and her fortune was almost gone. She spent the rest of her years forgotten and nearly penniless. Further description of her can be found in chapter 4.

RECORDING

Complete Recorded Works. 5 vols. Document 551 to 555

SMITH, MOSES "WHISPERING" (Harmonica, vocal). Born: Union Church, Mississippi–January 25, 1932.

Moses Smith started playing harmonica at the age of thirteen. By the time he was eighteen, he had his own band. He moved to Baton Rouge, Louisiana, in 1957 and led his own band there. While he was in Baton Rouge, he played with Lightnin' Slim from 1958 to 1960 and again from 1964 to 1966. He made his first recording in 1963 on the Excello label. He worked outside of music from 1966 to 1970 and began recording again in the early 1970s. He toured Europe with Lightnin' Slim in 1972 and 1973, playing the Montreaux Blues Festival and other venues. He performed around Baton Rouge, Louisiana, during the late 1970s and 1980s and was a regular at the New Orleans Jazz and Heritage Festival. He was a regular member of Tabby Thomas's Mighty House Rockers.

RECORDINGS

Authentic R & B. Stateside SL10068
The Excello Story. Blue Horizon 2683–007
The Excello Years. Excello 28025
Montreaux Blues Festival. Excello 28026
Over Easy. Excello 8020
Rooster Crowed for Day. Flyright 518
Swamp Blues. Blue Horizon 7–66263
25 Years with the Blues. Blues Unlimited 5007

SMITH, RUBY (Vocal). Born: unknown; died: unknown.

Ruby Smith was a cousin of Bessie Smith. She did quite a bit of performing in the middle and late 1930s. Her record output was not very large, but she still proved to be quite popular.

SMITH, TRIXIE (Vocal). Born: Atlanta, Georgia–1895; died: New York City–September 21, 1943.

Trixie Smith was a very good singer who worked mostly in vaudeville. She recorded with Louis Armstrong in 1925 and with Charlie Shavers and Sidney Bechet in 1938. She also did some work on the Black Swan Label in 1921, on the Paramount label with Fletcher Henderson in 1923, on the Silvertone label in 1925, and with Jimmy Blythe on Paramount in 1926. From 1927 to 1940 she appeared in numerous revues in New York City.

RECORDING
1922–29. Blues Documents 2068

SMITH, WHISPERIN'. *See* Smith, Moses.

SONNY TERRY. *See* Terrell, Saunders.

SPANN, LUCILLE (MAHALIA LUCILLE JENKINS) (Vocal). Born: Bolton, Mississippi–June 23, 1938.

Lucille Spann began her singing career after meeting Otis Spann in a nightclub where she worked as a barmaid. She was featured in Otis's band for a number of years, and in 1969 they were married. After Spann's death she continued to perform with Muddy Waters, and in the early 1970s she recorded for Al Smith. On her album, *Cry Before I Go,* which is on ABC Bluesway, she was backed by Detroit Junior on piano, Willie Smith on drums, James Green on bass, and Mighty Joe Young and Eddie Taylor on guitar. Her popularity outside of Chicago began to drop in the late 1970s, and by the 1980s not much was heard about her.

SPANN, OTIS (Piano, vocal). Born: Belzoni, Mississippi–March 21, 1930; died: Chicago, Illinois–April 25, 1970.

Otis Spann learned to play by ear at the age of seven and won first prize in a local blues contest the following year. He began working professionally at the age of fourteen and moved to Chicago in 1947. There he joined the band of his half brother, Muddy Waters. Spann worked with Waters for about twenty years, after which he formed his own band and also did some work as a single. He recorded with many blues artists, including Howlin' Wolf, Little Walter, Sonny Boy Williamson (Rice Miller), Chuck Berry, Bo Diddley, Big Mama Thornton, and James Cotton. He made his first recordings under his own name on the Candid label. Others followed on Bluesway, London, Vanguard, Testament, Prestige, and Bluestime. He also led the Waters band on several recordings and toured Europe a number of times.

RECORDINGS
The Blues Never Die. Fantasy/OBC OBCCD–530–2
Bosses of the Blues, Vol. 2 (with Eddie "Cleanhead" Vinson). Bluebird 8312–2–RB
Good Morning, Mr. Blues. Storyville 4041
Otis Spann: Chicago Blues. Testament 2211
Otis Spann Is the Blues. Candid CD9001
Walking the Blues. Candid CD9025

SPECKLED RED. *See* Perryman, Rufus.

SPIVEY, VICTORIA (Piano, vocal). Born: Houston, Texas–October 15, 1906; died: New York City–October 3, 1976.

Victoria Spivey's father was a member of a Texas string band. Her first professional work was with Lazy Daddy Fillmore's blues-jazz band. In the early 1920s she worked mostly in the Galveston-Houston area with people like Blind Lemon Jefferson, Joe Pullum, and Moanin' Bernice Edwards. In 1926 her recording of "Black Snake Blues" became a nationwide hit, and in 1929 she completed a starring role in King Vidor's musical extravaganza *Hallelujah!* During 1931 she worked as bandleader for the Hunters Serenaders. After her stint in the band business, she played reviews all over the Midwest, one of which included her sisters Leona, Sweet Peas, and Elton (Za Zu Girl) and her brother Sam. In 1933 she headed the Dallas Tan Town Topics and toured throughout Oklahoma and Texas. She also worked with Bessie Smith during this period. In 1934 she met dancer Billy Adams and had a steady association with him until 1951. After a ten-year period of semiretirement, she began a comeback in 1961 by recording enough material for four albums for the Prestige/Bluesville label. Her last years were spent in New York City, where she operated her own record company, Spivey Records.

RECORDINGS

Idle Hours (with Alonzo Johnson). Fantasy/OBC OBC–518–2
1927–30. Document 590
Victoria Spivey with the Easy Riders Jazz Band. GHB 17

STACKHOUSE, HOUSTON (Harmonica, violin, mandolin, guitar). Born: Wesson, Mississippi–September 28, 1910; died: ca. 1980.

Houston Stackhouse started playing music when he was fourteen years old, first on harmonica, then on violin, and on guitar a bit later, in 1926. One of the first bands with which he worked was the Mississippi Sheiks, Number Two. His career boasted long associations with Tommy Johnson and Sonny Boy Williamson (Alex "Rice" Miller) and a stint on "King Biscuit Time" on KFFA in Helena, Arkansas. All of his professional work was done in Arkansas and Mississippi, with only one trip to Chicago in 1973. His recordings consist of six sides, all made in 1967.

STEPHENS, JAMES "GUITAR SLIM" (Piano, guitar, vocal). Born: Spartanburg, South Carolina–1918.

In the late 1920s James Stephens left home to travel the medicine-show circuit for eight years. He was active in music throughout the 1930s and 1940s, but left the business around 1950 to work as a gardener and landscaper.

STEWARD, ALEXANDER T. "ALEC" (Guitar, vocal). Born: Charles City, Virginia–March 16, 1902; died: New York City–May 11, 1972.

Alec Steward moved to New York in the 1920s and later worked with Sonny Terry, Brownie McGhee, Leadbelly, Big Bill Broonzy, and Lonnie Johnson. During the 1940s he recorded under several names (Guitar Slim, the Blues King, the Back Porch Boys, and Slim Seward). He backed up Sonny Terry on a 1953 session for Elektra Records and in 1965 recorded an album under his own name for Prestige/Bluesville. Several of his earlier MGM and Tru-Blue records were reissued on the Arhoolie album *Guitar Slim and Jelly Belly.*

STIDHAM, ARBEE (Guitar, saxophone, harmonica, vocal). Born: DeValls Bluff, Arkansas–February 9, 1917.

At thirteen Arbee Stidham worked for a while with Bessie Smith. Later, in his teens, he traveled throughout Arkansas, played several times on radio station KARK in Little Rock, and worked regularly in Memphis. Halfway through his career he had to give up the saxophone for health reasons. He replaced it with the guitar, an instrument that he was reluctant to play in public until Big Bill Broonzy conned him into working at the Club Zanzibar in Chicago. Stidham's first recording session was for RCA Victor in 1947. Sidemen were Ransom Knowling, Judge Riley, Otto "Sax" Mallard, Bill Casimir, and Tampa Red. He did other sessions for Victor, Checker, Sittin' In With, Abco, Diamond, Prestige/Bluesville, Blues City, Folkways, and Mainstream Records as well. He retired from music around 1974.

STOVAL, JEWELL "BABE" (Guitar, vocal). Born: Tylertown, Mississippi–October 14, 1907; died: New Orleans, Louisiana–September 21, 1974.

Long a popular performer in New Orleans' French Quarter, Jewell Stoval sang blues, gospel, and traditional folk tunes. His first recordings were done on the Verve label in 1965. In the early 1970s he recorded an album on the Rounder label called *South Mississippi Blues*. Though not widely known, Stoval became a familiar figure on the local scene and at the annual New Orleans Jazz and Heritage Festival.

SUMLIN, HUBERT (Guitar, drums, vocal). Born: Greenwood, Mississippi–November 16, 1931.

Hubert Sumlin started playing the guitar when he was around eleven years old. He formed his own band and worked around Greenwood during the mid- and late 1940s. He played with James Cotton from 1950 to 1953. In 1954 he moved to Chicago and toured with Muddy Waters from that year until 1956. He did quite a bit of work in Europe in the 1960s. He worked sporadically with Howlin' Wolf's band throughout his career. He recorded as both sideman and leader on Black and Blue, Vogue, Sun, Amiga,

Blue Horizon, VJ, and Black Top Records. Still stationed in Chicago in the 1980s and early 1990s, he continues to work extensively in Europe.

RECORDINGS

Blues Party. Black Top 1036
Healing Feeling. Black Top 1053
Heart and Soul. Blind Pig BP–73389
Funky Roots. Vogue 512503

SUNNYLAND SLIM. *See* Luandrew, Albert.

SYKES, ROOSEVELT "THE HONEYDRIPPER" (Piano, organ, vocal). Born: Elmar, Arkansas–January 31, 1906; died: New Orleans, Louisiana–July 11, 1980.

Roosevelt Sykes was influenced by such great Arkansas piano players as Baby Sneed, Joe Crump, and Jesse Bell. He moved to St. Louis while he was in his early twenties and studied music there with Lee Green. In St. Louis he first began to compose. He was discovered by Jesse Johnson in 1929 and was taken to New York to make his first recordings. That same year he moved to Chicago and made that city his home base for the next thirty years, playing first with small groups and trios and later with his own ten-piece band, the Honeydrippers. In 1962 Sykes moved back to the South and lived there until his death. He remained active in music, touring the United States and Europe, doing concerts and recording dates, up to the time of his death.

RECORDINGS

Blue and Ribald. Yazoo 1033
Dirty Mother for You. Bluestime 2008
Feel Like Blowin' My Horn. Delmark DS–632
Gold Mine. Delmark DS–616
Hard Driving Blues. Delmark DS–607
The Honeydrippers, 1929–41. Blues Documents 2013
Music Is My Business. EPM Musique FDC5514
Raining in My Heart. Delmark DS–642
Urban Blues. Fantasy 24717

FILM

Roosevelt Sykes: The Honeydripper plus Jay McShann. Kay Jazz Video KJ096. *Sykes*: 27 minutes, black and white; *McShann*: 30 minutes, color.

SYLVESTER, HANNAH (Vocal). Born: Philadelphia, Pennsylvania–ca. 1900; died: New York City–October 15, 1973.

Hannah Sylvester was a singer of tough, raw blues. Her early works are extremely hard to find since she did not make many records. "Papa, Better Watch Your Step" and "Gulf Coast Blues" are excellent examples of her style. In the 1960s, she recorded "Mr. Cab" and "Big Black Limousine" for Spivey Records. From 1962 to the time of her death she worked outside of music.

TAMPA RED. *See* Whittaker, Hudson.

TAYLOR, CORA "KOKO" (Vocal). Born: Memphis, Tennessee–September 28, 1938.

Koko Taylor's singing career began in a church choir in Memphis. She moved to Chicago in 1953 and was soon in constant demand to perform with established stars such as Buddy Guy, Junior Wells, Elmore James, Muddy Waters, and Howlin' Wolf. In 1963 she did two singles on USA Records and a bit later had two huge hits on Chess: "What Kind of Man Is This?" and "I Got What It Takes." Finally, in 1965, she became famous nationally with "Wang Dang Doodle," a million seller. In 1972 Koko was recorded at the jazz and blues festivals in Ann Arbor and with Muddy Waters at Montreux, Switzerland. She toured Europe again in 1973, this time with the Chicago Blues Festival. While she was there, she cut an album for the French Black and Blue label. Taylor continued to perform and record with moderate success throughout the 1980s and early 1990s. Her releases during that time include *Queen of the Blues* (1985), *Live from Chicago* (1987), *What It Takes* (1991), and *South Side Lady* (1992).

RECORDINGS

The Earthshaker. Alligator ALCD–4711
From the Heart of a Woman. Alligator ALCD–4724
I Got What It Takes. Alligator ALCD–4706
Jump for Joy. Alligator 4784
Koko Taylor. Chess 9263
Live from Chicago. Alligator ALCD–4754
Queen of the Blues. Alligator 4740
South Side Lady. Black and Blue 59.542–2
Teaches Old Standards New Tricks. Chess CHC–91558
What It Takes: The Chess Years. Chess CHD–9328

TAYLOR, EDDIE (Guitar, vocal). Born: Benoit, Mississippi–January 29, 1923.

Eddie Taylor recorded under his own name for the VJ label from 1955 to 1957. From 1962 on into the late 1960s he appeared as a sideman on virtually every Jimmy Reed record. He has not been very active for the past twenty-five years. His album *I Feel So Bad* was reissued on the Hightone label in 1991.

RECORDINGS

I Feel So Bad. Hightone HCD–8027
My Heart Is Bleeding. L & R 42009
Ride 'Em on Down. Charly CD171

Still Not Ready for Eddie. Antone's 005
Street Talkin'! (with Elmore James and Jimmy Reed). Muse MCD–5087

TAYLOR, JOHNNY LAMAR "LITTLE JOHNNY" (Harmonica, vocal). Born: Memphis, Tennessee–February 11, 1943.

Little Johnny Taylor's first singing jobs were in gospel groups around Los Angeles in the early 1950s. He toured and recorded with the Mighty Clouds of Joy on the Victor label. He also recorded with the Stars of Bethel on Imperial in the mid–1950s. He was associated with the "Johnny Otis Blues Show" in the late 1950s and has been a top-quality rhythm-and-blues performer ever since. Taylor has recorded on Swingin', Galaxy, and Ronn. In 1988 he scored with a hit called *Part Time Love*, but was not able to back it up with anything else. He did mostly nightclub gigs in the South during the 1980s and was not very active in the early 1990s.

RECORDINGS

Greatest Hits. Fantasy 4510
I Shoulda' Been a Preacher. Red Lightnin' 0030
Part Time Love. Ace CH–229
Stuck in the Mud. Ichiban 1022
Ugly Man. Ichiban 1042

TAYLOR, KOKO. *See* Taylor, Cora.

TAYLOR, THEODORE ROOSEVELT "HOUND DOG" (Guitar, vocal). Born: Natchez, Mississippi–April 12, 1917; died: Chicago, Illinois–December 17, 1975.

Hound Dog Taylor began his professional career in 1935 in Greenville, Mississippi. He moved to Chicago in 1940 and became a regular on the Maxwell Street blues scene. He purchased his first electric guitar in 1957 and recorded for the first time that same year. In 1970 he and his group, the House Rockers, played the Ann Arbor Blues Festival and became an instant hit. He made his first album in 1971 and began to play concerts at places like the Manhattan Academy of Music, the Performance Center in Boston, and a string of universities around the United States.

RECORDINGS

And the Houserockers. Alligator ALCD–4701
Beware of the Dog. Alligator ALCD–4707
Genuine Houserocking Music. Alligator ALCD–4727
Natural Boogie. Alligator ALCD–4704

TERRELL, SAUNDERS "SONNY TERRY" (Harmonica, vocal). Born: Greensboro, Georgia–October 24, 1911; died: Mineola, New York–March 11, 1986.

Sonny Terry lost his sight in both eyes during his teens. DeFord Bailey, the first black to appear at the Grand Ole Opry, motivated him to turn to harmonica playing as a means of livelihood. He worked in North Carolina's tobacco towns with Blind Gary Davis, teamed up with Blind Boy Fuller for a while, and made his first recordings in 1937. He and Brownie McGhee joined forces in 1939 and remained together for the rest of Terry's life. They played *Cat on a Hot Tin Roof* on Broadway from 1955 to 1957 and in the road-show version during 1958. Both Sonny and Brownie were of the country blues tradition and were capable of intensely moving vocals and complex sounds that blossomed from their harmonica and guitar.

RECORDINGS

Brownie McGhee & Sonny Terry. MCA MCAC–1369
Brownie McGhee & Sonny Terry. Smithsonian/Folkways CDSF–40011
California Blues. Fantasy 24723
Chain Gang Blues. Collectables COLCD–5195
The Folkways Years. Smithsonian/Folkways CDSF40033
Just a Closer Walk with Thee. (with Brownie McGhee). Fantasy OBCCD–541–2
1938–1955. Document 536
Sonny and Brownie. A & M 75021–0829–2
Sonny Is King. Fantasy/OBC OBC–521
Sonny's Story. Fantasy/OBC OBCCD–503–2
Sonny Terry. Collectables COLCD–5307
Sonny Terry. Krazy Kat 807
Whoopin'. Alligator 4734

FILMS

Rev. Gary Davis and Sonny Terry: Masters of the Country Blues. Yazoo Video 000501. 60 minutes, color.
Sonny Terry. Seattle Folklore Society. 25 minutes, black and white.
Sonny Terry: Whoopin' the Blues. Pleasant Pastures Ltd. 14 minutes, color.
Sonny Terry and Brownie McGhee. Seattle Folklore Society. 25 minutes, black and white.

TERRY, SONNY. *See* Terrell, Saunders.

TEX, JOE (Vocal). Born: Rogers, Texas–August 8, 1933; died: Navasota, Texas–August 12, 1982.

Joe Tex performed for many years as a rhythm-and-blues singer before cashing in on the soul music explosion of the 1960s. He recorded such soul classics as "Hold on to What You Got" (1964), "Skinny Legs and All" (1967), "Men Are Getting Scarce" (1968), and "I Gotcha" (1972). After an extended absence from the scene for religious reasons, he returned to recording in 1977, when recorded the novelty tune "Ain't Gonna Bump No More (with No Big Fat Woman)" for Epic Records. His real name was Joseph Arrington.

RECORDINGS

Best of. Atlantic 81278–4

The Best of Joe Tex. King KL5–935

Greatest Hits. Curb/CEMA D21K–77520

THARPE, SISTER ROSETTA (Vocal). Born: Cotton Plant, Arkansas–March 20, 1921; died: Temple University Hospital, Philadelphia, Pennsylvania–October 9, 1973.

At the age of seventeen Sister Rosetta Tharpe was in Harlem's famous Cotton Club Revue. In the 1940s she worked with both Cab Calloway and Lucky Millinder and performed at the Cafe Society as a single. Her religious beliefs began to assert themselves after her first recording sessions for Decca Records. In 1949 she recorded a number of gospel songs with her mother, Katie Bell Nubin, and never ventured back into the blues.

RECORDING

I Believe I'm Gonna Make It. Rhino R4–70191

THOMAS, BLANCHE (Vocal). Born: New Orleans, Louisiana–October 16, 1922; died: New Orleans, Louisiana–April 21, 1977.

Blanche Thomas, a blues singer of ferocious force, was known around the Crescent City as "Queen of the Blues." In the 1960s and 1970s she appeared regularly with clarinetist Louis Cottrell in the French Quarter. In 1974 she played the New Orleans Jazz and Heritage Festival, featured as one of that city's top-named performers. She toured with the New York Jazz Repertory Company doing concert dates throughout Europe in 1975.

THOMAS, ERNEST "TABBY" (Piano, vocal). Born: Baton Rouge, Louisiana–January 5, 1929.

Ernest Thomas performed at an amateur talent show in San Francisco with Etta James and Johnny Mathis in 1952. In 1953 he cut his first record for Delta Records of Jackson, Mississippi. In 1955 he recorded in Crowley, Louisiana, on Feature Records and had a local hit with a tune called "Tomorrow." He also had a local hit with "Hoodoo Party" which he recorded on Excello Records in Crowley in 1962. He played the New Orleans Jazz and Heritage Festival in 1979. Later, he opened Tabby's Blues Box in Baton Rouge, Louisiana. His lounge featured blues artists four nights a week. He worked mostly in south Louisiana during the 1980s and 1990s. His album *Blues Train* was issued on Ace Records in 1989. He continues to play regularly around Baton Rouge with his own band, The Mighty House Rockers.

RECORDINGS

Blues Train. Ace CH–209

Hoodoo Party. Flyright 621

King of Swamp Blues. Maison de Soul 1026

Rockin' with the Blues. Maison de Soul 1010
25 Years with the Blues. Blues Unlimited 5007

THORNTON, WILLIE MAE "BIG MAMA" (Drums, harmonica, vocal). Born: Montgomery, Alabama–December 11, 1926.

Coming from a large family, Willie Mae Thornton had to go out and work at the age of fourteen when her mother died. Her first job, scrubbing floors in a saloon, gave her the opportunity to perform one night when the regular singer quit. She soon left Montgomery and went on the road with Sammy Green's Hot Harlem Review. With Green she traveled the blues circuit and heard such greats as Bessie Smith, Memphis Minnie, and Big Maceo. She remained with the Hot Harlem Review until 1948, when she settled in Houston, Texas. She made her first recording there as a featured singer with the Harlem Stars and continued recording, singing in local clubs, and giving concerts for the next ten years. She scored her biggest success in 1953 when she recorded Lieber and Stoller's "Hound Dog" and helped turn it into a hit record one year before Elvis Presley picked it up with great success. In the late 1950s she played drums and harmonica in small bands around San Francisco, and in 1961 she wrote and recorded "Ball and Chain," a moderate hit that was later recorded by rock star Janis Joplin. After playing at the Monterey Jazz Festival in 1964, she went on a tour of Europe and recorded "Hound Dog" on Fantana Records in Hamburg, Germany. At the same time she cut an album for Arhoolie in London. She recorded for Arhoolie again in 1966. This time she used James Cotton on harmonica, Otis Spann on piano, and Muddy Waters on guitar. Her association with Arhoolie continued into the 1980s. It released *Ball n' Chain* on compact disc in April of 1990. Vanguard Records released *Sassy Mama* (a reissue) in 1992.

RECORDINGS

Ball n' Chain (with Lightnin' Hopkins). Arhoolie CD–305
In Europe. Arhoolie (Japan) PCD2518
Jail. Vanguard VSD79351
The Original Hound Dog. Ace CDCHD940
Sassy Mama. Vanguard VMD–79354

TUCKER, TOMMY. *See* Higgenbotham, Robert.

TURNER, B. K. "BLACK ACE" (Guitar, vocal). Born: Hughes Springs, Texas–December 21, 1907; died: Malakoff, Texas–November 7, 1972.

B. K. Turner had a radio show on station KFJZ in Fort Worth, Texas, in the late 1930s. His recording career included some work for Decca in 1937 and Arhoolie Records in 1960.

TURNER, JOSEPH "BIG JOE" (Vocal). Born: Kansas City, Missouri–May 18, 1911; died: unknown.

Joseph Turner worked briefly with Benny Goodman during the swing era and also did a feature appearance on John Hammond's Carnegie Hall Spirituals to Swing concert. Turner met Pete Johnson in the mid–1920s in Kansas City, Missouri. They worked together until the late 1930s. His success was short-lived, and he ultimately faded into limbo until 1951, when he signed with Atlantic Records in New York City. "Chains of Love," his first release on that label, marked the beginning of a new career, and a succession of hits followed, including "Honey Hush," "Sweet Sixteen," and, in 1965, "Shake, Rattle, and Roll." "Corrina, Corrina," with its shuffle beat, was released in the spring of 1956.

RECORDINGS

Bosses of the Blues (with T-Bone Walker). Bluebird 8311–4–RB
The Boss of the Blues. Atlantic CD8812
Flip, Flop, and Fly. Pablo PACD 2310–937–2
Greatest Hits. Atlantic 81752
I've Been to Kansas City. MCA C42351
Jumpin' the Blues. Arhoolie 2004
Life Ain't Easy. Pablo 2310–883
Live! P-Vine PCD908

FILMS

Big Joe Turner, Count Basie, and Jay McShann: The Last of the Blue Devils. Rhapsody Films. 90 minutes, color.
Big Joe Turner and Hampton Hawes: L. A. Allstars. Rhapsody Films. 28 minutes, color.
The English Concert. VHS Video 40. 43 minutes, color.

VAUGHAN, STEVIE RAY (Guitar, vocal). Born: Dallas, Texas–1956; died: helicopter crash–1990.

Blues guitarist/vocalist Stevie Ray Vaughan was born in Dallas, Texas, in 1956. He started playing in bands by the age of eight. He dropped out of high school to begin his professional career in music. He recorded quite a bit during his short career. He died in a helicopter crash.

RECORDINGS

Couldn't Stand the Weather. Epic FE39304
Family Style. Epic ZK–46225
In Step. Epic EK–45024
Live Alive. Epic EGK–40511
The Sky Is Crying. Epic ET–47390
Soul to Soul. Epic FET–40036
Texas Flood. Epic BFT–38734

FILMS

Live at the Mocambo, 1983. SMV Video 49111–2. 30 minutes, color.
Pride and Joy, 1983–1989. SMV Video 49069–2. 36 minutes, color.

VINCENT, MONROE "POLKA DOT SLIM" (Harmonica, drums, vocal). Born: Woodville, Mississippi–December 9, 1919; died: Woodville, Mississippi–December 9, 1982.

Polka Dot Slim is more associated with Louisiana blues than with the music of his native Mississippi. He worked the New Orleans/Baton Rouge area beginning in the 1930s, performing solo as well as with Lightnin' Slim and Guitar Joe Willis. He recorded under the name "Vince Monroe" for the Excello label and as "Mr. Calhoun" for Zynn Records.

RECORDING

Real Blues from New Orleans. Bandy 70009

VINSON, EDDIE "CLEANHEAD" (Alto saxophone, vocal). Born: Houston, Texas–December 18, 1917.

Eddie Vinson started on piano, then took up alto saxophone and made his professional debut with Chester Boone's band in 1932. After a long stint with both Milt Larkins and Floyd Ray, he joined Cootie Williams's band in New York in 1942. He left Cootie in 1945 to form what turned out to be a sixteen-piece band. He has since worked long stints in Kansas City, co-led a band with Arnette Cobb in Houston, toured Europe with Jay McShann, and led his own big band in California. He performed in the 1980s at festivals and concerts throughout the world.

RECORDINGS

Back in Town. Charly CD50
Blues in the Night, Vol. 1: The Early Show. Fantasy FCD–9647–2
Blues in the Night, Vol. 2: The Late Show. Fantasy FCD–9655–2
Bosses of the Blues, Vol. 2 (with Otis Spann). Bluebird 8312–2–RB
Cleanhead and Cannonball (with Julian "Cannonball" Adderley). Landmark LCD–1309–2
Fun in London. JSP204
I Want a Little Girl. Pablo 2310–866
Kidney Stew. Black and Blue 233021
Live at Sandy's. Muse MR–5208
Meat's Too High. JSP223
Mr. Cleanhead Steps Out. Saxophonograph BP507
Old Kidney Stew Is Fine. Delmark DC–631
Sings the Blues. Muse MC–5310

VINSON, WALTER JACOBS (Guitar, vocal). Born: Bolton, Mississippi–February 2, 1901; died: Chicago, Illinois–April 22, 1975.

Walter Vinson began playing with Lonnie Chatmon while still very young, and in 1928 they decided to form a permanent partnership. In 1928 and 1929 they made their first recordings, accompanying Bo Chatmon and Mary Butler. In February 1930 they traveled to Shreveport, Louisiana, where they recorded for Okeh Records as the Mississippi Sheiks. The session produced two well-known tunes, "Stop and Listen" and "Sitting on Top of the

World." Except for one session for Bluebird Records in 1935, the Mississippi Sheiks never recorded again. Vinson recorded under his own name in 1935, 1936, and 1941 for Bluebird Records and in 1960 for Riverside. He also appeared at the University of Chicago Folk Festival and the Smithsonian Festival of American Folklife in 1972.

WALKER, AARON "T-BONE" (Guitar, vocal). Born: Linden, Texas–May 28, 1910; died: Los Angeles, California–March 17, 1975.

As a young man Aaron Walker led Blind Lemon Jefferson around the streets of Dallas, Texas. He later worked carnivals and medicine shows, spending some time with Ida Cox's band and groups led by Charlie and Edward Christian. He moved to California in 1934 and worked with Freddie Slack and Les Hite before getting his own band together. In the mid–1940s Chicago was his home base for a while. He recorded for Rhumboogie, Capitol, Black and White, Comet, Columbia, Constellation, Mercury, Atlantic, ABC, Bluesway, Polydor, Imperial, Delmark, Brunswick, Warner Brothers, and a host of other labels. Some of his hits include "Stormy Monday" and "Mean Old World." He was one of the first bluesmen to play the electric guitar and was an influence on nearly every blues guitarist who came after him.

RECORDINGS

Bosses of the Blues (with Big Joe Turner). Bluebird 8311–4–RB
The Complete Imperial Recordings: 1950–1954. EMI E22V–96737
Dirty Mistreater. MCA 1366
Feeling the Blues. Black and Blue 59.552–2
The Hustle Is On. Sequel NEXCD 124
I Want a Little Girl. Delmark DC–633
Low Down Blues. Charly CD7
T-Bone Blues. Atlantic 8020–2

BOOK

Dance, Helen Oakley. *Stormy Monday: The T-Bone Walker Story*. Baton Rouge: Louisiana State University Press, 1987.

WALKER, CHARLES (Guitar, vocal). Born: Macon, Georgia–July 26, 1922; died: New York City–June 24, 1975.

Charles Walker's career started in 1955 in Newark, New Jersey, where he played with a trio that consisted of piano, tub bass, and himself on guitar. He moved to New York in 1956, and in that same year he made his first recordings there for Holiday Records. For the last twenty years of his life, Walker managed to keep a band together to work mostly club dates. Although he recorded on Vest, Atlas/Angleton, P and P, Fury, and Oblivion Records, none of his work is currently available on the market.

WALKER, PHILLIP (Guitar, vocal). Born: Welsh, Louisiana–February 11, 1937.

Phillip Walker moved with his family to Port Arthur, Texas, in 1945, and he began playing guitar in 1951. In 1952 he started to play professionally. He was with Rosco Gordon and Lonesome Sundown in the latter part of that year, and from 1953 to 1957 he worked with Clifton Chenier. He moved to El Paso, Texas, with Long John Hunter in 1957 and stayed there until 1959, when J. R. Fulbright took him to Los Angeles to record for Elko Records. In 1963 he recorded for Austin McCoy's AMC Records. In 1966 Walker and his wife, "Bea Bop" (Ina Beatrice Walker), toured Texas with James K. Jones on piano, Ollie Count on bass, and Johnny Tucker playing drums. In the early 1970s he made recordings for Vault and Joliet Records. He had little activity in the 1980s.

RECORDINGS

Blues. Hightone 8013
The Bottom of the Top. Hightone 8020
From La to L.A. (with Lonesome Sundown). Rounder C–2037
Someday You'll Have These Blues. Alligator 4715
Tough As I Want to Be. Rounder C–2038

WALKER, T-BONE. *See* Walker, Aaron.

WALLACE, BEULAH THOMAS "SIPPIE" (Piano, vocal). Born: Houston, Texas–November 11, 1898; died: unknown.

Sippie Wallace spent her childhood in Houston, Texas, a city noted for its strong blues tradition. She got her first New York job in 1932 and afterwards toured for many years, mostly on the TOBA circuit. In 1966 she played the Royal Albert Hall in London, England, accompanied by Little Brother Montgomery on piano. Wallace remained active during the 1970s, playing at festivals and concert halls throughout the country.

RECORDINGS

Jug Band (with Otis Spann). Mountain Railroad 52672
1923–1929. Document 593
Sings the Blues. Storyville 4017

FILM

Sippie: The Life and Music of Sippie Wallace. Kay Jazz Video KJ073. 23 minutes, color.

WARREN, ULYSSES SAMUEL (Guitar, bass). Born: Aubrey, Arkansas–October 14, 1933.

Ulysses Warren first started playing guitar by ear in various string bands. He later took lessons and landed a job at King Records as a staff writer and studio musician. After his stint at King he became an independent producer and produced recordings by Bobby Taylor and Lil Green. He and his own band recorded "Fried Chitterlings, Parts I and II" on his Chi-Towns label in Chicago. Warren worked as musician or producer with a great many Chicago bluesmen, including Willie Mabon, Little Walter, Freddie King, Sonny Boy Williamson (Rice Miller), Elmore James, and Monk Higgins. He seems to have retired from the business in the 1980s and has not been active as a leader or sideman.

WASHINGTON, AARON GEORGE (Guitar). Born: Willington, South Carolina–January 2, 1902; died: unknown.

Aaron Washington played in a string band in Asheville, North Carolina, around 1919. The instrumentation included mandolin, fiddle, banjo, guitar, and bass fiddle. He was closely associated with Rev. Gary Davis from 1922 to 1926, taking him places to work and sometimes playing beside him on guitar. He continued to work sporadically until the late 1950s, when he retired from music completely.

WASHINGTON, ALBERT (Guitar, piano, vocal). Born: Rome, Georgia–August 17, 1935.

Albert Washington first started in music by singing spirituals with the Gospelaires. He began performing as a bluesman and made his first recordings in 1962 for Fence Records. He also recorded for Bluestown, VLM, Counterpart, Rye, Deluxe, Fraternity, and Jewel. His most popular songs were "Loosen These Pains" and "Turn On the Bright Lights." Although his career really never got off the ground, he continued to perform locally in and around Cincinnati, Ohio, throughout the 1980s. There were no available recordings on the national market in the early 1990s.

WASHINGTON, DINAH RUTH JONES (Vocal, piano). Born: Tuscaloosa, Alabama–August 29, 1924; died: Detroit, Michigan–December 14, 1963.

Raised in Chicago, Dinah Washington played piano for her church choir. She began singing in bars at eighteen. From 1943 to 1946 she worked with the Lionel Hampton band. In 1947 she began recording for Mercury and soon gained acceptance to the point that by 1950 Mercury was using her to cover pop hits for the black market. She finally broke into the pop market in 1959 and 1960 with "What a Difference a Day Makes." Her career was at its height at the time of her death.

RECORDINGS

The Bessie Smith Songbook. EmArcy 826663–4
Classic Dinah. Pair PDK2–1138
Dinah. EmArcy 842139–4
Dinah '63. Blue Note B41F–94576
If You Don't Believe I'm Leaving. Jukebox Lil1102
In Love. Roulette B41F–97273
Jazz Sides. EmArcy 824883–4

Mellow Mama. Delmark DC451
Sings the Blues. Mercury 832573–4
A Slick Chick on the Mellow Side. EmArcy 814184–4
What a Difference a Day Makes. Mercury 818815–4

WASHINGTON, WALTER "WOLFMAN" (Guitar, vocal). Born: New Orleans, Louisiana–ca. 1950.

An extremely popular young New Orleans blues musician, Walter Washington has been active nationally and internationally, performing at blues clubs and festivals.

RECORDINGS
Good and Juicy. Charly LIM 100
Heatin' It Up. Rounder CD–2098
Out of the Darkness. Rounder CD–2068
Rainin' in My Life. Maison de Soul C–1022
Sada. Pointblank/Charisma 91743–4
Wolf Tracks. Rounder CD–2048

WATERS, ETHEL (Vocal). Born: Chester, Pennsylvania–October 31, 1896; died: Chatsworth, California–September 1, 1977.

In her early teens Ethel Waters played theaters in Philadelphia and Baltimore, going by the name "Sweet Mama Stringbean" because of her tall, thin frame. She moved to New York in 1917 and established herself as top billing there. In 1921 and 1922 she toured with Fletcher Henderson and the Black Swan Troubadours and recorded several hit records for Paramount, Columbia, and Black Swan. She was featured in many shows and reviews during the 1920s and 1930s, including a stint in Europe. In 1932 she recorded with Duke Ellington and in 1933 with Benny Goodman. From 1935 to 1939 she headed her own touring show. She scored a big success with a dramatic role in *Mamba's Daughter* in 1939, and during the 1940s she worked chiefly as a nightclub artist and actress. Her television exposure consisted of being featured in a "Route 66" segment ("Goodnight Sweet Blues") in 1961, the "Ed Sullivan Show" in 1963, and an appearance on the "Pearl Bailey Show" in 1971.

RECORDINGS
1924–1928. Wolf WJS1009
1938–40. Rosetta 1314
On Stage and Screen (1925–1940). Sony Music Special Projects BT–2792.

BOOK
Waters, Ethel, with Charles Samuels. *His Eye Is on the Sparrow.* New York: Jove Publications, 1978.

WATERS, MUDDY. *See* Morganfield, McKinley.

WEBSTER, KATIE (Piano, organ, vocal). Born: Houston, Texas–September 1, 1939.

Katie Webster is perhaps southwest Louisiana's best female vocalist. She is currently based in Lake Charles and has performed since 1959 with most of that area's best musicians. She is a well-known figure around southwest Louisiana, having recorded extensively on Hollywood, Storyville, Kry, Rocko, Zynn, Spot, Action, Jin, and Goldband Records under her own name as well as with other popular artists. She suffered a bit of inactivity during the late 1970s and mid–1980s. Most of her work was done at gigs in Texas and Louisiana. She enjoyed a comeback in the late 1980s with performances in Europe that flowed into the 1990s. She had album releases on Arhoolie Records in 1986 and Alligator Records in 1988, 1989, and 1991.

RECORDINGS

Katie Webster. Flyright CD12
The Swamp Boogie Queen. Alligator 4766
Two-Fisted Mama. Alligator 4777
200% Joy. Ornament 7.529
Whoo Wee Sweet Daddy. Swamp Boogie 8701
You Can Dig It. Goldband 7785
No Foolin'. Alligator ALCD–4803
You Know That's Right. Arhoolie C–1094

WELLS, AMOS "JUNIOR" (Harmonica, vocal). Born: Memphis, Tennessee–December 9, 1934.

Junior Wells moved to Chicago while he was still in his teens, by which time his ability as a harmonica player was quite apparent. He began recording in 1953 with Muddy Waters on the State label. He has since recorded for Chief, Profile, Bright Star, and Vanguard, which produced his hit "Hoodoo Man." He teamed up with Buddy Guy in 1958 and has been a fixture at Theresa's, a basement bar on Chicago's South Side, for a number of years. The 1970s, 1980s, and early 1990s found Wells getting progressively more and more popular. He is now in demand at blues clubs and festivals throughout the world.

RECORDINGS

Blues Hit Big Town. Delmark 640
Chilly Walls. Flyright 605
Coming at You. Vanguard 79262
Hoodoo Man Blues. Delmark DD–612
In My Younger Days. Red Lightnin' 007
It's My Life, Baby. Vanguard VDS–73120
Messin' with the Kid. Charly CDCHLY219
On Tap. Delmark DD–635
Southside Blues Jam (with Buddy Guy and Otis Spann). Delmark DC–628

WELLS, VIOLA (Vocal). Born: Newark, New Jersey–December 14, 1902; died: unknown.

Viola Wells recorded on the Savoy label in 1944 and 1945. On these recordings her accompanists included Freddy Webster, Eddie "Lockjaw" Davis, Cozy Cole, and Frankie Newton. She recorded four titles on the Spivey label, of which only one has been issued, "See See Rider." For CBS she also did test sessions that included not only blues but also popular numbers and spirituals. As of this date, none of these has been issued.

WEST, CHARLIE (Piano, vocal). Born: Andalusia, Alabama–September 27, 1914; died: Chicago, Illinois–April 16, 1976.

Charlie West recorded a few songs for Vocalion and Bluebird Records in 1937. His last club date was in 1957 in Chicago. Aside from occasional house parties and the like, he remained relatively inactive as a professional musician during the two decades prior to his death.

WHEATSTRAW, PEETIE (Guitar, piano, vocal). Born: Ripley, Tennessee–December 21, 1902; died: East St. Louis, Illinois–December 21, 1941.

Peetie Wheatstraw was only thirty-nine years old when he died in an auto accident. He performed and recorded prolifically throughout the 1930s, leaving his mark upon all who came in contact with him. Professionally known as the Devil's Son-in-Law, Wheatstraw, who was influenced by Leroy Carr, was the composer of a small number of powerful blues songs, including his hit "Bring Me Flowers While I'm Living."

RECORDINGS

The Devil's Son-In-Law. Blues Documents 2011

"Kokomo" Arnold and Peetie Wheatstraw. Blues Classics BC–4

BOOK

Garon, Paul. *The Devil's Son-in-Law: The Story of Peetie Wheatstraw and His Songs*. London: Studio Vista, 1971.

WHITE, BOOKER T. WASHINGTON "BUKKA" (Guitar, piano, harmonica). Born: Houston, Mississippi–November 12, 1906; died: Memphis, Tennessee–February 26, 1977.

White's father taught him to play the guitar. He performed locally while working outside of music in Brazell, Mississippi, until 1920. He moved to St. Louis, Missouri, in the early 1920s and performed there, with frequent travels through the South, until 1930. In that year he moved to Memphis, Tennessee, and recorded there for the Victor label. He recorded for Vocalion Records in Chicago in 1937 and again in 1940. In 1939, while serving time in Parchman Farm Prison, he recorded for the Library of Congress label. From 1944 to 1963 he worked outside of music in Memphis, Tennessee. The mid–1960s found him back in the blues world. From then until his death, he made a number of recordings and performed throughout the United States and Europe.

RECORDINGS

Legacy of the Blues—vol. 1. GNP Crescendo 10011
Sky Songs. Arhoolie CD–323
Three Shades of Blues. Biograph BCD–107

FILMS

Along Old Man River (starring Bukka White, Robert Pete Williams, Furry Lewis, Sonny Terry, Brownie McGhee, and Roosevelt Sykes). Kay Jazz Video KJ020. 50 minutes, black and white.
Booker T. Washington White: Bukka White. Seattle Folklore Society. 25 minutes, black and white.

WHITE, CLEVE "SCHOOLBOY" (Harmonica). Born: Baton Rouge, Louisiana–June 10, 1928.

Strongly influenced by Sonny Boy Williamson (Rice Miller), White performed throughout south Louisiana during the 1950s. He recorded "Here I Go" and "Really, I Apologize" on Ace Records in Jackson, Mississippi, in 1957. He moved to Los Angeles in 1960 and retired from music for the next ten years. In 1970 he moved to San Francisco and began to perform again. He played university and club dates throughout the 1970s and early 1980s, but has been inactive since then.

WHITE, JOSH (Guitar, vocal). Born: Greenville, South Carolina–February 11, 1915; died: Manhasset, Long Island–September 5, 1969.

Josh White quit school early to become a lead boy for a series of blind bluesmen, including Blind Lemon Jefferson and Blind Blake. He recorded with Blind Joe Taggard for Paramount Records in 1928. His own recording career began in the 1930s when he performed gospel songs as the Singing Christian and blues as Pinewood Tom. White was a favorite of President and Mrs. Franklin D. Roosevelt and performed a number of times at the White House.

RECORDINGS

Blues Singer and Balladeer. Storyville 123
The Legendary. MCA 24170
1929–41. Document 597

WHITE, PRINCESS (Vocal). Born: Philadelphia, Pennsylvania–January 14, 1881; died: Mamaroneck, New York–March 21, 1976.

Princess White started in show business as a dancer when she was five years old. In 1898 she toured Australia and Europe with Salicia Bryan and her Pics. From 1900 to 1917 she appeared with the Charlie Gaines Carnival, with Wilbur Sweatman, and with the Silas Green Tent Show. She also worked with Ma Rainey, Ethel Waters, Ida Cox, and Butterbeans and Susie.

She retired from music in 1948 and devoted most of her time to church work until 1975, when she made her first album, *Sittin' on Top of the World,* at the age of ninety-four. Her last performance was at a concert at the Emelin Theater in Mamaroneck, New York. She sang two songs, "Sittin' on Top of the World" and "Peepin' in the Wrong Keyhole," walked backstage, sat down in a chair, collapsed, and died.

RECORDING

Sittin' on Top of the World. Barron VLP–401

WHITTAKER, HUDSON "TAMPA RED" (Guitar, vocal). Born: Smithville, Georgia–December 25, 1900; died: unknown.

Tampa Red Whittaker taught himself to play the guitar by watching his brother and local guitar players. While he was in his early twenties, he moved to Chicago and began to develop his own style of blues, a style that was to evolve into what is today referred to as urban blues. Throughout his career he played with a number of well-known blues artists, including Big Walter Horton and Sonny Boy Williamson (Rice Miller), and was considered king of the Chicago blues scene for some twenty years. The height of his career lasted from 1935 to 1953, during which time he recorded over 150 singles. Although a number of his songs have been recorded by more recent bluesmen, Tampa Red faded into obscurity, recording only two albums and giving only one public performance after 1953.

RECORDINGS

Bottleneck Guitar. Yazoo 1039
Crazy with the Blues. Oldie Blues 8001
Don't Tampa with the Blues. Fantasy/OBC OBCCD–516–2
Guitar Wizard. Blues Classics BC–25
It's Tight like That. Blues Documents 2001
Keep Jumping. Wolf WBJ001
1928–1942. Story of the Blues CD–3505–2

WILLIAMS, JOE. *See* Goreed, Joseph.

WILLIAMS, JOSEPH L. "JODY" (Guitar, harmonica). Born: Mobile, Alabama–February 3, 1935.

Jody Williams and Bo Diddley began learning the guitar at about the same time and later played together for a number of years. Williams's work as house musician for Chess Records led him to record with Muddy Waters, Sonny Boy Williamson (Rice Miller), Otis Spann, and Billy Boy Arnold. In 1954 he became bandleader for Howlin' Wolf. The sessions that he did under his own name included his first for Blue Lake Records on December 9, 1955, and one for Argo in 1957. Williams moved to Chicago in 1941 and continued to be a staple on that city's blues scene through the early 1980s.

WILLIAMS, ROBERT PETE (Guitar, vocal). Born: Zachary, Louisiana–March 14, 1914; died: Zachary, Louisiana–December 31, 1982.

Robert Williams started playing music on a cigar-box guitar when he was eighteen years old. He did not get into the blues professionally until he was twenty, and by then he was playing exclusively in a modal fashion. He has recorded on Vanguard, Prestige/Bluesville, Takoma, and Folklyric Records. Williams lived in Louisiana on a farm between Zachary and Baton Rouge and was usually on the bill at most blues festivals throughout the United States and Europe until the time of his death. Further description of him can be found in chapter 3.

RECORDINGS
Legacy of the Blues, Vol. 9. GNP Crescendo GNPD–10019
Robert Pete Williams. Storyville 225
Those Prison Blues. Arhoolie 2015
When I Lay My Burden Down. Southland 4

FILM
Robert Pete Williams. Seattle Folklore Society. 25 minutes, black and white.

WILLIAMS, SPENCER (Piano). Born: New Orleans, Louisiana–October 14, 1880; died: New York City–July 1965.

Spencer Williams was reared in Storyville by Madam Lulu White, one of New Orleans' most notorious characters. He worked as a "professor" for a while as a teenager. Best known as a composer, he wrote, among many other songs, "Basin Street Blues," "Mahogany Hall Stomp," "Shim Me Sha Wabblie," and "Tishomingo Blues."

WILLIAMSON, JOHN A. "HOMESICK JAMES" (Guitar, harmonica, vocal). Born: Somerville, Tennessee–April 30, 1910; died: unknown.

John Williamson was taught to play the guitar by his mother. He left home when he was thirteen and played throughout the South for several years. After some persuasion from his long-time friend Sleepy John Estes, Homesick James decided to move to Chicago in 1930. From that time on he was associated musically with B. B. King and other big-name bluesmen. He recorded for Blues on Blues Records and in 1970 headed a successful European tour with the American Blues Festival. The 1970s and 1980s were filled with performances in Europe, Canada, and the United States (mostly at festivals). He recorded for Black and Blue, Today, and Polydor Records during that time.

RECORDINGS
Goin' Back Home. Trix 3315
With Snooky Pryor. Wolf 0120409

WILLIAMSON, JOHN LEE "SONNY BOY" (Harmonica, vocal). Born: Jackson, Tennessee–March 30, 1914; died: Chicago, Illinois–June 1, 1948.

John Lee "Sonny Boy" Williamson, more than anyone else, shaped the course of Chicago's blues of the 1940s and 1950s and lifted the harmonica into prominence as a major blues instrument. He is truly one of the giants in blues history. His entire recording career, from 1937 to 1947, was spent with RCA Victor/Bluebird Records. Reissues of some of these sessions can be found in three volumes on Blues Classics. A fuller description of him can be found in chapter 3.

RECORDINGS

Complete Recordings, 1940 to 1942. Wolf 135
1937–1941, Vol. 1. Blues Classics BC–3
1937–1941, Vol. 2. Blues Classics BC–20
1937–1941, Vol. 3. Blues Classics BC–24

WILLIAMSON, SONNY BOY. *See* Miller, Rice.

WILLIAMSON, SONNY BOY. *See* Williamson, John Lee.

WILLIS, CHICK (Guitar, vocal). Born: Atlanta, Georgia–September 24, 1934.

Although Chick Willis is a first cousin of Chuck Willis, he was most influenced musically by Guitar Slim. He toured as a valet for Chuck from 1955 to 1958, the year his cousin died. While he was on the road, Chick learned to play the guitar and in 1956 cut his own record, "You're Mine," for Ebb Records in Los Angeles. He has since recorded for LaVal, Big Beat, and Mark IV Records. Most of his recorded output, however, is on the Ichiban label. His most recent work for it includes *Back to the Blues* (1991) and *Holdin' Hands with the Blues* (1992). He worked through the 1980s, mostly on the West Coast.

RECORDINGS

Back to the Blues. Ichiban ICH–1106
Chick Sings Chuck. Ichiban ICH–1012
Footprints in My Bed. Ichiban ICH–1054
Holdin' Hands with the Blues. Ichiban ICH–1134-CD
Stoop Down Baby. Collectables 5193

WILLIS, CHUCK (Guitar, vocal). Born: Atlanta, Georgia–ca. 1930; died: 1958.

Chuck Willis's first professional job was with Red McAllister's band. He recorded "Don't Deceive Me (Please Don't Go)" on the Okeh label in 1953 and Ma Rainey's "See See Rider" on that same label four years later. By 1956 Willis had moved to Atlantic Records, where his recording of his own composition "It's Too Late" won him a BMI award. In 1958, the year of his death, Willis recorded his most popular song, "What Am I Living For?" and "Hang Up My Rock and Roll Shoes."

RECORDING
My Story. Sony Music Special Products A–36389

WILSON, EDITH GOODALL (Vocal). Born: Louisville, Kentucky–September 2, 1906; died: Chicago–early 1980s.

Edith Wilson's paternal great-grandfather was John C. Breckinridge, a former vice president of the United States. She appeared in concerts and club dates with such greats as Duke Ellington, Jimmy Lunceford, and Bill "Bo Jangles" Robinson and performed in *Plantation Revue* (1922), *Rhapsody in Black* (1935), and *Hot Chocolates* (1929–30) with Louis Armstrong and Fats Waller. She will probably be remembered most of all for her impersonation of Kingfish's mother-in-law on the "Amos and Andy Show." She was also one of the stars of the Blackbirds and toured Europe six times. In 1964 Edith was the first black artist to be made a Kentucky colonel.

RECORDING
He May Be Your Man. Delmark 637

WILSON, HARDING "HOP" (Guitar, harmonica). Born: Grapeland, Texas–April 27, 1921; died: Houston, Texas–August 27, 1975.

Wilson learned to play the guitar and harmonica when he was a young boy. He worked mostly outside of music from the mid–1930s to the mid–1950s. Around 1956 he toured Texas and Louisiana with drummer Ivory Lee Semien. He recorded on the Goldband label in 1958 and 1959. In 1969 he recorded for Ivory Records in Houston, Texas. Throughout the 1960s and early 1970s he worked both in and out of music in Houston, Texas.

RECORDING
Hop Wilson and his Buddies: Steel Guitar Flash! Ace CHD–240

WINTER, EDGAR (Guitar, vocal). Born: Beaumont, Texas–December 28, 1946.

Brother of Johnny Winter, Edgar Winter performed music together with his brother as children in various venues around Texas. He joined his brother's band when his career started to take off. In 1969 he formed the Edgar Winter Group, featuring Rick Derringer. This was considered by some to be one of his best bands. In 1975 he recorded the album *Songs for the New Depression* with Bette Midler. His own albums include *White Trash* (1973), *They Only Come Out at Night* (1973), and *Recycled White Trash* (1974). He did not have much performance activity during the 1980s, although there were album releases on Epic in 1987, 1990, and 1992 and on Rhino Records in 1989.

RECORDINGS
The Edgar Winter Collection. Rhino R2–70895
Entrance. Epic EK–48536
Mission Earth. Rhino R2–70709
Shock Treatment. Epic EK–32461
They Only Come Out at Night. Epic EK–31584
White Trash. Epic EK–30512

WINTER, JOHNNY (Guitar, vocal). Born: Beaumont, Texas–February 23, 1944.

A self-taught guitar player, Johnny Winter came from a musical family. He worked the Beaumont area talent contests in the mid–1950s with his brother Edgar. He performed professionally in the late 1950s throughout Texas and Louisiana with Gene Terry and the Downbeats, and in Chicago in the early 1960s with Mike Bloomfield. He started recording, as a sideman, in the mid–1960s and formed his own band in 1968 to record for Sonobeat Records in Austin, Texas. He has been active as a professional musician doing concert and club dates and recording sessions ever since.

RECORDINGS
Back in Beaumont. Thunderbolt THBL078
Birds Can't Row Boats. Relix 2034
Early Winter. President PRCVII6
Guitar Slinger. Alligator ALCD4735
Johnny Winter. Columbia PC9826
The Johnny Winter Story. P-Vine PCD1611
Livin' the Blues. Showcase SHLP132
Second Winter. Columbia PC9947
Serious Business. Alligator 4742
Third Degree. Alligator 4748

WITHERSPOON, JAMES "JIMMY" (Bass, vocal). Born: Gurdon, Arkansas–August 8, 1923.

Jimmy Witherspoon, who made his recording debut with the Jay McShann Band, is perhaps one of the most popular blues singers in the world today. He has performed and recorded everything from jazz to popular material and has always placed his stamp of individuality on every song he has sung. He started singing when he was five years old in the First Baptist Church choir in Gurdon, Arkansas, and has been performing the blues successfully ever since the mid–1930s. He has recorded on a large number of labels, including United Artists, Blue Note, Prestige, Bluesway, and Columbia. Witherspoon lives in California and has performed throughout the United States and the world, always getting top billing.

RECORDINGS
Big Blues. JSP CD 205
Blue Spoon. Prestige 7327
Evenin' Blues. Fantasy/OBC OBC–511

Jimmy's Blues. MCA 1367
Meets the Jazz Giants. Charly CD 169

WRIGHT, BILLY (Vocal). Born: ca. 1918; died: Atlanta, Georgia–October 28, 1991.

Billy Wright gained the title "Prince of the Blues" in the 1940s when he was Atlanta's top rhythm-and-blues artist. His penchant for flashy costumes influenced Little Richard and many others. His 1950 hit "Blues for My Baby" was one of the first recorded rhythm-and-blues songs to overtly show gospel influences.

RECORDINGS
Don't You Want a Man Like Me? Ace CHA193
Goin' Down Slow. Savoy SJL1146
The Prince of the Blues. Route 66 KIX13

YANCEY, ESTELLA "MAMA" (Piano, guitar, vocal). Born: Cairo, Illinois–January 1, 1896; died: Chicago, Illinois–late 1970s.

Estella "Mama" Yancey worked mostly with her husband Jimmy Yancey around Chicago from 1919 to the late 1930s. She recorded with Jimmy on the Session label in 1943 and for Atlantic Records in 1951. She also recorded with Don Ewell on the Windin' Ball label in Chicago in 1952, with Little Brother Montgomery for Riverside in 1961, and with Art Hodes on Verve Folkways in 1965. Except for festival dates and special appearances at blues clubs and universities, she did little work in the 1970s.

RECORDINGS
Chicago Piano, Vol. 1. Atlantic 82368–2
Maybe I'll Cry. Red Beans 001

YANCEY, JAMES EDWARD "JIMMY" (Piano). Born: Chicago, Illinois–February 20, 1898; died: Chicago, Illinois–September 17, 1951.

Husband of blues singer Estella "Mama" Yancey, Jimmy Yancey began singing and dancing with a vaudeville company at the age of six. Shortly thereafter he toured with various troupes led by Bert Earle, Jeannette Adler, and Cozy Smith. He also did a long stint on the Orpheum circuit and toured Europe before World War I. Jimmy settled in Chicago in 1915 and worked as a pianist at house-rent parties and various clubs until 1925. In that year he started working at Comiskey Park as a groundsman and made that his major source of income for the next twenty-five years. In 1948 he did a solo gig at the Beehive in Chicago and appeared at Carnegie Hall with his wife during the Kid Ory concert tour. Unfortunately, Yancey did not play much during the last years of his life. He was constantly plagued by ill health.

RECORDINGS
Chicago Piano, Vol. 1. Atlantic 82368–2
In the Beginning. Solo Art SACD1
Jimmy Yancey. Oldie Blues 2802
Piano Blues, 1939–40. Swaggie 824

YOUNG, JOHNNY (Harmonica, guitar, mandolin, vocal). Born: Vicksburg, Mississippi–January 1, 1918; died: Chicago, Illinois–April 18, 1974.

Johnny Young's main source of inspiration was his uncle, Anthony Williams, who played violin, guitar, mandolin, and banjo in a string band in Rolling Fork, Mississippi. Johnny played harmonica with Robert Nighthawk in Mississippi and then with Sleepy John Estes and Hammie Nixon in Tennessee before moving to Chicago in 1940. In Chicago he worked with John Lee "Sonny Boy" Williamson, Memphis Slim, Sunnyland Slim, Muddy Waters, Howlin' Wolf, Snooky Pryor, and a host of other blues stalwarts. In 1947 he recorded for Ora Nelle Records and in 1948 for Planet/Old Swingmaster. He was not heard from again until 1963, when he did a few sides for Testament Records. In the late 1960s and early 1970s he made recordings for Milestone, Vanguard, Arhoolie, Blues on Blues, Bluesway, Spivey, Decca (British), Rounder, Storyville (Danish), and Horizon Records.

RECORDINGS
And His Chicago Blues Band. Arhoolie 1029
And His Friends. Testament 2226
Chicago Blues. Arhoolie C/CD325
Chicago Blues (with Johnny Young and Big Walter Horton). Arhoolie 1037

YOUNG, JOSEPH "MIGHTY JOE" (Guitar, vocal). Born: Shreveport, Louisiana–September 23, 1927.

Joe Young became involved in music at an early age, first by watching his father play, then trying to copy what he heard. He moved to Milwaukee, Wisconsin, in his early teens and while there took a few guitar lessons from the Columbia Musical Company. Since he was less than a hundred miles from Chicago, the hub of electric blues/rock, he headed there in 1956 and joined the band of the legendary Howlin' Wolf as lead guitarist. In the next few years he held the same position in the bands of Jimmy Rogers and Billy Boy Arnold. He then formed his first band in the Chicago area. Work was scarce in Chicago in the late 1950s. Young found himself working only one or two nights a week for very little money in the lesser-known local blues haunts. Figuring that it would be better to play with the stars, he joined up as second guitarist in the famous Otis Rush band of the early 1960s. He remained with Rush from 1960 to 1963, at which time he again started his own band, and he has remained on his own ever since.

It was also in the early 1960s that several of the smaller record companies that specialized in the changing blues and rhythm-and-blues field began to take an interest in Young. His first single, entitled "Why Baby" (Fire Records), soared into Chicago's top ten within a few weeks, bringing Young into larger demand throughout Chicago's black nightclub circuit. This was followed by two other singles, "We Love You, Baby" (Webco Records) and "Sweet Kisses" (Celtex Records), both of which also soared into Chicago's rhythm-and-blues top ten. Although none of these releases was successful nationally, Young was red-hot on the Chicago scene.

By the late 1960s the small record companies in Chicago had all but vanished. The name of Mighty Joe Young, however, had gotten stronger. He was in heavy demand as a session guitarist by Willie Dixon, Jimmy Rogers, Koko Taylor, Albert King, and Magic Sam, to name a few. Young and his guitar can be heard on several Tyrone Davis hits recorded during this period, including the million-selling "Can I Change My Mind" and the Duotones' million-selling "Shake a Tail Feather."

In the early 1970s a new wave of interest in the electric blues of Chicago began to appear. Young was called to cut his first album, *Blues with a Touch of Soul*, for Delmark Records. Following this he did an album entitled *Mighty Joe Young (The Legacy of the Blues, Vol. 4)* for the Sweden-based Sonet Gramafon.

In 1974 Young signed a recording contract with Ovation Records. His first album, entitled *Chicken Heads,* was released in late 1974. Proving himself to be a songwriter, Young composed seven of the ten selections on this album. In 1976 Ovation released a second album by Young, simply entitled *Mighty Joe Young.*

In the past Young had ventured very little out of the Chicago area, but with the success of *Chicken Heads* he was on the move nationally. His music holds a strong interest in many foreign markets, including Germany, England, Japan, Switzerland, New Zealand, and Australia. His international popularity brought about his first foreign tour in 1975 throughout parts of France and Spain. Young performed with his band mostly in Chicago during the 1980s. Although he continued to work abroad also, his popularity seemed not to be enough to warrant much recording. He has released nothing new on the national blues market in the early 1990s.

RECORDINGS

Blues with a Touch of Soul. Delmark 629
Bluesy Josephine. Black and Blue 59.521–2
Legacy of the Blues, Vol. 4. GNP Crescendo GNPD–10014

ZENO, CHESTER (Rubboard). Born: Lafayette, Louisiana–ca. 1929; died: Lafayette, Louisiana–1989.

Chester Zeno was a mainstay in Clifton Chiener's Zydeco Band for many years. His style of playing, the rhythms that he played, and the dance and body movements that he incorporated into his performances were influences to every rubboard player that came after him. He was forced to retire from music in the mid–1980s because of sickness. He never returned.

Bai Konte playing the 21-string Mandinka harp, a West African instrument of incredible complexity. (Photo by Austin Sonnier, Jr.)

Alphonse "Boise-Sec" Ardoin performing at the Southwest Louisiana Zydeco Festival in 1989. (Photo by Austin Sonnier, Jr.)

Lurrie and Carey Bell at the Springblues Festival in Ecaussines, Belgium, in 1989. (Photo by Jacques Depoorter. Courtesy of *Blues Life* magazine.)

Robert "Bobby" Bland performing in Houston, Texas, in 1982. (Photo by Austin Sonnier, Jr.)

Eddie Boyd at home in Finland in the mid-1980s. (Courtesy of Eddie Boyd.)

Clifton Chenier performing in Lafayette, Louisiana, in 1981. (Photo by Austin Sonnier, Jr.)

Eddy Clearwater at the Banana Peel in Ruiselede, Belgium, in 1989. (Photo by Jacques Depoorter. Courtesy of *Blues Life* magazine.)

Albert Collins at the Bluesesta Fette in Utrecht, Holland, in 1989. (Photo by Jacques Depoorter. Courtesy of *Blues Life* magazine.)

"Blind" John Henry Davis in the late 1970s. (Photo by Amy O'Neal. Courtesy of Alligator Productions.)

Willie Dixon, Chicago's most celebrated blues songwriter and producer.

Margie Evans in Europe in the late 1980s. (Courtesy of *Blues Life* magazine.)

Canray Fontenot performing at the Southwest Louisiana Zydeco Festival in 1989. (Photo by Austin Sonnier, Jr.)

Lowell Fulson in Europe in 1989. (Photo by Larry Benicewicz. Courtesy of *Blues Life* magazine.)

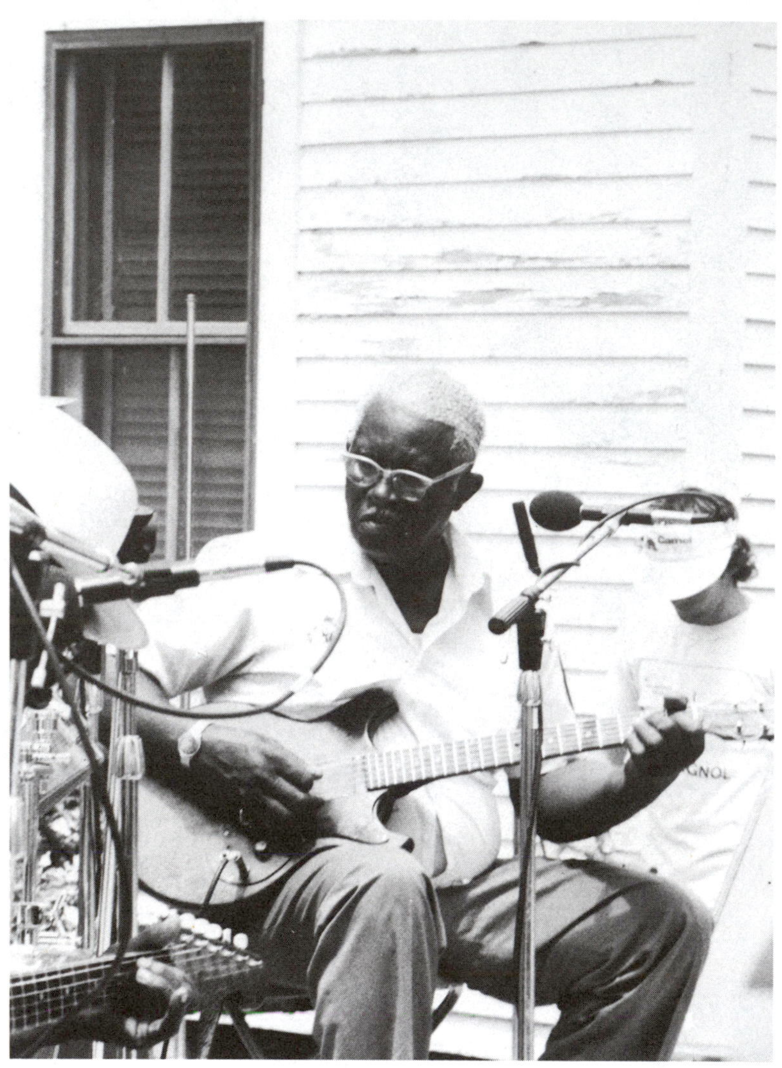

Silas Hogan at the Baton Rouge Festival in 1985. (Photo by Austin Sonnier, Jr.)

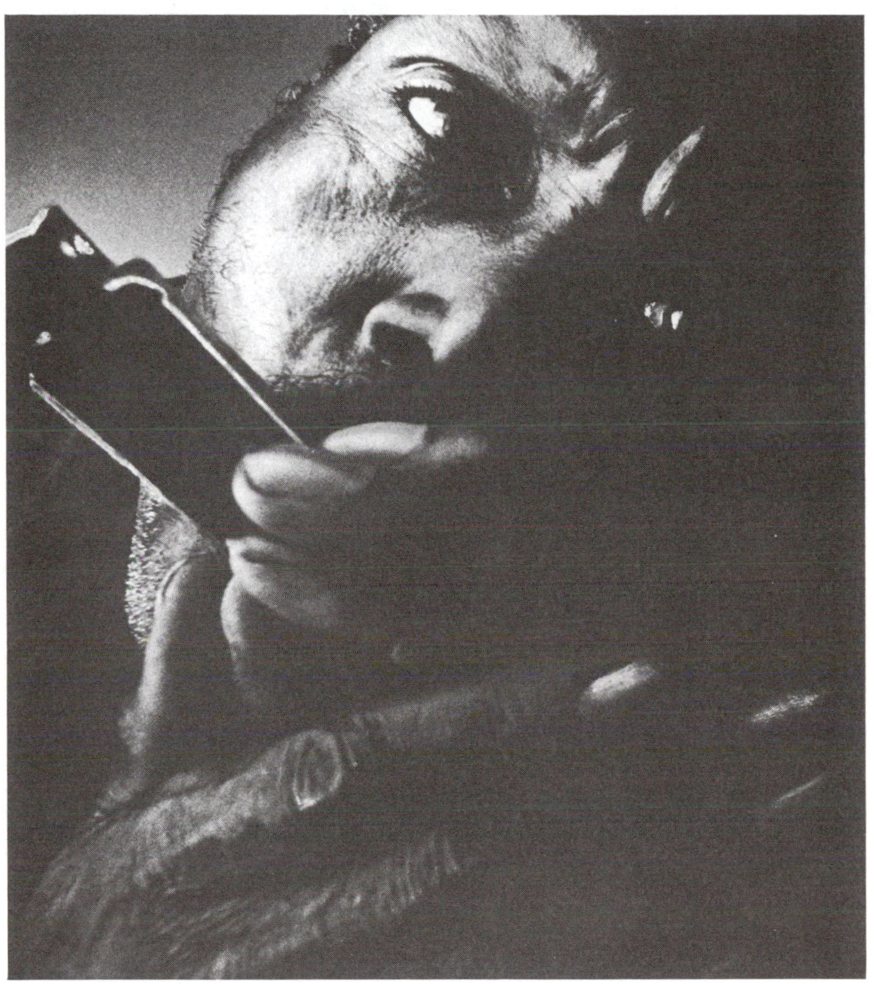

"Big" Walter Horton in the late 1970s (Photo by Peter Amft. Courtesy of Alligator Productions.)

Arthur "Peg-Leg Sam" Jackson at the New Orleans Jazz and Heritage Festival in 1980. (Photo by Austin Sonnier, Jr.)

Etta James at the Belgium Rhythm and Blues Festival in 1990. (Photo by Jacques Depoorter. Courtesy of *Blues Life* magazine.)

Ernie K-Doe at the Baton Rouge Blues Festival in 1985. (Photo by Austin Sonnier, Jr.)

Arthur "Guitar" Kelly at the Baton Rouge Blues Festival in 1985. (Photo by Austin Sonnier, Jr.)

Riley "B. B." King at the Belgium Rhythm and Blues Festival in Peer, Belgium, in 1989. (Photo by Jacques Depoorter. Courtesy of *Blues Life* magazine.)

Walter "Furry" Lewis at New Orleans' Preservation Hall in 1978. (Photo by Shirley House. Courtesy of Shirley and Richard House.)

Jerry McCain at the Banana Peel in Ruiselede, Belgium, in 1991. (Photo by Jacques Depoorter. Courtesy of *Blues Life* magazine.)

Johnny Monette as a young bluesman in 1966. (Courtesy of Johnny Monette.)

Eurreal "Little Brother" Montgomery at the New Orleans Jazz and Heritage Festival in 1980. (Photo by Austin Sonnier, Jr.)

Chicago blues giant McKinley "Muddy Waters" Morganfield in the late 1970s.

Charles Musselwhite at the Vredenburg in Utrecht, Netherlands, in 1992. (Photo by Jacques Depoorter. Courtesy of *Blues Life* magazine.)

Louis Myers in Europe in 1989. (Courtesy of *Blues Life* magazine.)

Raful Neal performing at the Baton Rouge Blues Festival in 1985. (Photo by Austin Sonnier, Jr.)

Gertrude "Ma" Rainey in the mid-1930s. (Courtesy of the Austin Sonnier collection.)

Fenton Robinson in Chicago in the late 1970s. (Photo by Jan Loveland. Courtesy of Alligator Productions.)

Charles Isaiah "Dr." Ross at the Banana Peel in Ruiselede, Belgium, in 1988. (Photo by Jacques Depoorter. Courtesy of *Blues Life* magazine.)

Alton "Rockin' Dopsie" Rubin at the Cajun Music Festival in Lafayette, Louisiana, in 1985. (Photo by Austin Sonnier, Jr.)

Otis Rush at the Poorthuis in Peer, Belgium, in 1990. (Photo by Jacques Depoorter. Courtesy of *Blues Life* magazine.)

Frank "Son" Seals performing on the street in Chicago. (Photo by Jan Loveland. Courtesy of Alligator Productions.)

Hubert Sumlin in Europe. (Courtesy of *Blues Life* magazine.)

Roosevelt Sykes at the New Orleans Jazz and Heritage Festival in 1981. (Photo by Austin Sonnier, Jr.)

Koko Taylor, one of the most popular contemporary urban blues singers. (Photo by Doug Fulton. Courtesy of Alligator Productions.)

Monroe "Polka Dot Slim" Vincent performing solo at the New Orleans Jazz and Heritage Festival in 1979. (Photo by Austin Sonnier, Jr.)

Walter "Wolfman" Washington at the Banana Peel in Ruiselede, Belgium, in 1990. (Photo by Jacques Depoorter. Courtesy of *Blues Life* magazine.)

Katie Webster (left) and Maxine Howard in Europe. (Courtesy of *Blues Life* magazine.)

Robert Pete Williams at the New Orleans Jazz and Heritage Festival in 1978. (Photo by Austin Sonnier, Jr.)

Joseph "Mighty Joe" Young.

Chester Zeno sporting his rubboard technique with Clifton Chenier's Red Hot Peppers. (Photo by Austin Sonnier, Jr.)

SELECTED FILMOGRAPHY

Afro-American Work Songs in a Texas Prison. Folklore Research Films. 29 minutes, black and white.

Along Old Man River (starring Bukka White, Robert Pete Williams, Furry Lewis, Sonny Terry, Brownie McGhee, and Roosevelt Sykes). Kay Jazz Video KJ020. 50 minutes, black and white.

Always a Pleasure. Flower Films. 58 minutes, color.

Another Kind of Music. Phoenix Films. 24 minutes, color.

Banjo Man. Texture Films. 26 minutes, black and white.

Beale Street. Real to Reel. 103 minutes, black and white.

Beale-Street Mama: And Other All Black Shorts. Limited Edition Videos LEV JL12. 90 minutes, black and white.

Bear Dog, Bulldog: Talking Traditions and Singing Blues in Arkansas Schools. Co-Media, Inc. 30 minutes, color.

Chuck Berry: Rock and Roll Music. BMG Video 791146, color.

Big Bill Broonzy. TCB Releasing Ltd. 18 minutes, black and white.

Big Brother and the Holding Company: Comin' Home. BMG Video 74321–100863. Color.

Big City Blues (starring James Brewer, Son Seals, Queen Sylvia Embry, Bill Branch, and others). Kay Jazz Video KJ075. 28 minutes, color.

The Big T.N.T. Show. Budget Films. 93 minutes, black and white.

A Black Experience. Dibie-Dash Productions. 25 minutes, color.

Black Music in America, From Then 'Til Now. Budget Films. 38 minutes, color.

Black Music in America: The Seventies. Budget Films. 32 minutes, color.

Black Music in Passage. PBS Video. 60 minutes, color.

Black Roots. Icarus Films. 61 minutes, color.

The Blues. Arhoolie Production Company. 25 minutes, black and white.

The Blues. Audio Brandon Films. 21 minutes, color.

Blues Alive. RCA/Columbia Pictures, Home Video. 91 minutes, color.

Blues Alive. RCA/Columbia Pictures Int. 58 minutes, color.

Blues Alive. (starring Buddy Guy, Albert Collins, Otis Rush, Ruth Brown, Sam Myers, Junior Wells, Charles Brown, and others). BMG Video 791151. Color.

Blues Country. Production Services. 86 minutes, color.

Blues Country to City. GPN Educational Media. 30 minutes, color.

Les Blues des Balfa (the Balfa Brothers). Flower Films. 30 minutes, color.

Blues from the South. Neyrac Films. 52 minutes, color.

Blues House Party (starring John Jackson, Cora Jackson, Flora Molton, John Cephas, and others). Eleanor Ellis Houseparty Productions. 60 minutes, color.

Blues One. Skylark Savoy Productions. 58 minutes, color.

Blues Summit in Chicago (Johnny Winter and others). Verve Films. 60 minutes, color.

Born for Hard Luck. Tom Davenport Films. 30 minutes, color.

Bottle Up and Go. Center for Southern Folklore. 18 minutes, color.

Clarence Gatemouth Brown. Phoenix Films. 58 minutes, color.

Brownsville Blues. Televista Projects. 22 minutes, color.

A Bundle of Blues. Paramount Pictures. 10 minutes, black and white.

Sam Chatmon: Sitting on Top of the World. Mississippi Authority for Educational Television. 28 minutes, color.

Clifton Chenier: Hot Pepper. Kay Jazz Video KJ006. 54 minutes, color.

Clifton Chenier: The King of Zydeco. Arhoolie Video ARV401. 55 minutes, color.

Chicago Blues (starring Buddy Guy, Johnnie Lewis, Floyd Jones, J. B. Hutto, Muddy Waters, and others). Kay Jazz Video KJ004. 50 minutes, color.

Eddy Clearwater (record party with Carey and Lurrie Bell). Gerry Chodkowski. 60 minutes, black and white.

Cobra Snake for a Necktie. Picture Start. 23 minutes, color.

Elizabeth Cotten. Seattle Folklore Society. 25 minutes, black and white.

Papa John Creach: Setting the Record Straight. Kay Jazz Video KJ083. 58 minutes, color.

Arthur Crudup: Born in the Blues. WETA-TV, Washington, D.C. 29 minutes, color.

Blind Gary Davis. University of California. 12 minutes, black and white.

Rev. Gary Davis. Seattle Folklore Society. 26 minutes, black and white.

Rev. Gary Davis and Sonny Terry: Masters of the Country Blues. Yazoo Video 000501. 60 minutes, color.

Drywood (the Ardoin family and Canray Fontenot). Kay Jazz Video KJ067. 37 minutes, color.

Sleepy John Estes. Televista Projects. 60 minutes, black and white.

Jesse Fuller: Lone Cat. Seattle Folklore Society. 26 Minutes, black and white.

Good Mornin' Blues. PBS Video. 59 minutes, color.

Gravel Springs Fife and Drums. Center for Southern Folklore. 10 minutes, color.

John Hammond: From Bessie to Springsteen (with Bessie Smith, Billie Holiday, Stevie Ray Vaughan, Aretha Franklin, and others). SMV Video 490572. Color.

W. C. Handy. Vignette Films. 14 minutes, color.

Jimi Hendrix: At the Atlanta Pop Festival. BMG Video 791279. 60 minutes, color/black and white.

Honky Tonk. Televista Projects. 120 minutes, black and white.

John Lee Hooker. Seattle Folklore Society. 25 minutes, black and white.

Hootie's Blues. TCB Relasing Ltd. 30 minutes, color.

Lightnin' Hopkins. Seattle Folklore Society. 25 minutes, black and white.
Lightnin' Hopkins: The Blues According to. Kay Jazz Video KJ053. 47 minutes, color.
Lightnin' Hopkins: A Program of Songs. University of Washington Press. 8 minutes, black and white.
Sam Lightnin' Hopkins. Indiana University. 30 minutes, color.
Son House. Seattle Folklore Society. 25 minutes, black and white.
Son House and Bukka White: Masters of the Country Blues. Yazoo Video 00500. 60 minutes, color.
Hungry Licks. Fantasy Films. 30 minutes, color.
Alberta Hunter. Kultur 1270. 60 minutes, color.
John Jackson: An American Songster. Rhapsody Films. 30 minutes, color.
John Jackson: A Musical Portrait (with Larry Johnson, Phil Wiggins, and John Cephas). Kay Jazz Video KJ076. 30 minutes, color.
Lee Jackson and His Music. Gerry Chodkowski. 30 minutes, black and white.
J'ai Ete au Bal (I Went to the Dance) (Cajun and zydeco music from southwest Louisiana). Arhoolie Video BF 103. 84 minutes, color.
Jazz Women, 1932–1952 (starring Sister Rosetta Tharpe, Billie Holiday, Ida Cox, and others). Rosetta Records RRV1320. 28 minutes, black and white.
Larry Johnson. TCB Releasing Ltd. 20 minutes, color.
Floyd Jones: Dark Roads. Gerry Chodkowski. 30 minutes, black and white.
Louis Jordan: Five Guys Named Moe. Jazz Classics Video JCVC 2004. 56 minutes, black and white.
Louis Jordan: 1941–1945. Jazz Classics Video JCVC 105. Black and white.
Jump the Blues Away. Jazz Visions Music Video 081–333–3. 30 minutes, color.
B. B. King: Blues Master. DCI Music Video. 3 vols. 65 to 85 minutes each, color.
B. B. King: Live in Africa, 1974. BMG Video 791010. Color.
Alexis Korner: Eat a Little Rhythm and Blues. BBC Video. 71 minutes, color.
The Ladies Sing the Blues. View Video 1313. 60 minutes, black and white.
Land Where the Blues Began. Phoenix Films. 58 minutes, color.
Leadbelly: Three Songs. Film Images. 8 minutes, color.
Let the Good Times Roll. Corinth Films. 99 minutes, color.
Furry Lewis. Seattle Folklore Society. 25 minutes, black and white.
Mance Lipscomb. Seattle Folklore Society. 25 minutes, black and white.
Mance Lipscomb and Lightnin' Hopkins: Masters of the Country Blues. Yazoo Video 000502. 60 minutes, color.
Taj Mahal: That's All. PBS Video. 29 minutes, color.
Maxwell Street Blues (starring Robert Nighthawk, Jim Brewer, Arvella Gray, Floyd Jones, Playboy Vinson, John Henry Davis, and Carrie Robinson). Kay Jazz Video KJ031. 56 minutes, color.
Percy Mayfield: Poet Laureate of the Blues. Rhapsody Films. 30 minutes, color.
Fred McDowell. Seattle Folklore Society. 15 minutes, black and white.
Walter Brownie McGhee. Seattle Folklore Society. 25 minutes, black and white.
Memphis Southside Blues. Televista Projects. 30 minutes, black and white.
Messin' with the Blues. Rhino Home Video RNVD–1991. 54 minutes, color.
Mississippi Blues. Corinth Films. 90 minutes, color.
Mississippi Delta Blues. Anthony Herrera. 29 minutes, color.
Mississippi Delta Blues. Center for Southern Folklore. 18 minutes, black and white.

Mississippi Delta Blues. MACE Delta Arts Projects. 58 minutes, color.

Mississippi Delta Bluesmen: Give My Poor Heart Ease. Center for Southern Folklore. 20 minutes, color.

Mr. Boogie Woogie. Real to Reel Productions. 30 minutes, color.

Mark Naftalin's Blue Monday Party (starring John Lee Hooker and Charlie Musselwhite). VT Productions. 30 minutes, color.

Mark Naftalin's Blue Monday Party (starring Lowell Fulson and Percy Mayfield). VT Productions. 30 minutes, color.

Piano Players Rarely Ever Play Together (starring Professor Longhair, Allen Toussaint, and Tuts Washington). Kay Jazz Video KJ084. 59 minutes, color.

Rhythm and Blues. GPN Educational Media. 30 minutes, color.

Roots of American Music: Country and Urban Music, Part I. University of Washington Press. 40 minutes, color.

Roots of American Music: Country and Urban Music, Part II. University of Washington Press. 33 minutes, color.

Roots of American Music: Country and Urban Music, Part III. University of Washington Press. 23 minutes, color.

St. Louis Blues. Budget Films. 17 minutes, black and white.

St. Louis Blues. TCB Releasing Ltd. 18 minutes, black and white.

Son Seals: Big City Blues. Rhapsody Films. 28 minutes, color.

Selected Negro Work Songs. Visual Aids Service. 9 minutes, black and white.

Johnny Shines: Black and Blue. University of Alabama Television. 58 minutes, color.

Shoutin' the Blues. Serious Business Co. 6 minutes, color.

Bessie Smith. Filmmakers Co-op/Canyon Cinema. 14 minutes, black and white.

Bessie Smith and Friends, 1929–1941. Jazz Classics Video JCVC–103. black and white.

Sunnyland Slim. Moviemakers Company. 12 minutes, color.

Roosevelt Sykes: The Honeydripper plus Jay McShann. Kay Jazz Video KJ096. 27 minutes, black and white (*Sykes*); 30 minutes, color (*McShann*).

Sonny Terry. Seattle Folklore Society. 25 minutes, black and white.

Sonny Terry and Brownie McGhee. Seattle Folklore Society. 25 minutes, black and white.

Sonny Terry: Whoopin' The Blues. Pleasant Pastures Ltd. 14 minutes, color.

James "Sonny Ford" Thomas: Delta Blues Singer. Center for Southern Folklore. 45 minutes, black and white.

Three Generations of the Blues. KPBS-TV, San Diego, California. 60 minutes, color.

Big Joe Turner: The English Concert. VHS Video 40. 43 minutes, color.

Big Joe Turner, Count Basie, and Jay McShann: The Last of the Blue Devils. Rhapsody Films. 90 minutes, color.

Big Joe Turner and Hampton Hawes: L.A. Allstars. Rhapsody Films. 28 minutes, color.

Up from the Cradle of Jazz. Second Line Productions. 59 minutes, color.

Stevie Ray Vaughan: Live at the Mocambo, 1983. SMV Video 49111–12. 30 minutes, color.

Stevie Ray Vaughan: Pride and Joy, 1983–1989. SMV Video 49069–2. 36 minutes, color.

Various Blues Artists (starring Bessie Smith, Big Bill Broonzy, Sonny Boy Williamson, T-Bone Walker, and Sonny Terry). VHS Video 13. 47 minutes, color.

Sippie: The Life and Music of Sippie Wallace. Kay Jazz Video KJ073. 23 minutes, color.

Muddy Waters: Chicago Blues. Rhapsody Films. 49 minutes, color.

Booker T. Washington White: Bukka White. Seattle Folklore Society. 25 minutes, black and white.

Big Joe Williams. Seattle Folklore Society. 25 minutes, black and white.

Joe Williams. Kultur 1277. 60 minutes, color.

Robert Pete Williams. Seattle Folklore Society. 25 minutes, black and white.

Sonny Boy Williamson II. TCB Releasing Ltd. 10 minutes, black and white.

U. P. Wilson: Blues Guitar Tornado. Red Lightnin' Video RLVD 0083. Color.

Johnny Woods. Televista Projects. 60 minutes, black and white.

Big John Wrenches. Gerry Chodkowski. 30 minutes, black and white.

Zodico: Creole Music and Culture. Gulfsouth Films. 30 minutes, color.

Zydeco Gumbo (starring Clifton Chenier, John Delafose, Boozoo Chavis, Terence Semian, and Willis Prudhomme). Rhapsody Films. 28 minutes, color.

SELECTED BIBLIOGRAPHY

Abdul, Raoul. *Blacks in Classical Music*. New York: Dodd, Mead, and Company, 1977.

Abrahams, Roger D. *Afro-American Folktales: Stories from Black Traditions in the New World*. New York: Pantheon Books, 1985.

Akpabot, Samuel E. *Ibibio Music in Nigerian Culture*. East Lansing: Michigan State University Press, 1975.

Albertson, Chris. *Bessie*. New York: Stein and Day, 1972.

Allen, William F. *Slave Songs of the United States*. New York: Peter Smith, 1929.

Anderson, Sherwood. *Mid-American Chants*. New York: B. W. Huebsch, 1918.

Arom, Simha. *African Polyphony and Polyrhythm: Musical Structure and Methodology*. Cambridge: Cambridge University Press, 1991.

Asch, M., and A. Lomax. *The Leadbelly Songbook*. New York: Oak Publications, 1962.

Ashanti, Faheem C. *Rootwork and Voodoo in Mental Health*. Durham, N.C.: Tone Books, 1987.

Baker, Houston A., Jr. *Blues, Ideology, and Afro-American Literature: A Vernacular Theory*. Chicago: University of Chicago Press, 1984.

Balliett, Whitney. *American Singers*. New York: Oxford University Press, 1979.

Bane, Michael. *Who's Who in Rock*. New York: Facts on File, 1981.

Bastin, Bruce. *Red River Blues: The Blues Tradition in the Southeast*. Urbana: University of Illinois Press, 1986.

Baudrillard, J. *Fatal Strategies*. New York: Semiotext, 1990.

Baugh, John. *Black Street Speech*. Austin: University of Texas Press, 1983.

Bebey, Francis. *African Music: A People's Art*. New York: Lawrence Hill, 1975.

Bennett, Lerone, Jr. *Before the Mayflower: A History of the Negro in America, 1619–1964*. Harmondsworth, Middlesex, England: Penguin, 1981.

Berkow, Ira. *Maxwell Street: Survival in a Bazaar*. Garden City, N.Y.: Doubleday, 1977.

Bernhardt, Clyde E. *I Remember: Eighty Years of Black Entertainment, Big Bands, and the Blues*. Philadelphia: University of Pennsylvania Press, 1986.

Berry, Chuck. *Chuck Berry: The Autobiography*. New York: Harmony Books, 1987.

Berry, Jason, Jonathan Foose, and Tad Jones. *Up from the Cradle of Jazz: New Orleans Music since World War II*. Athens: University of Georgia Press, 1986.

Berry, Mary Frances, and John Blassingame. *Long Memory: The Black Experience in America*. New York: Oxford University Press, 1982.

Beyer, Jimmy. *Baton Rouge Blues*. Baton Rouge, La.: Arts and Humanities Council of Greater Baton Rouge, 1980.

Billingsley, Andrew. *Climbing Jacob's Ladder: The Enduring Legacy of African-American Families*. New York: Simon and Schuster, 1992.

Blassingame, John W. *Black New Orleans, 1860–1880*. Chicago: University of Chicago Press, 1973.

Bodin, Ron. *Voodoo, Past and Present*. Lafayette, La.: University of Southwestern Louisiana, Center for Louisiana Studies, 1990.

Bogaert, Karel. *Blues Lexicon: Blues, Cajun, Boogie Woogie, Gospel*. Antwerp: N. V. Scriptoria, 1971.

Bogart, Max. *The Jazz Age*. New York: Macmillan, 1969.

Bogle, Donald. *Brown Sugar: Eighty Years of America's Black Female Superstars*. New York: Harmony Books, 1980.

Bontemps, Arna, and Jack Conroy. *They Seek A City*. Garden City, N.Y.: Doubleday, Doran, 1945.

Boskin, J. *Sambo: The Rise and Demise of an American Jester*. New York: Oxford University Press, 1990.

Botkin, B. A. *Lay My Burden Down: A Folk History of Slavery*. Chicago: University of Chicago Press, 1945.

Bradford, Perry. *Born with the Blues*. New York: Oak Publications, 1965.

Brendt, Joachim-Ernst. *Blues*. Munich: Nymphenburger Verlangshandlung, 1957.

Brooks, Edward. *The Bessie Smith Companion*. New York: Da Capo Press, 1983.

Broonzy, William Lee Conley, and Yannick Bruynoghe. *Big Bill Blues*. Paris: Ludd, 1987.

Broven, John. *Rhythm and Blues in New Orleans*. Gretna, La.: Pelican Publishing Company, 1978.

———. *South to Louisiana*. Gretna, La.: Pelican Publishing Company, 1983.

Brown, Charles T. *The Jazz Experience*. Dubuque, Iowa: William C. Brown, 1989.

Brown, Karen M. *Mama Lola: A Vodou Priestess in Brooklyn*. Berkeley: University of California Press, 1991.

Brunvand, Jan Harold. *The Study of American Folklore*. 2d ed. New York: W. W. Norton, 1978.

Buerkle, Jack V., and Danny Barker. *Bourbon Street Black*. New York: Oxford University Press, 1973.

Burlin, Natalie Curtis. *Hampton Series Negro Folk-Songs*. New York: G. Schirmer, 1918.

Butler, Judith. *Gender Trouble*. New York: Routledge, 1990.

Carpenter, Niles. *The Sociology of City Life*. New York: Longmans, Green, 1923.

Carruth, Hayden. *Sitting In: Selected Writings on Jazz, Blues, and Related Topics*. Iowa City: University of Iowa Press, 1986.

Center for Southern Folklore. *The Heritage of Black Music in Memphis*. Memphis: Center for Southern Folklore, 1986.

Charles, Ray, and David Ritz. *Brother Ray: Ray Charles' Own Story*. New York: Dial Press, 1978.

Charters, Samuel. *The Bluesmen*. 2 vols. New York: Oak Publications, 1967–77.

———. *The Country Blues*. New York: Rinehart and Company, 1959.

———. *Robert Johnson*. New York: Oak Publications, 1973.

———. *The Roots of the Blues: An African Search*. New York: Pedigree/Putnam, 1982.

Chase, Gilbert. *America's Music from the Pilgrims to the Present*. Urbana: University of Illinois Press, 1978.

Chernoff, John Miller. *African Rhythm and African Sensibility: Aesthetics and Social Action in African Musical Idioms*. Chicago: University of Chicago Press, 1979.

Chilton, John. *Billie's Blues: Billie Holiday's Story, 1933–1959*. New York: Stein and Day, 1975.

Collier, James L. *The Making of Jazz*. New York: Dell, 1978.

Collins, John. *African Pop Roots*. London: Foulsham, 1985.

Cone, James H. *The Spirituals and the Blues: An Interpretation*. New York: Orbis Books, 1991.

Cook, Bruce. *Listen to the Blues*. New York: Charles Scribner's Sons, 1973.

Crummell, A. *Africa and America*. Springfield, Mass.: Willey and Co., 1891.

Cuney-Hare, Maude. *Negro Musicians and Their Music*. Washington, D.C.: Associated Publishers, 1937.

Dadie, Bernard. *Climbie*. London: Heinemann, 1984.

Dance, Daryl C. *Long Gone: The Mecklenberg Six and the Theme of Escape in Black Folklore*. Knoxville: University of Tennessee Press, 1987.

Dance, Helen Oakley. *Stormy Monday: The T-Bone Walker Story*. Baton Rouge: Louisiana State University Press, 1987.

Dannett, Sylvia. *Profiles of Negro Womanhood*. Vol. 2. Yonkers, N.Y.: Educational Heritage, 1966.

Davis, Ronald L. *A History of Music in American Life, 1620–1865, Vol. 1, The Formative Years, 1620–1865*. Melbourne, Fla.: Krieger, 1982.

Davis, Ronald L. F. *Good and Faithful Labor: From Slavery to Sharecropping in the Natchez District, 1860–1890*. Westport, Conn.: Greenwood Press, 1982.

Davis, Wade. *The Serpent and the Rainbow*. New York: Warner Books, 1987.

DeLerma, Dominique-Rene. *Bibliography of Black Music*. Vol. 2, *Afro-American Idioms*. Westport, Conn.: Greenwood Press, 1981.

———. *Reflections on Afro-American Music*. Kent, Ohio: Kent State University Press, 1973.

Dennison, S. *Scandalize My Name*. New York: Garland Publishing, 1982.

Deren, Maya. *Divine Horsemen: The Living Gods of Haiti*. Kingston, N.Y.: McPherson and Company, 1984.

Dexter, Dave. *The Jazz Story*. Englewood Cliffs, N.J.: Prentice-Hall, 1964.

Dixon, Christa K. *Negro Spirituals: From Bible to Folk Songs*. Philadelphia: Fortress Press, 1976.

Dixon, Robert M. W., and John Godrich. *Recording the Blues*. New York: Stein and Day, 1970.

Dixon, Willie, and Don Snowden. *I Am the Blues: The Willie Dixon Story*. London: Quartet Books, 1989.

Drake, St. Clair. *Black Folk Here and There: An Essay in History and Anthropology*. 2 vols. Center for Afro-American Studies, University of California, 1990.

Drake, St. Clair, and Horace R. Cayton. *Black Metropolis: A Study of Negro Life in a Northern City*. 1945. Reprint. New York: Harcourt, Brace and World, 1970.

Ekwensi, Cyprian. *People of the City*. Rev. ed. London: Heinemann, 1963.

Epstein, Dena J. *Documenting the History of Black Folk Music in the United States: A Librarian's Odyssey*. Chicago: University of Chicago Press, 1976.

———. *Sinful Tunes and Spirituals: Black Folk Music to the Civil War*. Urbana: University of Illinois Press, 1981.

Evans, David. *Big Road Blues*. Berkeley: University of California Press, 1982.

———. *Tommy Johnson*. London: Studio Vista, 1971.

Fahey, John. *Charley Patton*. London: Studio Vista, 1970.

Faison, Edward, Jr. *African-American Folk Tales*. New York: Vantage Press, 1989.

Feather, Leonard. *The History of the Blues*. New York: Charles Hansen Books, 1972.

———. *Inside Jazz*. New York: Da Capo Press, 1977.

Ferris, William, Jr. 1978. *Blues from the Delta*. Garden City, N.Y.: Doubleday, 1978; New York: Da Capo Press, 1984.

Fisher, Miles M. *Negro Slaves Songs in the United States*. Ithaca: N.Y.: Cornell University Press, 1953.

Flax, J. *Thinking Fragments*. Berkeley: University of California Press, 1990.

Floyd, Samuel A., Jr., and Marsha J. Reisser. *Black Music in the United States: An Annotated Bibliography of Selected Reference and Research Materials*. Millwood, N.Y.: Kraus International Publications, 1983.

Fox, Ted. *Showtime at the Apollo*. New York: Holt, Rinehart, and Winston, 1983.

Fry, Gladys-Marie. *Night Riders in Black Folk History*. Knoxville: University of Tennessee Press, 1975.

Garland, Phyl. *The Sound of Soul*. Chicago: Henry Regnery, 1969.

Garon, Paul. *Blues and the Poetic Spirit*. New York: Da Capo Press, 1978.

———. *The Devil's Son-in-Law: The Story of Peetie Wheatstraw and His Songs*. London: Studio Vista, 1971.

Garvin, Richard M., and Edmond G. Addeo. *The Midnight Special: The Legend of Leadbelly*. New York: B. Geis Associates, 1971.

Gates, Henry Lewis, Jr., ed. *Race, Writing, and Difference*. Chicago: University of Chicago Press, 1986.

George, Nelson. *The Death of Rhythm and Blues*. New York: Pantheon Books, 1988.

Gillett, Charlie. *The Sound of the City*. New York: Pantheon Books, 1983.

Gilroy, P. *There Ain't No Black in the Union Jack*. London: Hutchinson, 1987.

Gleason, Ralph J. *Celebrating the Duke and Louis, Bessie, Billie, Bird, Carmen, Miles, Dizzy, and Other Heroes*. New York: Dell, 1976.

Glissant, E. *Caribbean Discourse*. Charlottesville: University Press of Virginia, 1989.

Glover, Tony. *Blues Harp*. New York: Oak Publications, 1965.

Goffin, Robert. *Jazz: From the Congo to the Metropolitan*. Garden City, N.Y.: Doubleday, Doran, 1944.

Govenar, Alan, and Benny Joseph. *The Early Years of Rhythm and Blues: Focus on Houston*. Houston, Tex.: Rice University Press, 1990.
Graham, Ronnie. *The Da Capo Guide to Contemporary African Music*. New York: Da Capo Press, 1988.
Grant, Robert B. *The Black Man Comes to the City*. Chicago: Nelson-Hall, 1972.
Green, Mildred Denby. *Black Women Composers: A Genesis*. Boston: Twayne Publishers, 1983.
Groom, Bob. *The Blues Revival*. London: Studio Vista, 1971.
Grossman, Stefan. *Delta Blues Guitar*. New York: Oak Publications, 1969.
———. *Ragtime Blues Guitarists*. New York: Oak Publications, 1970.
Grossman, S., Stephen Calt, and Hal Grossman. *Country Blues Songbook*. New York: Oak Publications, 1973.
Guralnick, Peter. *Feel Like Going Home*. New York: Outerbridge and Dienstfrey, 1971.
———. *The Listener's Guide to the Blues*. New York: Facts on File, 1982.
———. *Lost Highway*. Boston: Godine Publishing, 1979.
———. *Sweet Soul Music: The Southern Dream of Freedom*. New York: Harper and Row, 1986.
Gutman, Herbert G. *The Black Family in Slavery and Freedom*. New York: Random House, 1977.
Hadley, Frank J. *The Grove Press Guide to the Blues on CD*. New York: Grove Press, 1993.
Hager, Steven. *Hip Hop: The Illustrated History of Break Dancing, Rap Music, and Graffiti*. New York: St. Martin's Press, 1984.
Hamm, Charles. *Music in the New World*. New York: W. W. Norton, 1983.
Handy, D. Antoinette. *Black Women in American Bands and Orchestras*. Metuchen, N.J.: Scarecrow Press, 1981.
Handy, William C. *Blues: An Anthology*. New York: Macmillan, 1972.
———. *Father of the Blues: An Autobiography*. New York: Macmillan, 1941.
Handy, William C., and Abbe Niles. *A Treasury of the Blues*. New York: C. Boni, 1949.
Haralambos, Michael. *Right On: From Blues to Soul in Black America*. New York: Da Capo Press, 1979.
———. *Soul Music: The Birth of a Sound in Black America*. New York: Da Capo Press, 1985.
Harris, Sheldon. *Blues's Who's Who*. New Rochelle, N.Y.: Arlington House, 1979.
Harrison, Daphne Duval. *Black Pearls: Blues Queens of the 1920s*. New Brunswick, N.J.: Rutgers University Press, 1988.
Hart, Mary L., Brenda M. Eagles, and Lisa N. Howorth. *The Blues: A Bibliographical Guide*. New York: Garland Publishing Company, 1989.
Haskins, James. *Black Music in America*. New York: Thomas Y. Crowell, 1987.
———. *The Cotton Club*. New York: New American Library, 1977.
———. *Voodoo and Hoodoo*. Lanham, Md.: Scarborough House, 1990.
Henderson, D. *'Scuse Me While I Kiss the Sky: The Life of Jimi Hendrix*. New York: Bantam Books, 1983.
Hirshey, Gerri. *Nowhere to Run: The Story of Soul Music*. New York: Times Books, 1984.

Hitchcock, H. Wiley, and Stanley Sadie, eds. *The New Grove Dictionary of American Music*. London: Macmillan, 1986.

Holiday, Billie, and William Dufty. *Lady Sings the Blues*. Garden City, N.Y.: Doubleday, 1956.

Horne, Lena, and Richard Schickel. *Lena*. Garden City, N.Y.: Doubleday, 1965.

Howard, Joseph H. *Drums in the Americas*. New York: Oak Publications, 1967.

Howe, Martin. *Blue Jazz*. Bristol: Perpetua Press, 1934.

Hughes, Langston. *The First Book of Jazz*. New York: F. Watts, 1955.

Jackson, Mahalia, with Evan McLeod Wylie. *Movin' On Up*. New York: Hawthorn Books, 1966.

Jones, Hettie. *Big Star Fallin' Mama: Five Women in Black Music*. New York: Viking Press, 1974.

Jones, LeRoi. *Blues People*. New York: William Morrow, 1963.

Jones, Quincy. *Listen Up: The Lives of Quincy Jones*. New York: Warner Books, 1990.

Katz, Bernard, ed. *The Social Implications of Early Negro Music in the United States*. New York: Arno Press and the New York Times, 1979.

Keil, Charles. *The Tiv Song: The Sociology of Art in a Classless Society*. Chicago: University of Chicago Press, 1979.

———. *Urban Blues*. Chicago: University of Chicago Press, 1991.

Kmen, Henry. *Music in New Orleans: The Formative Years, 1791–1841*. Baton Rouge: Louisiana State University Press, 1966.

Krehbiel, Henry E. *Afro-American Folksongs: A Study in Racial and National Music*. New York: G. Schirmer, 1914.

Laguerre, Michel S. *Voodoo and Politics in Haiti*. New York: St. Martin's Press, 1989.

Lang, Iain. *Background of the Blues*. London: Workers' Music Association, 1943.

Leadbitter, Mike. *Delta Country Blues*. Bexhill-on-Sea, England: Blues Unlimited, 1968.

———, ed. *Nothing But the Blues*. London: Hanover Books, 1971.

Leadbitter, Mike, and Eddie Shuler. *From the Bayou*. Bexhill-on-Sea, England: Blues Unlimited, 1969.

Leadbitter, Mike, and Neil Slaven. *Blues Records, January 1943 to December 1966*. London: Hanover Books, 1968.

Lee, George W. *Beale Street: Where the Blues Began*. College Park, Md.: McGrath, 1969.

Lester, Julius. *Black Folktales*. New York: Grove Weidenfeld, 1991.

Levine, Lawrence W. *Black Culture and Black Consciousness: Afro-American Folk Thought from Slavery to Freedom*. London and New York: Oxford University Press, 1977.

Lewis, David. *When Harlem Was in Vogue*. New York: Oxford University Press, 1989.

Lieb, Sandra. *Mother of the Blues: A Study of Ma Rainey*. Amherst: University of Massachusetts Press, 1981.

Locke, Alain LeRoy. *The Negro and His Music*. Salem, N.H.: Ayer, 1988.

Lomax, John A., and Alan Lomax. *Folk Song U.S.A.* New York: Duell, Sloan, and Pearce, 1947.

Lovell, John. *Black Song: The Forge and the Flame*. New York: Macmillan, 1972.

Majors, Monroe A. *Noted Negro Women*. Chicago: n.p., 1893.

Marsh, Dave. *Before I Get Old: The Story of the Who*. New York: St. Martin's Press, 1983.

Mauerer, Hans J. *The Pete Johnson Story*. Frankfurt, Germany: Hans J. Mauerer, 1965.

McCutcheon, Lynn Ellis. *Rhythm and Blues: An Experience and Adventure in Its Origins and Development*. Arlington, Va.: R. W. Beatty, 1971.

McKee, Margaret, and Fred Chisenhall. *Beale Black and Blue*. Baton Rouge: Louisiana State University Press, 1989.

Meadows, Eddie S. *Theses and Dissertations on Black American Music*. Beverly Hills, Calif.: Theodore Front Musical Literature, 1980.

Meltzer, Richard. *The Aesthetics of Rock*. New York: Da Capo Press, 1987.

Metraux, Alfred. *Voodoo in Haiti*. New York: Schocken Books, 1972.

Middleton, Richard. *Pop Music and the Blues: A Study of the Relationship and Its Significance*. London: Victor Gollancz, 1972.

Mitchell, George. *Blow My Blues Away*. New York: Da Capo Press, 1983.

Moore, Carman. *Somebody's Angel Child: The Story of Bessie Smith*. New York: Thomas Y. Crowell Company, 1969.

Moore, MacDonald S. *Yankee Blues: Musical Culture and American Identity*. Bloomington: Indiana University Press, 1985.

Mossell, Gertrude. *The Work of the Afro-American Women*. Philadelphia: Geo. S. Ferguson Company, 1894.

Mudimbe, V. Y. *The Invention of Africa: Gnosis, Philosophy, and the Order of Knowledge*. Bloomington: Indiana University Press, 1988.

Murray, Albert. *The Hero and the Blues*. Columbia: University of Missouri Press, 1973.

———. *Stomping the Blues*. New York: McGraw-Hill, 1976.

Murray, Charles Shaar. *Crosstown Traffic*. London: Faber, 1990.

Napier, Simon A., comp. *Back Woods Blues*. Bexhill-on-Sea, England Blues Unlimited, 1968.

Nathan, Hans. *Dan Emmett and the Rise of Early Negro Minstrelsy*. Norman: University of Oklahoma Press, 1962.

Neff, Robert, and Anthony Connor. *Blues*. Boston: David R. Godine, 1975.

Nicholas, A. X., ed. *Woke Up This Mornin': Poetry of the Blues*. New York: Bantam Books, 1973.

Nite, Norma N. *Rock On*. 3 vols. New York: Thomas Y. Crowell Company, 1974.

Nketia, Joseph H. *The Music of Africa*. New York: W. W. Norton, 1974.

Nobles, Wade W. *Africanity and the Black Family: The Development of a Theatrical Model*. Institute for the Advanced Study of Black Family Life and Culture, 1985.

Oakley, Giles. *The Devil's Music: A History of the Blues*. New York: Horizon, 1977.

Odum, Howard W., and Guy B. Johnson. *The Negro and His Songs*. Chapel Hill: University of North Carolina Press, 1925.

Oliver, Paul. *Bessie Smith*. London: Cassell and Company, 1960.

———. *The Blackwell Guide to Blues Records*. Oxford: Basil Blackwell, 1989.

———. *Conversation with the Blues*. New York: Horizon, 1965.

———. *Savannah Syncopators: African Retentions in the Blues.* London: Studio Vista, 1970.
———. *Screening the Blues.* London: Cassell and Company, 1968.
———. *The Story of the Blues.* London: Barrie and Rockliff, 1969.
Olsson, Bengt. *Memphis Blues and Jug Bands.* London: Studio Vista, 1970.
Oster, Harry. *Living Country Blues.* Hatboro, Pa.: Folklore Associates, 1969.
Otis, Johnny. *Listen to the Lambs.* New York: W. W. Norton, 1968.
Palmer, Robert. *Deep Blues.* New York: Viking Press, 1981.
Paparell, Frank. *Five Boogie Woogie Blues Piano Solos by Pinetop Smith.* New York: Leeds Music Corp., 1941.
Parish, Lydia. *Slave Songs of the Georgia Sea Islands.* New York: Creative Age Press, 1942.
Pasteur, Alfred B., and Ivory L. Toldson. *Roots of Soul: The Psychology of Black Expressiveness.* Garden City, N.Y.: Anchor Doubleday, 1982.
Pearson, Nathan W., Jr. *Goin' to Kansas City.* Urbana: University of Illinois Press, 1987.
Placksin, Sally. *American Women in Jazz.* New York: Wideview Books, 1982.
Pomerance, Alan. *Repeal of the Blues: How Black Entertainers Influenced the Civil Rights Movement.* New York: Carol Publishing Group, 1991.
Porterfield, Nolan. *Jimmie Rodgers: The Life and Times of America's Blue Yodeler.* Urbana: University of Illinois Press, 1979.
Ramsey, Frederic. *Been Here and Gone.* New Brunswick, N.J.: Rutgers University Press, 1960.
Rigaud, Milo. *Secrets of Voodoo.* San Francisco: City Lights Publishing Company, 1985.
Riva, Anana. *Voodoo Handbook of Cult Secrets.* San Francisco: City Lights Books, 1974.
Rivelli, Pauline, and Robert Levin, eds. *Giants of Black Music.* New York: Da Capo Press, 1980.
Roach, Hildred. *Black American Music: Past and Present.* Boston: Crescendo Publishing Company, 1973.
Roberts, John Storm. *Black Music of Two Worlds.* New York: William Morrow, 1982.
Rooney, Jim. *Bossmen: Bill Monroe and Muddy Waters.* New York: Dial Press, 1971.
Rowe, Mike. *Chicago Blues: The City and the Music.* New York: Da Capo Press, 1981.
———. *Chicago Breakdown.* New York: Drake Publishers, 1975.
Russell, Tony. *Blacks, Whites, and Blues.* New York: Stein and Day, 1970.
Sackheim, Eric, comp. 1975. *The Blues Line: A Collection of Blues Lyrics.* New York: Schirmer Books, 1975.
St. Julien, Aline. *Colored Creole: Color Conflict and Confusion in New Orleans.* New Orleans: Ahidiana-Habari, 1977.
Sampson, Henry T. *Ghost Walks: A Chronological History of Blacks in Show Business.* Metuchen, N.J.: Scarecrow Press, 1988.
Sawyer, Charles. *The Arrival of B.B. King: The Authorized Biography.* Garden City, N.Y.: Doubleday, 1980.
Saxon, Lyle, comp. *Gumbo Ya-Ya.* Boston: Houghton Mifflin, 1945.

Schoen, Elin. *Tales of an All-Night Town*. New York: Harcourt Brace Jovanovich, 1979.

Schuller, Gunther. *Early Jazz: Its Roots and Musical Development*. New York: Oxford University Press, 1968.

Shapiro, Nat, and Nat Hentoff, eds. *Hear Me Talkin' to Ya*. New York: Dover Publications, 1966.

Shaw, Arnold. *Honkers and Shouters: The Golden Years of Rhythm and Blues*. New York: Collier Books, 1978.

———. *The World of Soul*. New York: Paperback Library, 1971.

Shirley, Kay, ed. *The Book of the Blues*. New York: Crown Publishers, 1963.

Silverman, Jerry. *Folk Blues*. New York: Macmillan, 1968.

Skates, John Ray. *Mississippi: A Bicentennial History*. New York: W. W. Norton, 1979.

Skowronski, JoAnn. *Black Music in America: A Bibliography*. Metuchen, N.J.: Scarecrow Press, 1981.

Smith, Jimmy. *Merry Memories of Marigold, Mississippi*. Memphis: JRS Publications, 1982.

Smith, Wallace C. *The Church in the Life of the Black Family*. Valley Forge, Penn.: Judson Press, 1985.

Spear, Allan H. *Black Chicago: The Making of a Negro Ghetto, 1890–1920*. Chicago: University of Chicago Press, 1967.

Spelman, E. *Inessential Woman*. Boston: Beacon Press, 1988.

Stagg, Tom, and Charlie Crump. *New Orleans: The Revival*. Dublin: Bashall Eaves, 1973.

Stapleton, Chris, and Chris May. *African Rock: The Pop Music of a Continent*. New York: Dutton, 1990.

Stearns, Marshall. *The Story of Jazz*. New York: Oxford University Press, 1958.

Sterling, Dorothy, ed. *We Are Your Sisters: Black Women in the Nineteenth Century*. New York: W. W. Norton, 1984.

Stewart-Baxter, Derrick. *Ma Rainey and the Classic Blues Singers*. New York: Stein and Day, 1970.

Surge, Frank. *Singers of the Blues*. Minneapolis: Lerner Publications, 1969.

Tallant, Robert. *Voodoo in New Orleans*. New York: Collier Books, 1974.

———. *Voodoo Queen*. Gretna, La.: Pelican Publishing Company, 1983.

Taylor, Frank C., with Gerald Cook. *Alberta Hunter: A Celebration in Blues*. New York: McGraw-Hill, 1987.

Terry, Richard R. *Voodooism in Music and Other Essays*. Salem, N.H.: Ayer Publishing Company, 1934.

Thompson, R. F. *Flash of the Spirit*. New York: Random House, 1983: New York: Vintage, 1984.

Titon, Jeff Todd. *Early Downhome Blues: A Musical and Cultural Analysis*. Urbana: University of Illinois Press, 1977.

Toll, R. C. *Blacking Up: The Minstrel Show in Nineteenth-Century America*. New York: Oxford University Press, 1974.

Toop, David. *The Rap Attack: African Jive to New York Hip Hop*. Boston: South End Press, 1984.

Topping, Ray. *New Orleans Rhythm and Blues Label Listings*. Bexhill-on-Sea, England: Flyright, 1980.

Tracy, Steven C. *Langston Hughes and the Blues*. Urbana: University of Illinois Press, 1980.

Traum, H., ed. *Guitar Styles of Brownie McGhee*. New York: Oak Publications, 1971.

Troen, Selwyn K., and Glen E. Holt, eds. *St. Louis*. New York: New Viewpoints, 1977.

Trotter, James M. *Music and Some Highly Musical People*. New York: Johnson Reprint Corporation, 1968.

Tudor, Dean, and Nancy Tudor. *Black Music*. Littleton, Colo.: Libraries Unlimited, 1979.

Turner, Tina, with Kurt Loder. *I, Tina*. New York: Avon Books, 1987.

Wachsmann, Klaus P., ed. *Essays on Music and History in Africa*. Evanston, Ill.: Northwestern University Press, 1971.

Wallace, Michele. *Black Macho and the Myth of the Superwoman*. New York: Warner Books, 1980.

Walton, Ortiz. *Music: Black, White, and Blue*. New York: William Morrow, 1972.

Waters, Ethel, with Charles Samuels. *His Eye Is on the Sparrow*. New York: Jove Publications, 1978.

Weisbrot, Robert. *Freedom Bound: A History of America's Civil Rights Movement*. New York: W. W. Norton, 1990.

Whitburn, Joel. *Top Rhythm and Blues Records, 1949–1971*. Menomonee Falls, Wis.: Whitburn Publishing Company, 1972.

White, Charles. *The Life and Times of Little Richard: The Quasar of Rock*. New York: Harmony Books, 1984.

Williams, Martin. 1989. *Jazz in Its Time*. New York: Oxford University Press, 1989.

Wilmer, Valerie. *The Face of Black Music*. New York: Da Capo Press, 1976.

Wittke, Carl. *Tambo and Bones*. Durham: Duke University Press, 1930.

Wood, Graham. *An A-Z of Rock and Roll*. London: Studio Vista, 1971.

Wooton, Richard. *Honky Tonkin': A Travel Guide to American Music*. London: Travelaid, 1980.

Work, John W. *American Negro Songs*. New York: Howell, Soskin, 1940.

Work, John W., ed. *Folk Songs of the American Negro*. New York: Negro Universities Press, 1907.

Zur Heide, Karl Gent. *Deep South Piano: The Story of Little Brother Montgomery*. London: Studio Vista, 1970.

SELECTED DISCOGRAPHY

COMPACT DISCS

Ace

Jesse Belvin: *Blues Balladeer*. CDCHD305
Bobby Bland: *Blues Boy*. CDCHD302
Bobby Bland: *The Voice*. CDCHD323
Blues around Midnight. CDCH235
Clifton Chenier: *Blues and Boogie*. CDCHD389
Clifton Chenier: *King of Zydeco*. CDCH234
Floyd Dixon: *Marshall Texas Is My Home*. Specialty SPCD–7011–2
Lowell Fulson: *Tramp/Soul*. CDCHD339
John Lee Hooker: *Blues Brother*. CDCHD405
John Lee Hooker: *Live at Sugar Hill*. CDCHD938
Walter Horton: *Mouth Harp Maestro*. CDCH252
Joe Houston: *Cornbread and Cabbage Greens*. CDCHD395
Elmore James: *Let's Cut It*. CDCH–192
Etta James: *R & B Dynamite*. CDCH210
Juke Joint: *Blues*. CDCH216
B. B. King: *The Fabulous*. CDFAB004
B. B. King: *Spotlight on Lucille*. CDCH187
B. B. King: *Sweet Little Angel*. CDCHD300
Lonnie Mack: *Lonnie on the Move*. CDCH351
Percy Mayfield: *Poet of the Blues*. Specialty SPCD–7001
Roy Milton: *And His Solid Senders*. Specialty SPCD–7004
Johnny Otis: *Creepin' with the Cats*. CDCHD325
Johnny Otis: *Good Lovin' Blues*. CDCH299
Little Richard: *The Fabulous*. CDCHM133

Little Richard: *His Greatest Recordings.* CHC–109
Little Richard: *The Specialty Sessions.* ABOXCD1
Guitar Slim: *The Things That I Used to Do.* CHD–110
Little Johnny Taylor: *The Galaxy Years.* CDCHD967
Sonny Terry and Brownie McGhee: *Back to New Orleans.* CDCH372
Big Mama Thornton: *The Original.* CDCHD940
Jimmy Witherspoon: *Blowin' in from Kansas City.* CDCHD279
Howlin' Wolf: *Rides Again.* CDCHD333

Aldabra

Robert Johnson: *Delta Blues, Vol. 1.* ALB1001CD
Robert Johnson: *Delta Blues, Vol. 2.* ALB1002CD
Leadbelly: *Convict Blues.* ALB1004CD
Memphis Minnie: *Traveling Blues.* ALB1005CD

Alligator

Lonnie Brooks: *Bayou Lightning.* ALCD–4714
Lonnie Brooks: *Turn on the Night.* ALCD–4721
Gatemouth Brown: *No Looking Back.* ALCD–4804
Gatemouth Brown: *Standing My Ground.* ALCD–4779
Nappy Brown: *Tore Up.* ALCD–4792
Roy Buchanan: *When a Guitar Plays the Blues.* ALCD–4741
Lil Charlie: *Disturbing the Peace.* ALCD–4761
Little Charlie: *All the Way Crazy.* ALCD–4753
Albert Collins: *Frostbite.* ALCD–4719
Albert Collins: *Frozen Alive.* ALCD–4725
Albert Collins: *Ice Pickin'.* ALCD–4713
Albert Collins: *Live in Japan.* ALCD–4733
James Cotton: *High Compression.* ALCD–4737
James Cotton: *Live from Chicago.* ALCD–4746
Lil Ed: *Rough Housin'.* ALCD–4749
Big Walter Horton: *And Carey Bell.* ALCD–4702
Lazy Lester: *Harp and Soul.* ALCD–4768
Professor Longhair: *Crawfish Fiesta.* ALCD–4718
Lonnie Mack: *Strikes with Lightning.* ALCD–4739
Charlie Musselwhite: *Ace of Harps.* ALCD–4781
Kenny Neal: *Devil Child.* ALCD–4774
Kenny Neal: *Walking on Fire.* ALCD–4795
A. C. Reed: *I'm in the Wrong Business.* ALCD–4757
Fenton Robinson: *I Hear Some Blues Downstairs.* ALCD–4710
Son Seals: *Bad Ax.* ALCD–4738
Son Seals: *Living in the Danger Zone.* ALCD–4798
Hound Dog Taylor: *And the Houserockers.* ALCD–4701
Hound Dog Taylor: *Beware of the Dog.* ALCD–4707
Hound Dog Taylor: *Genuine Houserocking Music.* ALCD–4727

Koko Taylor: *Audience with the Queen*. ALCD–4754
Koko Taylor: *The Earthshaker*. ALCD–4711
Koko Taylor: *From the Heart of a Woman*. ALCD–4724
Koko Taylor: *I Got What It Takes*. ALCD–4706
Koko Taylor: *Jump for Joy*. ALCD–4784
Sonny Terry: *Whoopin'*. ALCD–4734
Rufus Thomas: *That Woman Is Poison*. ALCD–4769
Big Twist: *Playing for Keeps*. ALCD–4732
Katie Webster: *No Foolin'*. ALCD–4803
Katie Webster: *The Swamp Boogie Queen*. ALCD–4766
Katie Webster: *Two-Fisted Mama*. ALCD–4777
Johnny Winter: *Guitar Slinger*. ALCD–4737

Antone's

Zuzu Bollin: *Texas Bluesman*. ANT0018
James Cotton: *Mighty Long Time*. ANT0015
Snooky Pryor: *Too Cool to Move*. ANT0017

Arhoolie

Clifton Chenier: *Bogalusa Boogie*. ARHCD347
Clifton Chenier: *Bon Ton Roulet*. ARHCD345
Clifton Chenier: *King of the Bayous*. ARHCD339
Clifton Chenier: *Live at St. Marks*. ARHCD313
Clifton Chenier: *Louisiana Blues and Zydeco*. ARHCD329
Clifton Chenier: *Out West*. ARHCD350
Clifton Chenier: *60 Minutes with the King of Zydeco*. ARHCD301
Mercy Dee: *Troublesome Mind*. ARHCD369
John Delafose: *Joe Pete Got Two Women*. ARHCD335
Snooks Eaglin: *Country Boy in New Orleans*. ARHCD348
Canray Fontenot: *Louisiana Hot Sauce*. ARHCD381
Jesse Fuller: *Frisco Bound*. ARHCD360
Lightnin' Hopkins: *The Gold Star Sessions, Vol. 1*. ARHCD337
Lightnin' Hopkins: *The Gold Star Sessions, Vol. 2*. ARHCD330
Lightnin' Hopkins: *Texas Blues*. ARHCD302
Mance Lipscomb: *Texas Songster*. ARHCD306
John Littlejohn: *Chicago Blues Stars*. ARHCD1043
Fred McDowell: *Mississippi Delta Blues*. ARHCD304
Charlie Musselwhite: *Memphis Charlie*. ARHCD303
Big Mama Thornton: *Ball and Chain*. ARHCD305
Bukka White: *Sky Song*. ARHCD323
Big Joe Williams: *Share Your Boogie*. ARHCD315
Sonny Boy Williamson: *King Biscuit Time*. ARHCD310

Atlantic

Atlantic Blues (Buddy Guy, Muddy Waters, J. B. Hutto, and others) 7823092
Atlantic Rhythm and Blues (Wilson Pickett, Hetty Wright, and others) 7823052
Big Joe Williams: *Rhythm and Blues Years*. 7816632

Bear Family

Esquerita: *Sock It to Me, Baby*. BCD 15504
Screamin' Jay Hawkins: *Spellbound*. BCD 15530
Louis Jordan: *Let the Good Times Roll*. BCD 15557
Little Richard: *The Formative Years*. BCD 15448
Howlin' Wolf: *Memphis Days, Vol. 1*. BCD 15460
Howlin' Wolf: *Memphis Days, Vol. 2*. BCD 15500

Beat Goes On

Bobby Bland: *Dreamer*. BGOCD63
Bobby Bland: *His California Album*. BGOCD64
Big Bill Broonzy: *Remembering Big Bill*. BGOCD91
John Lee Hooker: *Endless Boogie*. BGOCD70
John Lee Hooker: *Live at Cafe au Go Go*. BGOCD39
John Lee Hooker: *Simply the Truth*. BGOCD40
John Lee Hooker: *Urban Blues*. BGOCD122
B. B. King: *The Electric/His Best*. BGOCD37
B. B. King: *Friends*. BGOCD125
B. B. King: *In London*. BGOCD42
Otis Spann: *The Bottom of the Blues*. BGOCD92
Muddy Waters: *Mississippi Waters Live*. BGOCD109
Johnny Winter: *Nothing But the Blues*. BGOCD104

Bedrock

LowBlues/Chicago Harmonica Blues. BEDCD15
Pinetop Perkins: *With Chicago Beau*. BEDCD22

Bee Bump

Harmonica Fats: *I Had to Get Nasty*. BBCD02

Best of the Blues

Big Bill Broonzy: *1935–47*. BOB2CD
Leroy Carr/Scrapper Blackwell: *1929–35*. BOB10CD
Cow Cow Davenport: *1926–38*. BOB5CD
Champion Jack Dupree: *1940–50*. BOB9CD

Lightnin' Hopkins: *1947–67*. BOB3CD
Washboard Sam: *1936–42*. BOB1CD
Bumble Bee Slim: *1934–37*. BOB6CD
Peetie Wheatstraw: *1931–41*. BOB8CD
Josh White: *1933–41*. BOB7CD
Sonny Boy Williamson: *1937–47*. BOB11CD

Biograph

Rev. Gary Davis: *From Blues to Gospel*. BCD–123
Skip James: *Greatest of the Delta Blues Singers*. BCD–122
Johnny Shines: *Traditional Delta Blues*. BCD–121

Black and Blue

Buster Benton: *Blues at the Top*. 590012
Eddy Clearwater: *Blues Hand Out*. 597322
Lowell Fulson: *One More Blues*. 597242
Buddy Guy: *The Blues Giant*. 595002
Buddy Guy and Junior Wells: *Live in Montreaux (1978)*. 595302
Luther Johnson: *Luther's Blues*. 595192
Luther Johnson: *Someone in My Bedroom*. 233515
Sammy Price: *Midnight Boogie 1969*. 590252
Magic Slim: *Highway Is My Home*. 595252
T-Bone Walker and Roy Gaines: *Feeling the Blues*. 595522

Black Magic

Wild Child Butler: *Keep Doin' What You're Doin'*. BMCD9015
Fenton Robinson: *Blues in Progress*. BMCD9005
Big Bad Smitty: *Mean Disposition*. BMCD9018
Smoky Wilson: *And the William Clarke Blues Band*. BMCD9013

Black Swan

Ma Rainey: *The Paramounts Chronologically 1924–1925, Vol. 1*. WHCD–12001
Ma Rainey: *The Paramounts Chronologically 1924–1925, Vol. 2*. WHCD–12002

Black Top

Lynn August: *Creole Cruiser*. CDBT1074
Snooks Eaglin: *Teasin' You*. CDBT1072
Carol Fran/Clarence Holliman: *Soul Sensation*. CDBT1071

Blind Pig

James Cotton: *Take Me Back*. 2587
Pinetop Perkins: *After Hours*. 73088
Al Rapone/Zydeco Express: *Zydeco to Go*. 74090

Blue Horizon

Wild Child Butler: *The Devil Made Me Do It*. CDBLUHOIX

Blue Moon

Son House: *In Concert (1965)*. CDBM020
Mississippi John Hurt: *In Concert*. CDBM083

Blue Phoenix

Jimmy Johnson: *Heat See*. 233720

Blue Sting

Otis Clay: *Soul Man Live in Japan*. StingCD004
Louis Myers: *Tell My Story Movin'*. StingCD025
Sunnyland Slim: *Be Careful How You Vote*. StingCD019

Blues Documents

Cripple Clarence Lofton: *Complete, Vol. 1*. BDCD6006
Cripple Clarence Lofton: *Complete, Vol. 2*. BDCD6007
Charlie McCoy: *1928–32*. BDCD6018
Blind Willie McTell: *1940*. BDCD6001
Memphis Jug Band: *Complete Works, 1932–34*. BDCD6002
Memphis Minnie: *Vol. 1, 1935*. BDCD6008
Memphis Minnie: *Vol. 2, 1935–36*. BDCD6009
Memphis Minnie: *Vol. 3, 1937*. BDCD6010
Memphis Minnie: *Vol. 4, 1938–39*. BDCD6011
Memphis Minnie: *Vol. 5, 1940–41*. BDCD6012
Funny Papa Smith: *1930–1931*. BDCD6016
Walter Vinson: *1928–1941*. BDCD6017

Bluesville

Rev. Gary Davis: *Say No to the Devil*. OBCCD–5192
Lonnie Johnson: *Blues by Lonnie Johnson*. OBCCD5022
Blind Willie McTell: *Last Session*. OBCCD5172

Bullseye Blues

Charles Brown: *All My Life*. NETCD9501
Otis Clay: *Live in Japan*. CDBB9513
Luther Johnson: *I Want to Groove with You*. NETCD9506
Little Jimmy King: *And the Memphis Soul Survivors*. NETCD9509
Dalton Reed: *Louisiana Soul Man*. CDBB9506
Byther Smith: *Housefire*. NETCD9503

Castle Communications

Ray Charles: *The Collection*. CCSCD241
Jimi Hendrix: *Concerts*. CCSCD235
Jimi Hendrix: *Radio One*. CCSCD211
Taj Mahal: *The Collection*. CCSCD180
John Mayall: *The Collection*. CCSCD137
Johnny Winter: *The Collection*. CCSCD167

Charly

Blue Eyed Blues (Eric Clapton, Jeff Beck, and others.) CDBM20
The Blues Came down from Memphis. CDCHLY67
Blues upside Your Head. CDCHLY26
Gatemouth Brown: *San Antonio Ballbuster*. CDBM6
Robert Cray: *The Score*. CDBM16
Robert Cray: *Who's Been Talkin'*. CDBM161
Jack Dupree: *Blues for Everybody*. CDCHLY243
Wynonie Harris: *Good Rockin' Tonight*. CDCHLY244
Screamin' Jay Hawkins: *I Put a Spell on You*. CDCHLY181
Screamin' Jay Hawkins: *Real Life*. CDCHLY163
Luther Ingram: *If Loving You Is Wrong*. CDCHLY303
Elmore James: *Come Go with Me*. CDCHLY180
Little Willie John: *Fever*. CDCHLY246
Guitar Junior: *The Crawl*. CDBM1
Freddie King: *Texas Sensation*. CDCHLY247
John Mayall: *Chicago Line*. CDCHLY202
John Mayall: *Power of Blues*. CDCHLY212
Jimmy Reed: *Big Boss Blues*. CDCHLY3
Little Esther Phillips: *Better Beware*. CDCHLY248
Jimmy Reed: *Bright Lights, Big City*. CDBM17
Jimmy Rogers: *Hard Working Man*. CDBM3
Joe Tex: *The Very Best of*. CDCHLY133
Ike Turner: *Trailblazer*. CDCHLY263
Wolfman Washington: *Get On Up*. CDBM9
Junior Wells/Earl Hooker: *Messin' with the Kid*. CDCHLY219
Jimmy Witherspoon: *J's Blues*. CDCHLY270
Howlin' Wolf: *Howlin' for My Baby*. CDCHLY66

Chess

Chuck Berry: *Fruit of the Vine.* CDRED19
Chuck Berry: *The London Chuck Berry Sessions.* CHD–9295
The Blues, Vol. 6 (50's Rarities). CHCD9330
Jackie Brenston: *Rocket 88.* CDRED30
Big Bill Broonzy and Washboard Sam. CHCD9251
Jimmy Dawkins: *Chicago on My Mind.* 670419
Sugar Pie De Santo: *Use What You Got.* CDRED33
Bo Diddley: *Diddley Daddy.* CDRED2
Bo Diddley: *London Sessions.* CDRED21
Bo Diddley: *Oh Yeah!* CDRED31
Champion Jack Dupree: *I Had a Dream.* 670402
Lowell Fulson: *Hung Down Head.* CHCD9325
Buddy Guy: *Complete Chess Studio Recordings.* CHD29337
Buddy Guy: *Got My Eyes on You.* 670419
Buddy Guy: *Stone Crazy.* CDRED6
John Lee Hooker: *Hound Hog Blues.* 670416
"Big" Walter Horton: *Hard Hearted Woman.* 670420
Etta James: *Tell Mama.* CHD–9269
Laura Lee: *That's How It Is.* CDRED27
J. B. Lenoir: *I Don't Know.* 670406
Little Milton: *If Walls Could Talk.* 670407
Little Milton: *We're Gonna Make It.* CDRED18
Robert Nighthawk: *Forest City Joe.* CDRED29
Jimmy Reed: *Down in Mississippi.* 670415
Jimmy Rogers: *That's All Right.* CDRED16
Shoutin', Singin', and Making Love. CHCD9327
Koko Taylor: *Love You Like a Woman.* CDRED25
Koko Taylor: *What It Takes.* CHD–328
Irma Thomas: *Something Good: The Muscle Shoals Sessions.* CHD–93004
Tribute to Willie Dixon. CDRED37
Little Walter: *Boss Blues Harmonica.* 2–92503
Sonny Boy Williamson: *Bummer Road.* CHCD9324

Columbia

Willie Dixon: *The Big Three Trio.* C–46216
Willie Dixon: *I Am the Blues.* PCT–09987
Blind Boy Fuller: *East Coast Piedmont.* 467923–2
Billie Holiday: *The Legacy, 1933–58.* 469049–2
Lonnie Johnson: *Steppin' on the Blues.* C46221
Robert Johnson: *The Complete Recordings.* C2K–46222
Robert Johnson: *King of the Delta Blues Singers, Vol. 2.* PCT–30034
Huddie Leadbelly: *Leadbelly.* CK30035
Legends of the Blues (Son House, Bo Carter, and others). 467245–2
Memphis Minnie: *Hoodoo Lady, 1933–37.* 467888–2

Memphis Minnie: *I Ain't No Bad Girl*. CD44072
News and the Blues. CD46217
Esther Phillips: *The Best of*. CD45483
Raunchy Business/Hot Nuts and Lollipops. 467889–2
Bessie Smith: *The Complete Collection, Vol. 1*. 467895–2
Bessie Smith: *The Complete Collection, Vol. 2*. 468767–2

Crosscut

John Campbell: *A Man and His Blues*. CCD11019
Charlie Musselwhite: *Mellow Dee*. CCD1013
Magic Slim: *Gravel Road*. CCD11027

Delmark

Sleepy John Estes: *Electric Sleep*. DD619
Legend of Sleepy John Estes. DD603
Jimmy Dawkins: *All for Business*. DS634
J. B. Hutto: *Slidewinder*. DD636
Jimmy Johnson: *Johnson's Whacks*. DD644
Willie Kent: *Ain't It Nice?* DD653
Magic Sam: *Give Me Time*. DD654
Magic Sam: *West Side Soul*. DD615
Sunnyland Slim: *House Rent Party*. DD655
Dinah Washington: *Mellow Mama*. DC451
Junior Wells: *Hoodoo Man Blues*. DD612
Big Joe Williams and J. D. Short: *Starvin' Chain Blues*. DD609

Demon

Snooks Eaglin: *Baby, You Can Get Your Gun*. FiendCD96
Snooks Eaglin: *Out of Nowhere*. FiendCD146
Screamin' Jay Hawkins: *Black Music for White People*. Bizarre R2–70556
John Lee Hooker: *Detroit Lion*. Fiend CD154
Terrence Simien: *Zydeco On the Bayou*. FiendCD715
Joe Louis Walker: *Blue Soul*. Fiend CD159
Joe Louis Walker: *Live at Slim's*. Fiend CD212

Document

Kokomo Arnold: *Complete, Vol. 1*. DOCD5037
Kokomo Arnold: *Complete, Vol. 4*. DOCD5040
Beale Street Sheiks: *Complete, 1927–29*. DOCD5012
Blind Blake: *Complete, Vol. 1*. DOCD5024
Blind Blake: *Complete, Vol. 4*. DOCD5027

Barbecue Bob: *Complete, Vol. 1.* DOCD5046
Big Bill Broonzy: *Complete, Vol. 1.* DOCD5050
Gus Cannon: *Complete Works, Vol. 1.* DOCD5032
Earliest Negro Vocal Quartets: *1894–1928.* DOCD5061
Sleepy John Estes: *1929–1937.* DOCD5015
Joe Evans and Arthur McClain: *Two Poor Boys.* DOCD5044
Blind Boy Fuller: *Vol. 1, 1936.* DOCD5091
Blind Boy Fuller: *Vol. 6, 1940.* DOCD5096
The Greatest Songsters, 1927–1929 (John Hurt, Rabbit Brown, and others). DOCD5003
Sam Harris: *Complete Works, 1927–31.* DOCD5034
Son House and the Greatest Delta Blues Singers (Willie Brown and others). DOCD5002
Papa Charley Jackson: *1924–26.* DOCD5087
Skip James: *Complete 1931 Recordings.* DOCD5005
Blind Lemon Jefferson: *Complete, Vol. 1.* DOCD5017
Blind Lemon Jefferson: *Complete, Vol. 4.* DOCD5020
Lonnie Johnson: *Complete, Vol. 1.* DOCD5063
Lonnie Johnson: *Complete, Vol. 7.* DOCD5069
Tommy Johnson: *1928–1929 Complete.* DOCD5001
Charley Jordan: *Vol. 1, 1930–31.* DOCD5097
Furry Lewis: *1927–1929.* DOCD5004
Blind Willie McTell: *Vol. 1, 1927–31.* DOCD5006
Memphis Blues (Allen Shaw, Tom Dickson, and others). DOCD5014
Memphis Jug Band: *Complete Works, Vol. 1.* DOCD5021
Memphis Minnie and Kansas Joe: *1929–1930.* DOCD5028
Memphis Minnie and Kansas Joe: *Vol. 4.* DOCD5031
Mississippi Sheiks: *Complete, Vol. 1.* DOCD5083
Mississippi Sheiks: *Complete, Vol. 4.* DOCD5086
Charley Patton: *Complete Works, Vol. 1.* DOCD5009
Ragtime Blues Guitar: *1927–30.* DOCD5062
Tampa Red: *Vol. 1, 1928–29.* DOCD5073
Tampa Red: *Vol. 5, 1938–40.* DOCD5077
Frank Stokes: *Victor Recordings, 1928–29.* DOCD5013
Montana Taylor and Freddie Shayne. DOCD5053
Bessie Tucker: *1928–1929.* DOCD5070
Sunny Boy Williamson: *Complete, Vol. 1.* DOCD5055
Jimmy Yancey: *Complete Works, Vol. 1.* DOCD5041
Jimmy Yancey: *Complete Works, Vol. 4.* DOCD5043

Edsel

Jay Hawkins: *Feast of the Mau Mau.* EDCD252
Taj Mahal: *Natch'l Blues.* EDCD231
Taj Mahal: *Taj Mahal.* EDCD166
Johnny Otis: *Live at Monterey.* EDCD266
Johnny Winter: *Johnny Winter.* EDCD163

Epic

Stevie Ray Vaughan: *Live Alive*. EGK–40511
Stevie Ray Vaughan: *In Step*. EK–45024
The Vaughan Brothers: *Family Style*. ZK–46225
Muddy Waters: *Hoochie Coochie Man*. 461186–2

EPM

New Orleans Blues: *1923–40*. 997552

Essential

Ray Charles: *The Classic Years, 1950–1971*. ESBCD144
Ray Charles: *Genius and Soul - Jazz*. ESSCD009
Ray Charles and Betty Carter. ESSCD012
Albert King: *Red House*. ESSCS147
Taj Mahal: *Big Blues*. ESMCD002

Fan Club

Howlin' Wolf: *In Cambridge, Ma., 1966*. FCO82CD

Flapper

Billie Holiday: *Early Classics, 1935–38*. PastCD9756

Flyright

Blues Is Killing Me (Memphis Minnie and others.) FLYCD28
Juke Boy Bonner: *1960–1967*. FLYCD38
Clifton Chenier and Rockin' Dopsie. FLYCD17
Champion Jack Dupree: *The Joe Davis Sessions*. FLYCD22
Got My Mojo Working. FLYCD41
Slim Harpo: *I'm a King Bee*. FLYCD05
Lazy Lester: *Lazy Lester*. FLYCD07
Louisiana Swamp Blues. FLYCD09
Fred McDowell. FLYCD14
More Louisiana Swamp Blues. FLYCD24
Johnny Shines and Robert Lockwood. FLYCD10
Lightnin' Slim: *King of the Swamp Blues*. FLYCD47
Lightnin' Slim: *Rolling Stone*. FLYCD08
Lonesome Sundown. FLYCD16
Ike Turner: *1958–1959*. FLYCD39
Katie Webster: *Katie Webster*. FLYCD 12
Zydeco Blues (Fernest Arceneaux, Marcel Dugas) FLYCD36

GNP Crescendo

Clifton Chenier: *New Orleans*. GNPD2119

Good Time Jazz

Burt Bales and Paul Lingle: *They Tore My Playhouse Down*. GTJCD–12025–2

GRP

B. B. King: *Live at the Apollo*. GRD9637

Ichiban

Nappy Brown: *Apples and Lemons*. CDICH1056
Blues Boy Willie: *Be-Who?* CDICH1064

Indigo

Honeyboy Edwards: *Delta Bluesman*. IGOCD2003
Jimmy Witherspoon: *The Blues, the Whole Blues, and Nothing But the Blues*. IGOCD2001

Instant

Chuck Berry: *Rock n' Roll Music*. CDINS5002
Bo Diddley: *Hey! Bo Diddley*. CDINS5038

Jass

Copulatin' Blues. JASSCD1
Reefer Songs: JASSCD7
Sissy Man Blues. JASSCD13
Street Walking Blues. JASSCD26
Them Dirty Blues. JASSCD 11/12

Jazz Archives

Ethel Waters: *Push Out*. JACD747

Jazz Visions

Jump the Blues Away. JVCD–841–287–2

JSP

Nappy Brown and Big Jay McNeely: *Just for Me*. JSP218
Mojo Buford: *State of the Blues Harp*. JSP233
Butterbeans and Sussie: *Elevator Pappa*. JSP329
Lefty Dizz: *Ain't It Nice to Be Loved?* JSP229
Phil Guy: *All Star Chicago Blues Session*. JSP214
Walter Horton: *Little Boy Blue*. JSP208
Professor Longhair: *The Complete London Session*. JSP202
Junior Mance: *Smokey Blues*. JSP219
Louisiana Red: *Always Played the Blues*. JSP240
Louisiana Red: *Blues for Ida B*. JSP209
Dr. Ross: *I Want All My Friends to Know*. JSP243
Guitar Shorty: *My Way on the Highway*. JSP245
Rockin' Sidney: *Live with the Blues*. JSP213
Byther Smith: *Addressing the Nation*. JSP232
Hubert Sumlin: *Blues Guitar Boss*. JSP239
Eddie Cleanhead Vinson: *Fun in London*. JSP204
Eddie Cleanhead Vinson: *Meat's Too High*. JSP223
Big Moose Walker: *Swear to Tell the Truth*. JSP242

King

Battle of the Blues (Wynonie Harris/Roy Brown). KCD607
Little Willie John: *Sure Things*. KCD739
Freddy King: *Let's Hideaway and Dance Away*. KCD773

L&R

American Folk Blues Festival 1962 (Memphis Slim and others). CDLR42017
American Folk Blues Festival 1963 (Willie Dixon and others). CDLR42023
American Folk Blues Festival 1964 (Sonny Boy Williamson and others). CDLR42024
American Folk Blues Festival 1965 (Big Mama Thornton and others). CDLR42025
American Folk Blues Festival 1966 (Otis Rush and others). CDLR42069
American Folk Blues Festival 1967 (Koko Taylor and others). CDLR42070
American Folk Blues Festival 1970 (Shaney Horton and others). CDLR42021
American Folk Blues Festival 1972 (T-Bone Walker and others). CDLR42018

Magpie

Leroy Carr: *1933–1935*. PYCD07
Piano Blues: *Dallas, 1927–1929*. PYCD15
Piano Blues: *Paramount, Vol. 1*. PYCD01
Piano Blues: *Paramount, Vol. 2*. PYCD05
Piano Blues: *Vocalion, 1928–30*. PYCD03

Mainstream

Charles Brown: *Boss of the Blues*. MDCD908
Peppermint Harris: *Sittin' In with*. MDCD907
Smoky Hogg: *Sittin' In with*. MDCD906

Maison de Soul

Clifton Chenier: *Zydeco Legend*. CD105
Rockin' Dopsie: *Saturday Night Zydeco*. CD104

MCA

Bobby Bland: *Dreamer*. MCACD10415
Albert Collins: *Truckin'*. MCACD10423
B. B. King: *To Know You Is to Love You*. MCACD10414

Milestone

Blind Lemon Jefferson. MCD–47022–2
Ma Rainey. MCD–47021–2

Mr. R&B

Nappy Brown: *I Done Got Over*. RBD205
Ruth Brown: *Sweet Baby of Mine*. RBD16
Julia Lee: *Ugly Papa*. RBD603
Big Jay McNeely: *Road House Boogie*. RBD505
Jack McVea: *Two Timin' Baby*. RBD612

Munich

Lucinda Williams: *Happy Woman Blues*. MRCD149

Nighthawk

Professor Longhair: *Mardi Gras in New Orleans*. NHCD108

Prestige

Mose Allison: *Sings and Plays.* CDJZD007
Homesick James: *Blues on the Southside.* OBCCD5292
Jimmy Witherspoon: *Baby, Baby, Baby.* OBCCD5272

RCA Bluebird

Arthur Crudup: *That's All Right, Mama.* ND90653
How Blue Can You Get? ND86758
Washboard Sam: *Rockin' My Blues Away.* ND90652

Red Lightnin'

Albert Collins: *Molten Ice/Live 1973.* RLCD0089
Big Walter Horton: *Live at the El Mocambo.* RLCD0088

Rhino

Laverne Baker: *Live in Hollywood '91.* R2–70565
Slim Harpo: *The Best of.* R2–70169
Legends of the Guitar. R2–70716

Riverside

Ida Cox with the Coleman Hawkins Quintet: *Blues for Rampart Street.* RCD1758
Alberta Hunter: *With Lovie Austin and Her Blues Serenaders.* RCD510

Roots

Fontella Bass/Sugar Pie De Santo. RTS33024
Bo Diddley: *I'm a Man.* RTS33007
Lowell Fulson: *Reconsider Baby.* RTS33028
Buddy Guy: *Stone Crazy.* RTS33010
John Lee Hooker: *Walking the Blues.* RTS33016
Etta James: *Something Got a Hold on Me.* RTS33037
Little Milton: *We're Gonna Make It.* RTS33012
Memphis Slim: *Worried Life.* RTS33013
Bessie Smith: *Mother of the Blues.* RTS33015
Otis Spann: *This Is the Blues.* RTS33014
Koko Taylor: *Wang Dang Doodle.* RTS33030
Little Walter: *Blues with a Feeling.* RTS33006
Muddy Waters: *Live.* RTS33018
Muddy Waters: *Mannish Boy.* RTS77001
Howlin' Wolf: *The London Sessions.* RTS33017

Rounder

Johnny Adams: *From the Heart*. CD2044
Etta Bader: *One Dime Blues*. CD2112
Marcia Ball: *Gatorhythms*. CD3101
Marcia Ball: *Hot Tamale Baby*. CD3095
James Booker: *Classified*. CD2036
Gatemouth Brown: *Alright Again*. CD2028
Gatemouth Brown: *One More Mile*. CD2034
Buckwheat: *Waitin' for My Ya Ya*. CD2051
Boozoo Chavis: *The Lake Charles Atomic Bomb*. CD2097
Johnny Copeland: *Ain't Nothing But a Party*. CD2055
John Hammond: *Live at McCabe's, 1983*. CD3074
Professor Longhair: *Houseparty New Orleans*. CD2057
Nathan and the Zydeco Cha-chas: *Steady Rock*. CD2092
New Orleans Ladies. CD2078
Robert Nighthawk: *Live on Maxwell Street*. CD2022
Johnny Shines: *Hey Ba Ba Re Bop*. CD2020
Irma Thomas: *The New Rules*. CD2046
Irma Thomas: *Simply the Best: Live*. CD2110
Wolfman Washington: *Heatin' It Up*. CD2098
Wolfman Washington: *Out of the Darkness*. CD2068
Zydeco Live (Boozoo Chavis and others). CD2069
Zydeco Live (John Delafose and others). CD2070

Sequel

Charles Brown: *Hard Times and Cool Times*. NEXCD 133
Linda Jones: *For Your Precious Love*. NEXCD 167
Benny Latimore: *Sweet Vibration*. NEXCD 166
Smiley Lewis: *New Orleans Bounce*. NEXCD 130
Amos Milburn: *His Greatest Hits*. NEXCD 132
Little Milton: *The TR Sessions*. NEXCD 168

Silvertone

Buddy Guy: *Damn Right I've Got the Blues*. ORECD516

Skyranch

Bob Brozman: *Truckload of Blues*. SR652309
Marva Wright: *Heartbreaking Woman*. SR652307

Smithsonian/Folkways

Big Bill Broonzy: *Sings Folksongs*. CDSF40023
Elizabeth Cotten: *Freight Train*. CDSF40009

Rev. Gary Davis: *Pure Religion and Bad Company*. CDSF40035
Lightnin' Hopkins: *1959*. CDSF40019
Brownie McGhee: *Folkways Years, 1945–59*. CDSF40034
Sonny Terry: *The Folkways Years*. CDSF40033

Sonet

Boozoo Chavis: *Boozoo's Breakdown*. SNTCD1042
Queen Ida: *Cooking with*. SNTCD1021

Sony

The Beauty of the Blues. 47465CD
Good Time Blues. 46780CD
Legends of the Blues. 47467CD
Preachin the Gospel/Holy Blues. 46779CD

South Bound

Millie Jackson: *Feelin' Bitchy*. CDSEWM042

Stax

Shirley Brown: *Woman to Woman*. CDSXE002
Albert King: *The Best of*. CDSX007
Albert King: *I'll Play the Blues for You*. CDSXD969
Jean Knight: *Mr. Big Stuff* CDSX003
Otis Redding: *It's Not Just Sentimental*. CDSXE041
Little Sonny: *New King on the Blues Harmonica*. CDSX968
Carla Thomas: *Memphis Queen*. CDSXE027
Rufus Thomas: *Do the Funky Chicken*. CDSXE036

Story of the Blues

John Byrd and Walter Gordon: *Complete Recordings*. SB3517CD
Bill Gaither: *Leroy's Buddy, 1935–41*. SB3503CD
Jimmie Gordon: *The Mississippi Mudder, Vol. 2*. SB3518CD
Jimmie Gordon: *1934–1941*. SB3510CD
Mississippi Girls. SB3515CD
St. Louis Jimmy Oden: *1932–1948*. SB3528CD
Texas Piano Blues. SB3509CD
Washboard Sam: *1935–1947*. SB3502CD

Travelin' Man

Mississippi Blues, 1940–1942. (Willie Brown and others). TMCD07
Red River Blues, 1934–1943. TMCD08

Vanguard

John Fahe: *Yellow Princess.* VMCD79293
Buddy Guy: *Hold That Plane.* VMCD6315
John Hammond: *The Best of.* VSD 11/12
Jimmy Rushing: *The Essential.* VCD 65/66
Big Mama Thornton: *Jail.* VMDC78351
Doc Watson: *The Essential.* VMCD7308
Junior Wells: *It's My Life, Baby.* VDS–73120

Wolf

Eddy Clearwater: *Chicago Blues Session.* 120869CD
Michael Coleman: *Backbreaking Blues.* 120865CD
Merline Johnson: *Yas Yas Girl.* CDNBJ006
John Littlejohn: *Blues Party.* 120859CD
Louisiana Swamp Blues, Vol. 2 (Henry Gray and others). 120923CD
John Primer: *Poor Man Blues.* 120852CD
Maggie Slim: *Chicago Blues Session, Vol. 3.* 120849CD

Yazoo

Alabama Blues, 1927–1931. YAZCD1006
Scrapper Blackwell: *Virtuoso Guitar.* YAZCD1019
Blind Blake: *Ragtime Guitar's Foremost Fingerpicker.* YAZCD1068
Big Bill Broonzy: *Do That Guitar Rag.* YAZCD1035
Crying Sam Collins: *Jailhouse Blues.* YAZCD1079
East Coast Blues, 1926–1935. YAZCD1013
Blind Boy Fuller: *Trucking My Blues Away.* YAZCD1060
Jackson Blues, 1928–1938. YAZCD1007
Blind Willie Johnson: *Sweeter As the Years Go By.* YAZCD1078
Robert Johnson: *The Roots of.* YAZCD1073
Memphis Jamboree, 1927–1936. YAZCD1021
Charles Patton: *Founder of the Delta Blues.* YAZCD1020
Ma Rainey: *Ma Rainey's Black Bottom.* YAZCD1071
St. Louis Blues: The Depression, 1929–35. YAZCD1030
Frank Stones: *Creator of Memphis Blues.* YAZCD1056
Henry Thomas: *Texas Worried Blues.* YAZCD1080/81

CASSETTES

Ace

Blues around Midnight. CHC235
B. B. King: *The Best of, Vol. 1.* CHC198
B. B. King: *Sweet Little Angel.* CHDC300
Kings of the Blues. CHC276

Elmore James: *Let's Cut It*. CHC192
Etta James: *R&B Dynamite*. CHC210
Little Richard: *His Greatest Recordings*. CHC109
Howlin' Wolf: *Rides Again*. CHDC333

Aldabra

Robert Johnson: *Delta Blues, Vol. 1*. ALB1001MC
Robert Johnson: *Delta Blues, Vol. 2*. ALB1002MC
Memphis Minnie: *Traveling Blues*. ALB1005MC

Alligator

Lonnie Brooks: *Wound Up Tight*. ZCSN974
William Clarke: *Blowin' like Hell*. AC4788
Albert Collins: *Cold Snap*. ZCSN969
Lil' Ed: *Rough Housin'*. ZCSN966
Lonnie Mack: *Second Sight*. ZCSN968
Hound Dog Taylor: *And the Houserockers*. AC4701
Hound Dog Taylor: *Natural Boogie*. AC4704
Koko Taylor: *I Got What It Takes*. AC4706
Johnny Winter: *Third Degree*. ZCSN965

Arhoolie

C. J. Chenier: *Let Me in Your Heart*. C1098
Clifton Chenier: *Bon Ton Roulet*. C345
Clifton Chenier: *King of Zydeco at Montreaux*. C355
Clifton Chenier: *Live at St. Marks*. C313
Clifton Chenier: *Louisiana Blues and Zydeco*. C329
Clifton Chenier: *Out West*. C1072
Clifton Chenier: *60 Minutes with the King of Zydeco*. C301
John Delafose: *Joe Pete Got Two Women*. C335
Canray Fontenot: *Louisiana Hot Sauce*. C381
Lightnin' Hopkins: *Texas Bluesman*. C302
Mance Lipscomb: *Texas Songster*. C306
John Littlejohn: *Chicago Blues Stars*. C1043
Fred McDowell: *Mississippi Delta Blues*. C304
Charlie Musselwhite: *Memphis Charlie*. C303
Big Mama Thornton: *Ball and Chain*. C305
Big Mama Thornton: *Mama Thornton*. C204
Big Joe Williams: *Share Your Boogie*. C325
Sonny Boy Williamson: *King Biscuit Time*. C310

Beat Goes On

John Lee Hooker: *Free Beer and Chicken*. BGOMC123
John Lee Hooker: *Simply the Truth*. BGOMC40
John Lee Hooker: *Urban Blues*. BGOMC122

Bullseye Blues

Charles Brown: *All My Life*. C-BB9501
Otis Clay: *Live in Japan*. C-BB9513
Jack Dupree: *Back Home in New Orleans*. C-BB9502
Luther Johnson: *I Want to Groove with You*. C-BB9506

Charly

Gatemouth Brown: *San Antonio Ballbuster*. TCBM6
Buddy Guy: *The Treasure World*. TCBM11
John Lee Hooker: *Mambo Chillun*. TCBM19
John Lee Hooker: *This Is Hep*. TCBM7
Lightnin' Hopkins: *Morning Blues*. TCBM8
Elmore James: *The Sky Is Crying*. TCBM12
Robert Johnson: *Delta Blues Legend*. TCBM132
Guitar Junior: *The Crawl*. TCBM1
Albert King: *Albert Live*. TCBM18
Albert King: *So Many Roads*. TCBM2
John Mayall: *Life in the Jungle*. TCBM4
Jimmy Reed: *Bright Lights, Big City*. TCBM17
Jimmy Rogers: *Hard Working Man*. TCBM3
Wolfman Washington: *Get On Up*. TCBM9
Muddy Waters: *Rock Me*. TCBM10
Howlin' Wolf: *The Wolf Is at Your Door*. TCBM5

Columbia

Big Bill Broonzy: *Good Time Tonight*. 467247–4
Billie Holiday: *The Legacy, 1933–58*. 469049–4
Lonnie Johnson: *Steppin' on the Blues*. 467252–4
Robert Johnson: *Complete Recordings*. 467246–4
Legends of the Blues. 467245–4
Memphis Minnie: *Hoodoo Lady, 1933–37*. 467888–4
Bessie Smith: *The Complete Collection, Vol. 1*. 467895–4
Bessie Smith: *The Complete Collection, Vol. 2*. 468767–4

Edsel

Screamin' Jay Hawkins: *Frenzy*. CED104

Epic

Screamin' Jay Hawkins: *Cow Fingers and Mosquito Pie*. EK–47933
Stevie Ray Vaughan: *Couldn't Stand the Weather*. FE39304
Stevie Ray Vaughan: *Soul to Soul*. FET–40036
Stevie Ray Vaughan: *Texas Flood*. BFT–38734

Essential

Albert King: *Red House*. ESSMC147

FNAC

Paul Butterfield: *Rides Again*. 664023
Lost Blues Masters, Vol. 1. 664033

Indigo

Honeyboy Edwards: *Delta Bluesman*. IGOMC2003
Lightnin' Slim: *Blue Lightnin'*. IGOMC2002
Jimmy Witherspoon: *The Blues, the Whole Blues, and Nothing But the Blues*. IGOMC2001

Instant

Elmore James: *Dust My Broom*. TCINS5030

Rounder

Mississippi John Hurt: *Avalon Blues 1963*. ROUC1080
Mississippi John Hurt: *Worried Blues*. ROUC1082

Silvertone

Buddy Guy: *Damn Right I've Got the Blues*. OREC516
John Lee Hooker: *Mr. Lucky*. OREC519

Vanguard

Chicago—The Blues Today, Vol. 1. CV79216
Chicago—The Blues Today, Vol. 2. CV79217
Chicago—The Blues Today, Vol. 3. CV79218
Buddy Guy: *Hold That Plan*. VNP6315
John Hammond: *The Best of*. VMTC6314
Mississippi John Hurt: *The Best of*. VMTC6304
Mississippi John Hurt: *Last Sessions*. CV79327

Skip James: *Devil Got My Woman*. CV79273
Big Mama Thornton: *Jail*. CV79351
Junior Wells: *Coming at You*. CV79262
Junior Wells: *It's My Life, Baby*. VMTC6311

Yazoo

Kokomo Arnold and Carey Bell: *Bottleneck Trendsetters*. C1049
Scrapper Blackwell: *Virtuoso Guitar*. C1019
Blind Blake: *Ragtime Guitar*. C1068
Big Bill Broonzy: *Do That Guitar Rag*. C1035
Big Bill Broonzy: *The Young*. C1011
Bo Carter: *Greatest Hits, 1930–40*. C1014
Crying Sam Collins: *Jailhouse Blues*. C1079
East Coast Blues. C1013
Blind Boy Fuller: *Truckin' My Blues Away*. C1060
Skip James: *The Complete 1931 Session*. C1072
Blind Lemon Jefferson: *King of the Country Blues*. C1069
Blind Willie Johnson: *Sweeter As the Years Go By*. C1078
Furry Lewis: *In His Prime (1927–28)*. C1050
Blind Willie McTell: *The Early Years*. C1005
Mississippi Blues. C1001
Charley Patton: *Founder of the Delta Blues*. C1020
Ma Rainey: *Ma Rainey's Black Bottom*. C1071
Funny Papa Smith: *Original Howlin' Wolf*. C1030
Frank Stokes: *Creator of the Memphis Blues*. C1056
Roosevelt Sykes: *Country Blues Piano Ace*. C1033

VINYL ALBUMS

Ace

Billy Boy Arnold: *More Blues on Southside*. CH253
Lightnin' Hopkins: *Walking This Road by Myself*. CH256
Shakey Jake: *Mouth Harp Blues*. CH236
Etta James: *R&B Dynamite*. CH210
B. B. King: *The Memphis Masters*. CH50
B. B. King: *Sweet Little Angel*. CHD300
Johnny Otis: *Good Lovin' Blues*. CH299
Little Richard: *The Specialty Sessions*. ABOXLP1
Jimmy Witherspoon: *Blowin' in from Kansas City*. CHD279

Agram

Texas Alexander: *Texas Troublesome Blues*. AB2009
Kokomo Arnold: *Down and Out Blues, 1935–37*. AB2015

Scrapper Blackwell: *Blues That Made Me Cry*. AB2008
Lucille Bogan: *Women Don't Need No Men*. AB2005
Jim Jackson: *Kansas City Blues*. AB2004
James Stump Johnson: *Ducks Yes, Yes*. AB2007
Mary Johnson: *I Just Can't Take It, 1929–36*. AB2014
Alice Moore: *Lonesome Woman Blues*. AB2013
Washington Phillips: *Denomination Blues*. AB2006
Walter Vinson: *Rats Been on My Cheese*. AB2003
Sylvester Weaver: *Smoketown Strut*. AB2010

Aldabra

Robert Johnson: *Delta Blues, Vol. 1*. ALB1001

Bear Family

Lowell Fulson: *I Don't Know My Mind*. BFX 15279
Louis Jordan: *Rock and Roll Call*. BFX 15257
Louis Jordan: *Rockin' and Jivin'*. BFX 15201

Beat Goes On

Long John Baldry: *Long John's Blues*. BGOLP2
Bobby Bland: *His California Album*. BGOLP64
Johnny Winter: *Nothing But the Blues*. BGOLP104

Bedrock

Major Handy: *Wolf Couchon*. BED 7
Kenny Neal: *On the Bayou*. BED 6
Root Boy Slim: *Don't Let This Happen to You*. BED 1
Root Boy Slim: *Left for Dead*. BED4

Best of the Blues

Lucille Bogan: *1923–1930*. BOB17
Jazz Gillum: *1935–1946*. BOB4
Sara Martin: *1922–1928*. BOB19
Washboard Sam: *1936–1942*. BOB1
Bumble Bee Slim: *1934–1947*. BOB6
Victoria Spivey: *1926–1937*. BOB22
Georgia Tom: *1929–1939*. BOB18
Peetie Wheatstraw: *1937–1941*. BOB8

Blues Boy

Gatemouth Brown: *Atomic Energy*. BB305
Peewee Crayton: *After Hours Boogie*. BB307

Blues Documents

Blues from St. Louis 1929–1935. 2017
Lucille Bogan: *1923–1935.* 2046
Female Country Blues, Vol. 1. 2040
From Memphis to New Orleans, 1930–36. 2056
Harlem Hamfats, 1936–39. 2045
Rosa Henderson: *1923–24.* 2105
Sloppy Henry: *1924–1929.* 2063
Papa Charlie Jackson: *1924–1934.* 2036
St. Louis Jimmy: *1932–48.* 2058
Lil Johnson: *1935–37.* 2083
Jug and Washboard Bands, Vol. 1, 1924–1931. 2023
Virginia Liston: *1923–26.* 2103
Kansas Joe McCoy and Joe Williams, 1929–1941. 2032
Elzadie Robinson: *1926–1929.* 2081
Washboard Sam: *Volume One, 1937–47.* 2091
Irene Scruggs: *1924–1930.* 2095
Black Boy Shine: *1936–1937.* 2039
Bumble Bee Slim: *Volume One.* 2085
Trixie Smith: *1922–29.* 2068
Victoria Spivey: *1926–37.* 2079
Georgia Tom: *The Accompanist, 1928–31.* 2061
Sippie Wallace: *1924–27.* 2093
Peetie Wheatstraw: *Devil's Son-in-Law.* 2011
Georgia White: *1935–41.* 2080

Blues Southwest

Carey and Lorrie Bell: *Straight Shot.* BSW001
Silas Hogan: *The Godfather.* BSW003

Crosscut

Papa Lightfoot: *Natchez Trace.* CCR1001
Charlie Musselwhite: *Mellow Dee.* CCR1013
Magic Slim: *Gravel Road.* CCR1027

Crown Prince

Eddie Boyd: *Ratting and Running Around.* 400
Smoky Hogg: *Jivin' Little Woman.* 409
Willie Mabon: *The Seventh Son.* 402
Sticks McGhee: *Drinkin' Wine Spodee Odee.* 401

Delmark

Luther Allison: *Love Me Mama.* DS625
Carey Bell: *Blues Harp.* DS622

John Estes: *Broke and Hungry*. DS608
Honkers and Bar Walkers. DS438
J. B. Hutto: *Hawk Squat*. DS617
Jimmy Johnson: *North/South*. DS647
Robert Jr. Lockwood: *Steady Rollin' Man*. DS630
Yank Rachell: *Tennessee Jug Busters*. DS606
Speckled Red: *The Dirty Dozens*. DS601
Dave Spector and Barkin' Bill Smith: *Bluebird Blues*. DS650
Little Walter: *The Blues World of*. DS638
Big Joe Williams: *Piney Woods Blues*. DS602
Edith Wilson: *He May Be Your Man*. DS637
Mighty Joe Young: *Blues with a Touch of Soul*. DS629

Delta

Honeyboy Edwards: *White Windows*. DTA1

Demon

Johnny Adams: *Room with a View of the Blues*. 111
Robert Cray: *Bad Influence*. 23
Robert Cray: *False Accusations*. 43
Snooks Eaglin: *Baby You Can Get Your Gun*. 96
Irma Thomas: *The Way I Feel*. 112
Sandra Wright: *Wounded Woman*. 138

Document

Kokomo Arnold: *Master of the Bottleneck Guitar*. 512
Blue Ladies, 1934–1937. 579
Blue Ladies, Vol. 2, 1937–39. 580
Female Country Blues Singers, 1929–1931. 586
Frankie Half Pint Jaxon: *1937–1939*. 560
Lil Johnson: *Hottest Gal in Town*. 516
Pete Johnson: *1938–1939*. 547
Tampa Red and Georgia Tom: *1929–31*. 585
Banjo Idey Robinson: *Blues Skipped and Jazz*. 509
Elzadie Robinson: *1926–29*. 588
Washboard Sam: *Vol. 1, 1935–37*. 507
Bumble Bee Slim: *1931–1937*. 506
Clara Smith: *Vol. 1, 1923–1924*. 566
Clara Smith: *Vol. 2, 1924*. 567
Mamie Smith: *First Lady of the Blues*. 554
Mamie Smith: *Get Hot*. 552
Mamie Smith: *Goin' Crazy with the Blues*. 555
Mamie Smith: *Mamie Smith Blues*. 553
Victoria Spivey: *1927–1930*. 590
Georgia Tom: *1928–1932*. 563
Sippie Wallace: *1923–1929*. 593
Josh White: *1929–41*. 597
Leola B. Wilson and Kid Wesley Wilson: *1928–33*. 549

Double Trouble

Andrew Brown: *On the Case.* DT3010
Eddie King: *The Blues Has Got to Me.* DT3017

Earl

Bo Carter: *The Rarest, Vol. 2.* 618
Lee Green: *Blues and Barrelhouse Piano.* 609
Charlie McCoy and Walter Vinson: *1928–36.* 612
Memphis Minnie, *Vol. 2.* 617
Sylvester Weaver: *Remaining Titles, 1924–27.* 615
Josh White: *Earliest Recordings, Vol. 2.* 619

Edsel

King Curtis: *Instant Groove.* ED315
Son House: *Death Letter.* ED167
Albert King: *Laundromat Blues.* ED130
Ben E. King: *Comes the Night.* ED131
Taj Mahal: *Natch'l Blues.* ED231

Epic

Stevie Ray Vaughan: *In Step.* EK–45024
Stevie Ray Vaughan: *Live Alive.* EGK–40511
Stevie Ray Vaughan: *Texas Flood.* BFT–38734

Flyright

Slim Harpo: *Blues Hangover.* 520
Slim Harpo: *I Got Love If U Want It.* 558
Lightnin' Slim: *We Gotta Rock Tonight.* 612
Lonesome Sundown: *If Anyone Asks You.* 617
Katie Webster: *Jay Miller Sessions, Vol. 48.* 613

H. K. Records

Alabama Blues, 1927–51. 4004
Carolina Blues, 1936–1950. 4006
Chicago Blues, 1937–1941. 4007
Georgia Blues, 1924–1935. 4005
Memphis Blues, 1927–1937. 4002
Mississippi Blues, 1927–1937. 4001
Piano Blues, 1927–1930. 4010
Texas Blues, 1928–1929. 4003

Ichiban

Clarence Carter: *Between a Rock and a Hard Place*. ICH1068
Luther Johnson: *Takin' a Bite outta the Blues*. ICH1060

Instant

Chuck Berry: *Rock n' Roll Music*. INS5002
Bo Diddley: *Road Runner*. INS5004
T-Bone Walker: *Stormy Monday*. INS5022
Muddy Waters: *Chicago Blues*. INS5003
Howlin' Wolf: *Back Door Man*. INS5020

Jukebox

Charles Brown and Johnny Moore: *Sail On*. 1106
Ella Johnson: *Say Ella*. 604
Louis Jordan: *Cole Slaw*. 605
Louis Jordan: *G.I. Jive*. 602
Julia Lee: *Ugly Papa*. 603
Joe Liggins: *Darktown Strutters Ball*. 601
Nellie Lutcher: *Papa's Got to Have Everything*. 1100
Roy Milton: *Big Fat Mama*. 616
Roy Milton: *Grandfather of R&B*. 600
Joe Morris: *Lowdown Baby*. 610
Mable Scott: *Fine, Fine Baby*. 606
Big Joe Turner: *I Don't Dig It*. 618
Dinah Washington: *If You Don't Believe I'm Leaving*. 1102

King Biscuit

Freddie King: *Live in Germany, 1975*. KBR001
Professor Longhair: *Rare Recordings*. KBR002

L & R

Carey Bell: *Goin' on Main Street*. LR42051
Margie Evans: *Another Blues Day*. LR42060
Blind Joe Hill: *One Man Blues Band*. LR42059
J. B. Lenoir: *Alabama Blues*. LR42001
Louisiana Red: *Boy from Black Bayou*. LR42055

Matchbox

Texas Alexander: *Vol. 1*. 206
Texas Alexander: *Vol. 2*. 214

Texas Alexander: *Vol. 3*. 220
St. Louis Bessie: *1927–1930*. 223
Barbecue Bob: *1927–30*. 1009
Buddy Boy Hawkins: *1927–29*. 202
Famous Hokum Boys: *1930–31*. 1014
Peg Leg Howell: *1928–29*. 205
Bo Weevil Jackson: *1926*. 203
Papa Charlie Jackson: *1924–29*. 1007
Blind Lemon Jefferson: *The Remaining Titles*. 1001
Charley Lincoln: *Complete, 1927–30*. 212
Frank Stokes: *1927–1929*. 1002

Mr. R & B

Faye Adams: *I'm Going to Leave You*. 110
Nappy Brown: *That Man*. 100
Roy Brown: *Saturday Night*. 104
Johnny Copeland: *I'll Be Around*. 1001
Amos Milburn: *You Used Me*. 1000

Nighthawk

Professor Longhair: *Mardi Gras in New Orleans*. 108

Old Tramp

Jimmie Gordon: *1934–46*. OT1220
New Orleans Willie Jackson: *1926–28*. OT1215
Monkey Joe: *1938–39*. OT1208

Pearl

J. T. Brown: *Windy City Boogie*. PL9
Robert Nighthawk: *Bricks in My Pillow*. PL11

RCA

Otis Spann and Cleanhead Vinson: *Bosses of the Blues, Vol. 2*. NL88312

Red Lightnin'

Buster Benton: *Bluesbuster*. 026
King Biscuit Boy: *Mouth of Steel*. 049
Phil Guy: *Tough Guy*. 062
Clayton Love: *Come On Home*. 029
Byther Smith: *Tell Me How You Like It*. 061

Fingers Taylor: *Harpoon Man*. 058
Little Johnny Taylor: *I Shoulda' Been a Preacher*. 030
Tommy Tucker: *Mother Trucker*. 022
Johnny Watson: *Gangster Is Back*. 013
Junior Wells: *In My Younger Days*. 007

Rockin' Blues

Joe Hill Louis: *The Be-Bop Boy*. RB19921

Rosetta

Lil Green: *Chicago, 1940–47*. RR1310
Jailhouse/Women's Prison Blues. RR1316
Sister Rosetta Tharpe: *Sincerely*. RR1317

Route 66

Charles Brown: *Racetrack Blues*. KIX17
Roy Brown: *Laughing But Crying*. KIX2
Ruth Brown: *Baby of Mine*. KIX16
Floyd Dixon: *Opportunity Blues*. KIX1
Peppermint Harris: *I Got Loaded*. KIX23
Wynonie Harris: *Oh Babe!* KIX20
Ivory Joe Hunter: *Seventh Street Boogie*. KIX4
Bullmoose Jackson: *Big Fat Mamas Are Back in Style*. KIX14
Jimmy Liggins: *I Can't Stop*. KIX18
Little Willie Littlefield: *It's Midnight*. KIX10
Percy Mayfield: *The Voice Within*. KIX22
Amos Milburn: *Just One More Drink*. KIX7

Saxophonograph

Bull Moose Jackson: *Moose on the Loose*. BP506
Eddie Vinson: *Mr. Cleanhead Steps Out*. BP507

Sundown

Peppermint Harris and Elmore Nixon: *Shout and Rock*. 70912
Sonny Terry and Buster Brown: *Toughest Terry and Baddest Brown*. 70911

Testament

Chicago Blues: The Beginning, 1946. 2207
Chicago Stringband: Johnny Young and Company. 2220
Modern Chicago Blues (Otis Spann and others). 2203

Jack Owens: *Must Have Been the Devil.* 2222
Johnny Shines: *Band.* 2212

Tramp

Big Joe Lewis: *The Stars in the Sky.* TR9910

Wolf

Esther Bigeou: *Complete, 1921–23.* WJS1010
Son Bonds: *Delta Boys, 1934–41.* 129
Gene Campbell: *1929–31.* 112
Big Joe Duskin: *Down the Road a Piece.* 120609
Harlem Hamfats: *With Rosetta Howard.* WJS1007
Harmonica Blues, 1936–40. 109
Maggie Jones: *1923–24.* 137
Louisiana Blues Live at Tabby's Blues Box. 120922
Carl Martin: *Complete Recordings, 1930–36.* 123
Robert Lee McCoy: *1938.* 120
Luella Miller: *1926–27.* 125
Sonny Boy Nelson: *1936.* 128
John Primer: *Poor Man Blues.* 120852
Jaydee Short: *1930–33.* 118
Blind Joe Taggart: *Remaining Titles, 1926–34.* 122
Vera and Eddie Taylor: *I Found Out.* 120711
Ethel Waters: *1924–1928.* WJS1009
Robert Wilkins: *1928–35.* 111
Robert Pete Williams: *Live.* 120919

Yazoo

Buddy Boy Hawkins: *1927–34.* YAZLP1010
Cripple Clarence Lofton and Walter Davis. YAZLP1025

INDEX

Page numbers in bold type indicate biographical entries.

ABOUT THE AUTHOR

AUSTIN SONNIER, JR., is from Louisiana, a home of the blues. He is the author of *Willie Geary "Bunk" Johnson, The New Iberia Years* (1977) and *Second Linin': Jazzmen of Southwest Louisiana 1900–1950* (1989) and 27 articles on blues and jazz in U.S. and European publications. At present he is writing two books: *The Violin Tradition in New Orleans* and *Zydeco: La Musique Creole et Acadienne.*